Lecture Notes in Computer Science

T0237902

Commenced Publication in 1973
Founding and Former Series Editors:
Gerhard Goos, Juris Hartmanis, and Jan van Leeuwen

Jian Cao   Minglu Li   Min-You Wu
Jinjun Chen (Eds.)

Network and
Parallel Computing

IFIP International Conference, NPC 2008
Shanghai, China, October 18-20, 2008
Proceedings

 Springer

Volume Editors

Jian Cao
Shanghai Jiatong University
Department of Computer Science and Engineering
80 Dongcuan Road, Shanghai 200240, China
E-mail: cao-jian@sjtu.edu.cn

Minglu Li
Shanghai Jiatong University
Department of Computer Science and Engineering
80 Dongcuan Road, Shanghai 200240, China
E-mail: li-mli@cs.sjtu.edu.cn

Min-You Wu
Shanghai Jiatong University
Department of Computer Science and Engineering
80 Dongcuan Road, Shanghai 200240, China
E-mail: wu-my@cs.sjtu.edu.cn

Jinjun Chen
Swinburne University of Technology
Centre for Complex Software Systems and Services
Faculty of Information & Communication Technologies
1, Alfred Street, Hawthorn, Melbourne, Victoria 3122, Australia
E-mail: jchen@swin.edu.au

Library of Congress Control Number: Applied for

CR Subject Classification (1998): C.2, D.4.6, E.3, D.1.3, F.1.2

LNCS Sublibrary: SL 1 – Theoretical Computer Science and General Issues

ISSN   0302-9743
ISBN-10   3-540-88139-5 Springer Berlin Heidelberg New York
ISBN-13   978-3-540-88139-1 Springer Berlin Heidelberg New York

Springer is a part of Springer Science+Business Media

springer.com

© IFIP International Federation for Information Processing 2008
Printed in Germany

Typesetting: Camera-ready by author, data conversion by Scientific Publishing Services, Chennai, India
Printed on acid-free paper   SPIN: 12532995   06/3180   5 4 3 2 1 0

Preface

Welcome to the proceedings of the 2008 IFIP International Conference on Network and Parallel Computing (NPC 2008) held in Shanghai, China.

NPC has been a premier conference that has brought together researchers and practitioners from academia, industry and governments around the world to advance the theories and technologies of network and parallel computing. The goal of NPC is to establish an international forum for researchers and practitioners to present their excellent ideas and experiences in all system fields of network and parallel computing. The main focus of NPC 2008 was on the most critical areas of network and parallel computing, network technologies, network applications, network and parallel architectures, and parallel and distributed software.

In total, the conference received more than 140 papers from researchers and practitioners. Each paper was reviewed by at least two internationally renowned referees and selected based on its originality, significance, correctness, relevance, and clarity of presentation. Among the high-quality submissions, only 32 regular papers were accepted by the conferences. All of the selected conference papers are included in the conference proceedings. After the conference, some high-quality papers will be recommended to be published in the special issue of international journals.

We were delighted to host three well-known international scholars offering the keynote speeches, Sajal K. Das from University Texas at Arlington USA, Matt Mutka from Michigan State University and David Hung-Chang Du from University of Minnesota University of Minnesota.

We would like to take this opportunity to thank all the authors for their submissions to NPC 2008. We also thank the Program Committee members and additional reviewers for providing in-depth reviews. Our thanks also go to local conference organizers for their local arrangements.

Last but not least, we appreciate IFIP Working Group 10.3 on Concurrent Systems. We are also grateful to the Steering Committee of IFIP NPC.

October 2008

Jian Cao
Minglu Li
Ming-You Wu
Jingjun Chen

Organization

General Co-chairs

Minglu Li   Shanghai Jiaotong University, China
Taieb Znati   University of Pittsburgh, USA
Josep Torrellas   University of Illinois at Urbana-Champaign, USA

Program Co-chairs

Ming-You Wu   Shanghai Jiaotong University, China
Y. Thomas Hou   Virginia Tech, USA

Program Vice Co-chairs

Jian Cao   Shanghai Jiaotong University, China
Jingjun Chen   Swinburne University of Technology, Australia

Steering Committee

Kemal Ebcioglu (Chair)   Global Supercomputing Corporation, USA
Jack Dongarra   University of Tennessee, USA
Guang Gao   University of Delaware, USA
Jean-Luc Gaudiot   University of California, Irvine, USA
Chris Jesshope   University of Amsterdam, The Netherlands
Hai Jin   Huazhong University of Science and Technology, China
Guojie Li   Institute of Computing Technology, CAS, China
Yoichi Muraoka   Waseda University, Japan
Daniel Reed   Microsoft, USA
Zhiwei Xu   Institute of Computing Technology, CAS, China

Publicity Chair

Yadong Gui   Shanghai Supercomputer Center (SSC), China

Workshop Co-chairs

Chuliang Weng   Shanghai Jiaotong University, China
Haifeng Shen   Nanyang Technological University, Singapore

Publication Co-chairs

Guangtao Xue   Shanghai Jiaotong University, China
Xing Wang   Fudan University, China

Program Committee

Andy Pimentel   University of Amsterdam, The Netherlands
Depei Qian   Xi'an Jiaotong University, China
Franciszek Seredynski   Polish Academy of Sciences, Poland
Qingkui Chen   University of Shanghai for Science and
                       Technology, China
Xiaowei Shen   IBM T. J. Watson Research Center, USA
Sven-bodo Scholz   Hertfordshire University, UK
Yutaka Takahashi   Kyoto University, Japan
Makoto Takizawa   Tokyo Denki University, Japan
Xinmin Tian   Intel Corporation, USA
Cho-Li Wang   The University of Hong Kong, Hong Kong
Xicheng Wang   Dalian University of Technology, Chin
Xingwei Wang   Northeastern University, China
Paul Werstein   The University of Otago, New Zealand
Weng-Fai Wong   National University of Singapore, Singapore
Nong Xiao   National University of Defense Technology,
                       China
Qin Xin   The University of Bergen, Norway
Cheng-Zhong Xu   Wayne State University, USA
Chao-Tung Yang   Tunghai University, Taiwan
Laurence T. Yang   St. Francis Xavier University, Canada
Xun Yue   Shandong Agricultural University, China
Weimin Zheng   Tsinghua University, China
Si Qing Zheng   University of Texas at Dallas, USA
Bing Bing Zhou   University of Sydney, Australia
Hai Zhuge   Institute of Computing Technology, CAS, China
Albert Y. Zomaya   The University of Sydney, Australia
Ajith Abraham   Chun-Ang University, Korea
Ishfaq Ahmad   University of Texas at Arlington, USA
Makoto Amamiya   Kyushu University, Japan
Luc Bouge   IRISA/ENS Cachan, France
Pascal Bouvry   University of Luxembourg, Luxembourg
Jiannong Cao   Hong Kong Polytechnic University, Hong Kong
Yeh-Ching Chung   National Tsing Hua University, Taiwan
Chen Ding   University of Rochester, USA
Christine Eisenbeis   INRIA, France
Bjoern Franke   University of Edinburgh, UK
Cecile Germain   University of Paris Sud, France
Anura Jayasumana   Colorado State Univeristy, USA

Weijia Jia	City University of Hong Kong, Hong Kong
Yong-kee Jun	Gyeongsang National University, Korea.
Gabriele Kotsis	Johannes Kepler University Linz, Austria
Ricky Kwok	The University of Hong Kong, Hong Kong
Francis Lau	The University of Hong Kong, Hong Kong
Kuan-Ching Li	Providence University, Taiwan
Xiuqi Li	Florida Atlantic University, USA
Geyong Min	University of Bradford, UK
Koji Nakano	Hiroshima University, Japan
Lionel Ni	Hong Kong University of Science and Technology, Hong Kong
Jun Ni	The University of Iowa, USA
Yang Xiang	Central Queensland University, Australia
Josep Torrellas	University of Illinois at Urbana-Champaign, USA
Jong Hyuk Park	Kyungnam University, Korea

Table of Contents

Network Technologies

Network Applications

Network and Parallel Architectures

Parallel and Distributed Software

An AIAD-Based Adaptive Routing Protocol in Ad-Hoc Wireless Networks

Youn-Sik Hong[1] and Ki-Young Lee[2]

[1] Department of Computer Science and Eng.
[2] Department of Information and Telecommunication Eng.,
University of Incheon
177 Dowha-dong Nam-gu 402-749 Incheon, Korea
{*yshong*,kylee}@incheon.ac.kr

Abstract. AODV routing protocol is intended for use by mobile nodes in ad-hoc wireless networks. Even though it performs well in static and low-mobility environments, the performance degrades rapidly with increasing mobility. Our primary concern is to enhance the performance of AODV by reducing the volume of the control packets like RREQ and RREP during the route discovery process effectively due to the node mobility. The propagation delays of the all possible links vary according to changes in its topology. Carefully adjusting the values of these network parameters can reduce the occurrences of the control packets. Thus, we propose a novel method of smoothly adjusting them based on AIAD (additive increase additive decrease) under a consideration of current network status. We have tested our proposed method with both the conventional AODV and the method using timestamp based on the three performance metrics; i.e., node mobility, node velocity, and node density, to compare their performances.

Keywords: Ad-hoc Network, AODV, Expanding Ring Search, Node Mobility, Node Traversal Time.

1 Introduction

Ad-hoc wireless network architecture is a self-organizing and distributed controlled network formed by a set of stations (called *nodes*) that can freely and dynamically self-configure and organize themselves to set up a temporary wireless network [1]. In the ad-hoc network configuration, a node acts as a mobile terminal as well as a router to forward messages to neighboring nodes if possible. The network topology in an ad hoc network is highly dynamic due to the movement of nodes; hence an on-going session suffers frequent path breaks. A disruption may be occurred either due to the movement of the intermediate nodes in the path or due to the movement of end nodes. Routing protocols for ad-hoc networks must be able to perform efficient and effective mobility management.

Existing ad-hoc routing protocols may generally be categorized as *table-driven* and *source-initiated demand driven* [2]. In table-driven routing protocols, every node maintains the network topology information in the form of routing tables by

J. Cao et al. (Eds.): NPC 2008, LNCS 5245, pp. 1–12, 2008.

periodically exchanging routing information. These protocols suffer from excessive control overhead that is proportional to the number of nodes in the network and therefore is not scalable in ad-hoc wireless networks, which have limited bandwidth and whose topologies are highly dynamic.

Unlike the table-driven routing protocols, on-demand routing protocols execute the *path-finding* process and exchange routing information only when a path is required by a source node to communicate with a destination. One of the on-demand routing protocols is AODV (*Ad-hoc On-demand Distance Vector*) [5]. In AODV, a source node floods the Route Request (RREQ) packet in the network when a route is not available for the desired destination. When an intermediate node receives a RREQ, it either forwards it or prepares a Route Reply (RREP) if it has a valid route to the destination. All intermediate nodes having valid routes to the destination, or the destination node itself, are allowed to send RREP packets to the source. AODV reduces the need for the system wide broadcasts by localizing the propagation of changes in the network. Even though it performs well in static and low-mobility environments, the performance degrades rapidly with increasing mobility.

As shown in Fig 1, data packet transmission is slightly affected by the node mobility. However, as the node mobility increases the control packets like RREQs and RREPs increase rapidly. Then it causes route discovery latency to increase. Besides, the amount of energy consumption increases corresponding to the increased number of control packets. To the end, the overall performance should be degraded with high node mobility. Our primary concern is to enhance the performance of AODV by reducing the volume of these control packets effectively due to the node mobility.

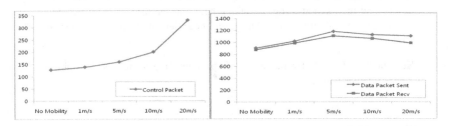

Fig. 1. The number of control packets (*left*) and the number of data packets (*right*) with node mobility

The rest of this paper is organized as follows. In section 2, we describe the expanding ring search algorithm and related works. In section 3, we present a proposed approach based on AIAD method. In section 4, a series of experimental results will be given and finally we conclude our paper in section 5.

2   Expanding Ring Search and Related Works

2.1   Expanding Ring Search

Consider the example depicted in Fig 2. In this figure, the source node 1 initiates a path-finding process by originating a RREQ to be flooded in the network for the

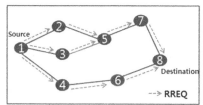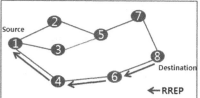

Fig. 2. AODV route discovery; propagation of the RREQ packets (left) and a path of the RREP packet to the source (right)

destination node 8. When the intermediate nodes 2, 3, and 4 receive the RREQ packet, they check their routes to the destination. In case a route to the destination is not available, they further forward it to their neighbors. If the RREQ reaches the node 8 through path 1-4-6-8 or any other alternate route, it also sends a RREP to the source.

To prevent unnecessary network-wide dissemination of RREQs, the source node should use an *expanding ring search* (ERS) technique [6]. Centered on the source node, ERS successively searches larger areas until a node with the information being searched is located. In the ERS, the source node initially uses a TTL (*time to live*) = TTL_START in the RREQ packet header and sets the timeout for receiving a RREP to RING_TRAVERSAL_TIME milliseconds [5]. If the RREQ times out without a corresponding RREP, the source node broadcasts the RREQ again with the TTL incremented by TTL_INCREMENT. This continues until the TTL set in the RREQ reaches TTL_THRESHOLD, beyond which a TTL = NET_DIAMETER is used for each attempt. Beyond this, the RREQ is not forwarded any further. Each time, the timeout for receiving a RREP is RING_TRAVERSAL_TIME. Table 1 gives default values for some important parameters associated with ERS techniques used in the AODV routing protocol.

Table 1. Default values for AODV parameters

Parameter name	value
NET_DIAMETER	35
NODE_TRAVERSAL_TIME	40 ms
NET_TRAVERSAL_TIME	2 × NODE_TRAVERSAL_TIME × NET_DIAMETER
RING_TRAVERSAL_TIME	2 × NODE_TRAVERSAL_TIME × TTL_VALUE
TTL_START	1
TTL_INCREMENT	2
TTL_THRESHOLD	7

NODE_TRAVERSAL_TIME (NTT) is a conservative estimate of the average one hop traversal time for packets and should include queuing delays, interrupt processing times and transfer times [5]. Typically NTT is set to a fixed value of 40ms. In that case, it does not reflect a full dynamic topology with respect to node mobility in ad-hoc wireless networks. For example, node i moves to the right in some distance from its neighbors as shown in Fig 3, while it still resides in a transmission range of them.

It causes a longer response time for the query from its neighbors. In TTL-based ERS, if the node cannot reply within a specified time-out period, the source node re-initiates a RREQ packet as shown in Fig 3(a). However, by setting the appropriate TTL value in the query as shown in Fig 3(b), the source node can control the search radius. Thus, by setting the appropriate NTT value the unnecessary RREQ packets should be minimized. Minimizing the cost of the initiating and the forwarding RREQ packets is crucial for resource-constraint multi-hop wireless network, which motivates this work.

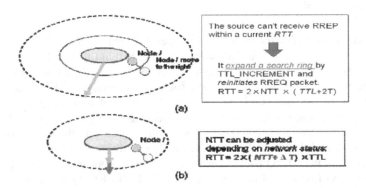

Fig. 3. An illustration of our proposed approach: (a) TTL-based ERS, (b) NTT-based ERS

2.2 Related Works

A number of heuristics for enhancements of the performance of AODV routing proto-col has been proposed. *Hassan and Jha* [7] explored to find an optimum TTL thresh-old *L* that would minimize the expected bandwidth cost of ERS. They give the follow-ing experimental results; search threshold L of 3 is optimum for three categories of networks, that is, large networks with small radius, medium networks with large ra-dius and medium networks with small radius. In the AODV, TTL_THRESHOLD is typically set to 7, which gives the search threshold of 3.

Some of the works tries to identify the inefficient elements of ERS. *Lee* et al[9] pro-posed a method of timestamp to compute NTT; every node adds the current time to the message (i.e., RREQ and RREP) before sending it out, and then the neighbor that re-ceives it computes a measured traversal time (called *M*) using the timestamp. A smoothed NTT is updated by using the similar equation of the round-trip-time estimator:

$$NTT = \alpha \times NTT + (1 - \alpha) M \tag{1}$$

where, α is a smoothing factor with a range of 0 and 1. *Kim* et al [10] presented a technique of estimating NTT that divides a time difference between the source node and the destination node by the number of hops. In addition, *Park* et al [11] proposed a blocking ERS (B-ERS for short). One of the differences from the TTL-ERS is that the B-ERS does not resume its route search procedure from the source node each time a rebroadcast is required. *Tripathi* et al [8] proposed four heuristics; one for them is the utilization of route caches at intermediate nodes for route discovery.

All of the works mentioned above have an emphasis on the adaptive control of AODV routing protocol with respect to node mobility. Since the timestamp based approaches [9] changes NTT too rapidly, the stability of the network becomes relatively low. Besides, with low mobility their performance will be degraded due to increases in the number of RREQ packets initiated by the source node. Even if B-ERS reduces in route discovery latency, it may suffer from dynamic changes in the network topology with high mobility. With the proposed heuristics proposed by *Tripathi* et al, the complexity of maintenance of multiple paths demands a larger memory and greater processing power for every node.

3 A Control Packet Minimized AODV Protocol

Our proposed method relies on packet based propagation of timestamp information to calculate more realistic NTT by considering the network status. While initiating a RREP, the destination node appends the timestamp information in the RREP packet. When the source node receives the RREP packet, it checks the timestamp *ST* available at the source node and the timestamp *DT* available at the destination node. Let *MT* denotes estimated time taken for a packet to be delivered from one node to one-hop neighboring node. Let the number of hops on the route path established between the source node and the destination node be denoted by H. Then the *MT* is calculated as:

$$MT = (ST - DT) / H \qquad (2)$$

A computed estimate *MT* of one-hop traversal time just gives a reference relative to a previous NTT. A new NTT should be adjusted depending on MT. For example, the path 8-6-4-1 in Fig.2 consists of three links. Assume that each of them has a propagation delay of 40ms, 30ms, and 20ms, respectively. In that case, MT is computed as 30ms. However, since the longest propagation delay should be considered, a NTT is not changed and still remains 40ms. If the propagation delays of the all links increase equally in 6ms due to node mobility, MT is 36ms and then the amount of the difference between NTT and MT becomes smaller. Thus, a new NTT should be increased by a certain amount Δ.

Table 2. The recalculated NTT with respect to the propagation delays of each link (unit: ms)

Propagation delay			MT	previous NTT	NTT − MT	New NTT
Link1	Link2	Link3				
40	30	20	30	40	10	40
46	36	26	36	40	4	40+Δ
34	24	14	24	40	16	40-Δ

On the contrary, if the delays of the all links decrease equally in 6ms, MT is 24ms and then the amount of difference between them becomes greater. So a new NTT should be decreased by Δ. The above explanations are summarized as shown in Table 2.

Then the following algorithm, called CP_AODV (*Control Packet minimized AODV*), is used to resolve the number of control packets including RREQ and RREP packets. To minimize the flooding of control packets, a NTT should be adjusted smoothly by AIAD (*additive increase additive decrease*) technique.

```
IF (min_threshold > NTT - MT)
{
     NTT = NTT + increment;
}
ELSE IF (max_threshold < NTT - MT)
{
     NTT = NTT - increment;
     IF (NTT < lower_bound)
     {
           NTT = lower_bound;
     }
}
```

The parameters *min_threshold, max_threshold,* and *increment* are adjustable with respect to the network status. Notice that *max_threshold > min_threshold.* When the amount of the difference between NTT and MT is less than *min_threshold,* the average propagation delay of the links seems to be increased. So a new NTT should be increased by a specific amount *increment.* On the contrary, when the amount of the difference between them is greater than *max_threshold,* the average delay seems to be shorter. Then a new NTT should be decreased by *increment.* The parameter *increment* is controlled adaptively depending on the movement of nodes. Our experimental results show that with less than 40ms of NTT the number of retransmission of the RREQ packets increases so rapidly and thus the overall performance is degraded. Thus, the lower bound on NTT is set to 40ms. While the amount of difference between them is in the range of *min_threshold* and *max_threshold,* the node mobility seems to be relatively low. Then the value of a current NTT remains as before.

4   Performance Evaluations

For the purpose of the simulation, AODV protocol implemented in QualNet 4.0 simulator [12] has been modified to incorporate the changes which have been proposed in this paper. Data payload is of 512 bytes. All the data packets are CBR (*continuous bit rate*) packets. Each node moves with randomly chosen maximum speed up to 10m/s. The simulation parameters are summarized as shown in Table 3. Notice that the control parameters used in the CP_AODV are set through our simulations as the following: *min_threshold* = 5, *max_threshold* = 10, *increment* = 5.

Table 3. Simulation set-up

attributes	value
space	1,500m x 1,500m
bandwidth	2MB
Number of nodes	49
Placement strategy	GRID
Transmission range	250m
Node velocity	0 ~ 10m/s
run time	600 seconds

The performance evaluation is based on the comparison of the three different metrics; node mobility, node velocity and node density. In order to get a realistic insight into the effects of the proposed method (CP_AODV), these metrics also have been evaluated for both the legacy AODV [6] and the modified AODV with the timestamp method [9] (*T-AODV* for short).

4.1 The Experiments for the Node Mobility

After reaching the destination the node begins to move again after pause time. In our experiments we varied it between 0 to 600 seconds. The network between the pause times 0 to 150 have a high mobility, whereas the network beyond 450 have a low mobility. The network between the pause times 150 to 450 have a moderate mobility. The pause time implies the level of the mobility in the network.

We classify RREQ messages into two types; a RREQ initiated by the source node and a RREQ forwarded by an intermediate node. The source node re-initiates the RREQ if there is no route reply within a time-out period. Thus, a possible measurement to evaluate the cost of network-wide flooding is the number of the RREQ packets initiated by the source node. RREQ packets are flooded in the network by intermediate nodes forwarding the requests to their neighbors. So, another measurement is the number of RREQ packets forwarded by them.

For the number of RREQ packets initiated by the source node, CP_AODV is remarkably less than AODV as shown in Fig 4. In addition, CP_AODV is better than

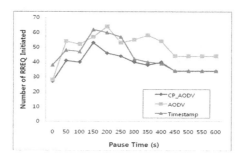

Fig. 4. The number of RREQ packets initiated by a source node

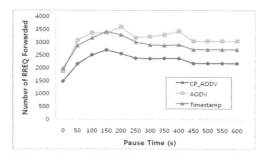

Fig. 5. The number of RREQ forwarded by intermediate nodes

T-AODV except in low mobility. For the number of RREQ packets forwarded by intermediate nodes, CP_AODV has significantly lower average packets than the two protocols (Fig 5). Typically, with CP_AODV the number of RREQ packets forwarded is reduced by 28% and 21% compared to AODV and T-AODV, respectively.

The decreased number of RREQ packets result in the decreased number of both RREP and RERR. For the number of RREP packets initiated by the destination node, CP_AODV has significantly low average packets in all levels of node mobility than both protocols as shown in Fig 6. In addition, with CP_AODV the number of RERR packets is reduced by more than 30% in average than the two protocols. Notice that both curves for RREP (Fig 6) and for RERR are similar to it for RREQ in Fig 4.

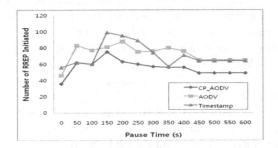

Fig. 6. The number of RREP packets initiated by a destination node

The proposed approach can save the amount of energy consumption by reducing the number of control packets including RREQs, RREPs and RERRs without increase in route discovery latency. The amount of energy consumption by CP_AODV, AODV and T-AODV are plotted against the pause time (i.e., *node mobility*) in Fig 7. Notice that the amount of energy consumption in Fig 7 includes both one for the route discovery process and one for data packet transmissions. Thus the shapes of the curves in Fig 7 are quite different from it in Fig 4. In all levels of node mobility, CP_AODV is remarkably less than AODV.

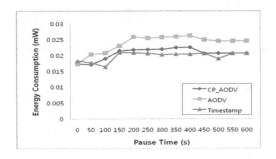

Fig. 7. Energy consumption versus node mobility

Notice that the amount of energy consumption is greater than T-AODV by 6% in average. The reason may be attributed to the fact that with T-AODV the number of data packets received by the destination node is relatively small. To be more precise, few observations can be made from our simulation results (Fig 8 and Fig 9). We see that there is no clear distinction for the throughput versus the pause time in Fig 8 for both CP_AODV and T-AODV. For the number of data packets received by the destination node, CP_AODV, however, is significantly higher than T-AODV by 10% as shown in Fig 8. We can say that T-AODV transmits less data packets compared to CP_AODV and thus its energy consumption becomes low.

CP_AODV achieves 5% and 3% better results for the throughput and the number of data packets received, respectively, compared to AODV irrespective of node mobility. From these observations, we can say that substantial reduction in the flooding of the control packets may result in a less route discovery latency. In turn, it causes low data packet traffic to increase the overall throughput.

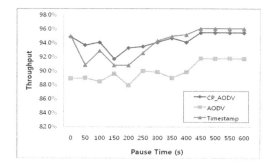

Fig. 8. The throughput versus the pause time

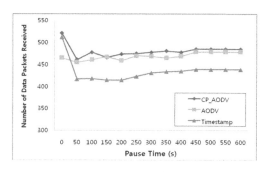

Fig. 9. The number of data packets received

4.2 The Experiments for Node Velocity

In this experiment each node moves with a nearly constant speed. When each node is set to the speed of 5m/s, it moves with the speed of 4~5 m/s. At the experiments in the previous section, it moves with the random speed of 0~10 m/s. Thus, this section focuses on the performance evaluation under the node speed ranges. Through this experiment, the pause time is set to 100 seconds and thus the network has a high mobility. The other parameters are used in Table 3. As you see in Fig 10, the average number of RREQ packets of CP_AODV turns out to be better. More specifically, it of

CP_ADOV has been measured 58.7, whereas that of AODV and that of T-AODV is 67.9 and 66.1, respectively. Besides, the standard deviation for the number of RREQs of CP_ADOV is the lowest among the three protocols. Thus, we can say that our proposed approach is more stable under the node speed ranges.

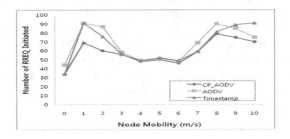

Fig. 10. The number of RREQ initiated versus node velocity

CP_AODV achieves substantial energy savings by 11~1.7% in average compared to both AODV and T-AODV. In addition, for the number of data packets delivered to the destination it is better than the two protocols by 14~2.4% in average (Fig 11). It cannot say that a network with slower movement of nodes achieves a better through-put than one with faster movement of nodes. In other words, to reduce the volume of control packets that needs to be exchanged between the source and the destination, all of the neighboring nodes keep the distance to exchange messages each other irrespective of node velocity.

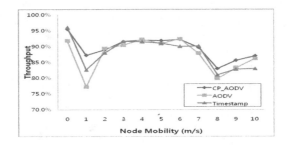

Fig. 11. The throughput versus node velocity

4.3   The Experiments for Node Density

In this experiment we vary the number of nodes starting from 36 up to 121 to evaluate the number of RREQ initiated (Fig 12), the amount of energy consumption and the number of data packets received by the destination (Fig 13). Since the rectangular field configuration is fixed as 1,500m x 1,500m, the distance between each pair of the neighboring nodes becomes shorter with a denser network. Depending on the number of nodes present in the ad-hoc network, we refer to the network as *sparse* which con-sists of less than 50 nodes. A *dense* network consists of more than 100 nodes.

Through this experiment, the network has a high mobility. In the following results (Fig 12-13), we omit the results of T-AODV because they are similar to them in the previous sections. Thus, through this subsection, CP_AODV is directly compared to the legacy AODV for simplicity and clarity.

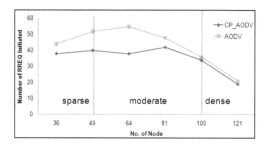

Fig. 12. The number of RREQ initiated versus the number of nodes

As in a dense network the number of pairs of the two neighboring nodes which locate within a possible transmission range of each other increase, the number of RREQ packets initiated by the source decreases significantly (Fig 12). That means in a dense network the possibility for finding a neighboring node to forward the request packets to the destination node is high. It causes the rate of RREQ packets initiated and forwarded to reduce remarkably. In a dense network, CP_AODV performs similar to AODV as shown in Fig 13. In addition, in a dense network no clear difference between them occurs for the amount of energy consumption.

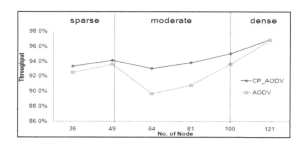

Fig. 13. The throughput versus the number of nodes

For sparse and moderate networks, overall performance of CP_AODV is found to be better than AODV. For the number of RREQ packets initiated, CP_AODV is 35.2 in average, whereas AODV is 42.7 in average. For both the amount of energy consumption and the number of data packets (Fig 13) CP_AODV is better than AODV by 13% and 2% in average, respectively. However, as the node density increases such the differences between them decreases. Thus our proposed method can achieve a better result with a sparse and moderate network than legacy AODV.

5   Concluding Remarks

We proposed a control packet minimized AODV protocol for rapidly changing the network topology in ad-hoc wireless networks due to node mobility. During the route discovery process, the volume of the control packets increases with the changes in the network topology due to the movement of nodes. To reduce them significantly, more realistic estimation of NTT is needed. To minimize the flooding of control packets, a NTT should be adjusted smoothly based on AIAD technique. CP_AODV protocol provides good improvement in terms of the number of control packets, the amount of energy consumption, the throughput and the number of data packets received by the destination, compared to the legacy AODV and the modified AODV with timestamp technique. These results have been obtained under three distinct metrics; node mobility, node velocity and node density. However, in a dense network, CP_AODV performs similar to AODV, whereas it achieves a better result with a sparse and moderate network.

References

1. Corson, S., Macker, J.: Mobile Ad hoc Networking (MANET): Routing Protocol Performance Issues and Evaluation Considerations. RFC 2501 (1999)
2. Royer, E.M., Toh, C.-K.: A review of current routing protocols for ad-hoc mobile wireless networks. IEEE Personal Communications Magazine, 46–55 (1999)
3. Toh, C.K.: Ad-hoc Mobile Wireless Networks: Protocols and Systems. In: ACM SIGCOMM. Prentice Hall PTR (2002)
4. Perkins, C.: Performance Comparison of Two On-Demand Routing Protocols for Ad-hoc Networks. In: Proc. of the IEEE Infocom, pp. 3–12 (2000)
5. Ad hoc On-Demand Distance Vector (AODV) Routing (RFC 3561),
   http://www.faqs.org/rfcs/rfc3561.html
6. Carlberg, K., Crowcroft, J.: Building Shared Trees Using a One-to-Many Joining Mechanism. ACM Computer Communication Review 27(1), 5–11 (1997)
7. Hassan, J., Jha, S.: Optimizing expanding ring search for multi-hop wireless networks. In: GLOBECOM, pp. 1061–1065 (2004)
8. Tripathi, S.M., Ghosh, R.K.: An Implementational Study of Certain Heuristics for the Performance Enhancements of AODV. In: Proc. of Euro-Micro Workshop on Parallel, Distributed and Network-based Processing, pp. 395–402 (2002)
9. Lee, J., Park, H., Lee, K., Suk, K.: Performance Improvement of AODV Routing Algorithm Using Timestamp. Journal of Korea Information and Communication Society (domestic) 31(8), 830–836 (2006)
10. Kim, H.-c., Chunng, S.-m.: A study of Optimization using state space survey in ad hoc network. Journal of Korea Institute of Military Science and Technology (domestic) 8(4), 68–76 (2005)
11. Park, I., Pu, I.: Energy Efficient Expanding Ring Search. In: 1st ASIA Int. Conf. on Modeling & Simulation (AMS), pp. 198–199 (2007)
12. http://www.scalable-networks.com

Adaptive Neighbor Selection for Service Discovery in Mobile Ad Hoc Networks*

Eunyoung Kang[1], Yongsoon Im[2], and Ungmo Kim[1]

[1] School of Computer Engineering, Sungkyunkwan University,
440-776, Suwon, Gyeonggi-do, Korea
{eykang,umkim}@ece.skku.ac.kr
[2] School of Broadcasting, Kookje College,
459-070, Pyeongtaek, Gyeonggi-do, Korea
ysim@kookje.ac.kr

Abstract. Service discovery to search for an available service in a mobile ad-hoc network is an important issue. Although mobile computing technologies grow ever more powerful and accessible, MANET, consisting of mobile devices without any fixed infrastructure, has such features as high mobility and resource constraints. Given these features, the costs of service discovery in mobile ad-hoc networks must be lower than those of service discovery in conventional fixed networks. In this paper, we design and evaluate a service discovery scheme to effectively discover services by using only local information in a mobile ad hoc network. Our service discovery protocol is based on the concept of peer-to-peer caching of service advertisement and node ID-based forwarding of service requests to solve these problems. Our protocol is that physical hop counts and the number of messages exchanged have been significantly reduced, since it does not require a central lookup server and does not rely on multicasting and flooding. The simulation results show that, in the proposed scheme, physical hop counts and the number of messages exchanged have been significantly reduced, compared with the other protocol.

Keywords: Service discovery, Peer-to-Peer Caching, MANET, Message Delivery.

1 Introduction

A mobile ad-hoc network (MANET) autonomously composed of mobile nodes independent of the existing wired networks or base stations has recently attracted substantial interest from industrial or research groups. Because it lacks infrastructure support,

* This work was supported in part by the MKE(Ministry of Knowledge Economy), Korea, under the ITRC(Information Technology Research Center) support program supervised by the IITA(Institute of Information Technology Advancement, IITA-2008-C1090-0801-0028) and by Foundation of ubiquitous computing and networking project (UCN) Project, the Ministry of Knowledge Economy(MKE) 21st Century Frontier R&D Program in Korea and a result of subproject UCN 08B3-B1-10M.

J. Cao et al. (Eds.): NPC 2008, LNCS 5245, pp. 13–23, 2008.
© IFIP International Federation for Information Processing 2008

each node acts as a router, forwarding messages for other nodes [1], [2]. In accordance with these trends, such mobile devices as PDAs, handheld devices and notebook computers have rapidly evolved. Due to the development of those mobile devices increasing user demand, file sharing or service discovery is emerging as an important issue.

With regard to file sharing or service discovery, there have been lots of researches on wired network P2P systems. Examples of representative unstructured P2P systems include Gnutella [3] and KaZaA [4]. Because Gnutella uses centralized directory services, it can easily find the location of each directory. But it causes a central directory server to produce a number of query messages, incurring bottlenecks. On the other hand, such structured P2P systems as Chord [5], CAN [6], and Pastry [7] are based on distributed hash tables (DHTs). A DHT-based overlay network makes out a table for searching by using a file and a key value obtained as a result of applying the file to its hash function. It is effective for peers involving themselves in a network to distribute and save the whole file information for searching because such searching is based on the key value corresponding to the file.

Notwithstanding advantages as demonstrated above, there is little application of these technologies to a mobile ad-hoc network. It is difficult to apply P2P applications based on a fixed network environment to ad-hoc networks different from those fixed wired networks, because their nodes are free to move. Although mobile computing technologies grow ever more powerful and accessible, mobile devices have a lower level of processing capacity and use batteries of limited power. They consume substantial power when they exchange messages. In this sense, it is requirement that costs are reduced for P2P applications with mobile devices in a wireless network. An ad-hoc network enables reduction of energy consumption, and reduction of wireless bandwidth needed for transmission, by reducing query messages among P2P applications in the network.

To solve these problems, this study proposes an improved service discovery protocol which is based on the concept of peer-to-peer caching of service advertisement and the lower node ID-based forwarding of service requests. First, it listen service information from neighbor node and store service information in own local service cache for the purpose of caching service advertisement. Second, it utilizes the lower node ID scheme to efficiently discover service information in MANET. Regarding lower ID delivery, a node with lower ID receives information from another node since messages are transmitted to the node of lower ID. The node of the lowest ID operates as a distributed index server. The number of messages exchanged in a network and average hop counts between a service requester and a service provider are reduced since the probability of responding service messages increases. The results of simulations showed that the proposed scheme reduced total network cost and power consumption by reducing messages and average hop counts(query delay), and improving response time, by comparison with any other system.

The remainder of this paper is organized as follows: in Section 2, the existing various approaches for service discovery are covered; Section 3 gives an explanation to the proposed service discovery architecture; an analysis of the architecture and its validity are exploited in Section 4; Finally, Section 5 concludes this paper, proposing the future study.

2 Existing Approaches for Service Discovery

Service discovery is an important area of research in wired networks and as well as wireless networks. There has been studied in the field of wired networks to develop peer-to-peer architectures as shown in [3-7]. To provide service discovery, the existing works use P2Ps including Gnutella [3] and KaZaA [4]. The former mainly uses central directory services. That is, each server identifies their location at which it registers its own services so that clients find services by sending service request queries to the corresponding directory where their own services are registered. On the other hand, service discovery protocols such as KaZaA generally use flooding search protocol, creating lots of query messages. These kinds of networks have to be controlled by a central server, leading to the problem of creating a large number of query messages. Structural P2P networks, such as Chord [5], CAN [6], and Pastry [7], are based on DHT in which each service is allocated ID in accordance with available keys. Due to the dynamic characteristics such as node mobility, resource (CPU, bandwidth, storage) constraints, and limited transmission range, using it on an ad-hoc network is not valid solution.

Jini [8], SLP2 [9], Salutation [10], Konark [11], Allia [12], and UPnP [13] are service discovery architectures of an ad-hoc network. These researches have been developed over the past few years to efficiently discover wired infrastructure-based services from wired and as well as wireless platforms. Jini, UPnP and SLP2 are service discovery protocols for a one-hop ad-hoc network environment. They are not suitable for an environment with high mobility, where lots of nodes participate in a network. In addition, Jini and SLP2 provide centralized service information management. Jini registers the service objects of a server through lookup services, and SLP2 manages the service information of a server through directory agents. On the other hand, UPnP, Saluatation, Konark, and Allia collect and manage information at their own cache through service advertisement based on a P2P system. Regarding Konark, multicast groups forwards messages. In Allia, various alliances among nodes are formed to forward messages to allied nodes. GSD [14] is based on group-based intelligent forwarding of service requested. The group means a service group to which the requested service belongs. They selectively forwards the request to neighboring nodes belongs to one of those groups. However, a node that has high degree of node connectivity often broadcast to neighboring nodes.

3 Proposed Service Discovery Architecture

3.1 Single Mobile Device Architecture

Fig. 1 shows components included in a single mobile device and the proposed service discovery architecture. The service discovery architecture is composed of 3 layers: application layer, service management layer and network communication layer.

Application layer provides users with applications such as audio-vide player, event alarm, network storage, etc.

Service management layer provides services related to discovery. If a requested service has not been found out in local cache, a service request message is sent to forwarding manager to start service discovery.

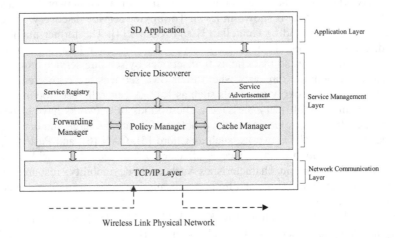

Fig. 1. Service Discovery Architecture

Forwarding manager plays a role in carrying service advertisement messages and request messages. Service discoverer picks out the shortest shortcut of neighboring nodes, by using service discovery protocol proposed in this paper to carry a request message. That is, a node with the shortest shortcut to a destination on those paths is chosen to carry service request message. Policy manager plays a role in controlling nodes through their current policies which describe service advertisement preference or replacement strategy or refresh rate, TTL(time-to-live).

Although whatever routing protocol may be used in the network communication layer, this paper uses on-demand AODV [15].

3.2 System Model

We consider a MANET that is a self-organized network of mobile nodes comprising such small mobile devices as PDAs, handheld devices, and notebook computers, which are connected with via wireless links.

The system model is as follows:

Mobile nodes are free to move at random, comprising a dynamic topology network. Each mobile node in the network has its own unique node ID. A file also has a unique file ID.

4   Proposed Service Discovery Protocol

This section describes cooperative neighbor caching of service information, the lower ID-based service discovery protocol, and cache management, for mobile ad-hoc networks.

4.1 Cooperative Neighbor Caching of Service Information

Our model is based on the concepts of peer-to-peer caching of service advertisement. A service provider saves information about services or files it provides at its local cache, then, advertises such service or file information to its neighboring node in accordance with the delivery scheme. All mobile nodes in a network serve as intermediate nodes, in accordance with the delivery scheme. This is relay messages, which are transmitted via cooperation with neighboring nodes, within the transmission range of a wireless network. Nodes in a network save and manage information received to at their local cache, for a specified period. We call this cache Service Routing Cache (SRC), in which each entry contains information such as; node Id, IP address, service name, power and ttl. Each node as a service provider acts both a server and a client when it requests a needed service. In MANET, we use AODV, which is well-known as a routing protocol in a mobile ad-hoc network. 'Hello' messages of AODV are periodical one-hop broadcast to neighboring nodes. To gather information about the neighbors of each node, we piggyback on hello messages including neighbor information, such as node ID, service name, degree of node connectivity, power and timestamp. Therefore, we do not use separate messages to obtain information about neighbors. A neighboring node management table is generated to manage information about neighboring nodes, based on 'hello' messages obtained from them. If there is not any 'hello' message from neighboring nodes after a specified period, they are now not neighbors, because they have moved. Information about the neighboring nodes is updated in the neighboring node management table. Nodes recently joining a network inform of their existence by making a broadcast to their neighboring nodes via 'hello' messages. If there is not any 'hello' message from neighboring nodes after a specified period, they are beyond transmission range or have left the network.

4.2 The Lower ID-Based Service Discovery

The basic idea of lower ID scheme is that each node only transmits messages to neighboring nodes with lower ID, instead of broadcasting them to all neighboring node. It can be used when the node advertises its service to another node, when a service requester sends a request message to search for a needed service, and when an intermediate node transmits the received message to neighbors. A service provider saves its services in a local cache SRC, and periodically advertises them to neighboring nodes. Figure 1 shows a simple example of a lower ID scheme.

In Figure 2(a), each node in a network advertises its service to another node on the network. We suppose that Nodes 1 to 4 have Files A to D, respectively, Node 3 transmits a service advertisement message to its neighboring Node 2 of lower ID. Then, Node 2 saves information about File C and the address of Node 3 in its local cache SRC. Node 4 transmits a service advertisement message to its neighboring Node 2 of lower ID, when Node 2 saves information about File D and the address of Node 4 in its local cache SRC. Similarly, Node 2 only transmits a service advertisement message to its neighboring Node 1 of lower ID. Iteration of this advertisement process results in Node 1 having the lowest ID, which no longer transmits SADM

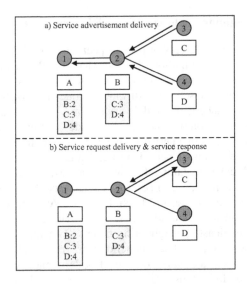

Fig. 2. Lower ID-based Service Advertisement and Service Discovery

```
SADM (msg)
//SADM: Service Advertisement Message
save service name and nodeid in local cache SRC;
for each neighbor n in neighboring node management table
    {
        if   n.nodeID < current.nodeID
            forward SADM to n.nodeID
    }
}
```

Fig. 3. When receive service advertisement message

messages. At that time, Node 1 functions as a distributed index server for file information, producing significantly fewer messages than in case of broadcasting. This
policy is associated with a service request message to search for file information. For
example, Node 3 in Figure 2(b) transmits a service request message to its neighboring
Node 2 of lower ID to discover File D. Node 2 contains information about File D,
which implies that the search for File D is a success. In the lower ID delivery scheme,
a node of lower ID acts as a server using message information transmitted in collaboration with its neighboring nodes in a distributed environment, without any centralized directory structure. This scheme is efficient because it can transmit messages to a
node of lower ID without flooding in a distributed environment, reducing the transmissions and messages used for service discovery. An algorithm for services advertisement is shown in Figure 3 and we show the searching process in Figure 4.

```
SRQM (request node ID, servicename)
// SRQM: Service Request Message
// SREM: Service Response Message
//Case 1: The current node has service name
If    node has servicename in local cache SRC
        return servicename
            reply SREM;
//Case 2: A neighbor node has service name
If    one of the neighboring nodes has a service name
        return servicenam
            reply SREM;
//Case 3: A SRQM is forwarded to a node of the lower ID
for each neighbor n in neighboring node management table
{
  if    n.nodeID < current.nodeID
        forward SRQM to n.nodeID
}
```

Fig. 4. An algorithm for service discovery

While a service request message is being forwarded, or when a service requested by a service provider is found, an available node produces a service response message based on information about that service. The service response message contains the IP address of a service that can provide services. Note that there may be several service response messages. Of service providers receiving these service response messages, the one with the highest value of service power (slack time) is selected to receive a service call.

4.3 Cache Management

There is a cache consistency issue in both the lower ID scheme and the higher degree scheme. Several research works prove that a strong cache consistency is maintained in the single-hop-based wireless environment [16]. However, it is too expensive to maintain strong cache consistency in an ad-hoc network, due to its bandwidth or power constraints; in fact, a weak consistency model is more attractive [17].

To maintain cache consistency, we use a simple weak consistency model based on a time-to-live mechanism, in which, if a service entry has not exceeded its service available time, we call it "valid service entry", it is considered to have a proper value. On other hand, if it does, we call it "invalid service entry", it is eliminated from the local cache SRC, because services are not effective any more. If a new copy of a node has a more recent service available time, only its service available time field is updated, if not, it is dropped. If the cache size has not enough free space that a new service can not be added, service rarely referred to are deleted or eliminated in accordance with the LRU deletion policy. An algorithm for cache management is shown in Figure 5.

```
// When cache replacement is necessary;
If   (not enough free space)
      If   (there is invalid service entry in the cache SRC)
            then remove a invalid service entry
      else
            remove a valid service entry that has the least
            available time
```

Fig. 5. When cache replacement is necessary

5   Results and Analysis of Simulation

In this section, we evaluate the capacity of the lower ID (LD) scheme in MANET. There will be a comparison of our protocol with a flooding-based system, which is a conventional search system.

5.1   Environment of Simulation

Simulation studies are performed using NS2 [18], a representative network simulation tool. AODV protocol is used as a routing protocol, with 1500m□1500m in the size of network area. Simulation scenarios are created with the number of nodes randomly distributed in the scenario area. The simulation is carried out with a change in the number of nodes ranging from 20 up to 100. Random way point model is used as the mobility model. A mobile scenario for mobile nodes where pause time on average is 2 seconds with average velocity and maximum velocity varying 3 to 20 m/sec and 5 to 30 m/sec, respectively, is designed for evaluating their performance. At the beginning of each simulation, some nodes are randomly selected out to act as a server. These selected servers provide randomly selected services. Table 1 shows the values of factors used in a simulation.

Table 1. Simulation Parameters

Parameter	Value
Number of nodes	20 to 100
Network Area (x, y)	1500m x 1500m
Mean query generate time (secs)	5
Hello Message Interval (secs)	5
Routing Protocol	AODV
Movement average speed (m/s)	3 to 20
Movement maximum speed (m/s)	5 to 30
Mobility Pattern	Random way-point
Duration	300s
Transmission range	250m
Server Rate	30%
Mac	Mac/802_11

5.2 Results of Simulation

The average search hop count, a measurement standard that evaluates algorithm performance is the number of average hops needed for the search. More nodes cache more related information, locality and service response will get higher and quicker, respectively. When a service requester found out available services, the number of physical hops for paths is reduced, it can quickly find them out without going through many nodes and that power of node is relatively less consumed. Figure 6 shows physical hop count from source node to destination node.

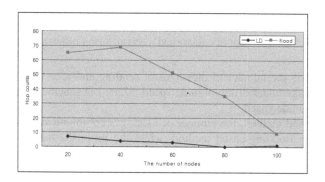

Fig. 6. Average physical hop count from source node to destination node

Figure 7 shows the number of messages nodes communicate. In flooding method, a number of messages are communicated by broadcasting messages for service advertisements and service searches to neighboring nodes, which means that a transmission of messages is delayed with nodes consuming lots of power.

To inspect the effects of node speed, we run simulation sets that use the two selected service discovery protocols, respectively. In these simulations, the number of nodes is fixed to 100. Each set includes four subsets of simulations, where average velocity is set to 5 m/s, 10 m/s, 15 m/s, 20 m/s, respectively. Figure 8 shows the effect

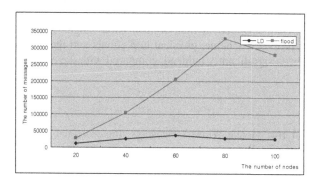

Fig. 7. Message count of sending and receiving

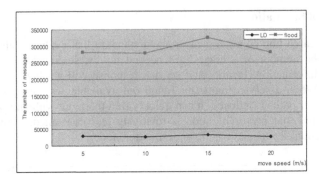

Fig. 8. Message count of sending and receiving under different node speed

of node speed on the number of messages of sending and receiving. LD scheme has the lower message under different node speed. Thus, LD scheme is effective protocol under different node speed.

In our proposed method, the number of messages communicated among nodes is a little more than flooding-based method, while the proposed method does not incur countless messages unlike flooding-based service discovery.

6   Conclusion

In this paper, we propose a service discovery scheme to effectively discover services by using only local information. The proposed scheme is suitable for a mobile ad-hoc network, where mobile devices with such features as high mobility and resource constraints comprise wireless networks without any infrastructure. While the flooding scheme incurs high costs in MANET, since there are lots of messages exchanged, our proposed scheme shows in simulation results that it is very effective in significantly reducing physical hop counts and the number of messages exchanged. A reduction in physical hop counts means reducing query delay by reducing response time, and a reduction in the number of messages exchanged implies a reduction in total network traffic costs and node workloads. Since nodes in MANET dynamically move and the neighboring nodes are changed in their transmission range. The simulation results show that, in the proposed scheme, physical hop counts and the number of messages exchanged have been significantly reduced, compared with the other protocol.

References

1. Toh, C.K.: Ad Hoc Mobile Wireless Networks. Protocols and Systems. Prentice-Hall, Englewood Cliffs (2002)
2. Meier, R., Cahill, V., Nedos, A., Clarke, S.: Proximity-Based Service Discovery in Mobile Ad Hoc Networks. In: Kutvonen, L., Alonistioti, N. (eds.) DAIS 2005. LNCS, vol. 3543, pp. 115–129. Springer, Heidelberg (2005)
3. The Gnutella web site, http://www.gnutella.com
4. The KaZaA web site, http://www.kazaa.com

5. Stoica, I., Morris, R., Karger, D., Kaashoek, M.F., Balakrishnan, H.: Chord A scalable peer-to-peer lookup service for internet applications. In: Proceedings of the 2001 conference on Applications technologies architectures and protocols for computer communications, pp. 149–160. ACM Press, New York (2001)
6. Ratnasamy, S., Francis, P., Handley, M., Karp, R., Schenker, S.: A scalable content addressable network. In: Proceedings of the 2001 conference on Applications technologies architectures and protocols for computer communications, pp. 161–172. ACM Press, New York (2001)
7. Rowstron, A.I.T., Druschel, P.: Pastry Scalable, decentralized object location, and routing for large-scale peer-to-peer systems. In: Guerraoui, R. (ed.) Middleware 2001. LNCS, vol. 2218, pp. 329–350. Springer, Heidelberg (2001)
8. Jini Architectural Overview: Technical White Paper, http://www.sun.com/software/jini/whitepapers/architecture.html
9. Guttman, E.: Service Location Protocol Automatic Discovery of IP Network Services. IEEE Internet Computing 3, 71–80 (1999)
10. White paper, Salutation Architecture overview (1998), http://www.salutation.org/whitepaper/originalwp.pdf
11. Helal, S., Desai, N., Verma, V., Lee, C.: Konark-A Service Discovery and Delivery Protocol for Ad-hoc Networks. In: Proc. of the Third IEEE Conference on Wireless Communication Networks (WCNC), New Orleans (March 2003)
12. Helal, O., Chakraborty, D., Tolia, S., Kushraj, D., Kunjithapatham, A., Gupta, G., Joshi, A., Finin, T.: Allia Alliance-based Service Discovery for Ad-Hoc Environments. In: Second ACM International Workshop on Mobile Commerce, in conjunction with Mobicom 2002, Atlanta GA, USA (2002)
13. Understanding UPnP. A White Paper, Microsoft Corporation (June 2000)
14. Chakraborty, D., Joshi, A., Yesha, Y., Finin, T.: Toward Distributed Service Discovery in Pervasive Computing Environments. IEEE Trans. on Mobile Computing 5(2), 97–112 (2006)
15. Perkins, C.E., Royer, E.M., Das, S.: Ad Hoc On-Demand Distance Vector Routing (AODV) Routing. RFC 3561, IETF (July 2003)
16. Cao, G.: Proactive Power-Aware Cache Management for Mobile Computing Systems. IEEE Trans. Computer 51(6), 608–621 (2002)
17. Yin., L., Cao, G.: Supporting Cooperative Caching in Ad Hoc Networks. IEEE Trans. on Mobile Computing 5(1), 77–89 (2006)
18. NS2 Object Hierarchy, http://www-sop.iniria.fr/planete/software/ns-doc/ns-current/aindex.html

A Formal Approach to Robustness Testing of Network Protocol

Chuanming Jing[1,3], Zhiliang Wang[2,3], Xia Yin[1,3], and Jianping Wu[1,2,3]

[1] Department of Computer Science & Technology, Tsinghua University
[2] Network Research Center of Tsinghua University
[3] Tsinghua National Laboratory for Information Science and Technology,
Beijing, P.R. China, 100084
{jcm,wzl,yxia}@csnet1.cs.tsinghua.edu.cn, jianping@cernet.edu.cn

Abstract. Robustness testing of network protocol aims to detect vulnerabilities of protocol specifications and implementations under critical conditions. However, related theory is not well developed and prevalent test practices have deficiencies. This paper builds a novel NPEFSM model containing sufficient inputs and their processing rules to formalize complex protocol. Based on this model, Normal-Verification Sequence is proposed to enhance verdict mechanism. We adopt various strategies to generate anomalous values for some fields of messages and further apply pairwise combination to systematically mutate messages. We propose compound anomalous test case to simplify test sequences and give its generation algorithm. Standard test specification language TTCN-3 is extended to describe compound anomalous test cases. As a case study, we test OSPFv2 sufficiently with a test system based on extended TTCN-3. Our method and test system can effectively discover vulnerabilities of protocol implementations as well as their inconsistencies with specifications.

1 Introduction

Network protocols are often partially specified. There are numerous invalid inputs for protocol implementations and how to handle these inputs is usually unspecified or specified ambiguously in protocol. Also protocol specifications contain optional requirements specified by "MAY" statements. These two cases provide certain flexibility to protocol implementations. As conformance testing only verifies whether an implementation conforms to its specification or not, the capability of error-detection is limited. National Vulnerability Database [1] reports that about 60% of the software vulnerabilities detected in 2007 were caused by input validation, format string vulnerability and buffer errors. Protocol robustness testing is the test to verify whether IUT (Implementation under Test) can function correctly in the presence of invalid inputs or stressful environmental conditions [2]. Robustness testing aims to detect vulnerabilities of protocol specifications and implementations, including [3]: vulnerabilities of malformed message parsing; vulnerabilities of state transitions; hole of buffer overflow etc. There have been large previous works about robustness testing [4-14]. Although their test practices have found vulnerabilities of protocol implementations, these approaches have certain limitations: 1) test cases generation lacks guidance of

J. Cao et al. (Eds.): NPC 2008, LNCS 5245, pp. 24–37, 2008.
© IFIP International Federation for Information Processing 2008

theory; 2) verdict mechanism needs improvement; 3) structure of test case is not optimal, resulting in large test costs; 4) test system is not generic to other protocols; 5) most use programming languages (e.g. C) to build test suite, so the readability, extensibility and maintainability of test suite are not good.

To cope with these deficiencies, we build a novel Nondeterministic Parameterized Extended Finite State Machine model. Our model has distinct benefits: 1) it contains sufficient inputs and their processing rules, thus it can guide robustness testing; 2) it supports variables, parameters of inputs/outputs and operations based on these values, thus it can model complex protocols. Based on this model, Normal-Verification Sequence is proposed to enhance verdict mechanism. Data-driven robustness testing focuses on inputting various invalid messages. We adopt various mutation strategies to generate anomalies for some fields of messages and further apply pairwise strategy [15,16] to systematically import anomalies to mutate multiple fields for each message. To inject test data efficiently and effectively, compound anomalous test case is proposed to simplify test sequences. The algorithm of test case generation is given. TTCN-3 [20] is extended to describe compound anomalous test cases. Implementing the function of generating test data automatically, the extended description is very simple and convenient to use. As a case study, we test OSPFv2 [21] sufficiently with a test system based on extended TTCN-3.

The rest of this paper is organized as follows. Related works are introduced in section 2. Section 3 proposes NPEFSM model. In section 4, pairwise strategy is used to combine anomalies and test case generation is discussed. We apply TTCN-3 to robustness testing and extend it in section 5. In section 6, we test OSPFv2 using our method. Conclusions and future work are given in section 7.

2 Related Works

Related works can be classified into research on model-based robustness testing [4,5] and test practices (often called Fuzz testing [6-14]). The model and framework for robustness testing are not well developed. [4,5] propose a formal framework, but mutation operations and fault injections are not done automatically. Hence it is difficult to generate large number of test cases.

Fuzz testing is a black-box testing method by injecting faults. The procedure is to generate test data, inject test data to IUT and make verdict. Currently, there are two methods to obtain numerous invalid messages: designing manually using script language [6-12]; generating semi-randomly data (e.g. most of tools listed in [13]). Various script languages are used to describe invalid messages such as BNF (Backus-Naur Form) [6], SBNF (Strengthened BNF)[7,8], SCL (Semantic Constraint Language) [9,10] and XML [11,12]. The production and injection of invalid PDUs are all done by tools implemented by C or Java. Also, other Fuzzing tools [13] can produce semi-random messages which are often blind to testing and each tool can only test a certain protocol due to weak extensibility. Intelligent Fuzzing requires injecting invalid inputs on the corresponding state. [7,8,11] all propose state identification by inferring from I/O sequences logged, but it is not practical for complex protocols. Related works about verdict mechanism are also not well developed. In test practice, they observe whether IUT is crashed or monitor the performance (e.g. CPU usage) of IUT under invalid injections. In [10,11], a simple sequence consisting of a valid request and corresponding reply is used to make verdict after fault injection.

So, it is highly desirable to have a formal approach to robustness testing. In our previous work [17], single-field mutation testing is studied. Based on this work, we give our full solutions for protocol robustness testing in this paper.

3   Formal Model and Testing Framework

3.1   Model Definition

Usual protocol specifications include variables and operations based on variable values. Extended Finite State Machine (EFSM) can be used in this situation. However, it is still not powerful enough to model some protocol systems where there are parameters associated with inputs and have effects on the predicates and actions of transitions [18]. Hence Parameterized Extended Finite State Machine (PEFSM) [18] is used to model protocol specifications. Robustness testing requires injecting many invalid messages. As most invalid messages and their processing rules are not well prescribed, state transitions after these invalid injections are often nondeterministic. So, we build a model for protocol robustness testing using NPEFSM (Nondeterministic Parameterized Extended Finite State Machine). Our model covers more detailed and precise nondeterministic features than traditional nondeterministic FSM and EFSM model.

Definition 1: NPEFSM for Protocol Robustness Testing
A Nondeterministic Parameterized Extended Finite State Machine (NPEFSM) is a 6-tuple $M=<I, O, \overline{X}, S, s_0, T>$, where:

1. $I=\{ i_1(\overrightarrow{v_1}), i_2(\overrightarrow{v_2}),...,i_p(\overrightarrow{v_p}) \}$ is the input alphabet with parameters $\overrightarrow{v}$; each input symbol
   $i_k(\overrightarrow{v_k})$ $(1 \leq k \leq p)$ carries a vector of parameter values $\overrightarrow{v_k}$;

   Also, we define $I=I_{spec} \cup I_{unspec}$. I_{spec} includes inputs that are prescribed in protocol specification and composed of valid PDUs as well as some invalid PDUs. I_{unspec} includes numerous inputs that are not prescribed definitely in protocol specification and composed of various invalid PDUs.

2. $O=\{ o_1(\overrightarrow{w_1}), o_2(\overrightarrow{w_2}),...,o_q(\overrightarrow{w_q}) \}$ is the output alphabet with parameters $\overrightarrow{w}$; each output symbol $o_k(\overrightarrow{w_k})$ $(1 \leq k \leq q)$ carries a vector of parameter values $\overrightarrow{w_k}$.

3. $\overline{X}$ is a vector denoting a finite set of variables with default initial values.

4. S is a finite set of states, $S=S_{spec}$, S_{spec} includes states prescribed in protocol specification. We introduce and define $S_?=\{s_{?i}|\ i=1,2,...\}$, $s_{?1}$, $s_{?2}$...are all nondeterministic states after nondeterministic or undefined transitions but within a range of states according to corresponding ambiguous protocol specification, i.e. for $i=1, 2,..., s_{?i}$ $\in S_i \subseteq S_{spec}$. So, $S = S_{spec} = S_{spec} \cup S_?$.

5. s_0: initial state.

6. T: a set of transitions. For $t \in T$, $t = s \xrightarrow{\ i(\overrightarrow{v})/o(\overrightarrow{w})\ /\ P(\overline{X},i(\overrightarrow{v}))\ /\ A(\overline{X},i(\overrightarrow{v}),o(\overrightarrow{w}))\ } s^*$ $(s \in S, s^* \in S)$ is a transition where s and $s^*$are the starting and ending state of this transition respectively; $i(\overrightarrow{v}) / o(\overrightarrow{w})$ is the input/output with parameters; $P(\overline{X}, i(\overrightarrow{v}))$ is a predicate of the variables and input parameters; the action $A(\overline{X}, i(\overrightarrow{v}), o(\overrightarrow{w}))$ is an operation on variables

as well as output parameters and this operation is based on current variable values and input parameter values.

$T=T_{deter}\cup T_{nondeter}=T_{deter}\cup(T_{nondeter-spec}\cup T_{nondeter-unspec})$. Each transition of T_{deter} is uniquely deterministic in protocol. $T_{deter}=\cup t$: $s_j \xrightarrow{i_j(\vec{v})/o_j(\vec{w})/P(\overline{X},i_j(\vec{v}))/A(\overline{X},i_j(\vec{v}),o_j(\vec{w}))} s_k$, where $s_j\in S_{spec}$, $s_k\in S_{spec}$; $i_j(\vec{v})\in I_{spec}$; $o_j(\vec{w})\in O$ $or\ o_j(\vec{w})=Null$. Each of $T_{nondeter-spec}$ is nondeterministic but specified clearly in protocol specification. $T_{nondeter-spec}=\cup t$:s_j $\xrightarrow{i_j(\vec{v})/o_j(\vec{w})/P(\overline{X},i_j(\vec{v}))/A(\overline{X},i_j(\vec{v}),o_j(\vec{w}))} s_{?k}$, where $s_j\in S_{spec}$, $s_{?k}\in S_?$; $i_j(\vec{v})\in I_{spec}$; $o_j(\vec{w})\in O$ $or\ o_j(\vec{w})=Null$. Each of $T_{nondeter-unspec}$ is nondeterministic and unspecified or specified ambiguously in specification. $T_{nondeter-unspec}=\cup t$: $s_j \xrightarrow{i_j(\vec{v})/-/true/-} s_{?k}$, where $s_j\in S_{spec}$, $s_{?k}\in S_?$; $i_j(\vec{v})\in I$, output and action are unspecified or specified ambiguously. □

Figure 1 shows a part of NPEFSM for OSPFv2 [21] Neighbor State Machine, predicates and actions are omitted. An example of transition is given in Table 1. The inputs and outputs are parameterized Database Description Packets (DDP). The parameters of DDP are DD sequence number (denoted as *Seq*) and I/M/MS (denoted as *Ims*). Predicate includes sequence number checking, I/M/MS checking and other validations. *y* is a variable used to check sequence number.

Figure 2 shows two kinds of state transitions under invalid injections. Figure 2(a) shows that after receiving an invalid input i_k ($i_k\in I_{spec}$), s_i transits to s_j according to related description in protocol specification. For example, OSPFv2 specification prescribes that receiving duplicate DDP will trigger "SeqNumberMismatch" and transit the state from "Exchange" or higher to "Exstart". Figure 2(b) shows that s_i transits to state $s_{?k}$ ($s_{?k}\in S_k=\{s_{ki}|\ i=1,2,...\}\subseteq S_{spec}$) because the transition after receiving i_j ($i_j\in I$) is prescribed indeterminately, ambiguously or even not prescribed in protocol specification. For example, during Database Exchanging, after receiving DDP, whether to check the syntax of each field of DDP.LSAHeader is not specified definitely. Suppose this syntax error: LSAHeader.LinkStateID="FFFFFFFF", if IUT checks this field, event "SeqNumberMismatch" will be triggered to transit the state to "Exstart". Otherwise, exchanging will go on until this fault can be found (maybe in LSA requesting process). So, after receiving i_j(DDP), $s_{?k}\in S_k=\{s_{k1}=$"Exstart", $s_{k2}=$"Exchange"$\}$ and $t_j\in T_{nondeter-unspec}$.

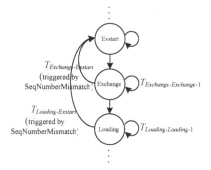

Fig. 1. A Part of NPEFSM for OSPFv2 Neighbor State Machine: Database Exchange

Table 1. An Example of Transition

Name	$T_{Exchange-Exchange}$-1
Start State	Exchange
End State	Exchange
Input	DDP(*Seq1, Ims1*)
Output	DDP(*Seq2, Ims2*)
Variables	*y,...*
Predicate	(*Seq1==y*)&& (*Ims1==011*)&&...
Action	*Seq2=y; y=Seq1+1;...*

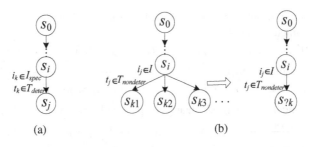

Fig. 2. (a) State transition prescribed definitely in protocol specification after invalid input **(b)** State transition prescribed ambiguously, indeterminately, or even not prescribed in protocol specification after invalid input

Some "MAY" statements in protocol specification also specify transitions belonging to $T_{nondeter\text{-}spec}$. We omit further exemplification.

Some special inputs can transit each of several states (denoted as S') to the same state, we propose Forced Transition as follows:

Definition 2: Forced Transition

Let $S' \subseteq S_{spec}$ and $s_j \in S_{spec}$.

$(\forall s \in S') \rightarrow s_j$ is a Forced Transition, iff, $\exists\ i_j(\vec{v}) \in I_{spec}$, such that $\forall s \in S'$,

$$s \xrightarrow{\ i_j(\vec{v})\,/\text{-}\,/\,true\,/\text{-}\ } s_j.$$

Especially, if $s_j = s_0$, such a forced transition is also called **Reset Transition**.

In Figure 3, if Forced Transition exists, $s_{?k}$ can receive certain input and transit to a deterministic state s_j according to Definition 2. In the former example about OSPFv2 Data Exchanging, event "SeqNumberMismatch" can force the machine to transit from $s_{?k}$ to s_j (s_j ="Exstart"), whether $s_{?k}$ ="Exstart" or "Exchange".

3.2 Robustness Requirement and Normal-Verification Sequence

The structure of a test case in conformance testing can be described as follows: **Test Case**=<State Leading Sequence, Executing Sequence, State Verification Sequence> [17, 18]. In robustness testing, we introduce a term called "anomalous test case" which can inject invalid data on corresponding state and make verdict. Instead of State Verification Sequence of conformance testing, Normal-Verification Sequence of robustness testing is executed to verify whether the state machine works properly. If it returns "Fail", we conclude that IUT behaves abnormally and has poor robustness. The structure of an anomalous test case can be described as follows: **Anomalous Test Case**=<State Leading Sequence, Invalid PDU Inputting, Normal-Verification Sequence>. The first step of robustness testing is to construct robustness requirement. In this paper, we use an intuitive and practical robustness requirement that IUT must keep normal state and continue normal operations conforming to protocol specification under invalid injections. According to the state transitions shown in Figure 2, we propose two types of Normal-Verification Sequences as follows:

Normal-Verification Sequence_1

Suppose at state s_i, an invalid PDU $i_j(\vec{v})$ is received and $i_j(\vec{v}) \in I_{spec}$.

If t: $\quad s_i \xrightarrow{\; i_j(\vec{v})/o_j(\vec{w})/P(\overline{X},i_j(\vec{v}))/A(\overline{X},i_j(\vec{v}),o_j(\vec{w})) \;} s_j$, *i.e. $t \in T_{deter}$. Normal-Verification Sequence= state verification sequence of s_j.*

Normal-Verification Sequence_2

Suppose at state s_i, an invalid PDU $i_j(\vec{v})$ is received and $i_j(\vec{v}) \in I$.

If t: $\quad s_i \xrightarrow{\; i_j(\vec{v})/o_j(\vec{w})/P(\overline{X},i_j(\vec{v}))/A(\overline{X},i_j(\vec{v}),o_j(\vec{w})) \;} s_{?k}$ *or t:* $s_i \xrightarrow{\; i_j(\vec{v})/-/true/- \;} s_{?k}$, *i.e. $t \in (T_{nondeter\text{-}spec} \cup T_{nondeter\text{-}unspec}) = T_{nondeter}$. Normal-Verification Sequence = state identification sequence of $s_{?k}$.*

State identification [18][19] will cause the robustness test sequences to be very complex, so we define another Normal-Verification Sequence to approximately replace Normal-Verification Sequence_2:

Normal-Verification Sequence_2-1

After receiving invalid PDU, the ending state transited to is $s_{?k} \in S_?$ and $s_{?k} \in S_k = \{s_{ki} \mid i=1,2,\ldots\} \subseteq S_{spec}$, If there exists Forced Transition: $(s_{?k} \in S_k) \rightarrow s_j$, Normal-Verification Sequence $\approx ((s_{?k} \in S_k) \rightarrow s_j) + $ (state verification sequence of s_j).

Forced Transition and Reset Transition are very common in network protocols. For OSPFv2, event "1-Way", "KillNbr", "SeqNumberMismatch" and "BadLSReq" can trigger Forced transition. So Normal-Verification Sequence_2-1 can be widely used.

A PEFSM can be unfolded into a FSM. In this paper, we do not discuss the construction of state verification sequence for FSM or PEFSM model which is a classical problem in conformance testing [18]. We further illustrate our robustness requirement. For anomalous test cases using Normal-Verification Sequence_1, robustness requirement is the same with conformance testing. For test cases using Normal-Verification Sequence_2-1, robustness requirement can be illustrated using a Probabilistic Finite State Machine (PFSM) shown in Figure 4. s^* is a trap state which is not an element of S_{spec}. P_1 is the probability of state transition from s_i to s^* after receiving an invalid input. P_2 is the probability of state transition from s^* to s^* after receiving an input which is used to trigger Forced Transition. Strict robustness requirement discussed before is $P_1=0$. In order to ease test practices, we adopt $P_1 \cdot P_2=0$ as our robustness requirement.

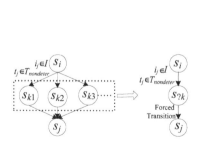

Fig. 3. Forced Transition of $s_{?k}$

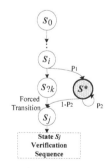

Fig. 4. Robustness requirement analysis

4 Test Case Generation

4.1 Invalid Inputs Generation

A PDU is composed of several fields denoted as f_1, f_2…Invalid PDUs can be syntactically or semantically invalid. The former disobey protocol specification data formats. The latter have valid syntax but conflict with protocol state, configuration and policies. We mutate several valid inputs to generate many messages either syntactically invalid or semantically invalid.

Single-field mutation rules: $Fun_{FieldMutation}()$
We define some typical invalid field values which attackers tend to exploit:

1) Field value mutation rules
In [17], we define Boundary value; Field values mismatch; Format error; Length, Checksum and Encapsulation error. We also define input partition values: {Min, Min+(Max-Min)/n, Min+2*(Max-Min)/n,…,Max}(Suppose Field $f_i \in$ (Min,Max)). n is a parameter set by tester. All these values can be used to replace a valid field value.

2) Field mutation rules:

- Removal and Addition: a field of PDU is removed or added;
- Overflow: one field is replaced with another field with bigger bytes;
- Permutation: sequence of fields in PDU changes.

Multi-field mutation rules using pairwise algorithm
Some fields of one message may have consistency with each other. Value changing of one field may influence values of other fields. Also, protocol implementations may not parse fields of receiving message in the sequence of one by one. So it is necessary to inject messages whose multiple fields are invalid. Suppose 8 fields of one PDU will be mutated and each field has 5 invalid values, total of mutated PDUs will be 5^8=390625. So exhaustive testing is impractical. In this paper we introduce pairwise combination which can guarantee that each pair of faults between any two fields is covered by at least one combination. Pairwise combination is a good trade-off between test effort and test coverage. Algorithm 1 adopts a heuristic pairwise algorithm called In-Parameter-Order [15,16] to generate test data.

Algorithm 1. pairwise (F, Q)

Input: $F=\{f_1, f_2,…, f_n\}$; $Q=\{ q_{f_1}, q_{f_2},…, q_{f_n} \}$; /*each q_{f_i} is a set of values for field f_i. */

Output: $T=\{T_1, T_2,…T_m\}$; /*each $T_i =\{v_{f1}, v_{f2},…,v_{fn}\}$, where $v_{f_j} \in q_{f_j}$ $(1 \leq j \leq n)$, i.e. T_i is a n-dimension vector containing values for field $f_1, f_2,…, f_n$, respectively.*/

1 $T=\{(v_1, v_2) \mid v_1$ and v_2 are values of f_1 and f_2 ,respectively}$;

2 if (n ==2) **return** T;

3 **for each** field f_i, i=3,4,…,n **do**

4   T= In-Parameter-Order (T, Q, f_i); /*see references [15,16] */

5 **return** T;

Then we give an example. Suppose $F=\{f_1, f_2, f_3, f_4\}$, each has four unsigned boundary values and one 2-partition values. $q_{f_1} = q_{f_4} = \{00,01,7F,FE,FF\}$; $q_{f_2} = \{0000,0001,7FFF,FFFE,FFFF\}$; $q_{f_3} = \{000000, 000001, 7FFFFF, FFFFFE, FFFFFF\}$. Applying Algorithm 1, we can get test data shown in Figure 5:

$$
T_{pairwise}(F(f_1,f_2,f_3,f_4)) = \begin{pmatrix} T_1 \\ T_2 \\ T_3 \\ T_4 \\ \cdots \\ T_{32} \end{pmatrix} = \begin{array}{cccc} f_1 & f_2 & f_3 & f_4 \\ 00 & 0000 & 000000 & 00 \\ 00 & 0001 & 000001 & 01 \\ 00 & 7FFF & 7FFFFF & 7F \\ 00 & FFFE & FFFFFE & FE \\ 00 & FFFF & FFFFFF & FF \\ 01 & 0000 & 000001 & 7F \\ 01 & 0001 & 000000 & FE \\ \cdots & \cdots & \cdots & \cdots \\ 00 & FFFF & 000000 & 7F \end{array}
$$

Fig. 5. Test generation using pairwise combination

In above example, compared to the exhaustive combination (test data set total: $5^4=625$), Algorithm 1 only generates 32 test data and each pair of faults between any two fields is covered by at least one PDU.

4.2   Robustness Test Case Generation

According to the definition of robustness testing (see section 1), the quantity and variety of invalid messages are important criterions for testing. There are numerous invalid PDUs and how to inject needs to be well studied. So we propose compound anomalous test case which can also simplify test sequences: 1) One compound anomalous test case focuses on several fields of one PDU (the combination of these fields can be denoted as $F_l \subseteq PDU$). If the verdict is "Fail", it means IUT cannot parse F_l with robustness; 2) Two or more anomalous messages with different invalid values of F_l should be injected in one compound anomalous test case. Values of other fields of these messages cannot be mutated and keep valid.

If $|F_l|=1$, it means only one field is mutated and the corresponding test case belongs to single-field robustness testing. If $|F_l|\geq 2$ (means multiple fields are mutated), this test case belongs to multi-field robustness testing. For test case returning "Fail" in multi-field testing, we should decompose it into several separated test cases executed further to analyze why it fails. As robustness testing is often done after conformance testing, the pass rate is often high, thus test execution of separated test cases will not consume much work. For test cases using Normal-Verification Sequence_1, the formats of Compound Anomalous Test Cases are constructed as follows:

Compound Anomalous Test Case-1$(m, pdu.F_l) = <$ State (s_0 to s_i) Leading Sequence, {Invalid pdu Inputting, State (s_j to s_i) Leading Sequence}$*m$, State Verification Sequence of $s_i >$.

Where, "{ }$*m$" means the sequences contained in "{ }" are executed m times. Also, the fields under test must be mutated before each executing loop. m means the number of invalid messages generated by mutation rules for $pdu.F_l$.

For test cases using Normal-Verification Sequence_2-1, the formats of Compound Anomalous Test Cases are constructed as follows:

Compound Anomalous Test Case-2 $(m, pdu.F_l)$ = <State $(s_0$ to $s_i)$ Leading Sequence, {Invalid pdu Inputting, State$(s_{?k}$ to $s_j)$Leading Sequence (suppose Forced Transition $(s_{?k} \in S_k) \to s_j$ exists), State$(s_j$ to $s_i)$ Leading Sequence }*m, State Verification Sequence of s_i >.

Figure 6 shows structures of compound anomalous test cases. Algorithm 2 is defined for Compound Anomalous Test Case-1 generation. We omit the algorithm of Compound Anomalous Test Case-2 generation due to space limitation.

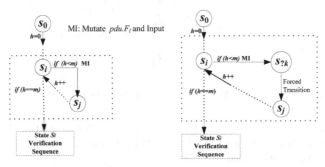

(a) Compound Anomalous Test Case-1   (b) Compound Anomalous Test Case-2

Fig. 6. Two Types of Compound Anomalous Test Cases ($pdu.F_l$ is under test)

Algorithm 2: Compound Anomalous Test Case-1 generation

Input: PDU $pdu=\{f_1, f_2,...,f_n\}$; /* pdu: a valid PDU */
    $F_l \subseteq pdu$; /* F_l :a fields set under test */
    s_i, s_j;/*inject anomalies on state s_i and the state transits to s_j in protocol specification*/
Output: $TestCase_{F_i}$;   /* test case for $pdu.F_l$ */

Initial Value: $TestCase_{F_i}$ =**Null**;

1   $Q=\{ q_{f_1}, q_{f_2},...,q_{f_n} \}$; $q_{f_1}, q_{f_2},...,q_{f_n}$ =**Null** ; /* q_{f_i} is a set of values for field f_i */

2   $T_{F_i} = \{T_1, T_2,...T_m\}$; $T_1, T_2,... T_m$=**Null**; /* see Algorithm 1 in section 4.1*/

3   **For each** $f_k \in F_l$ **do**

4   q_{f_k} = $Fun_{FieldMutation}$ (f_k); /*generate anomalous values, see section 4.1*/

5   **If** ($|F_l|$=1)   /*single-field robustness testing*/

6       $T_{F_i} = Q$;

7   **If** ($|F_l| \geq 2$)   /*multi-field robustness testing*/

8   T_{F_i} = pairwise (F_l, Q); /* see Algorithm 1 in section 4.1*/

9   $TestCase_{F_i}$.**add**(State $(s_0$ to $s_i)$Leading Sequence);

10 **For each** $T_h \in T_{F_i}$ **do**

11   **replace** each field of $pdu.F_l$ **with** values in T_h, respectively;

12      $TestCase_{F_i}$.**add** (Invalid pdu Inputting, State $(s_j$ to $s_i)$ Leading Sequence);

13 $TestCase_{F_i}$.**add**(State Verification Sequence of s_i);

14 **Return** $TestCase_{F_i}$;

Compound Anomalous Test Case-1 is similar to test case of conformance testing and we do not discuss its property. For Compound Anomalous Test Case-2, different invalid PDU is injected in each loop. We have deduced that the "Fail" probability for each loop is $P_1 \cdot P_2$ (see section 3.2 and Figure 4).Then the "Fail"probability of Compound Anomalous Test Case-2 can be deduced:

$$P_{fail}(m) = 1 - \prod_{i=1}^{m} (1 - P_{i\_1} \cdot P_{i\_2}) \text{ (where } P_{i\_1} \cdot P_{i\_2} \text{ is the fail rate for } ith \text{ invalid injection)}$$

From this equation, we can deduce that the fail rate increases as m increases. An intuitive reason is that the more invalid data are injected, the more holes may be discovered.

5 TTCN-3 Extensions and Test System

TTCN-3 [20] is developed by ETSI (European Telecommunications Standards Institute) and standardized by the ITU-T. Test suite described by TTCN-3 has good readability, extensibility and maintainability. But TTCN-3 is not flexible: 1) TTCN-3 cannot support mutation operations well, so we should define thousands of invalid test data using TTCN-3 [17]; 2) Using TTCN-3, it is difficult or even impossible to give the description of compound anomalous test cases.

We extend TTCN-3 in syntax for robustness testing as follows: 1) Add a new keyword "pairwise" which represents the complex algorithm of compound anomalous test case generation; 2) Add a new keyword "count", the value behind this keyword means the number of mutations for one field; 3) In the description statement using "pairwise", each field of the message in format of "global template" can be modified to be invalid so test suite need define only a little data.

If the parameters of "pairwise" statement are only for one field of one message, the test case belongs to single-field testing. Otherwise, it belongs to multi-field testing and pairwise combination will be used. Similar to extension using "pairwise", we can make extensions to accomplish other mutations rules (e.g. Removal, Overflow) defined in section 4.1. We omit these due to space limitation. "pairwise" statement supports describing two types of Compound Anomalous Test Cases. We give a description of test case belonging to Compound Anomalous Test Case-2:

```
testcase Onebyone_HL1_Opt( )   runs on MyTestComponentAsync
  system SystemComponent    {
    map(mtc:MyPortAsync, system:SystemPort1);
    P1( );
    pairwise HL1( Mask octetstring 4 count 5 record_value;
                  Hint octetstring 2 count 6;
                   Opt octetstring 1 count 8) {
       Onebyone_HL1();
    }
    Normal_Verification( );
  }
```

Most anomalies are generated automatically according to $Fun_{FieldMutation}()$ (see section 4.1). "**octetstring** n **count** m" means generating invalid data set which consists of

4 boundary unsigned values and m-4 partition values (see section 4.1), each is in the format of n octetstrings. Some anomalies can be defined manually in "Const Record" (e.g. "record_value" in above statements). When above statements (other keywords in bold are introduced in [20]) are compiled, invalid data for field HL1.Mask, HL1.Hint and HL1.Opt are generated (e.g. $q_{f_{Mask}}$ ={4 boundary values, (5-4) partition values and values in "record_value"}), further pairwise algorithm $T_{pairwise}(F(f_{Mask}, f_{Hint}, f_{Opt}))$ is executed to generate invalid messages. "Onebyone_HL1" is a function using Forced Transition. During test case executing, "Onebyone_HL1" will be executed continually for many loops until all the invalid test data are injected to IUT. Finally, Normal_Verification() is executed to make verdict.

Based on TTCN-3 and its extension, we have developed a test system called PITSv3 which is introduced sufficiently in [23]. We omit this due to space limitation.

6   Case Study: OSPFv2

OSPFv2 [21] defines five kinds of messages including: Hello, Database Description (DDP), Link State Request (LSR), Link State Update (LSU) and Link State Acknowledgment (Ack). It also defines five kinds of Link State Advertisements (LSAs). We design test suites for single-field and multi-field robustness testing respectively. We use Forced Transitions (e.g. "1-Way", "SeqNumberMismatch" and "BadLSReq" [21]) to construct Normal-Verification Sequence.

Table 2 lists test suite. Invalid messages are injected on corresponding state. In test practice, we use PITSv3 to connect with IUT through a link. We choose Zebra-0.94 [22] installed in Linux as IUT.

Table 2. Test suite of compound anomalous test cases for OSPFv2

| Test Group | Test Content | Number | |
	(State / Invalid PDU received)	Single-field	Multi-field
OSPF Head	Init / Hello	14	8
Hello	2-way / Hello	16	6
DDP0	Exstart / DDP0(without LSA Header)	8	4
DDP1	Exchange / DDP1(include one LSA Header)	22	12
LSR	Exchange / LSR	6	2
Ack	Exchange / Ack	16	6
LSA_HEAD	Exchange / LSU(include Router_LSA)	14	10
LSU_RLSA	Exchange / LSU(include Router_LSA)	16	10
LSU_NLSA	Full / LSU (include Network _LSA)	4	5
LSU_S3LSA	Full / LSU (include Type3 Summary _LSA)	4	1
LSU_S4LSA	Full / LSU (include Type4 Summary _LSA)	4	1
LSU_AsLSA	Full / LSU (include As External_LSA)	6	2
	Total	130	67

For single-field testing}, we set m with different values using "count" keyword in TTCN-3 (see section 4.2 and 5). During test, we choose m=5~30. Thus, about 650~3900 invalid messages are injected in total 130 test cases. Test results are shown in Figure 7 (Fail Rate I). Test verdicts of Fail Rate I base on robustness requirement (see section 3.2). Fail rate is 5.38% when m=5~20 and it increases to 6.92% when

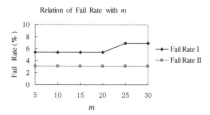

Fig. 7. Test results for single-field robustness testing of Zebra-0.94

m=25, 30. These results indicate that the more invalid data are injected, the more holes may be discovered (see section 4.2). During test, we also sum up test cases (Fail Rate II) returning "fail" due to critical vulnerabilities which cause IUT to crash or be quiescent (IUT may not crash, but can not reply to inputs). Fail Rate II shows that there are always 4 test cases (fail rate: 3.08%) returning "Fail" due to critical vulnerabilities as m increases from 5 to 30.

In multi-field testing, we assign m=5 (each field has 5 invalid values). Each test case can inject about 25~40 messages generated by pairwise algorithm. So invalid messages injected are about 1675~2680 in total 67 test cases. Test verdicts are based on robustness requirement (see section 3.2) and the fail rate is 8/67=11.9%.

Based on test results, critical vulnerabilities of Zebra-0.94 are analyzed: 1) Zebra cannot parse invalid messages with mutated "length" field in OSPF header robustly and the OSPF routine crashes. Analyzing the source code, we find that the checksum routine (in_cksum in checksum.c) does not compare the "length" field in OSPF header with the "length" field in the IP header so that the routine reads past the end of the heap into unauthorized memory space. 2)LSA header also exists the same vulnerability. The LSA checksum routine (ospf_lsa_checksum in ospf_lsa.c) does not verify the validity of the length field in the LSA header. This occurs only for LSA Header in LSU packets.

7   Conclusions and Future Work

It is desirable to test the robustness, reliability of network devices. The work and contribution of this paper are given as follows: we build a novel NPEFSM to effectively guide robustness testing; Normal-Verification Sequence is proposed to enhance verdict mechanism; we apply pairwise strategy to systematically import anomalies to mutate messages and further generate compound test cases which can simplify test sequences; TTCN-3 is extended to describe compound anomalous test cases. While our approach and test system are generic enough to be applied to all protocols, we will focus on application layer protocols (e.g. HTTP, SMTP) in future work as they typically handle human user level inputs that may have more faults. We will also apply our method to test real-time distributed systems.

Acknowledgment. This work is supported by the National Natural Science Foundation of China under Grant No. 60572082.

References

1. National Vulnerability Database, http://nvd.nist.gov/
2. IEEE Standard Glossary of Software Engineering Terminology. IEEE Std 610.12-1990, p. 64 (1990)
3. Pothamsetty, V., Akyol, B.: A Vulnerability Taxonomy for Network Protocols: Corresponding Engineering Best Practice Countermeasures. In: IASTED Internet and Communications conference, US Virgin Islands (November 2004)
4. Fernandez, J.-C., Mounier, L., Pachon, C.: A Model-Based Approach for Robustness Testing. In: The 17th IFIP International Conference on Testing of Communicating Systems (TestCom 2005), Concordia, Canada, May 30-June 2 (2005)
5. Saad-Khorchef, F., Rollet, A., Castanet, R.: A framework and a tool for robustness testing of communicating software. In: ACM Symposium on Applied Computing (SAC 2007), pp. 1461–1466 (2007)
6. Oulu University Secure Programming Group. PROTOS (2002), http://www.ee.oulu.fi/research/ouspg/protos/index.html
7. Xiao, S., Li, S., Wang, X., Deng, L.: ARF, Cisco Systems, Inc. Fault-oriented Software Robustness Assessment for Multicast Protocols. In: Proceedings of the Second IEEE International Symposium on Network Computing and Applications (NCA 2003) (2003)
8. Xiao, S., Deng, L., Li, S., Wang, X.: ARF, Cisco Systems, Inc. Integrated TCP/IP Protocol Software Testing for Vulnerability Detection. In: Proceedings of the 2003 International Conference on Computer Networks and Mobile Computing (ICCNMC 2003) (2003)
9. Turcotte, Y., Tal, O., Knight, S.: Security Vulnerabilities Assessment of the X.509 Protocol by Syntax-Based Testing. In: Military Communications Conference 2004 (MILCOM 2004), Monterey CA, October 2004, vol. 3, pp. 1572–1578 (2004)
10. Tal, O., Knight, S., Dean, T.: Syntax-based Vulnerability Testing of Frame-based Network Protocols. In: Proc. 2nd Annual Conference on Privacy, Security and Trust, Fredericton, Canada, October 2004, pp. 155–160 (2004)
11. Banks, G., Cova, M., Felmetsger, V., Almeroth, K., Kemmerer, R., Vigna, G.: SNOOZE: toward a Stateful NetwOrk prOtocol fuzZEr. In: Information Security Conference (ISC), Samos Island, Greece (September 2006)
12. Neves, N.F., Antunes, J., Correia, M., Veríssimo, P., Neves, R.: Using Attack Injection to Discover New Vulnerabilities. In: Proceedings of the International Conference on Dependable Systems and Networks (DSN 2006), June 2006, pp. 457–466 (2006)
13. FuzzingTools, http://www.scadasec.net/secwiki/FuzzingTools
14. Vasan, A.M.M.: ASPIRE: Automated Systematic Protocol Implementation Robustness Evaluation. In: Proceedings of the 2004 Australian Software Engineering Conference (ASWEC 2004), April 2004, p. 241 (2004)
15. Lei, Y., Tai, K.C.: In-parameter-order: a test generation strategy for pairwise testing. In: Proceedings Third IEEE Intl. High-Assurance Systems Engineering Symp., pp. 254–261 (1998)
16. Tai, K.C., Lei, Y.: A test generation strategy for pairwise testing. IEEE Trans on Software Engineering 28(1), 109–111 (2002)
17. Jing, C., Wang, Z., Shi, X., Yin, X., Wu, J.: Mutation Testing of Protocol Messages Based on Extended TTCN-3. In: Proceedings of the IEEE 22nd International Conference on Advanced Information Networking and Applications (AINA 2008), Japan, pp. 667–674 (2008)
18. Lee, D., Yannakakis, M.: Principles and Methods of Testing Finite-State Machines-A Survey. Proceedings of IEEE 84(8), 1089–1123 (1996)

19. Alur, R., Courcoubetis, C., Yannakakis, M.: Distinguishing tests for nondeterministic and probabilistic machines. In: Symposium on Theory of Computer Science, pp. 363–372. ACM, New York (1995)
20. ETSI: ETSI Standard ES 201 873-1 V3.2.1(2007-03): The Testing and Test Control Notation version 3; Part 1: TTCN-3 Core Language. European Telecommunications Standards Institute (ETSI), Sophia-Antipolis, France (2007)
21. Moy, J.: OSPF Version 2, RFC 2328 (April 1998)
22. Zebra-0.94, http://www.zebra.org/
23. Yin, X., Wang, Z., Wu, J., Jing, C., Shi, X.: Researches on a TTCN-3-based protocol testing system and its extension. Science in China Series F: Information Sciences (accepted, 2008)

Deadline Probing: Towards Timely Cognitive Wireless Network

Panlong Yang*, Guihai Chen, and Qihui Wu

Institute of Communication Engineering, PLAUST
Computer Science Department, Nanjing University. Nanjing, Jiangsu Province, China
plyang@computer.org, gchen@nju.edu.cn, qiwu@google.com

Abstract. A confidential and effective probing is fundamental to a cooperative and cognitive wireless network. Previous seminar works are not deadline sensitive, and often suffer from highly dynamic multi-channel environments. As they focus more on transmitting packets with the optimal channel, resources are not efficiently used when sufficient channels are available in multi-radio multi-channel systems. Decisions are made without time constraints, while in dynamic wireless environments, deadlines are always presented for both probing and data transmission process. In this paper, we propose a transmission deadline probing paradigm, and an optimal probing and transmission schedule with time constraints is proposed, which is a pure threshold policy. Simulation results show that, deadline probing paradigm effectively improves network resource utilization as multiple channels presented with probing and transmission deadlines.

Keywords: Cognitive Radio, Mobility, Scheduling, Wireless Network.

1 Introduction

As fundamental resources in self-organizing wireless network, channels qualities and link durations are important factors in achieving efficient data transmissions. On one hand, mobility causes dynamic topology changes between mobile devices in network, which would eventually lead to packet loss and additional routing messages. Routing protocol overhead and undelivered roaming packets degrade network performance dramatically. On the other hand, spatial and temporal varying characteristics of wireless channels would make the probing policy difficult and degrade scheduling efficiency. Great efforts are needed in finding an opportunistically optimal channel and time period to transmit packets [1] [2].

At the same time, many research works [10][5] have been done on selecting routes in highly dynamic and self-organizing wireless network. However, these works suffer from the following two aspects. One is that, although joint works

* This work is supported in part by the National Basic Research Program of China (973 Program) under grant No. 2006CB303004. China 863 project Grant No.2007AA01Z267. Jiangsu High-Tech Research Project of China under Grant No.BG2007391.

J. Cao et al. (Eds.): NPC 2008, LNCS 5245, pp. 38–49, 2008.

on routing, channel assignment and scheduling have been proposed, they are all based on a relative static network topology. For those algorithms based on globally optimizations, any changes on network topology would cause large amount of control messages overhead, which would degrade network performance as most of the time are spent on computing the optimal value and the optimal schedule. The other is that, unstable forwarder would cause intermittent links in network, which lead to frequent re-routing in network scale.

Deadline probing mechanism would intelligently select links with relatively long duration, and provide scheduling algorithm with time constraints. Scheduling according to both transmitting jobs and channel transmitting capability will make a more efficient usage on channels, and time constraints strengthen the scheduling algorithm in time scale.

The main contributions of this paper are listed as follows: Firstly, we propose an effective deadline probing algorithm in dealing with mobile wireless network environment. Link duration is the time constraints between two nodes, and by using the adaptive beacon messages, we explore the mobility factors of the moving node, and evaluate the link duration time, which is important to optimal channel assignment.

Secondly, we propose a multi-channel transmission schedule algorithm which considers traffic arrival rate and transmission deadline. Channels are assigned to the appropriate transmissions which is "suitable" to accomplish the transmitting job.

The remainders of this paper are organized as follows. We review the seminar works related in Section 2. Section 3 we formulate our problems. In section 4, we propose a deadline probing algorithm. Section 5 transmission schedule is modeled as a sequential job assignment algorithm with deadline constraints. Numerical results and simulation results are presented in section 6. Section 7 concludes the paper.

2   Related Work

Many seminar works have been done in order to opportunistically utilize the multiple available channels [1][2][4] with relative good quality. In [4], Ji et al propose a scheme named Medium Access Diversity (MAD) to probe channel with time and space varying quality at the MAC layer. By effectively using the multi-channel diversity, the user can select the receiver with best channel condition. Channel probing with opportunistic transmission has been widely studied recently. Similar problems have been studied in [1][2][4].

In all those applications, optimal channel probing can be achieved in order to set a tradeoff between obtaining useful channel information and consuming valuable probing times. It is usually assumed in these applications that, more channels are ready for transmission, and the only thing probing policy needs to consider is to select the best one among them, with a joint considerations on probing cost. In multi-channel systems, independent optimization on one channel transmission is not sufficient. In the perspective view of overall network throughput, if wireless channels are enough, selecting one channel for transmission would reduce overall channel utilization.

Seminar work in [1] presents a pure threshold based algorithm on optimal stopping strategy of channel probing. It is a tradeoff between channel quality reward and probing cost. [2] propose a distributed scheme, which models the probing procedure as a contention and threshold based process. Seminar work in [1] assumes that channel state is independent of the state of other channels during transmission. It is true if we take channel state as the only metric for opportunistic transmission. However, in real network deployment, if the channels are not enough, the links in network would congest for limited number of channels. Selecting one channel would face challenges, one is that the larger reward channels would possibly be preferred by all nodes, and the correlations between channels[1] would somehow make the contention even worse. Another challenge is that, as the time progresses, more channels are probed, and the rest of the channels are unused by other transmissions are becoming less, which would the contention on channel selection.

These works also assume that channel sates are rather stable in a relative long period, but it is not true since channel quality is a parameter varying with time [5][6].

3   Problem Formation

3.1   Deadline Probing Model

The movement model of each node in network is random way point (RWP), where each node in network randomly selects a position as its destination in a convex region, and selects a speed randomly with a uniformly distributed region $[v_{min}, v_{max}]$, and the node moves toward its destination at its chosen speed directly. Transmission power can be adaptively adjusted in the transmission power set $\Pi = \{P_1, P_2, ..., P_m\}$. There are m levels of transmission range respectively, which form the range set $\Gamma = \{R_1, R_2, ..., R_m\}$. At the physical layer, we simplified our model to free-space model and a SINR based receiving, as defined in [11]; while at the MAC layer, we use the IEEE 802.11 model. As mentioned in the following sections, our proposed scheduling and mobility awareness mechanism are independent to MAC layer protocols, and only need a power adjustable transmission scheme.

In mobile wireless network, duration time between nodes in dynamic topology is hard to achieve. The first problem is that in highly dynamic network, transit links are always existing in network entirely. These links would lead network communication into fluctuation state, and no effective mobility mining is available as links in network are unstable. The second reason is that, nodes are moving in different velocity, with different speed and direction. As RSSI estimation methods have been applied [10], it will suffer from weak and unstable radio signals.

In order to solve these problems, we need a mobility-aware mechanism in evaluating the link stability. And we assume that, no localization and speed measurement instrument is available to nodes in network.

3.2   Channel Quality Probing and Scheduling

We consider a wireless system consisting of n channels. There are $\mathcal{N}$ nodes in graph $\mathcal{G} = \langle \mathcal{V}, \mathcal{E} \rangle$, with $\mathcal{M}$ edges such that $e(i,j) = \langle v_i, v_j \rangle \in \mathcal{E}$. With each channel $j \in \Omega$, the channel quality would be a random variable X_j. It is assumed that, each channel must be probed before being used for transmission after a period of that in order to avoid the channel quality variation[6][5]. We also assume that, channel quality values are independently and identically distributed if homogeneous network is given. While in a heterogeneous network, distribution of different channels varies.

As we use multiple channels to transmit packets dynamically and concurrently, the top k among all channels having been probed are selected in terms of their channel quality value X_j, which could be modeled as the following equations:

$$MaxE[J_N(\boldsymbol{u}_1^N)] = E \sum_{1 \leq k \leq N} u_k X_k \qquad (1)$$

with $\boldsymbol{u}_1^N = (u_1, u_2, ..., u_N)$ satisfying the constraints. $u_j \in \mathcal{U}_j = \{0,1\}, j = 1, 2, ..., N, \sum_{1 \leq k \leq N} u_k = n$. $J_N(*)$ denotes the reward value, in this paper, it denotes the probed channel bandwidth. $E[*]$ denotes the expectation of reward value. It has been proved in [7] that, at each step j, with $N - j + 1$ channels still available and a_j already selected for transmission. And the optimal result is up to a threshold value $\tilde{s}(j, a_j)$ such that the channel j with quality value X_j is selected if larger than $\tilde{s}(j, a_j)$ and is rejected otherwise. Although such threshold probing criteria is optimal for multi-channel probing problem, it does not consider limitations on channel probing duration and number of admissible channels.

As multiple channels can be probed, another question naturally arises that, as the packets for transmission arrive sequentially, locally assign packets to different channels would be important, as packets should be successfully transmitted before the probing deadline reaches, and not all transmission need to be transmitted on optimal channels. And the local channel assignment algorithm can be described as:

Problem. *How to assign sequentially arriving packets to multiple channels with different bandwidth in order to maximize number of successful transmissions, where each packet transmission has a transmission deadline?*

4   Deadline Probing Algorithm

4.1   Threshold Based Filtering

As shown in Fig. 1, node i and node j are located on position in planar labeled O and P respectively. According to deadline probing algorithm, probing range

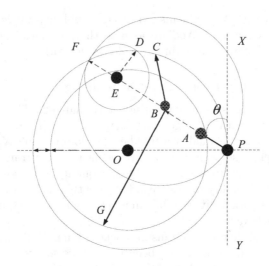

Fig. 1. Threshold based neighbor selection

is $\left\|\overrightarrow{OP}\right\| = R$, with maximum transmitting power. And the one-phase tolerant transmission range is $\left\|\overrightarrow{OQ}\right\| = (1-\Delta)R$. And we denote Δ as "tolerance factor". Node j is moving along direction at $\overrightarrow{BP}$. We assume that, $\angle BPX = \phi$. Since

$$\left\|\overrightarrow{BN}\right\| = \|BP\| - \|PN\| = 2\|PM\| - (\|PM\| - \|MN\|)$$
$$= \|PM\| + \|MN\|$$

and $\left\|\overrightarrow{PM}\right\| = R \cdot \sin\theta, \left\|\overrightarrow{MN}\right\| = \sqrt{(1-\Delta)^2 R^2 - (R\cos\theta)^2}$.

And it can be concluded that,

$$\left\|\overrightarrow{BN}\right\| = R.\sin\theta + \sqrt{(1-\Delta)^2 R^2 - (R\cos\theta)^2} \tag{2}$$

Available link duration is denoted as $U(\theta, v, \Delta)$. Threshold based stability means that link duration $\left\|\overrightarrow{BN}\right\| \geq U_{thre}$ and we can get the θ_{min} and θ_{max}, and accordingly the tolerant factor Δ. According to series of equations listed above, we can get the value that, $\theta_{min} = \arcsin\frac{U_{thre}}{R}$ and $\theta_{max} = \pi - \arcsin\frac{U_{thre}}{R}$.

And the reduction factor

$$\Delta = 1 - \sqrt{1 - \left(U_{thre}/R\right)^2} \tag{3}$$

There are two factors that are not available: direction and velocity, which affect the link stability most in random way point model. In the following subsection, we will make an investigation on direction and velocity awareness on random way point mobility model.

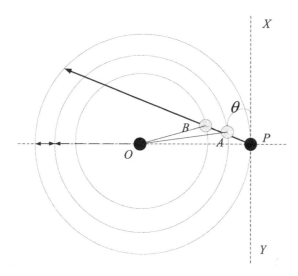

Fig. 2. Direction and velocity awareness mechanism

4.2 Relative Direction and Velocity Awareness

Threshold based filtering can effectively filter out the transitory links with duration below , but the velocity is not available, and the direction is not available also. In this subsection, we assume the centering node is static, and the relative direction and velocity can be achieved according to the following equations. As shown in Fig. 2, we can have that

$$\|PA\| = v \cdot t_1 = R \cdot \sin\theta - \sqrt{(1-\Delta_1)^2 R^2 - (R\cos\theta)^2} \tag{4}$$

$$\|PB\| = v \cdot t_2 = R \cdot \sin\theta - \sqrt{(1-\Delta_2)^2 R^2 - (R\cos\theta)^2} \tag{5}$$

$\frac{\|PA\|}{\|PB\|} = \frac{t_1}{t_2}$ and we can get an equation that:

$$t_1 \cdot \left[\sin\theta - \sqrt{(1-\Delta_1)^2 - \cos^2\theta}\right] = t_2 \cdot \left[\sin\theta - \sqrt{(1-\Delta_2)^2 - \cos^2\theta}\right] \tag{6}$$

Obviously, if $\Delta_1 = \Delta_2$, then $t_1 = t_2$. If we intentionally choose $\Delta_1 \neq \Delta_2$, we can calculate parameter θ. Let left $f(\theta)$ denote left part of equation 6, and let $g(\theta)$ denote right part of equation 6.

$f(\theta) = \sin\theta - \sqrt{(1-\Delta_1)^2 - \cos^2\theta}$ and $g(\theta) = \sin\theta - \sqrt{(1-\Delta_2)^2 - \cos^2\theta}$

$\frac{f(\frac{\pi}{2})}{g(\frac{\pi}{2})} = \frac{1-\sqrt{(1-\Delta_1)^2}}{1-\sqrt{(1-\Delta_2)^2}} = \frac{\Delta_1}{\Delta_2}$

As $\theta = \frac{pi}{2}$, we have

$$\frac{f(\frac{\pi}{2})}{g(\frac{\pi}{2})} = \frac{1 - \sqrt{(1 - \Delta_1)^2}}{1 - \sqrt{(1 - \Delta_2)^2}} = \frac{\Delta_1}{\Delta_2} \tag{7}$$

As $\theta = \arccos(1 - \Delta_2)$

$\frac{f(\arccos(1-\Delta_2))}{g(\arccos(1-\Delta_2))} = \frac{\sqrt{1-(1-\Delta_2)^2} - \sqrt{(1-\Delta_1)^2 - (1-\Delta_2)^2}}{\sqrt{1-(1-\Delta_2)^2}}$ And we have $d\left[\frac{f(x)}{g(x)}\right]\Big/dx < 0$,
thus the function is monotonic.

As figure Fig.2 shows, two phase probing improves the performance of deadline probing algorithm, where the mobile direction and speed if we set different tolerant factors in two phase probing process. According to our deadline probing paradigm, both direction and speed of the moving node can be evaluated through adaptive power adjustment and probing mechanism.

5   Channel Assignment with Job Complete Deadline

5.1   Model Description

In our channel assignment model, arriving packets should be assigned immediately or rejected. Either there is a single deadline that is exponentially distributed with rate α, or there are n independent deadlines exponentially distributed. Packets being rejected for transmission should be buffered and re-scheduled so as to to be transmitted on next probing period. In this paper, we aim at maximizing the probability that at least k transmitting jobs out of n are correctly completed before the deadline. On each channel j of node v_i, there is a competency value p_j, which is defined as follows.

Definition 1: Competency value p_j for channel j is the probability that a metric on channel quality, it can be the successful transmission rate or a normalized bandwidth, where $0 \leq p_j \leq 1$ probed according to threshold based strategy.

Each channel $j \in \Omega$ would have competency value p_j, and transmit data on the channel j with quality X_j. The is channel j can be correctly used link i with rewards $p_i X_j$. The channel quality can be achieved through probing, and appealing to renewal theory, the channel is available for transmission can be modeled as a queuing system, where the arrival rate can be applied in characterizing channel availability for transmission.

According to sequential assignment problem studied in [8], we have the following theorem in achieving maximized number of success transmissions. There are the following characteristics of our problem:

1: The channel resource is limited; 2: Request arrival rate for the resource is a stochastic process; 3: The rewards associated with the channel resource is known before transmission; 4: A deadline exists, where unfinished transmissions would be rejected from transmission; 5: Reject or accept the transmission should be decided on-line; 6: The objective is to maximize the expected reward accumulated by the deadline.

Let us consider the link competency values so that $p_1 \geq p_2 \geq p_3, ..., p_n \geq 0$. Let X be a random value on success probability of packet transmission. Obviously, $0 \leq X \leq 1$, and it is dominated by packet arrival time and packet transmission time. The problem is how to assign m different packet transmissions to n channels, which would achieve a maximized number of success transmissions.

The optimal assignment policy can be modeled as:

$$Max \qquad u_{ij} p_i x_j$$

$$subject \quad to \qquad p_i \in \{0, 1\} \quad x_j \in \{0, 1\} \quad u_{ij} \in \{0, 1\}$$

$$i \in \{1, ...n\} \quad j \in \{1, ..., m\}$$

$$\sum_{i=1}^{n} u_{ij} \leq 1 \quad \sum_{j=1}^{m} u_{ij} \leq 1$$

If packet numbered i is assigned to channel j, u_{ij} would accordingly be set to 1, else it would be 0.

5.2   General Results

If there are no limits on number of packets waiting for transmissions, and the deadlines for each packet are independent, we will get the following theorem [8].

Theorem 1. *Given an optimal assignment policy, there are thresholds values on transmitting job difficulty, denoted as $1 = v_0 > v_1 > v_2, ..., v_n > v_{n+1} = 0$, such that to assign transmission job value x to channel i if $v_i < x \leq v_{i-1}$.*

THEOREM 1 means that, channel assignment policy can be reduced to pure threshold policy, where channel assignment is done according to the rank of the "job difficulty", and it shows to us that, the optimal assignment policy is a pure threshold based policy.

Lemma 1. *Let π denotes assignment policy and the optimal threshold corresponding to policy π can be computed according to the following iterative equation.*

$$v_i = \frac{\lambda P[X > v_i]}{\lambda P[X > v_i] + i\alpha} E[X | X > v_i]. \tag{8}$$

Corollary 1: If the transmission deadline parameter on channel with best transmission quality is $i \cdot \alpha$, and have the same deadline threshold as the ith arrival packet, that is the deadline parameter of the first arrival packet is $i \cdot \alpha$, it will have the same threshold as the ith channel has the deadline parameter of α, because $v_1(i \cdot \alpha) = v_i(\alpha)$.

5.3   Reward on Transmitting Packets

In this paper, we denote the random value x, as the transmitting reward $x_i = P[F_i = T_i + A_i < D_i]$, where T_i is the transmission duration of packet labeled with i, and $T_i = \frac{l_i}{b}$. A_i is the arrival time of the packet, and the ending time of a packet can be denoted as $F_i = T_i + D_i$. And D_i is the delay constraint. A question naturally arises, that is, how to set the bandwidth value b? It is shown in [11][6] that, channel bandwidth is correlated with channel quality, and $T_i = \frac{l_i}{b_j}$. One simple method is that, each reward value x is evaluated equally with best channel quality $sup_{\{p_j \in \mathcal{P}\}}\{p_j\}$. Under this policy, packets with shorter length would be preferred over longer ones, and more likely to be transferred on channels with higher quality. Because according to this criteria, shorter packets would have larger x, and shorter packets are more likely to be transmitted on high quality channels.

Considering network throughput, each packet should be transmitted on its suitable transmission channel. That is, if the packet has larger length, it should be transmitted on high quality channel.

And according to this lemma, we can easily get the following results. If the packet labeled i is accepted for transmission, and let l_i denote the packet length, $t(i)_j = \frac{l_i}{b_j}$ denote the transmission time value of packet i. $x(i)_j$ is monotonic with the order of channel j. As $1 = v_0 > v_1 > v_2, ..., v_n > v_{n+1} = 0$, with increasing of j, $x(i)_j$ decreases. There are three possible results as we select channel j to transmit packet i. They are $j^* > j$, $j^* = j$ and $j^* < j$ respectively.

Lemma 2. *If a transmission can be accepted for transmission, suitable channel i^* exists, and the value is $x(i^*)$.*

Proof. There are three cases as we arbitrarily select one channel for transmission. The first case is $x < v_i$; The second case $x > v_{i-1}$; And the third case is $vi < x < v_{i-1}$. $x(i)$ is non-increasing as i increases. In the third case, it proves that, channel $i = i^*$. In the first case, we should decrease i, whereas, the reward value x would increase. Since the transmission can be accepted, there is $0 \geq i^* < i$, and $vi^* < x < v_{i^*-1}$. In the second case, we should increase i, where the reward value is decreased accordingly.

Since threshold values are monotonic, our suitable channel finding algorithm (SCF) works as follows:

Step 1: Compute x according to $P[F_i = T_i + A_i < D_i]$
        when channel i is used for transmission
Step 2: if $x < v_i$, $i = i - 1$, go to step 1;
        if $x > v_{i-1}$ then $i = i + 1$, go to step 1;
        if $vi < x < v_{i-1}$, end the algorithm.

At first, the transmission job T_i randomly select a channel j and evaluate the transmission difficulty x, if $v_j < x(i) \leq v_{j-1}$, the transmission channel would be j. Else if $x(i) \leq v_j$, we should select channel $j - 1$, if . Else if $x(i) > v_j$, we should select channel $j + 1$.

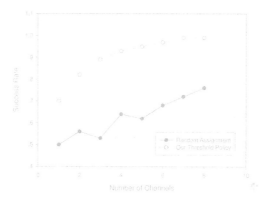

Fig. 3. Different transmission schedule comparisons

5.4   Sub-optimal Criteria

Iteratively computing the threshold value would be difficult as distribution of job difficulty is complex. At the same time, we are also interested on achieving at least k successful transmissions with maximal probability.

In this subsection, we first considering a special case where there only two channels available, and the object is to maximize probability that at least one packet is successfully transmitted over the two channels. Assume that there are two channels and $p_1 \geq p_2$, and the deadline is exponentially distributed with rate α. The theorem has been proved in [8] as follows:

Theorem 2. *The optimal policy is to assign a channel with value x to link-set 1 if $x > v_1$, to assign it to link-set 2, if $v_1 \geq x > t$, and to reject it otherwise, where*

$$v_1 = \frac{\lambda q_1 E[X_1]}{\alpha + \lambda q_1} \tag{9}$$

$$t = \frac{\lambda q_1 v_1 (1 - p_1 E[X_1])}{(\lambda q_1 + \lambda q_2 + \alpha)(1 - p_1 v_1)} + \frac{\lambda q_2 E[X_2]}{\lambda q_1 + \lambda q_2 + \alpha} \tag{10}$$

Also, $V(p_1, p_2) = p_1 v_1 + (1 - p_1 v_1) p_2 t$

Comparing with the policy that try to maximized number of successful transmissions, the first threshold v_1 in both cases is the same, since there is only one channel to be assigned, and it is independent to the second channel. The second threshold $t > v_2$, as the object that we set threshold value t is to maximize the probability of at least one transmission is successful.

Let $V_{k,n}(\boldsymbol{p}|x)$ be the value of $P\{N \geq k\}$ under policy π when there are n links with competency value array $\boldsymbol{p}$, and the channel with reward x has just arrived.
$V_{k,n}(\boldsymbol{p}) = p_n v_n V_{k-1,n-1}(\boldsymbol{p}^n) + (1 - p_n v_n) V_{k,n-1}(\boldsymbol{p}^n)$ for all $n > 0, 0 < k \leq n$.
$V_{0,n}(\boldsymbol{p}) = 1$ for all n,
$V_{k,n}(\boldsymbol{p}) = 0$ for all $k > n$.

We find that, the k out of n optimal criteria and maximum number criteria are correlated with channel states and the distribution of transmission jobs. We will make a further discussion in our simulation works.

6   Simulation Results and Numerical Analysis

We build the simulator and it is written in C++ language. In this simulation, we build a 10 nodes network, where channel reward value are uniformly distributed between $(0.7, 0.9)$, deadline parameter α is uniformly distributed between $(0, 4)$. Packet length is triangular distributed with average packet length $E[L] = 5$. Appealing to free-space radio propagation model and SINR based receiving [11], we set our simulation environment, where the transmission range is $250m$.

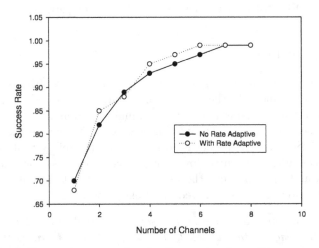

Fig. 4. Comparisons on rate adaptive mechanism with success rate

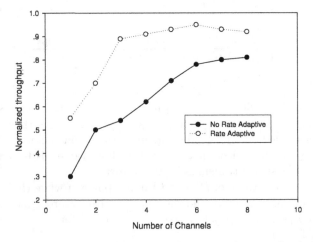

Fig. 5. Comparisons on rate adaptive mechanism with normalized throughput

In Fig3, we make a comparison on success probability between random assignment policy and our threshold based policy.

In Fig4, we make an evaluation on rate adaptive algorithm with neighbor coordination, which is shown in section4.

Simulation show that although rate adaptive algorithm does not improve success rate obviously, it really improves network throughput due to its consideration on packet length, which is shown in Fig5.

7 Conclusions

In this paper, we model optimal probing problem as a knapsack problem with deadlines, and channels probed are sequentially accepted or rejected according to threshold value. Transmission schedule policy is built according to pure threshold criteria, where transmission jobs are assigned to different channels, leading to a maximized number of successful transmissions as deadlines are considered as well. Future work will include a more accurate model on channel reward values and transmission priority. Quantum of different channels should be fully considered, which will affect channel utilization in entire network scale.

References

1. Chang, N.B., Liu, M.: Optimal channel probing and transmission scheduling for opportunistic spectrum access. In: ACM Mobicom, September 2007, pp. 795–825 (2007)
2. Zheng, D., Ge, W., Zhang, J.: Distributed opportunistic scheduling for ad-hoc communications: an optimal stopping approach. In: ACM Mobihoc, pp. 795–825 (2007)
3. Guha, S., Munagala, K., Sarkar, S.: Jointly optimal transmission and probing strategies for multichannel wireless systems. In: 40th Annual Conference on Information Sciences and Systems, pp. 955–960 (2007)
4. Ji, Z., Yang, Y., Zhou, J., Takai, M., Bagrodia, R.: Exploiting medium access diversity in rate adaptive wireless lans. In: Proc. of IEEE Asilomar Conference on Signals, Systems, and Computers (September 2004)
5. Wang, H., Mandayam: Opportunistic file transfer over a fading channel under energy and delay constraints. IEEE Transactions on Communications, 632–644 (2005)
6. Wu, D., Negi, R.: A Wireless Channel Model For Support of Quality of Service. IEEE Transactions on Wireless Communications, 630–643 (2003)
7. Derman, C., Lieberman, G., Ross, S.: A Sequential Stochastic Assignment Algorithm. Management Science, 349–355 (1972)
8. Righter, R.: Stochastically Maximizing the Number of Successes in a Sequential Assignment Problem. Journal of Applied Probability, 351–364 (1990)
9. Gunter, Stefan, G., et al.: Queueing Networks and Markov Chains. Publishing House of Electronics Industry (1998)
10. Lenders, V., Baumann, R.: Link-diversity Routing: A Robust Routing Paradigm for Mobile Ad Hoc Networks. Technical Report (2006)
11. Rappaport, T.S.: Wireless Communication: Principles and Practice. Prentice Hall, Englewood Cliffs (1995)

SRDFA: A Kind of Session Reconstruction DFA

Jinjing Huang, Lei Zhao*, and Jiwen Yang

School of Computer Science and Technology, Soochow University, China 215006
weijintu@163.com, zhaol@suda.edu.cn

Abstract. Session reconstruction is a crucial step in web usage mining. This paper proposes a kind of session reconstruction DFA called SRDFA, which can do session reconstruction for these webpages with or without frame. Moreover, SRDFA can be used to do session reconstruction on those websites which open URLs in new windows. This paper also takes an example to show that sessions reconstructed by SRDFA are more close to users' actual browsing path.

Keywords: web usage mining, session reconstruction, DFA.

1 Introduction

With the rapid development of Internet, more and more people pay attention to web usage mining [1,11], which can discover frequent access patterns based on user's access log. Web usage mining not only can provide personalized service to users, but also be beneficial to the designers to reconstruct the website.

In order to discover the frequent access patterns, the first thing we should do is to preprocess access log to obtain user's sessions which are used for mining association rules [2]. The precision of sessions will affect the acquisition of frequent itemsets [8,12] directly, so how to get the accurate sessions from users' log is the chief problem. Furthermore, the structure of website becomes more and more complex: on the one hand, the technology of dynamic website design is popular and the designers would like to make web applications based on B/S frame. At the same time, a large number of webpages with frame appear in web applications. On the other hand, in some websites whose URLs can be opened in new windows so that users can browse website in asynchronous parallel mode. As a result, the traditional methods of session reconstructions are no longer feasible to this new situation. Based on the theory of DFA, this paper proposes one kind of session reconstruction DFA called SRDFA, which can respectively be suitable for webpages with frame or not; in addition, it can be seen that SRDFA is also available to do session reconstruction for these websites which open URLs in new windows.

---

* Corresponding author.

J. Cao et al. (Eds.): NPC 2008, LNCS 5245, pp. 50–60, 2008.

2   Related Work

The object of web usage mining is user's access log with the format of CLF or ECLF [3]. In the stage of preprocessing, there are mainly two kinds of methods for session reconstruction: time-oriented heuristics and navigation-oriented heuristics. Paper [4,5,9] introduce the two heuristics.

In time-oriented heuristics, session data is reconstructed by analyzing the session duration time or the time between consecutive web page requests (page stay time) [4]. Session duration time represents the total time of one session is limited with a threshold of δ (usually δ=30mins) and page stay time means the time spent on any page is limited with a threshold of δ (usually δ=10mins)[4].

Supposed that there are a series of page requests $p_1, p_2, \ldots, p_k$, the access time of which are $t_1, t_2, \ldots, t_k$ respectively. According to the first time-oriented heuristics, if $t_k - t_1 \leq 30mins$, these pages can constitute one session. However, based on the second time-oriented heuristics, if pages $p_1, p_2, \ldots, p_k$ form a session, then time spent on each page is less than 10 minutes ($t_{i+1} - t_i \leq 10mins$).

In navigation-oriented heuristics [4,9], pages of one session can access each other through direct or indirect hyperlink. If $p_1, p_2, \ldots, p_k$ have already been constituted a session, p_{k+1} can be joined into this session if there exist a hyperlink from p_i to $p_{k+1}(i \in [1, k])$. If many pages contain such hyperlink, p_i is the nearest one to p_k.

After session reconstruction, sessions can not be used for mining association rules directly, for the reason that the log data sometimes isn't intact. In other words, such pages generated by clicking "back" button in the previous page are not recorded in service log, because they have already been stored in the local cache. For instance, page p_1 has hyperlinks toward page p_2 and p_3 , user A first clicks this hyperlink to reach page p_2 , then he comes back to p_1 by clicking "back" button, and then go to page p_3 from p_1. Obviously, the real access path of user A is $p_1 \rightarrow p_2 \rightarrow p_1 \rightarrow p_3$, however, the access path in log file is $p_1 \rightarrow p_2 \rightarrow p_3$. Some papers such as [4] and [10] study this problem and paper [10] proposes the method of path supplement.

Reference [6] and [7] have already done some research on session reconstruction and path supplement. In the two papers, DFA theory is applied to do session reconstruction, however, this DFA isn't suitable for webpage with frame. Thus this paper proposes a kind of session reconstruction DFA called SRDFA, which is different from that one in reference [6]. SRDFA is not only suitable for these webpages with frame, but also is applicable to these websites which open URLs in new windows.

3   SRDFA

Considering the flexibility of web design, if we only use time-oriental or navigation-oriental heuristics to reconstruct sessions, maybe a real session is separated into several ones. Moreover, today many websites open some URLs in new windows, which results in that traditional algorithm of path supplement can not reveal the actual access path. Based on the fact this paper proposes a kind of DFA to do session reconstruction called SRDFA, which can automatically accomplish session reconstruction for a section of users' access log.

3.1 Webpages without Frame

For the webpages without frame, we can use the DFA to reconstruct sessions as figure 1 depicts. Paper [6] has introduced this DFA in details.

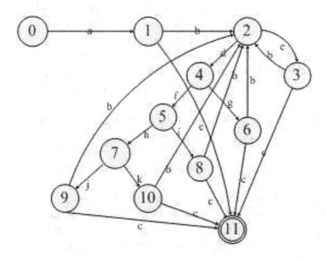

Fig. 1. The DFA used in webpages without frame

One DFA is composed of five elements defined as $M = (S, \sum, f, S_0, Z)$. In figure 1, $S = \{1, 2, \ldots, 11\}, \sum = \{a, b, \ldots, k\}, S_0 = 0, Z = 11$, and the meaning of each state and character has been explained in paper [6].

3.2 Webpages with Frame

Nowadays, due to the adoption of new technology, the contents of access log have become more complex. For example, Webpage with frame is a kind of special webpage, which divides the browser window into several regions as table 1 shows. And each region is filled with different page.

The webpage shown in table 1 is made up of three regions, which in fact are different pages. In this case, the contents of catalogue and banners framework usually display statically while the main framework changes its contents after users click different hyperlinks. Generally speaking, page B usually is welcome page, so it can be cleaned from the log. In catalogue framework, many hyperlinks about different subjects are provided for users.

Table 1. The structure of webpage with frame

Banners framework(B)	
Catalogue framework(C)	Main framework(M)

Before session reconstruction we should extract some fields such as HostID, Date, URL (the address of page request), Referrer (the refer page of the current page), Agent from the cleaned log. However, for webpages with frame (such as struts framework website based on MVC mode), URL should be understood in a broad sense instead of just as address.

Take a website based on MVC mode as an example. User submits a request to web application through a table or a URL. After receiving this request, the controller begins to search for the corresponding action. If no such action, the controller will send the response to JSP or static page (html/xml) directly; but if such action exists, then the field of URL is filled with a string of characters ended with .do, which can be viewed as a generalized URL. Table 2 shows the log data of a dynamic framework website based on MVC mode.

Table 2. Data of a dynamic framework website based on MVC mode

HostId	Date	URL	Referrer
A	[19/Mar/2008:15:40:23 +0800]	a.jsp	-
A	[19/Mar/2008:15:40:25 +0800]	b.do	a.jsp
A	[19/Mar/2008:15:40:35 +0800]	c.do	b.do
A	[19/Mar/2008:15:41:38 +0800]	d.do	a.jsp
A	[19/Mar/2008:15:42:56 +0800]	d.do	d.do
A	[19/Mar/2008:15:43:28 +0800]	d.do	d.do
A	[19/Mar/2008:15:45:12 +0800]	d.do	d.do

In some dynamic web applications, there is a fact that after clicking the different hyperlinks in one page, the address of URL displaying in the page is same although we get different contents. In order to find out which hyperlink user clicked, we have to resort to the access log. In some website different actions are generated from different hyperlinks, we just need to confirm the clicked action which is recorded in the field of URL. For example, supposed that page A has 3 hyperlinks B, C, D, and they correspond to 3 actions $b.do, c.do, d.do$ respectively. If user clicks hyperlink B, then the field of URL will be recorded as $b.do$. Therefore, we can easily identify which hyperlink was clicked. Let's review the table 2, we can find the user traversed on the same action that is $d.do$ from record 5 to 8. The reasons for this case are as follows: firstly, several hyperlinks in one page may share the same action; secondly, some URL in dynamic website contains parameters which are removed in the step of log cleaning. For example, suppose URL is "d.do?BH=076001&BM=JZGGNJXXX" which includes two parameters BH and BM. After the step of log cleaning, the URL converts into "d.do". Regardless of which situation, $d.do$ should be considered as an important action. So the designer would pay more attention to page $a.jsp$ which generates action $d.do$, and it is better to provide a short cut for user to access $a.jsp$ conveniently.

3.3   Path Supplement Based on Multi Window

First of all, the data structure of record in session is defined as table 3 shows.

Table 3. The data structure of record

IP	user
date	the access time of page request
url	url of page request (generalized url)
refer	the refer page of current page
new_window	whether opened from new window

Suppose page p_1 has two hyperlinks towards page p_2 and p_3 respectively which are opened in new windows. It means that page p_1 is not close when page p_2 or p_3 are opened. Besides, there is a hyperlink toward page p_5 in page p_2. Then suppose the session is p_1, p_2, p_5, p_3 before doing path supplement. According to the traditional path supplement algorithm, p_2 and p_1 should be inserted after p_5 for the reason that $p_3.refer \neq p_5.url$. Therefore, the new session is p_1, p_2, p_5, p_2, p_1, p_3. However, because of the particularity of this website, while p_5 is open, p_1 isn't close. So user can click p_3 in the page p_1 directly after visiting p_5, rather than coming back to page p_1 by clicking "back" button in page p_5. Obviously, the real session is p_1, p_2, p_5, p_1, p_3.

As describing in section 3.2, when the main framework changes its content, the catalogue framework is not variable, so users can easily change their interests to watch pages about different subjects by clicking hyperlinks in the catalogue framework, rather than coming to the main page through clicking the "back" button.

The algorithm of path supplement based on multi window [7] as follows:

Suppose p and q are any two consecutive records in a session, and $q.refer = s.url \neq p.url$.

(1) If $s.url$ isn't in the current session, put the current session into database and regard record q as the first record of a new session, then go to (6).

(2) Suppose the next record of s is t and judge the section of records from s to p consecutive or not. If it is, then go to (3); Otherwise to find the discontinuous record r, if $r = s$, then insert q after r, go to (6); if $r \neq s$, go to (4).

(3) From t to p, there is one record whose URL is opened in a new window or not. If there isn't such record, then go to (5). Otherwise, suppose this record is

x and the record in front of x is y. If there are several records are opened in new windows, x is the one closest to s. If $y = s$, insert s and q after p, go to (6); If $y \neq s$, insert the section of records from y to s after p, then insert q, go to (6).

(4) From record t to r, there is one record whose URL is opened in a new window or not. If there isn't such record, then go to (5). Otherwise, suppose the record is x and the record in front of x is y. If there are several records are opened in new windows, x is the one closest to s. If $y = s$, insert s and q after r, go to (6); If $y \neq s$, insert the section of records from y to s after r, then insert q, go to (6).

(5)Do path supplement with the traditional method ("back" mode).

(6)Path supplement finishes.

3.4   Session Reconstruction DFA

Because of the flexibility of web applications, such DFA introduced in section 3.1 can not be used in the webpages with frame. Thus we design a new DFA called SRDFA, which adds several states to the original DFA. On the first aspect, SRDFA contains some states for webpages with frame. On the second aspect, SRDFA does the path supplement based on two modes which are "back" mode and "multi window" mode.

Figure 2 is SRDFA which can automatically finish session reconstruction for a section of users' access log.

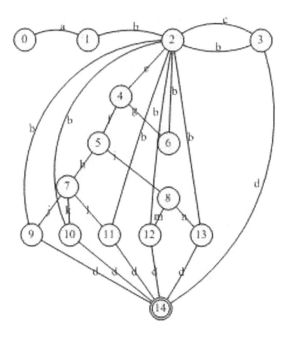

Fig. 2. SRDFA

Suppose p and q are two consecutive records of log, the meaning of each state in SRDFA as follows:

State 0: the beginning state, start to accept the first record of access log;

State 1: accept the next record;

State 2: judge the two consecutive records belong to the same user or not;

State 3: current session terminates;

State 4: judge the time interval of two consecutive is greater than10 minutes or not;

State 5: judge whether $q.refer = p.url$ or not;

State 6: the same as 3;

State 7: judge which method of path supplement should be used;

State 8: judge whether $q.refer = q.url$ or not;

State 9: do path supplement by the "back" mode;

State 10: do path supplement by "multi window" mode;

State 11: the same as 3;

State 12: accept the next record until its URL isn't equal to $p.url$, and terminate the current session;

State 13: insert the current record into the current session;

State 14: the terminal state, session reconstruction finishes.

The meaning of each character as follows:

a: the first record p;

b: the next record q;

c: $p.IP \neq q.IP$ (the consecutive pages belong to different users);

d: there is no next record in the log;

e: $p.IP = q.IP$ (the consecutive pages belong to the same user);

f: $q.date - p.date \leq 10mins$ (the time interval between p and q is less than 10 minutes);

g: $q.date - p.date > 10mins$ (the time interval between p and q is greater than 10 minutes);

h:$q.refer \neq p.url$ (p is not the refer page of q);

i: $q.refer = p.url$ (p is the refer page of q);

j: records from $q.refer$ to p are consecutive and their URLs are not opened in new windows;

k: records from $q.refer$ to p aren't consecutive or they are consecutive but there exist one record whose URL is opened in a new window;

l: $q.refer$ isn't in current session;

m: $q.url = q.refer$;

n: $q.url \neq q.refer$.

4   Experimental Results

Table 4 is a section of access log from a dynamic struts framework website based on MVC mode. In table 4, URLs are replaced by letters and Record-Id represents the sequence of these records.

In this website, *a.jsp* plays the role of catalogue framework. URLs opened from catalogue page are all opened in new windows according to the section 3.3. Thus, *b.jsp* and *f.jsp* are view as opened in new windows from *a.jsp* in this log.

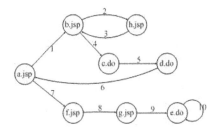

Fig. 3. The actual path of 192.168.151.79

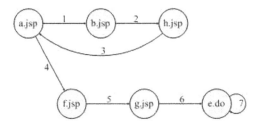

Fig. 4. The actual path of 192.168.151.65

In table 4, there are two different users 192.168.151.79 and 192.168.151.65. Figure 3 and figure 4 are the actual access paths of these two users respectively and numbers above the arrow represent the sequence of browsing the website.

For this section of log, if we just use the first time-oriented heuristics which has been described in section 2, we can obtain sessions like this :{*a.jsp, b.jsp, a.jsp, b.jsp, h.jsp, c.do, d.do, f.jsp, g.jsp, e.do, e.do, e.do*} and{*a.jsp, b.jsp, h.jsp, f.jsp, g.jsp, e.do, e.do*}. In addition, if we adopt the second time-oriented heuristics, sessions {*a.jsp, b.jsp*}, {*a.jsp, b.jsp, h.jsp, c.do, d.do, f.jsp, g.jsp, e.do, e.do, e.do*}, {*a.jsp, b.jsp, h.jsp, f.jsp, g.jsp, e.do, e.do*} can be obtained.

After that, path supplement should be done. Take {*a.jsp, b.jsp, h.jsp, f.jsp, g.jsp, e.do, e.do*} as an example, if we use the traditional method just considering "back" mode, then {*a.jsp, b.jsp, h.jsp, b.jsp, a.jsp, f.jsp, g.jsp, e.do, e.do*} can be obtained.

Obviously, the results can not really reflect the actual access path, which means previous methods aren't suitable for this framework website. Thus, we

Table 4. Data of a dynamic framework website based on MVC mode

Record-Id	HostId	Data	URL	Referrer
1	192.168.151.79	[19/Mar/2008:17:01:23 +0800]	a.jsp	main.jsp
2	192.168.151.79	[19/Mar/2008:17:01:36 +0800]	b.jsp	a.jsp
3	192.168.151.79	[19/Mar/2008:17:12:56 +0800]	a.jsp	main.jsp
4	192.168.151.79	[19/Mar/2008:17:13:26 +0800]	b.jsp	a.jsp
5	192.168.151.79	[19/Mar/2008:17:15:18 +0800]	h.jsp	b.jsp
6	192.168.151.79	[19/Mar/2008:17:15:37 +0800]	c.do	b.jsp
7	192.168.151.79	[19/Mar/2008:17:16:18 +0800]	d.do	c.do
8	192.168.151.79	[19/Mar/2008:17:20:02 +0800]	f.jsp	a.jsp
9	192.168.151.79	[19/Mar/2008:17:20:16 +0800]	g.jsp	f.jsp
10	192.168.151.79	[19/Mar/2008:17:22:16 +0800]	e.do	g.jsp
11	192.168.151.79	[19/Mar/2008:17:22:38 +0800]	e.do	e.do
12	192.168.151.79	[19/Mar/2008:17:23:53 +0800]	e.do	e.do
13	192.168.151.65	[19/Mar/2008:18:15:12 +0800]	a.jsp	main.jsp
14	192.168.151.65	[19/Mar/2008:18:15:26 +0800]	b.jsp	a.jsp
15	192.168.151.65	[19/Mar/2008:18:16:03 +0800]	h.jsp	b.jsp
16	192.168.151.65	[19/Mar/2008:18:17:23 +0800]	f.jsp	a.jsp
17	192.168.151.65	[19/Mar/2008:18:17:42 +0800]	g.jsp	f.jsp
18	192.168.151.65	[19/Mar/2008:18:18:16 +0800]	e.do	g.jsp
19	192.168.151.65	[19/Mar/2008:18:18:23 +0800]	e.do	e.do

adopt SRDFA to do session reconstruction. Suppose p and q are any two consecutive records of the log and the simple process of session reconstruction by SRDFA is as follows:

(1)Accept the first record denoted as p on the state 0, then come to state 1 to accept the next record denoted as q; On the state 2, it can be found that p and q belong to the same user (192.168.151.79), thus come to state 4; The time interval between p and q is less than 10mins, so come to state 5; After that, come to state 8 because $p.url = q.refer(a.jsp)$; On the state 8, we can judge that $q.refer(a.jsp) \neq q.url(b.jsp)$, so come to state 13; Insert record q into the current session on this state, then continue to accept the next record. At this moment, p and q are the second and third record respectively.

(2)Accept the third record by the aforementioned method. On the state 4, we can find the time interval of p and q is greater than 10mins, so come to state 6; On this state, the current session $\{a.jsp, b.jsp\}$ is terminated and is put into the database, then the next record is accepted. Reset p and q, thus p is the third record while q is the fourth one.

(3)Accept $b.jsp$, $h.jsp$ by the same method, the current session is $\{a.jsp, b.jsp, h.jsp\}$, then continue to accept the next URL ($c.do$). Based on the theory of section 3.2, $c.do$ is viewed as a generalized URL. On the state 5, it can be found that $q.refer \neq q.url(b.jsp \neq h.jsp)$, so come to state 7; On the state, the SRDFA jumps to state 9 and does path supplement by "back" mode, so the current session is $\{a.jsp, b.jsp, h.jsp, b.jsp, c.do\}$.

(4)Then put the next record into current session based on the method described above, the current session is $\{a.jsp, b.jsp, h.jsp, b.jsp, c.do, d.do\}$. Then accept the next record whose URL is $f.jsp$, and come to state 7 from state 5 as $q.refer \neq q.url(a.jsp \neq e.do)$; b.jsp is opened in new window, so do path supplement by "multi window" mode on state 10. The current session is $\{a.jsp, b.jsp, h.jsp, b.jsp, c.do, d.do, a.jsp, f.jsp\}$.

(5)Continue to accept next two records $g.jsp$ and $e.do$, and the current session is $\{a.jsp, b.jsp, h.jsp, b.jsp, c.do, d.do, a.jsp, f.jsp, g.jsp, e.do\}$. Accept next URL $(e.do)$, then $q.url = q.refer(e.do = e.do)$ is found on the state 8, so come to state 12, and record $e.do$ doesn't need repeat join in the session. Continue to accept next record until its URL is not e.do or is null. Then put current session $\{a.jsp, b.jsp, h.jsp, b.jsp, c.do, d.do, a.jsp, f.jsp, g.jsp, e.do\}$ into the database.

(6)The rest records accepted by the aforementioned method and the paper dosen't explain in details. The SRDFA accepts records until the next URL is null, then comes to the terminal state (state 14). There are three sessions in the database $\{a.jsp, b.jsp\}$, $\{a.jsp, b.jsp, h.jsp, b.jsp, c.do, d.do, a.jsp, f.jsp, g.jsp, e.do\}$ and $\{a.jsp, b.jsp, h.jsp, a.jsp, f.jsp, g.jsp, e.do\}$.

According to figure 3 and figure 4, it is obviously found that sessions reconstructed by SRDFA more close to the actual paths of users, which provide more accurate data for mining association rules. Besides, SRDFA can be used in webpages with or without frame and applied to the website which open URLs in new windows, so SRDFA has more advantages than the traditional methods of session reconstruction.

5   Conclusion

The user's web log becomes more and more complex, which brings new challenge and opportunity to web usage mining. This paper proposes a kind of session reconstruction DFA called SRDFA. On the one hand, it can be applied to webpages with frame or not respectively; On the other hand, it is also suitable for these websites which open URLs in new windows. The experiment results show sessions reconstructed by SRDFA more close to users' actual access paths. The future work is that we can optimize the SRDFA with addition of states for transaction reconstruction, which means we can obtain transactions used for mining association rules directly by the DFA.

6   The References Section

References

1. Srivastava, J., Cooley, R., Desphande, M., Tan, P.: Web Usage Mining, Discovery and Applications of usage patterns from web data. SIGKDD Explorations 1(2), 12–23 (2000)
2. Ye, Y., Chiang, C.-C.: A Parallel Apriori Algorithm for Frequent Itemsets Mining. In: Proceedings of the Fourth international Conference on Software Engineering Research, Management and Applications. IEEE, Los Alamitos (2006)

3. Luotnen A.: The Common Log File Format,
   http://www.w3.org/Daermon/User/Config/Logging.html
4. Bayir, M.A., Toroslu, I.H., Cosar, A.: A New Approach for Reactive Web Usage
   Data Processing. In: Proceedings of the 22nd International Conference on Data
   Engineering Workshops. IEEE, Los Alamitos (2006)
5. Berendt, B., Mobasher, B., Spiliopoulou, M., Nakagawa, M.: A Framework for the
   Evaluation of Session Reconstruction Heuristics in Web Usage Analysis. INFORMS
   Journal of Computing, Special Issue on Mining Web-Based Data for E-Business
   Applications 15(2) (2003)
6. Jinjing, H., Lei, Z., Jiwen, Y.: Web Sessions Reconstruction based on DFA. Computer Engineering and Applications (accepted) (chinese)
7. Jinjing, H., Lei, Z., Jiwen, Y.: Path Supplement in Session Reconstruction based
   on multi window. Computer Applications and Software (accepted)(chinese)
8. Ye, Y., Chiang, C.-C.: A Parallel Apriori Algorithm for Frequent Itemsets Mining.
   In: Proceedings of the Fourth international Conference on Software Engineering
   Research. IEEE, Los Alamitos (2006)
9. Cooley, R., Mobasher, B., Srivastava, J.: Data Preparation for Mining World Wide
   Web Browsing Patterns. Knowledge and Information Systems 1(1) (1999)
10. Liehu, L., Haipeng, Z., Yafeng, Z.: Data preprocessing Method Research for Web
    Log Mining. Computer Technology and Development 17(7), 45–48 (2007) (chinese)
11. Cooley, R., Mobasher, B., Srivastava, J.: Web mining: Information and pattern
    discovery on the world wide web. In: Proceedings of the 9th IEEE Internatioal
    Conference on Tools with Artificial Intelligence (ICTAI 1997), Newposrt Beach,
    CA (1997)
12. El-Sayed, M., Ruiz, C., Rundensteiner, E.A.: FS-Miner: Efficient and Incremental
    Mining of Frequent Sequence Patterns in Web logs. In: WIDM 2004, Washing-
    ton,USA (2004)

Measuring the Normality of Web Proxies' Behavior Based on Locality Principles

Yi Xie and Shun-zheng Yu

Department of Electrical and Communication Engineering,
Sun Yat-Sen University, Guangzhou 510275, P.R. China
xieyicn@163.com, syu@sysu.edu.cn

Abstract. Web Proxy and cache play important roles in the modern Internet. Although much work has been done on them, few studies were focused on the fact that these trusted intermediaries may be utilized to launch Web-based attacks and to shield the attackers' malicious behavior. This paper fills an void in this area by proposing a new server-side detection scheme based on the behavior characteristics of proxy-to-server Web traffic. Proxy's access behavior is extracted from the temporal locality and the bytes of the requested objects. A stochastic process based on Gaussian mixtures hidden semi-Markov model is applied to describe the dynamic variability of the observed variables. The entropies of those pending Web traffics launched by proxies fitting to the model are used as the criterion for attack detection. Experiments based on the real Web traffic and an emulated attack are implemented to valid the proposal.

1 Introduction

Since 1994, Web proxies and caches have been widely deployed to reduce network traffic and provide better response time for Web accesses. The primary aim of proxy is to allow users to access the Web within a firewall. This type proxy runs on a firewall machine and waits for a request from inside the firewall, then, forwards the request to the remote server outside the firewall, reads the response and then sends it back to the client. Apart from letting clients access resources on the Web, proxies have various uses including sharing of various resources, caching, anonymization, transformation of requests/responses, transfer between different protocol system, and filtering/modifying requests/responses. Although many studies have been done on Web proxy, most of them were only focused on performance improvement (e.g., hit ratio, prefetch algorithm, item update model) instead of the security issues.

In this paper, we study the server-side security issues caused by Web proxies and explore the early detection for a new type Web-based attack which is launched by utilizing the vulnerabilities of Web proxy based on HTTP protocol. Being different from other traditional Web-based attacks whose aim is only to shut down the victim or steal customs' privacy information or illegally use Web applications, such attack usually prevents legitimate users from using the service by consuming server's available CPU slots and memory resources. In order

J. Cao et al. (Eds.): NPC 2008, LNCS 5245, pp. 61–73, 2008.
© IFIP International Federation for Information Processing 2008

to avoid the server-side detection and Web proxies' bypassing, attackers may keep the victim server alive and locate behind proxies during the attack period. The malicious attack behavior are tunneled to the Web server by utilizing various types of HTTP requests (e.g., dynamic Web pages or HTTP requests with "*No-Cache*" headers).

The motivations of proposing a scheme for such attack exist in many aspects: (i) This type attack utilizes the HTTP and the opening TCP port 80 to pass all low-layer firewalls and anomaly detection systems, thus, most detection methods based on IP header or TCP connection (e.g., those surveyed in [1]) become invalid. (ii) According to the "request-response" mechanism of HTTP, Web server has to return response for each incoming request. This working method creates the chance of attack. Furthermore, attackers may also use the normal but expensive computational complexity HTTP requests to consume the server-side resources, thus, it is difficult for those designed for flooding attacks and SQL injection attacks (e.g., [2] [3]) to discover the anomaly signals of such attack. (iii) Attackers are often unseen to the Web server because of the anonymization function of hierarchical proxy architecture. (iv) Measuring the system resource consumption rate (e.g., CPU or memory utilization) maybe a good way to discover the abnormalities caused by such attack. However, this method is not conducive to the early detection or realtime monitoring because when the monitor finds the system resources are occupied abnormally, attack has been successfully going on for a very long time. To the best of our knowledge, few work has been done on this field. This paper proposes a novel server-side anomaly detection scheme to meet this new challenge and fills an void in this area based on proxies' access behavior. The remainder of this paper is organized as follows. In section 2, we introduce rational of our scheme. We valid the proposal by the experiments in section 3 and conclude this work in section 4.

2   Rationale of the Proposed Scheme

Much previous work has approved that statistics is a good method for anomaly detection. Thus, our scheme is also based on statistical methods. One difference between our method and other existing anomaly detection systems is that we implement the anomaly detection by measuring the normality of proxies' application-layer access behavior instead of the IP headers or TCP connections. In order to achieve this aim, we introduce a new way based on temporal locality to extract the access behavior of Web proxies. Then a stochastic process based on Gaussian mixtures hidden semi-Markov Model is used to describe the variety of the normal access behavior and implement the anomaly detection for the pending proxy-to-sever Web traffic.

2.1   Stack Distance Model for Temporal Locality

Temporal locality of reference is one of the cornerstones of computer science. Primitively, it was born from efforts to make virtual memory systems work well.

After that, temporal locality has been widely applied in many fields, e.g., Memory behavior [4], CPU cache [5], program behavior [6], Characterizing reference pattern of Web access [7] and Web proxy cache replacement strategy and performance improvement [8].

Intuitively, temporal locality refers to the property/likehood that referencing behavior in the recent past is a good predictor of the referencing behavior to be seen in the near future, whereas resource popularity metric only represents the frequency of the requests without indicating the spacing between the requests, i.e., the correlation between a reference to a document and the time since it was last accessed.

The temporal locality of Web traffic can be defined by the following probability function:

$$F(t) \stackrel{\text{def}}{=} Prob[document\ i\ is\ referenced\ at\ time \tag{1}$$
$$x + t \mid document\ i\ was\ last\ referenced\ at\ time\ x]$$

Stack distance model is often utilized to capture the temporal locality relationships in most previous work, e.g., [7]. We denote a reference stream $\mathcal{R}_i = \{r_1, r_2, \cdots, r_i\}$, where r_i denotes the ith requested document's name. Index i indicates that i requests have already arrived at a server. We define the least recently used (LRU) stack $\mathcal{L}_i$, which is an ordering of all documents of a server by recency of usage. Thus, at index i, the LRU stack is given by $\mathcal{L}_i = \{u_1, u_2, \cdots, u_N\}$, where $u_1, u_2, \cdots, u_N$ are documents of the server and u_1 is the most recently accessed document, u_2 the next most recently referenced, etc. In other words, u_1 is just accessed at index i, i.e., $r_i = u_1$. Whenever a reference is made to an document, the stack must be update. Considering that $r_{i+1} = u_j$, then the stack becomes $\mathcal{L}_{i+1} = \{u_j, u_1, u_2, \cdots, u_N\}$. Suppose now that $\mathcal{L}_{i-1} = \{u_1, u_2, \cdots, u_N\}$ and $r_i = u_j$, i.e., the request r_i is at distance j in stack $\mathcal{L}_{i-1}$. Let d_i denote the stack depth of the document referenced at index i. Then, a new relation can be obtained by the following equation "$if\ r_i = u_j\ then\ d_i = j$", where j denotes the stack depth of the requested document at index i. An example of this LRU stack model is shown in Figure 1. Based on the initial stack ($\mathcal{L}_0 = \{C, E, A, D, B\}$), the final stack distance sequence correspondent to the

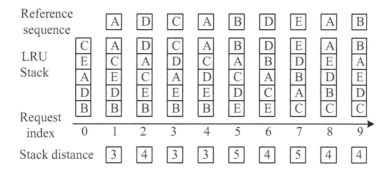

Fig. 1. Least recently used stack model

input reference string ($\mathcal{R}_9$={$A, D, C, A, B, D, E, A, B$}) is {$3, 4, 3, 3, 5, 4, 5, 4, 4$}. In other words, the reference symbol stream $\mathcal{R}_i = \{r_1, r_2, \cdots, r_i\}$ is transformed to a numerical stream $\mathcal{D}_i = \{d_1, d_2, \cdots, d_i\}$ based on stack distance model.

2.2 Profiling the Access Behavior

Since we focus on the anomaly detection of proxy-to-server Web traffic, we need to profile the normal proxy behavior. Much previous work on Web proxy [7] [8] has approved stack of object references is a good model for characterizing the behavior of proxies and caches. The main advantage of stack distance model for describing the Web proxies' access behavior is that a request string can be converted into a distance string that preserves the pattern of activity, but does not depend on document names. For these reasons, we apply the stack distance model to extract the proxy behavior characteristics in this paper.

Considering downloading is another main factor affecting the server performance, we also take into account the bytes of requested documents. One problem of obtaining the bytes of requested documents is, if the requests are for dynamic Web pages, front-end detection system may not know the exact values of bytes before the server responds the requests. If we put the detection system on the outgoing path, it will be not conducive to the realtime detection. Thus, we use a compromise solution to resolve this issue here. We build a database to record the bytes of previously visited documents or routines (e.g., JAVA scripts). When a request arrives at the front-end detection system, the system looks up the database and estimate the bytes of its corresponding response. If the requested document or routine can not be found in the database, we will use the mean bytes of the documents/routines recorded in database. In order to avoid confusion between the estimated bytes value and the actual one, we call the response bytes used in this paper as "prospective return bytes (PRBs)". The PRBs of the corresponding document or routine recorded in the database will be updated by exponential forgetting based on the server's response if the incoming request is legitimate:

$$s_i(j) = (1 - \rho)s_i(j - 1) + \rho s_{ij}, \ 1 \geq \rho \geq 0 \tag{2}$$

where ρ is the decay rate, $s_i(j)$ and s_{ij} is the new PRBs and the real response bytes value of the ith object (document/routin) requested at the jth time.

Thus, assuming a HTTP reference stream $\mathcal{R}_i = \{r_1, r_2, \cdots, r_i\}$, we have two corresponding numerical streams: $\mathcal{D}_i = \{d_1, d_2, \cdots, d_i\}$ and $\mathcal{S}_i = \{s_1, s_2, \cdots, s_i\}$, where s_i denote the PRBs of the document referenced at index i.

If we use $\mathbb{M}(t)$ to denote the set of HTTP requests which appear during the tth second, and use $\mathbb{N}(t)$ to denote the size (i.e., the number of requests) of $\mathbb{M}(t)$, then, the average stack distance value and average PRBs per second can be respectively calculated by the following equations:

$$\{\bar{d}_t, \bar{s}_t\} = \frac{1}{\mathbb{N}(t)} \sum_{\forall i : r_i \in \mathbb{M}(t)} \{d_i, s_i\}, \quad t = 1, 2, \ldots \tag{3}$$

For brevity of notation, we use o_t to denote a time series which is made up of $\bar{d}_t$ and $\bar{s}_t$, i.e., $o_t = (\bar{d}_t, \bar{s}_t)$, where t is the index of second. Previous work [7] [8] indicated that Web temporal locality streams are statistically self-similar or long-range dependence and that this property can be used to explain aspects of the request string that are the result of spatial locality [7]. This means that correlations between object references can occur at widely varying timescales. Such characteristics can have a significant impact on profiling the proxy-to-server traffic. Therefore, better understanding of the nature of the temporal locality is useful to profile the access behavior of proxy-to-server Web traffic. In order to achieve this aim, we use a stochastic process to describe the dynamic variation of stack distance value instead of the traditional ways designed for proxy performance improvement based on pure statistical method (e.g., mean or variance).

Among existing stochastic models, hidden semi-Markov Models (HsMMs) [9] is one of the useful tools to describe most practical stochastic signals without too many assumptions. A major advantage of using the HsMM is its efficiency in estimating the model parameters to account for an observed sequence. Furthermore, it can capture various statistical properties of time series, including long-rang and short-rang dependence, non-stationary and the non-Markovian [10]. Thus, HsMMs have been widely applied in many areas such as mobility tracking in wireless networks, activity recognition in smart environments, and inference for structured video sequences.

In this paper, we assume the time series $\{o_1, o_2, \cdots, o_T\}$ is controlled by an underlying Markov Chain. Each underlying Markov state represents one type joint probability distribution of average stack distance value and average PRBs per second, or say a type of proxy's access behavior pattern. Transition of the hidden Markov states implies the change of proxy's access behavior pattern from one kind to another one. Residential duration of the Markov state can be considered as persistence of the request profile.

Let $x_1, x_2, \cdots, x_M$ be states of a semi-Markov chain, q_t denote the state of the semi-Markov chain at time t and $\lambda = \{\pi_m, a_{mn}, b_m(o_t), p_m(d)\}$ be the parameters of a given HsMM, where $\pi_m \equiv Pr[q_1 = x_m|\lambda]$ is the initial state probability function, $a_{mn} = Pr[q_t = x_n|q_{t-1} = x_m, \lambda]$ the state transition probability function, $b_m(o_t) = Pr[\text{output vector of the model is } o_t|q_t = x_m, \lambda]$ the output probability function and $p_m(d) = Pr[\text{duration of } q_t \text{ is } d|q_t = x_m, \lambda]$ the state duration probability function.

The rational and parameter estimation of discrete HsMM can be found in [9]. In this paper, we simplify the HsMM by applying the Gaussian mixtures into the output probability function $b_m(o_t)$, i.e.:

$$b_m(o_t) = \sum_{k=1}^{\kappa} c_{mk} b_{mk}(o_t) = \sum_{k=1}^{\kappa} c_{mk} \mathcal{N}(o_t, \mu_{mk}, \Sigma_{mk}), \qquad (4)$$

where κ is known; $c_{mk} \geq 0$ for $1 \leq m \leq M$, $1 \leq k \leq \kappa$; $\sum_{k=1}^{\kappa} c_{mk} = 1$ for $1 \leq m \leq M$; and $\mathcal{N}(o, \mu, \Sigma)$ denotes the multi-dimensional normal density function of mean vector $\boldsymbol{\mu}$ and covariance matrix Σ. We also assume the transition of hidden states obeys the Birth-death process, i.e., $a_{mn} = 0$ when $|n - m| > 1$.

We directly use the forward and backward variables and three joint probability functions defined in [9] , i.e. :

$$\alpha_t(m, d) \overset{\text{def}}{=} P[\boldsymbol{o}_1^t, q_t = x_m, \tau_t = d | \lambda] \tag{5}$$

$$\beta_t(m, d) \overset{\text{def}}{=} P[\boldsymbol{o}_{t+1}^T | q_t = x_m, \tau_t = d, \lambda] \tag{6}$$

$$\zeta_t(m, n) \overset{\text{def}}{=} P[\boldsymbol{o}_1^T, q_{t-1} = x_m, q_t = x_n | \lambda] \tag{7}$$

$$\eta_t(m, d) \overset{\text{def}}{=} P[\boldsymbol{o}_1^T, q_{t-1} \neq x_m, q_t = x_m, \tau_t = d | \lambda] \tag{8}$$

$$\gamma_t(m) \overset{\text{def}}{=} P[\boldsymbol{o}_1^T, q_t = x_m | \lambda] \tag{9}$$

where τ_t denotes the state duration of q_t. Then, We define the probability that the kth component of the mth mixture generated observation $\boldsymbol{o}_t$ as

$$\gamma_t(m, k) \overset{\text{def}}{=} \Pr(q_t = m, Y_{mt} = k | \boldsymbol{O}, \lambda) \tag{10}$$
$$= \gamma_t(m) \frac{c_{mk} b_{mk}(\boldsymbol{o}_t)}{b_m(\boldsymbol{o}_t)}$$

where Y_{mt} is a random variable indicating the mixture component at time t for state m. When there are E observation sequences the eth being the length of T_e, the parameters of this parametric HsMM can be iteratively calculated by:

$$\hat{\pi}_m = \sum_{e=1}^{E} \gamma_1^e(m) / E \tag{11}$$

$$\hat{a}_{mn} = \frac{\sum_{e=1}^{E} \sum_{t=1}^{T_e} \zeta_t^e(m, n)}{\sum_{e=1}^{E} \sum_{t=1}^{T_e} \sum_{n=1}^{M} \zeta_t^e(m, n)} \tag{12}$$

$$\hat{c}_{mk} = \frac{\sum_{e=1}^{E} \sum_{t=1}^{T_e} \gamma_t^e(m, k)}{\sum_{e=1}^{E} \sum_{t=1}^{T_e} \gamma_t^e(m)} \tag{13}$$

$$\hat{\boldsymbol{\mu}}_{mk} = \frac{\sum_{e=1}^{E} \sum_{t=1}^{T_e} \gamma_t^e(m, k) \boldsymbol{o}_t^e}{\sum_{e=1}^{E} \sum_{t=1}^{T_e} \gamma_t^e(m, k)} \tag{14}$$

$$\hat{\Sigma}_{mk} = \frac{\sum_{e=1}^{E} \sum_{t=1}^{T_e} \gamma_t^e(m, k)(\boldsymbol{o}_t^e - \boldsymbol{\mu}_{mk})(\boldsymbol{o}_t^e - \boldsymbol{\mu}_{mk})^{\text{T}}}{\sum_{e=1}^{E} \sum_{t=1}^{T_e} \gamma_t^e(m, k)} \tag{15}$$

$$\hat{p}_m(d) = \frac{\sum_{e=1}^{E} \sum_{t=1}^{T_e} \eta_t^e(m, d)}{\sum_{e=1}^{E} \sum_{t=1}^{T_e} \sum_{d=1}^{D} \eta_t^e(m, d)} \tag{16}$$

Most previous work have approved Viterbi algorithm is a good method for decoding. Thus, we modify the Viterbi algorithm designed for hidden Markov Model [11] for our HsMM based on the following recursion for $\delta_t(m)$, the posterior probability of the best state sequence ending in state m at time t:

$$\delta_t(m) = \max_d \delta^*_{t-d}(m) p_m(d) b_m(\boldsymbol{o}_{t-d+1}, ..., \boldsymbol{o}_t) \qquad (17)$$

$$\delta^*_t(m) = \max_m \delta^*_t(m) a_{mn} \qquad (18)$$

2.3   Detection Scheme

We use an average logarithmic likelihood $\varepsilon(t)$ (i.e., entropy) of observations $(\boldsymbol{o}_1^t)$ fitting to the given HsMM (λ) as the detection criterion at the tth second. The $\varepsilon(t)$ is defined as Equation (19):

$$\varepsilon(t) \overset{def}{=} \frac{1}{t} log\{P[\boldsymbol{o}_1^t|\lambda]\} = \frac{1}{t} log\{\sum_{m,d} \alpha_t(m,d)\} \qquad (19)$$

The whole anomaly detection scheme is outlined in Figure 2. The details are shown as the following. When a proxy's reference string reaches the ingress of the victim Web server, the detection scheme begins to work. First, Information Extraction (IE) module is performed on the incoming observed data for calculating the average stack distance and requested file size (i.e., $\boldsymbol{O}_t = \boldsymbol{o}_1, \boldsymbol{o}_2, \cdots, \boldsymbol{o}_t$). If the data are used for training model, they will be sent to the Iteration Calculation (IC) module which will output the parameters (λ) of the model to the Forward Process (FP). Otherwise, the observed data may be directly sent to the FP which will form the decision of pending reference string's normality based on its entropy. If the decision is positive, the switch between the Data Pool (DP) and the Service Queue (SQ) will be kept on opening to prevent those suspected HTTP requests from entering the SQ module and affecting the Web server performance. In order to avoid the overflow of DP, we can start a timer while a new reference stream enters the DP. When the value of timer is zero, the corresponding reference stream will be deleted. Once, the decision of the pending request stream is negative, switch will be put on for transmitting the correspondent reference string to the SQ module where the proxy's requests are

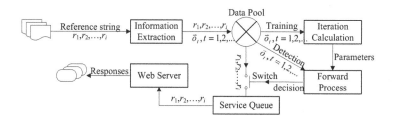

Fig. 2. Detection scheme for proxy-to-server Web traffic

waiting for Web Server's response according to the First in First out (FIFO) policy or other Quality of Service (QoS) strategies.

3   Experiments and Numerical Results

In this section, we use a 72 hours real Web traffic which includes 258 proxies to valid our detection scheme. The simulation is implemented in the NS2 simulator [12] by two application-layer modules (i.e., "Web cache application" and "PackMime-HTTP: Web Traffic Generation"). There are three phases in our simulation: the first 24 hours traffics are used for constructing a stable temporal locality stack for proxies; the second 24 hours traffics are used for model training and the remaining are used for testing. During the attack period, we let the emulated "bad" clients replay the normal users' requests, most of which are for dynamic contents(e.g., database searching) and large byte documents (e.g., audio and video). Once the "bad" requests are produced, they are sent to the proxies. Thus, both the "bad" requests and the "good" requests of proxies are sent to the victim Web server.

The time unit of the final observation o_t is second. This time series is then blocked into frames. Each frame spans 10 seconds or 10 observed vectors. Consecutive frames overlap by 5 seconds. On the other words, each frame is multiplied by a Hamming Window with width of 10 seconds and applied every 5 seconds.

3.1   Statistical Analysis for Observed Data

In Figure 3 , we compare the joint distributions of stack distance and PRBs between period of the normal Web traffic and the emulated attack period. We can find that most points of both the normal and attack periods fall into the low-value area. Furthermore, during the emulated attack period, the largest stack distance value is much smaller than that of the normal period. This result shows that it is not easy for us to distinguish the attack requests from the normal requests sent by proxies only by the statistical properties.

We plot the distribution of logarithmic stack distance values and PRBs of different testing data in Figure 4 and Figure 5, respectively. All these figures are Gaussian-like distributions with similar means and variances. These results also show, it is ineffective for the pure statistical methods to distinguish the abnormal requests from the normal ones.

3.2   Detection Based on HsMM

A five-state HsMM is used in this experiment. The model parameters are obtained based on the previous HsMM algorithm. In Figure 6 and Figure 7, we use a 500 seconds Web traffic fragment of one of the sample proxies to show the stochastic processes of stack distance values and PRBs based on HsMM. Comparing both the hidden state processes of normal and emulated attack

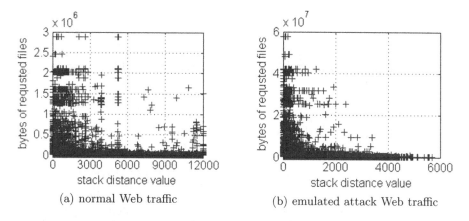

Fig. 3. Joint distribution of stack distance and bytes in different periods

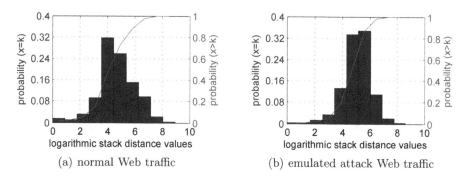

Fig. 4. Marginal distribution of stack distance in different periods

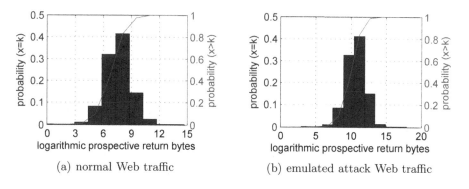

Fig. 5. Marginal distribution of prospective return bytes in different periods

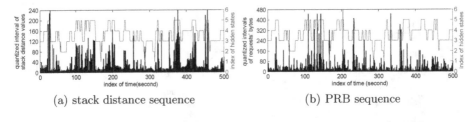

(a) stack distance sequence   (b) PRB sequence

Fig. 6. Profiling the normal proxies behavior by hidden states

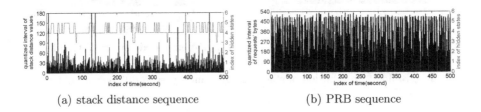

(a) stack distance sequence   (b) PRB sequence

Fig. 7. Profiling the abnormal proxies behavior by hidden states

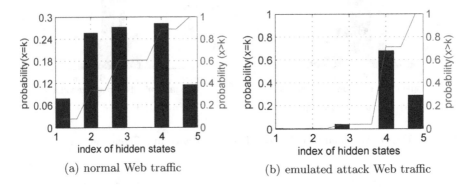

(a) normal Web traffic   (b) emulated attack Web traffic

Fig. 8. Distribution of hidden states in different periods

testing periods, we can find the obvious differences: dynamic range of state transition of normal Web traffic is wider and more homogeneous than that of the evaluated attack Web traffic. This shows the hidden semi-Markov states can be used to extract the proxy behavior and to recognize the abnormality.

Since the hidden semi-Markov state sequences are different between the normal proxy traffic and the abnormal one, the distribution of hidden state can be used intuitively for the anomaly detection. In Figure 8, we show the histograms of hidden states.

It is not credible to draw a conclusion only based on the intuitionists results. In order to build an automatical and numerical detection system, we use the entropy defined in Equation (19) as the measure criterion. We show the entropy

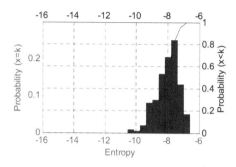

Fig. 9. Entropy of training data

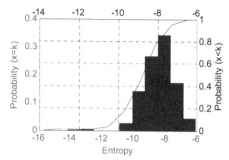

Fig. 10. Entropy of normal testing data

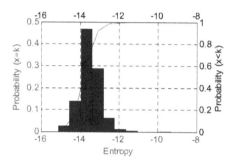

Fig. 11. Entropy of emulated attack data

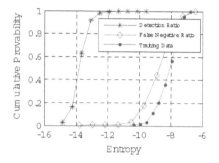

Fig. 12. Detection performance

distribution and the corresponding cumulative distribution of the training data in Figure 9, from which we find most entropies of normal proxy-to-server Web traffic are belong to [-10,-7]. Since the entropy distribution of normal proxy-to-server is concentrated, it can be used as a criterion to achieve the anomaly detection for the proxy-to-server Web traffic.

Two data sets are used to test the model performance. The first one is used to validate the False Positive Rate (FPR) of the model. It includes the normal proxy-to-server Web traffics which occur after the training data and are produced by those proxies that never appear in the training process. The second one including the emulated attacks is used to verify the scheme's Detection Rate (DR). Two attack forms are considered in this experiments, which include the dynamic page attack and the downloading attack. We plot the entropy distributions and the corresponding cumulative distributions of these two data sets in Figure 10 and Figure 11, respectively.

Comparing Figure 9 with Figure 10 and Figure 11, we see, although the sources and the time are quite different between the training data and the normal test data, most entropies of them fall into the same range . The result means the statistical properties of our observations does not depend on or bind with the name of requested documents which are varying with time. Thus, the model is fairly stable for the normal proxy-to-server Web traffic. However, as shown in Figure 11, the entropy distribution of the traffic mixed with emulated attack requests are quite different from those of previous ones, which shows the model is sensitive to the unusual request pattern. This characteristic is very useful for detecting the potential abnormity of proxy-to-server Web traffic. In Figure 12, we plot the receive operating characteristic (ROC) curve which shows the $FPR = 0.1\%$ and $DR = 98\%$ when the decision threshold of entropy takes the value of -12.

4   Conclusion

An early detection scheme focusing on a Web-based attack which utilizes the proxy-to-server Web traffic to shield the attack behavior, is proposed in this paper. Based on the stack distance of temporal locality, Gaussian mixtures HsMM is applied to profile the access behavior characteristics of proxy-to-server traffic and carry out the anomaly detection. The numerical results of experiment demonstrate that the proposed method is expected to be practical in monitoring the attacks hidden in the proxy-to-server traffic.

Acknowledgment

This work was supported by the key Program of NSFC-Guangdong Joint Funds (Grant No.U0735002) and the National High Technology Research and Development Program of China (Grant No.2007AA01Z449). It was performed while the author was with George Mason University as a visiting PHD student.

References

1. Patcha, A., Park, J.: An overview of anomaly detection techniques: Existing solutions and latest technological trends. Computer Networks 51(12), 3448–3470 (2007)
2. Ranjan, S., Swaminathan, R., Uysal, M., Knightly, E.: DDoS-Resilient Scheduling to Counter Application Layer Attacks under Imperfect Detection. In: Proceedings of IEEE INFOCOM, Barcelona, Spain, April, pp. 1–13 (2006)
3. Zhang, L., White, G.: Anomaly detection for application level network attacks using payload keywords. In: IEEE Symposium on Computational Intelligence in Security and Defense Applications, 2007. CISDA 2007, April 1-5, 2007, pp. 178–185 (2007)
4. Smith, A.: Cache Memories. ACM Computing Surveys (CSUR) 14(3), 473–530 (1982)
5. Hill, M., Smith, A.: Evaluating Associativity in CPU Caches. IEEE Transactions on Computers 38(12), 1612–1630 (1989)
6. Spirn, J.: Distance String Models for Program Behavior. Computer 9(11), 14–20 (1976)
7. Almeida, V., Bestavros, A., Crovella, M., de Oliveira, A.: Characterizing reference locality in the WWW. In: Fourth International Conference on Parallel and Distributed Information Systems, 1996, pp. 92–103 (1996)
8. Mahanti, A., Eager, D., Williamson, C.: Temporal locality and its impact on Web proxy cache performance. Performance Evaluation 42(2-3), 187–203 (2000)

9. Yu, S.Z., Kobayashi, H.: An efficient forward-backward algorithm for an explicit-duration hidden Markov model. Signal Processing Letters 10(1), 11–14 (2003)
10. Yu, S.Z., Liu, Z., Squillante, M., Xia, C., Zhang, L.: A hidden semi-Markov model for web workload self-similarity. In: 21st IEEE International on Performance, Computing, and Communications Conference, 2002, pp. 65–72 (2002)
11. Rabiner, L.: A tutorial on hidden Markov models and selected applications inspeech recognition. Proceedings of the IEEE 77(2), 257–286 (1989)
12. NS2 (Ns2), http://www.isi.edu/nsnam/ns/

Feedback Control-Based Database Connection Management for Proportional Delay Differentiation-Enabled Web Application Servers

Wenping Pan, Dejun Mu, Hangxing Wu, Xinjia Zhang, and Lei Yao

College of Automation, Northwestern Polytechnical University, Xi'an, Shaanxi 710072,China
paninxian@gmail.com

Abstract. As an important differentiated service model, proportional delay differentiation (PDD) aims to maintain the queuing delay ratio between different classes of requests or packets according to pre-specified parameters. This paper considers providing PDD service in web application servers through feedback control-based database connection management. To achieve this goal, an approximate linear time-invariant model of the database connection pool (DBCP) is identified experimentally and used to design a proportional-integral (PI) controller. Periodically the controller is invoked to calculate and adjust the probabilities for different classes of dynamic requests to use database connections, according to the error between the measured delay ratio and the reference value. Three kinds of workloads, which follow deterministic, uniform and heavy-tailed distributions respectively, are designed to evaluate the performance of the closed-loop system. Experiment results indicate that, the controller is effective in handling varying workloads, and PDD can be achieved in the DBCP even if the number of concurrent dynamic requests changes abruptly under different kinds of workloads.

1   Introduction

It has become an important issue for Internet servers to provide quality of service (QoS) guarantees to different network applications and clients. Many researchers have highlighted the importance of QoS guarantees in web servers under heavy-load conditions, and there has existed much work focusing on response delay guarantees in web servers [8][12][3][10]. Response delay is a key performance metric for web applications. From a client's perspective, response delay of a request includes three parts, connection delay, processing delay and communication delay. For a dynamic request, processing delay is an important part of users' perceived response time. Most dynamic requests use database connections for data access. Under heavy-load conditions, dynamic requests need to compete for limited number of database connections, which incurs the delay in the DBCP. In order to implement PDD in the DBCP, we divide dynamic requests into two different classes according to their priorities and design a controller to adjust the probabilities for these classes to get idle database connections from the pool. In this approach, requests with different priorities can be served with different delays.

The rest of the paper is organized as follows. Section 2 describes PDD in the DBCP. Section 3 presents the system identification, the controller design, as well as the

J. Cao et al. (Eds.): NPC 2008, LNCS 5245, pp. 74–85, 2008.

system implementation and extension. Section 4 describes the experiments and gives the experimental results. Section 5 reviews related work and section 6 concludes the paper.

2 Proportional Delay Differentiation in Database Connection Pools

2.1 Connection Management in DBCP

It is a resource intensive and time consuming operation to open a database connection. As to a specified web application, if each http request opens and then closes a database connection for data access, a significant amount of processing time will be spent on the connection process, which obviously increases users' perceived response time. To solve these kinds of problems, DBCP has been widely adopted in web application servers. DBCP promotes the performance of web applications by reusing active connections rather than opening a new connection for each request. DBCP maintains a pool filled with active connections [11]. Once a new connection request comes in, after checking if there are any idle connections in the pool, DBCP returns one connection if true. If all connections in the pool are busy and the maximum pool size has not been reached, DBCP will create several new connections. When the pool reaches its maximum size, a newly incoming connection request will be queued up waiting for a connection available until the pre-specified waiting time is out, no matter how urgent or important the request is.

2.2 PDD in DBCP

Although DBCP reduces the response time for dynamic requests and enhances the performance of web application servers, it provides service only in a best-effort model and doesn't take the priorities of requests into account. For many business websites, service differentiation becomes necessary because web applications are deployed for online trading and e-commerce. There have existed many mechanisms [4] [17] [22]for service differentiation in web server end-systems, but none of them focuses on the delay differentiation in the DBCP for web application servers. In this paper, we achieve PDD in a DBCP using classical feedback control theory.

PDD, which was first proposed in [23], has gained much attention in recent years [2] [20] [21][13][12][18]. The basic principle of PDD is that requests or packets with high priority will receive better performance compared with those with low priority. Suppose that requests or packets in networks can be classified into n classes. Let $\bar{d}_i$ be the average queuing delay of class i and δ_i be the specified delay differentiation parameter for class i. PDD aims to ensure that the delay ratio between class i and j equals the ratio between δ_i and δ_j, as is in Eq.(1). The class with a higher priority usually has a smaller delay differentiation parameter.

$$\frac{\bar{d}_i}{\bar{d}_j} = \frac{\delta_i}{\delta_j}, where\ 1 \leq i \leq n,\ 1 \leq j \leq n. \tag{1}$$

In this paper, dynamic requests in web application servers are classified into two classes, class A with high priority and class B with low priority. When there is no idle database connection in the DBCP, each class of requests will queue up to compete for the next database connection available, as is in Fig.2. According to PDD, the request from class A will get service in a smaller queueing delay than those from class B, and the average delay ratio between class A and class B will be kept as a constant value.

3   Design of a Feedback Controller

3.1   System Identification

As is shown in Fig. 2, let $\bar{d}_A(k)$ and $\bar{d}_B(k)$ denote the average queuing delays for class A and B in the kth sampling period. Let $P_A(k)$ and $P_B(k)$ denote the probabilities for class A and B to get idle database connections in the kth sampling period. Suppose that the DBCP can be approximately modeled as a mth order linear time-invariant system, which can be described as

$$Y(k) = \sum_{i=1}^{m} [a_i Y(k-i) + b_i X(k-i)] \tag{2}$$

where

$$Y(k) = \frac{\bar{d}_A(k)}{\bar{d}_B(k)}$$

$$X(k) = \frac{P_B(k)}{P_A(k)}$$

$$P_B(k) + P_A(k) = 1.$$

We need to decide the order m and the parameter vector θ, i.e. $(a_1, \cdots, a_m, b_1, \cdots, b_m)^T$ of the model.

The test-bed is described in section 4. Experimental setup is as follows. The total number of worker threads is configured to be 100, and the pool size is set to be 20. Two client machines, one with high priority and the other with low priority, are started to simulate 50 real clients to send dynamic requests. Requests are classified into class A or B by the classifier according to their source IP, as is shown in Fig. 2. White noise input has been widely used for system identification. In our experiment, we generate a white noise input sequence according to

$$\epsilon(k) = [\epsilon(k-p) + \epsilon(k-q)] \bmod 2 \tag{3}$$

where $p = 8$, $q = 5$ and the sequence period is 255. At the kth sampling instant, $X(k)$ is set to be 1 if $\epsilon(k) = 1$, or else 1.5. The experiment lasts for 40 minutes.

We calculate θ using the recursive least square (RLS) estimation algorithm [14]. According to RLS, θ can be calculated by Eq. (4).Suppose that $\theta_0 = 0$ and $P_0 = 15I$, we can calculate θ under different order $m(1 \le m \le 6)$.

$$\theta_{N+1} = \theta_N + \frac{P_N \varphi_{N+1}}{\varphi_{N+1}^T P_N \varphi_{N+1} + 1} Y_\triangle(N+m+1) \tag{4}$$

where

$$P_{N+1} = P_N - \frac{P_N \varphi_{N+1} \varphi_{N+1}^T P_N}{\varphi_{N+1}^T P_N \varphi_{N+1} + 1}$$

$$\varphi_{N+1} = (Y(N+m-1), \cdots, Y(N),$$
$$X(N+m-1), \cdots, X(N))^T$$

$$Y_\triangle(N+m+1) = Y(N+m+1) - \varphi_{N+1}^T \theta_N$$

And then we decide the order m using $F - test$ method [14]. We define a loss function $J(m)$, as is shown in Eq. (5), to describe the error between θ and the real parameter vector when the system order is m, and we also construct a statistic $V(n_1, n_2)$, as is shown in Eq. (6), to evaluate the variation of $J(m)$ when the system order is changed from n_1 to n_2. According to $F - test$, $V(n_1, n_2)$ follows the distribution $F(2(n_2 - n_1), L - 2n_2)$ when $n_2 > n_1 \geq m$ and L is large enough, where L is the length of experimental samples.

$$J(m) = \sum_{k=m+1}^{m+N} \left\{ Y(k) - \sum_{i=1}^{m} [a_i Y(k-i) + b_i X(k-i)] \right\}^2 \tag{5}$$

$$V(n_1, n_2) = \frac{J(n_1) - J(n_2)}{J(n_2)} \frac{N - 2n_2}{2(n_2 - n_1)} \tag{6}$$

Through the experiment, we get that, when $n_2 = 2$ and $n_1 = 1, V(1,2) < F_{0.05}$ $(2, 80)$ holds with the confidence of 95%. It means that, when the system order is changed from 1 to 2, there is no significant reduction of the loss function. So $m = 1$, and the DBCP can be modeled as a first order linear time-invariant system with a parameter vector

$$\theta = (-0.0172, 0.7463)^T. \tag{7}$$

3.2   Controller Design

We design a PI controller for the approximate linear model to implement PDD in a DBCP. Integral control is able to eliminate the steady state error and PI controller is easy to be implemented in programme. We can use transfer functions, as are shown in Eq. (8)(9)(10), to describe the PI controller, the linear model given by Eq. (2), and the closed-loop system, which is shown in Fig.1. Performance specifications the closed-loop system should meet are as follows. The steady state error is zero and the settling time is no more than 300 seconds.

$$D(z) = K_P + \frac{K_I T(z+1)}{2(z-1)} \tag{8}$$

$$G(z) = \frac{\sum_{i=1}^{m} b_i z^{m-i}}{z^m - \sum_{i=1}^{m} a_i z^{m-i}} \tag{9}$$

$$G_C(z) = \frac{D(z)G(z)}{1 + D(z)G(z)} \tag{10}$$

$$\triangle x(k) = x(k) - x(k-1)$$

$$= K_P[(1 + \frac{TK_I}{K_P})e(k) - e(k-1)] \tag{11}$$

To construct a system that satisfies the pre-specified performance, we use Root Lotus tool in MATLAB to place the closed-loop poles and get the parameters K_P and K_I for the PI controller. According to the incremental algorithm, we can get the output increment of the controller at the kth sampling time by Eq. (11) and finally we get $\triangle x(k) = 0.42e(k) - 0.1e(k-1)$.

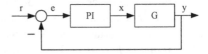

Fig. 1. Feedback control diagram with a PI controller

3.3 The Closed-Loop System

We give a description of the closed-loop system components from the perspective of control theory. As is shown in Fig.2, at the kth sampling instant, the monitor is invoked to calculate the average queueing delays $\bar{d}_A(k)$ and $\bar{d}_B(k)$ during the last sampling interval for two classes of requests. Then the controller compares the delay ratio $\frac{\bar{d}_A(k)}{\bar{d}_B(k)}$ with the desired value $\frac{\delta_A}{\delta_B}$, and calculates a new probability ratio $\frac{P_B(k)}{P_A(k)}$ according to the error measured. According to Eq.(11), we can get $\frac{P_B(k)}{P_A(k)} = \triangle x(k) + \frac{P_B(k-1)}{P_A(k-1)}$. Suppose that $\frac{P_B(0)}{P_A(0)} = 1$, we can get $\frac{P_B(k)}{P_A(k)} = 1 + \sum_{i=1}^{k} \triangle x(i)$. The scheduler acts as an actuator. Once a database connection is available, the scheduler generates a random sample r from the uniform distribution $U(0,1)$. If $r \leq P_A(k) = \frac{1}{2+\sum_{i=1}^{k} \triangle x(i)}$, class A gets the connection, or else class B. To reduce the overhead for generating random samples, a sequence of random samples S, can be generated and stored in the scheduler before it works.

3.4 System Implementation and Extension

We firstly introduce the implementation of the closed-loop system based on the Tomcat application server [1]. As a standard JSP/Servlet container, Tomcat supports data access using JSP pages and java classes of Servlet based on DBCP. When a dynamic request, which is mapped to a JSP page or a Servlet class, calls the function $getConnection()$, the classifier puts the request into a virtual queue, Queue A or Queue B, as is in Fig.2, according to its source IP. At the same time the monitor records its arrival time at the queue. When a database connection becomes available, the scheduler decides which queue will get the connection and makes the function $getConnection()$ return from the queue. When the request at the queue head gets the connection available, the monitor will record its departure time and get its queueing delay. When a request finishes data access by calling $closeConnection()$, a connection immediately becomes available for

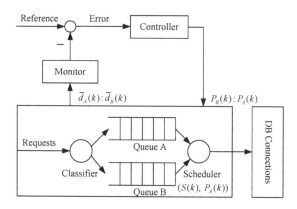

Fig. 2. Control loop for PDD

reusing. Periodically, the monitor will recalculate $\frac{\bar{d}_A(k)}{\bar{d}_B(k)}$, and the PI controller, which is implemented as a java thread, will changes $\frac{P_B(k)}{P_A(k)}$ according to Eq.(11). Member functions, such as $SetReferenceValue()$, are also implemented in the DBCP. All of our implementation, which just needs to modify the code of the DBCP, is transparent to web application developers and website managers. It also brings convenience for us to deploy the DBCP in other web application servers.

Secondly, we discuss how our implementation for two classes of requests can be extended to the general case for n ($n \geq 2$) classes. We can divide n classes into $n-1$ overlapped groups where group $j(1 \leq j \leq (n-1))$ includes class j and $j+1$. Each group has a PI controller and some pre-specified delay differentiation parameters. PDD for each group is the case for two classes, just as described in above. Suppose that at the kth sampling time, the average delay for class $i(1 \leq i \leq n)$ is $\bar{d}_i(k)$, and the probability for class i to get connections is $P_i(k)$ ($\Sigma_{i=1}^{n}P_i(k) = 1$), the controller output $x_j(k+1)$ for group j can be calculated according to Eq.(11). We can get $P_1(k+1), \ldots, P_n(k+1)$ by solving Eq.(12).In this way, the DBCP can provide PDD service for more than two classes of dynamic requests.

$$\begin{cases} \frac{P_j(k+1)}{P_{j+1}(k+1)} = x_j(k+1), \;\; (1 \leq j \leq (n-1)) \\ \Sigma_{i=1}^{n}P_i(k+1) = 1 \end{cases} \tag{12}$$

Thirdly, we discuss how to reduce the average delay for each service class by using the shortest-job first (SJF) scheduling policy. In the closed-loop system in above, dynamic requests of each class are served in a first-come-first-serve (FCFS) manner. For static requests, it has been proven that shortest-remain-processing-time (SRPT) scheduling policy can reduce the mean response time by nearly a factor of ten [25]. However, job sizes for dynamic requests are always unknown in advance and many dynamic requests can not be interrupted. As a result, SRPT scheduling policy can not be used directly in the DBCP. In [24], SJF scheduling policy was implemented for web sites interactions processing. In our implementation of PDD in the DBCP, the sizes of dynamic requests are generated in advance and SJF scheduling policy may bring performance improvement for dynamic requests processing when providing PDD service meanwhile.

4   Experiments

4.1   Test-Bed and Workloads

Our test-bed consists of a dispatcher, a back-end server, and three client machines, each with a 2.80GHz Pentium processor and 512 MB RAM. Three client machines run Linux-2.4.18 and generate web traffic using the modified SURGE [7] workload generator, which can simulate a number of real-world clients to send dynamic requests. The back-end server runs Tomcat 5.5.17 and Oracle 9i for handling dynamic requests. The feedback control-based DBCP works in Tomcat. On the dispatcher machine, Apache 2.0.53 works as a load balancer and uses Mod_jk [1]communicating with the back-end server. In such a scalable architecture, static requests can be processed by the cache module in Apache, and more back-end servers can be added to share the dynamic workload of the whole system according to pre-specified load-balancing strategies.

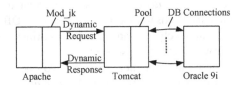

Fig. 3. Architecture of the server system

   Previous researchers have illustrated that, the processing time of a static request is approximately linear with the size of the requested file [3], which follows the well-known heavy-tailed distribution. However, it is difficult to find out the distribution of the processing time for dynamic requests because most of them are CPU-intensive or I/O-intensive. For this reason, we designed three kinds of workloads for our experiments. The first workload designed follows a deterministic distribution, where all the dynamic requests have the same processing time, 350ms. The second one fits a uniform distribution, where the processing time of a request ranges from 0 to 700ms. The third one follows a bounded Perato distribution, as is in Eq. (13), which is a typical heavy-tailed distribution with an upper bound. In practice, we generate the third workload using an equivalent bimodal distribution [16], as is in Eq. (14) where $x_a = 50$, $x_b = 6050$, $\alpha = 0.95$, that corresponds to the bounded Pareto distribution.

$$F(x) = \frac{1-(m/x)^{\gamma}}{1-(m/M)^{\gamma}} \qquad (13)$$
$$where\ M \gg m,\ M \geq x \geq m,\ \gamma \in (0,2)$$

$$f(x) = \alpha\delta(x-x_a) + (1-\alpha)\delta(x-x_b)$$
$$where\ \alpha \approx 1,\ \delta(x) = \begin{cases} 1, & x=0; \\ 0, & else \end{cases} \qquad (14)$$

4.2   Experimental Setup and Results

Three kinds of experiments are conducted to evaluate the performance of the closed-loop system. Firstly, we want to compare the impacts of different sampling periods on the closed-loop system and choose the best sampling period T. From the perspective of control theory, the settling time of a closed-loop discrete system is related to its sampling period. In principle, a smaller period leads to a shorter settling time. However, a too small sampling period may make the system enter an oscillatory state and cannot settle down. The experimental setup is as follows. The total number of worker threads is configured to be 100, and the pool size is set to be 15. The reference value is 0.5, i.e. $\frac{\bar{d}_A}{\bar{d}_B} = \frac{1}{2}$. We conduct experiments three times under the uniform workload, and each time with a different sampling period. At the beginning of each experiment, two client machines are started to simulate 50 clients to generate dynamic requests, one with high priority and the other with low priority. The third client machine with low priority is started at 200 seconds to send requests for 10 minutes, which simulates 100 clients to generate bursty traffic. Each experiment lasts for 30 minutes.

Fig.4 shows the results under different sampling periods. When the sampling period T is changed from 10 seconds to 15 seconds, the measured curve of delay ratio becomes much more smooth. But when T is changed from 15 seconds to 20 seconds, there is no significant improvement. To make a tradeoff between stability and response rate, we select 15 seconds as the sampling period for the rest of our experiments.

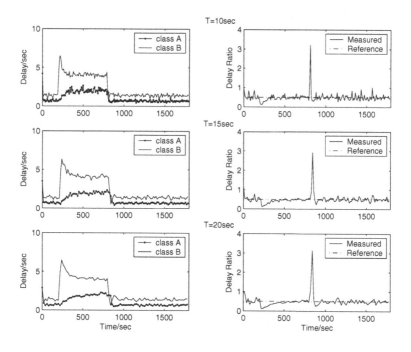

Fig. 4. PDD under different sampling periods

Secondly, we focus on PDD in the DBCP under different kinds of workloads. Parameters of the closed-loop system are configured as in the first kind of experiments. We conduct two experiments, which are under deterministic and heavy-tailed workload respectively. All client machines work as in the first kind of experiments, and there is also a traffic burst during 200 seconds and 800 seconds generated by the third machine. Each experiment lasts for half an hour.

Fig.5 shows the results under different workloads. The figure also includes the result from the first kind of experiment under uniform workload. The DBCP achieves PDD successfully under different workloads, although the average delay for each class is fluctuated all the time. Compared with the other two workloads, heavy-tailed workload makes the average delay for each class vary much more quickly. That is maybe the result of workload distribution. According to Eq. (14), the size of large requests is nearly 121 times of the size of small ones. A large request will significantly increase the service demand in the web application server. However, when the number of concurrent requests changes, the controller reacts quickly to the load variation and ensures that requests with high priority are served with small delays, no matter under what kind of workload.

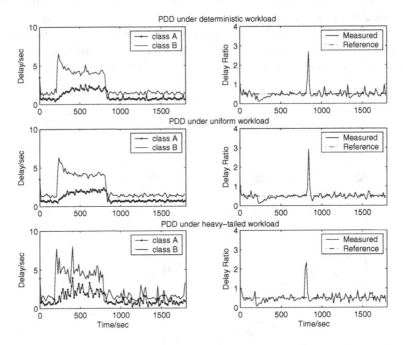

Fig. 5. PDD under different workloads

Thirdly, we want to compare the performance of the closed-loop systems with different scheduling policies. The experiment lasts for 20 minutes. As can be seen from Fig.6, under the uniform workload, the average delay for each service class with SJF scheduling policy is smaller than that with FCFS scheduling policy. The feedback control-based DBCP is capable of providing PDD service no matter what kind of scheduling policy is used.

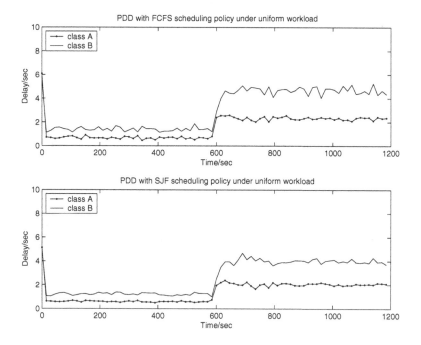

Fig. 6. PDD with different scheduling policies

5   Related Work

Many researchers have highlighted the importance of integrating resource management with quality of service in server systems. In [5], a CPU scheduling algorithm has been proposed to dynamically allocate CPU cycles to Apache processes. In [6], resource containers were proposed as as a kernel mechanism to provide service differentiation by accurate accounting of resource usage. In [8], an observation-based approach was proposed for QoS guarantees at the kernel level by handling bottleneck resources, the CPU cycles and the accept queue. Other kernel-based resource allocation mechanisms for service differentiation can be found in [17]. In [4], a feedback control framework was proposed to guarantee relative/absolute delay in web servers at the connection level and controllers were designed to allocate service threads to clients with different priorities. To reduce latencies and overhead from closing and re-establishing connections, persistent connections are supported as a default by HTTP/1.1. A persistent connection can transmit a sequence of requests, so connection delay just affects the response time of the first request over the connection and request level QoS becomes necessary. Many researchers focused on other QoS metrics e.g. relative hit ratio of web cache [15], relative rejection ratio of requests [9] and system slowdown [19].

Our solution differs from the above works in many respects. Firstly, most of their work only addresses workloads with static requests, whereas this paper fundamentally focuses on dynamic requests and database-driven websites. Secondly, compared with existing work, our work focuses on providing differentiated service at a request level rather than a connection level, and important dynamic requests can get high priority when being handled. Thirdly, in our solution, we implement the controller in the DBCP rather than in the kernel of an operating system, and the DBCP can be deployed in other web application servers besides Tomcat conveniently.

6   Conclusion

It is a great challenge for Internet servers to provide service differentiations in an unpredictable and highly-dynamic environment. Proportional differentiated service is an important service model and response delay is the key performance metric for web application servers. This paper describes the approach for proportional delay differentiations in web application servers through feedback control-based database connection management. We implement a PI controller in a real DBCP for web application servers and design three kinds of workloads for simulation of the closed-loop system. We experimentally demonstrate that, the controller is effective in handling different kinds of workloads and the feedback control-based DBCP is capable of providing service differentiation. Feedback control theory presents its potential for better resource management and QoS guarantees in web application servers.

References

1. The apache tomcat document, http://tomcat.apache.org
2. Abbad, M., Zahratahdi, T.: An algorithm for achieving proportional delay differentiation. Operations Research Letters 36(2), 196–200 (2008)
3. Abdelzaher, T.F., Shin, K.G., Bhatti, N.: Performance guarantees for Web server endsystems: A control-theoretical approach. IEEE Transactions on Parallel and Distributed Systems 13(1), 80–96 (2002)
4. Abdelzaher, T.F., Stankovic, J.A., Lu, C., Zhang, R., Lu, Y.: Feedback performance control in software services. IEEE Control Systems 23(3) (June 2003)
5. Almeida, J., Dabu, M., Manikutty, A., Cao, P.: Providing differentiated levels of service in web content hosting. In: Proceedings of the SIGMETRICS Workshop on Internet Server Performance (1998)
6. Banga, G., Druschel, P., Mogul, J.C.: Resource containers: A new facility for resource management in server systems. In: Proceedings of the Symposium on Operating Systems Design and Implementation (1999)
7. Barford, P., Crovella, M.E.: Generating representative web workloads for network and server performance evaluation. Measurement and Modeling of Computer Systems, 151–160 (1998)
8. Chandra, A., Pradhan, P., Tewari, R., Sahu, S., Shenoy, P.: An observation-based approach towards self-managing web servers. Computer Communications, 1–15 (2005)
9. Huang, C., Cheng, C., Chuang, Y., Jang, J.R.: Admission control schemes for proportional differentiated services enabled internet servers using machine learning techniques. Expert Systems with Applications 31, 458–471 (2006)
10. Kanodia, V., Knightly, E.W.: Ensuring latency targets in multiclass web servers. IEEE Transaction on Parallel and Distributed Systems 13(10) (October 2002)
11. Lea, D.: Concurrent Programming in Java: Design Principles and Patterns, 2nd edn. Addison Wesley Longman, Inc., Amsterdam (2000)

12. Lee, S.C., Lui, J.C., Yau, D.K.: A proportional-delay diffserv-enabled web server: Admission control and dynamic adaptation. IEEE Transactions on Parallel and Distributed Systems 15(5), 385–400 (2006)

13. Lim, K.M., Paik, J., dong Ryoo, J., Joo, S.-S.: Prediction error adaptation of input traffic for absolute and proportional delay differentiated services. In: Proceedings of the 3rd international conference on Quality of service in heterogeneous wired/wireless networks, August 2006, pp. 38–47 (2006)

14. Ljung, L.: System Identification: Theory for the User. Tsinghua University Press, Beijing (2002)

15. Lu, Y., Abdelzaher, T.F., Saxena, A.: Design, implementation, and evaluation of differentiated caching services. IEEE Transactions on Parallel and Distributed Systems 15(5), 440–452 (2004)

16. Psounis, K., Molinero-Fernndex, P., Prabhakar, B., Papadopoulos, F.: Systems with multiple servers under heavy-tailed workloads. Performance Evaluation 62(7), 456–474 (2005)

17. Voigt, T., Tewari, R., Freimuth, D.: Kernel mechanisms for service differentiation in overloaded web servers. In: Proceedings of the Usenix Annual Technical Conference (2001)

18. Wang, K.C., Ramanathan, P.: End-to-end throughput and delay assurances in multihop wireless hotspots. In: Proceedings of the 1st ACM international workshop on Wireless mobile applications and services on WLAN hotspots, September 2003, pp. 93–102 (2003)

19. Wei, J., Xu, C.: Design and implementation of a feedback controller for slowdown differentiation on internet server. In: WWW 2005, May 2005, pp. 10–14 (2005)

20. Wei, J., Xu, C.Z.: Consistent proportional delay differentiation: A fuzzy control approach. Computer Networks 51(8), 2015–2032 (2007)

21. Wu, C.C., Wu, H.M., Lin, W.: High-performance packet scheduling to provide relative delay differentiation in future high-speed networks. Computer Networks (December 2007)

22. Ye, N., Gel, E.S., Li, X., Farley, T., Lai, Y.: Web server qos models: applying scheduling rules from production planning. Computers and Operations Research 32(5), 1147–1164 (2005)

23. Dovrolis, C., Stiliadis, D., Ramanathan, P.: Proportional Differentiated Services: Delay Differentiation and Packet Scheduling. In: Proceedings of the ACM SIGCOMM, vol. 10(1), pp. 12–26 (1999)

24. Elnikety, S., Nahum, E., Tracey, J., Zwaenepoel, W.: A method for transparent admission control and request scheduling in e-commerce web sites. In: WWW 2004, May 2004, pp. 276–286 (2004)

25. Harchol-balter, M., Schroeder, B., Bansal, N., Agrawal, M.: Size-Based Scheduling to Improve Web Performance. ACM Transactions on Computer Systems 21(2), 207–233 (2003)

Research on the Detection of Distributed Denial of Service Attacks Based on the Characteristics of IP Flow

Dongqi Wang, Guiran Chang, Xiaoshuo Feng, and Rui Guo

Northeastern University, Computing Centre 310-1,
Shenyang, China
zorrorily@163.com,chang@neu.edu.cn
{shuoner,happyachilles}@163.com

Abstract. IP Flow is classified into the Micro-flow and the Macro-flow, which provides a way of selecting proper features used to detect DDoS. Five abstracted features' capabilities of recognizing DDoS are analyzed through experiments. With these features as inputs, a neural network classifier is used to detect DDoS. Experiments' results show that these IP Flow based features can be very helpful to DDoS detection if they are put together.

Keywords: DDoS; IP Flow; Detection; Neural Network.

1   Introduction

Distributed Denial of Service (DDoS) attack presents a very serious threat to the internet. There are mainly two kinds of researches on DDoS detection: One is how to select the features to be tested. Another is looking for effective techniques to find out the abnormities shown by features during the attack, which is to be detected. Feature selecting methods can be divided into wrapper approach and filter approach [1]. Wrapper approach exploits machine learning algorithm to evaluate the goodness of features, and performance of learning algorithm is used as evaluation criterion. On the other hand, filter approach uses underlying characteristics of features as evaluation criterions. One example of wrapper approach is [2] in which Gavrilis Dimitris et al. used neural network classifier's performance as a genetic algorithm's evaluation criterion to identify a hypo-optimal feature set. The examples of filter approach are [3] and [4]. Xu Tu et al. [3] employed an underlying characteristic of network flow OWCD to detect DDoS, Cheng Guang et al. [4] get features through sampling measurement of statistics in high speed network. In order to find out the features' abnormities during an attack, researchers had employed many kinds of techniques, such as neural network, hidden Markov model, SVM, data mining [5-8] and so on.

   In this paper, a filter approach which selects five statistical features from IP flow is proposed, and a neural network classifier is designed to find out the

J. Cao et al. (Eds.): NPC 2008, LNCS 5245, pp. 86–93, 2008.

abnormities shown by these features during an attack. The information such as protocols used by attackers, packet's size of an attack etc, as byproducts, can be gained during the generation of the features, which are very useful for filtering DDoS attack.

2   IP Flow Based Feature Selection

IP flow is composed of IP packets arriving one after another. As the basic data carrying unit of Internet, IP packet holds the upper layer's information and can be easily caught and handled. In the following part of this section IP flow will be divided into the Micro-Flow and the Macro-Flow and we are going to research how to select effective IP flow based detecting features.

2.1   The Concepts of Micro-Flow and Macro Flow

The Micro-Flow. A Micro-Flow is a packet set who is composed of packets belonging to the same time interval of Internet, and all these packets have the same specific characteristics [9,10]. These same specific characteristics are called keys [10]. A group of commonly used keys are ¡Protocol, SrcIP, SrcPort, DestIP, DestPort¿. Protocol is the protocol used by the upper layer, SrcIP and SrcPort are the source IP address and the source port number separately. DestIP and SrcIP are the destination IP address and the destination port number separately.

The definition of Micro-Flow is helpful in two ways. First, each key group corresponds to one connection from SrcIP to DestIP, so keys can be used to describe DDoS connection. Second, a key group contains much information which can be used by routers and firewalls to operate each packet.

The Macro-Flow. All the packets belonging to one time interval compose a set which is called the Macro-Flow. Macro-Flow is pooled by Micro-Flows.

The definition of Macro-Flow is helpful in two ways too. First, Detecting features can be formed on the base of Macro-Flow. Second, the information contained in the Macro-Flow is the complementarities to keys.

In experiments, we intercept network traffic by time interval i equals to 10s randomly. On one hand, in order to form the Micro-Flow based features, we classify packets by different keys. On the other hand, we abstract the Macro-Flow based features from the whole i directly.

2.2   IP Flow Based Features

Micro-Flow Based Features:

1. Average Number of Packets in Per Flow(ANPPF). Continuously and randomly generated "legitimate" IP are usually used in attack, so the generating speed of Micro-Flow is quickened, and the packet amount in per flow decrease. There are commonly 1-3 packets in per flow [9].

$$ANPPF = (\sum_{j=1}^{FlowNum} PacketsNum_j)/FlowNum \qquad (1)$$

PacketsNumj is the quantity of packets in the jth flow of a time interval. FlowNum is the quantity of packets of the whole interval. Figure 1 shows the experimental comparison of ANPPF between normal traffic and DDoS traffic (110i-180i).The ANPPF of DDoS traffic which is near 1(attacking traffic is the mix of DDoS traffic generated by tfn2k and normal traffic of internet. ANPPF of tfn2k generating traffic is 1) differs from normal ANPPF (ruleless distribution) significantly.

2. Percentage of Correlative Flow (PCF). During attack, though the victim still has capability to reply to attacking packets' "requests", the replying packets can not get to the zombies, because the attacking IP addresses are faked. If flow x is from SrcIPx=A to DestIPx=B, and flow y is from SrcIPy=B to DestIPy=A, then we call flow x and y is a pair of Correlative Flow.

$$PCF = CFNum/FlowNum \qquad (2)$$

CFNum is two times of the pairs of Correlative Flow. PCF represents the "there is going-out but no coming-back" characteristic of DDoS. As is shown in figure 2, when DDoS happens (110i-180i), PCF is near 0, while the PCF of normal traffic is 0.4-0.6. The difference between them is distinguishable.

3. One Direction Generating Speed (ODGS). Flow generating speed quickens when attack happens or busy time comes. In order to distinguish these two kinds of situations, ODGS is proposed.

$$ODGS = (FlowNum - CFNum)/interval \qquad (3)$$

ODGS reflects the sudden increase of traffic when DDoS happens, and it also reflects the "there is going-out but no coming-back" characteristic of DDoS. Figure 4 gives the experimental comparison of ODGS between normal traffic (110i-180i) and abnormal traffic. ODGS' order of magnitude in normal traffic (102i) is much smaller than that in the abnormal traffic (104i).

4. Ports Generating Speed (PGS).

$$PGS = PortsNum/interval \qquad (4)$$

PortsNum is the number of distinct port in one time interval. Some researchers select the size of port[2] as a detecting feature, while we find that many newly emerged services and applications (such as famous p2p application BT) use port number bigger than 1024, so approach of [2] is not suitable anymore. Through

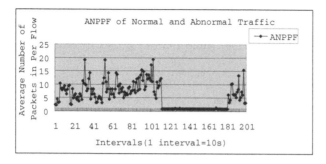

Fig. 1. ANPPF of Normal and Abnormal Traffic

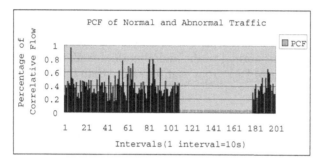

Fig. 2. PCF of Normal and Abnormal Traffic

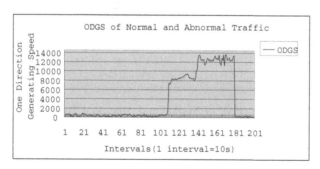

Fig. 3. ODGS of Normal and Abnormal Traffic

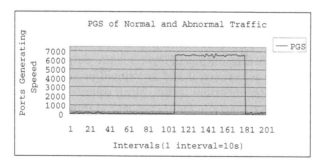

Fig. 4. PGS of Normal and Abnormal Traffic

deeper investigation, we realize that attackers continuously and randomly generate port too, so PGS is proposed. As is shown in figure 4, the PGS of normal traffic is not bigger than 200, while PGS of attacking traffic (110-180i)is over thousands.

Macro-Flow Based Feature:

Percentage of Abnormal Packets(PAP.) In order to increase the efficiency of attacking, attacking packets' content parts are usually unfilled or only filled with very few useless bytes (such as famous attacking tools tfn2k, trinoo). This kind of procedure results in the increase of abnormal small packets (for example, some TCP packets are only a little bigger than 40bytes, and UDP packets are only a little bigger than 28bytes). PAP presents this characteristic of DDoS attack by counting the percentage of abnormal packets in the one i(a Macro-Flow). Figure 5 is the comparison of PAP of normal traffic and abnormal traffic. As we can see, there is a significant change of PAP from near 0 to more than 0.9 when DDoS happens (110i-180i).

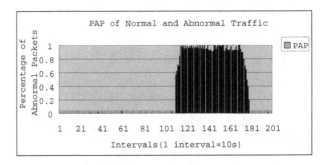

Fig. 5. PAP of Normal and Abnormal Traffic

3   Neural Network Classifier

To detect the abnormities shown by features we choose to use a BP neural network with two layers. There are 5 neurons (because there are 5 features) in layer 1, and these neurons all use hyperbolic tangent sigmoid function as their transfer function. Layer 2 has only one neuron using logarithmic sigmoid function as the transfer function. The output of layer 2 is the output of the whole neural network, and its value is between 0 and 1. Value 0 presents the normal traffic, and value 1 presents the abnormal traffic. Mean squared error function is used as our error performance function, and Levenberg Marquardt (LM) algorithm is chosen to adjust weights and thresholds.

These five features mentioned earlier are used as the inputs of neural networks to do convergence test of different adjusting algorithms. In the experiment, weights and thresholds are randomly initialized, and inputs (PAP, ANPPF, PCF,

ODGS, PGS) belonging to 50 intervals are applied. Table 1 is the comparison of four commonly used adjusting algorithms' convergence performance, and the values in table 1 are the average values of 50 tests to each algorithm. As is shown, LM algorithm suits us better from convergence rate to error performance on average level.

Table 1. The Comparison of BP Algorithms

	BFGS	OSS	RPOP	LM
Average Convergence Time	0.9141s	1.079s	0.658s	0.6893s
Average Iteration Times	74.25	100	100	74.87
Average Error Performance	10^{-10}	10^{-7}	10^{-7}	10^{-18}

4 Detecting Experiments

On one hand, victims usually do not want to publicize the details of the attack they had suffered. On the other hand, currently, few data can describe the whole profile of DDoS attack. So we use both the UCLA's data set [11] and the data generated by our own simulation.

In our own simulation, 200 time intervals randomly intercepted from an outgoing router (kilo mega) of the central node are used as the normal samples of neural network. Another 200 time intervals are randomly intercepted when we use 50 hosts running tfn to attack one server behind this router, and these intervals containing both attack traffic and normal traffic are used as the attack samples.

UCLA's data is stored as pure text, and each row of the text is a packet composed of SrcIP, DestIP, SrcPort, DestPort, packet length and ACK (TCP packet) et. The attack launched in our own simulation is constant rate attack, so we choose the constant rate UDP attack data of UCLA as the attack samples.

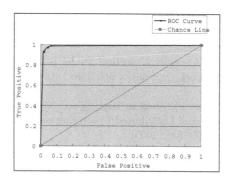
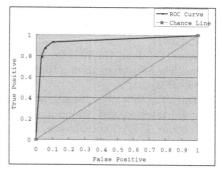

Fig. 6. Our Own Data ROC Curve   **Fig. 7.** UCLA ROC Curve

The ROC curves in figure 6 and figure 7 show the sensitivity and accuracy of the neural network. A ROC curve is a plot with the false positive rate on the X axis and the true positive rate on the Y axis. The area below the curve reflects the sensitivity of the neural network. As we can see, the curve is close to both the Y axis and the point (0, 1) which means that we obtained low false positives and the classification capability is good.

5   Conclusion

In this paper we present five effective detecting features base on the characteristics of IP flow: PAP, ANPPF, PCF, ODGS and PGS. These five features can exploit the abnormalities during DDoS attack. Byproducts of features generation are helpful for filtering. We prove the capabilities of these five features through experimental comparison between their normal values and values in attack. A neural network using LM algorithm to adjust the rights and thresholds is used to detect abnormalities shown by features. Experiments using our own simulating data and UCLA data are carried out separately, and the experimental result are satisfying. As an effective approach, ours is easy to understand and easily to be carried out. It can be used as a part of common security tool in the core network, and it can also be attached a filter to in the edge network to relieve the threat of DDoS. Our future work is to improve the classifier's performance in real-time. Filtering Research based on this approach will also be done.

References

1. Park, J.S., Shazzad, K.M., Kim, D.S.: Toward modeling lightweight intrusion detection through correlation-based hybrid feature selection. In: Infromation Security and Cryptology. First SKLOIS Conference, CISC 2005, Beijing,China, pp. 279–289 (2005)
2. Dimitris, G., Ioannis, T., Evangelos, D.: Feature Selection for Robust Detection of Distributed Denial-of-Service Attacks Using Genetic Algorithms. Methods and Applications of Artificial Intelligence 3025, 276–281 (2004)
3. Tu, X., Da-ke, H.: Time series Analysis for One-Way Connection Density of Network Flow. Journal of SiChuan University (Engineer Science Edition) 39(3), 136–140 (2007)
4. Guang, C., Jian, G., Wei, D.: A Real-Time Anomaly Detection Model Based on Sampling Measurement in a High-Speed Network. Journal of Software 14(3), 594–599 (2003)
5. Xiang, Y., Zhou, W.: Intelligent DDoS Packet Filtering in High Speed Network. In: 3rd International Symposium on Parallel and Distributed Processing and Applications, ISPA 2005, Nanjing, China, pp. 395–408 (2005)
6. Yi, X., Shun-zheng, Y.: A novel model for detecting application layer DDoS attacks. In: First international on Computer and Computational Sciences, vol. 2, pp. 56–63. IEEE press, Hanzhou (2006)

7. Seo, J., Lee, C., Shon, T., et al.: A New DDoS Detection Model Using Multiple SVMs and TRA. In: Embedded and Ubiquitous Computing -EUC 2005 Workshops. EUC 2005 Workshops: UISW, NCUS, SecUbiq,USN, and TAUES, Nagasaki,Japan, pp. 976–985 (2005)
8. Neng, G., Deng-guo, F., Ji, X.: A Data-Mining Based DoS Detection Technique. Chinese Journal of Computers 29(6), 944–951 (2006)
9. Maglaris, C.S.V.: Detecting incoming and outgoing DDoS attacks at the edge using a single set of network characteristics. In: Proceedings 10th IEEE Symposium on Computers and Communications, Murcia, Spain, pp. 469–475 (2005)
10. Song, S., Ling, L.: Flow-based Statistical Aggregation Schemes for Network Anomaly Detection. In: 2006 IEEE International Conference on Networking, Sensing and Control, pp. 786–791. IEEE Press, Ft.Lauderdate (2006)
11. Ucla.Sanitized UCLA CSD traffic traces,
    http://lever.cs.ucla.edu/ddos/traces/

Password-Authenticated Key Exchange between Clients in a Cross-Realm Setting*

Shuhua Wu and Yuefei Zhu

Department of Networks Engineering,
Zhengzhou Information Science Technology Institute,
Zhengzhou 450002, China
wushuhua726@sina.com.cn

Abstract. The area of password-based authenticated key exchange protocols has been the subject of a vast amount of work in the last few years due to its practical aspects. AuthA is an example of such a technology considered for standardization by the IEEE P1363.2 working group. Unfortunately in its current form AuthA, including some variants, only considered the classic client and server (2-party) scenarios. In this paper, based on a variant of AuthA, we consider a quite different paradigm from the existing ones and propose a provably secure password-authenticated key exchange protocol in a cross-realm setting where two clients in different realms obtain a secret session key as well as mutual authentication, with the help of respective servers. In our protocol, any honest server is unable to gain any information on the value of that session key. Moreover, our protocol is reasonably efficient and has a per-user computational cost that is comparable to that of the underlying 2-party encrypted key exchange.

Keywords: Password; provably secure; cross-realm; authenticated key exchange.

1 Introduction

The Password-based Authenticated Key Exchange (PAKE) is a protocol which allows two communicating parties to prove to each other that they know the password (that is, mutual authentication), and to generate a fresh symmetric key securely such that it is known only to these two parties (that is, key exchange). However, since people like to choose simply-guessed strings (e.g. personal identity, nickname, birthday, etc.) as their passwords, many password-based protocols are vulnerable to replay attack or dictionary attacks [1]. Designing a secure password-based protocol is a precise task that has attracted many cryptographers. Due to its practical aspects, the area has been the subject of a vast amount of work in the last few years [1,2,3,4,5,6,7,8,9]. AuthA is an example of such a technology considered for standardization by the IEEE P1363.2 working

---

* This work was partially supported by a grant from the National High Technology Research and Development Program of China (863 Program) (No. 2007AA01Z471).

J. Cao et al. (Eds.): NPC 2008, LNCS 5245, pp. 94–104, 2008.

group[11,12]. Unfortunately in its current form AuthA, including some variants, only considered the classic client and server scenarios and assume that they share a common password. In a word, AuthA is 2-party password-authenticated key exchange (2PAKE).

With diversity and development of communication environments in the fields such as mobile networks, home networking and etc., the end-to-end security is considered as one of main concerns [10,13]. For example, from a users point of view, in a mobile computing environment, a secure end-to-end channel between one mobile user in cell A and another user in cell A or cell B may be a primary concern. Although 2PAKE protocols are quite useful for client-server architectures, they are not suitable for large scale end-to-end communication environments since 2PAKE protocols require every pair of communication entities to share a password. It is very inconvenient in key management for client-client communications in large-scale communication environments. To avoid this inconvenience, some of proposed PAKE protocols are extended to take into account the 3-party scenario [14,15,16,17,18,19], in which a trusted server exists to mediate between two communication parties to allow mutual authentication. Such protocols only demand that each communication entity shares a password with a trusted server. However, in practices, they are less considered in a cross-realm setting like in kerberos system [20,21]. In a cross-realm setting, two clients are in two different Kerberos realms and hence two servers (who are connected with a symmetric key) are involved. Some researchers, e.g. [18], think it unnecessary to consider this case since they have presumed that all servers in the general case know all users' passwords. Actually, in the protocols with a cross-realm setting, it is important to guarantee that one server should not obtain the password of a client in another realm.

Kerberos system is the first solution to password-authenticated key exchange in a cross-realm setting but one of the most serious problems in the Kerberos system is a dictionary attack. To solve this dictionary attack, Byun et al. recently proposed a password-authenticated key exchange protocol in a cross-realm setting [14], which is a variant of cross-realm authentication in the Kerberos system. However, S. Wang et al. subsequently found the protocol due to Byun et al. was insecure [22]. Later, two schemes for password-authenticated key establishment in a cross-realm setting were proposed in [24,25] but both of them were still pointed out to be insecure in [26]. To the best of our knowledge, no more work address the problem in the cross-realm setting and achieves provable security. Moreover, as noted in [22], a scheme in a single-server setting(3-party setting) cannot be easily lift up to a scheme in a cross-realm setting since it is a quite different paradigm from the former. In this paper, based on a variant of AuthA in [5], we propose a provably secure password-authenticated key exchange protocol in a cross-realm setting. Note it is not a trivial work. Difficulties in designing a secure client-client password-based authenticated key exchange scheme arise from the existence of insider attacks while insider attacks do not need be considered explicitly in the case of 2-party protocols. Our protocol has several attractive features. As in [18], we trust as little as possible the third party and assume that the servers are honest but curious, which roughly means that, even though the servers' help is required to establish a session key between two users in the system, the servers should not be able to gain any information on the value of that session key. Please note that key distribution schemes usually do not achieve this property. We can show that our protocol has key privacy with respect to the server. Moreover, our scheme is reasonably efficient and has a per-user computational cost that is comparable to that of the underlying 2-party encrypted key exchange.

The remainder of this paper is organized as follows. In Section 2, we introduce the formal model of security for password-based authenticated key exchange in a cross-realm setting. Next, in Section 3, we recall the algorithmic assumptions upon which the security of our protocol is based upon. Section 4 then presents our password-based key exchange protocol along with its security claims and rigorous proof. Efficiency analysis is also presented in this section. In the last section, we conclude this paper.

2   Security Model for Password-Based Key Exchange

A secure password-based key exchange is a key exchange protocol where the parties use their passwords in order to derive a common session key sk that will be used to build secure channels. Loosely speaking, such protocols are said to be secure against *dictionary attacks* if the advantage of an attacker in distinguishing a real session key from a random key is less than $O(n/|\mathcal{DC}|) + \epsilon(l)$, where $|\mathcal{DC}|$ is the size of the dictionary $\mathcal{DC}$, n is the number of active sessions and $\epsilon(l)$ is a negligible function depending on the security parameter l.

In this section, we introduce the formal security models which will be used in next section when we show that our protocol is secure in the random-oracle model. The model is a slightly different variant of that introduced in [19], in which two trusted servers are contained.

2.1   Protocol Syntax

PROTOCOL PARTICIPANTS. The end-to-end system we consider is made up of three disjoint sets: $\mathcal{S}$, the set of trusted servers; $\mathcal{C}$, the set of honest clients; and $\mathcal{E}$, the set of malicious clients. We also denote the set of all clients by $\mathcal{U}$. That is, $\mathcal{U} = \mathcal{C} \cup \mathcal{E}$. In a cross-realm setting, we assume S to contain two trusted servers.

As in [18], the inclusion of the malicious set $\mathcal{E}$ among the participants is one the main differences between the 2-party and the multi-party models. Such inclusion is needed in the multi-party model in order to cope with the possibility of insider attacks. The set of malicious users did not need to be considered in the 2-party due to the independence among the passwords shared between pairs of honest participants and those shared with malicious users.

LONG-LIVED KEYS. Two servers are connected with a symmetric key. Each participant $U \in \mathcal{U}$ holds a password pw_U. Each server $S \in \mathcal{S}$ holds a vector $pw_S = \langle pw_S[U] \rangle_{U \in \mathcal{U}}$ with an entry for each client, where $pw_S[U]$ is the transformed password, following the definition in [3]. In a symmetric model, $pw_S[U] = pw_U$, but they may be different in some schemes. The set of passwords pw_E, where $E \in \mathcal{E}$, is assumed to be known by the adversary.

2.2   The Security Model

The interaction between an adversary $\mathcal{A}$ and the protocol participants occurs only via oracle queries, which model the adversary capabilities in a real attack (see literature for more details [3,5].) The types of oracles available to the adversary are as follows:

- $Execute(U_1^{i_1}, S_1^{j_1}, S_2^{j_2}, U_2^{i_2})$: This query models passive attacks in which the attacker eavesdrops on honest executions among the client instances $U_1^{i_1}$ and $U_2^{i_2}$ and trusted server instances $S_1^{j_1}$ and $S_2^{j_2}$. The output of this query consists of the messages that were exchanged during the honest execution of the protocol.
- $SendClient(U^i, m)$: This query models an active attack, in which the adversary may intercept a message and then modify it, create a new one, or simply forward it to the intended client. The output of this query is the message that client instance U^i would generate upon receipt of message m.
- $SendServer(S^j, m)$: This query models an active attack against a server. It outputs the message that server instance S^j would generate upon receipt of message m.
- $Reveal(U^i)$: If a session key is not defined for instance U^i or if a $Test$ query(see section 2.3) was asked to either U^i or to its partner, then return $\perp$. Otherwise, return the session key held by the instance U^i.

2.3   Security Notions

In order to define a notion of security for the key exchange protocol, we consider a game in which the protocol $\mathcal{P}$ is executed in the presence of the adversary $\mathcal{A}$. In this game, we first draw some passwords from a dictionary $\mathcal{DC}$, provide coin tosses and oracles to $\mathcal{A}$, and then run the adversary, letting it ask any number of queries as described above, in any order.

AKE Security. In order to model the secrecy (semantic security) of the session key, we consider a game $Game^{ake}(\mathcal{A}, \mathcal{P})$, in which one additional oracle is available to the adversary: the $Test(U^i)$ oracle.

- $Test(U^i)$: This query tries to capture the adversary's ability to tell apart a real session key from a random one. In order to answer it, we first flip a (private) coin b and then forward to the adversary either the session key sk held by U^i (i.e., the value that a query $Reveal(U^i)$ would output) if $b = 1$ or a random key of the same size if $b = 0$.

The $Test$-oracle can be queried at most once by the adversary $\mathcal{A}$ and is only available to $\mathcal{A}$ if the attacked instance U^i is Fresh, which is defined to avoid cases in which adversary can trivially break the security of the scheme. In this setting, we say that a session key sk is Fresh if all of the following hold: (1) the instance holding sk has accepted, (2)both the related clients are honest; and (3) no *Reveal*-query has been asked to the instance holding sk or to its partner (defined according to the session identification). Let **Succ** denote the event in which the adversary successfully guesses the hidden bit b used by $Test$ oracle. The AKE advantage of an adversary $\mathcal{A}$ is then defined as $Adv_{\mathcal{P},\mathcal{DC}}^{ake}(\mathcal{A}) = 2Pr[\mathbf{Succ}] - 1$, when passwords are drawn from a dictionary $\mathcal{DC}$. The protocol $\mathcal{P}$ is said to be (t,ε)-AKE-secure if $\mathcal{A}$'s advantage is smaller than ε for any adversary $\mathcal{A}$ running with time t. The definition of time-complexity that we use henceforth is the usual one, which includes the maximum of all execution times in the games defining the security plus the code size [23].

3   Algorithmic Assumptions

The security is proved by finding a reduction to the hardness of the Computational Diffie-Hellman (CDH) problem and the security of the underlying message authentication schemes. We will briefly introduce these algorithmic assumptions in this section.

3.1   CDH Assumption

We assume a finite cyclic group $\mathbb{G}$ of l-bit prime order q generated by an element g, in which the operation is denoted multiplicatively. The CDH assumption states that given g^x and g^y, where x and y are drawn at random from Z_q, it is hard to compute g^{xy}. Under the computational Diffie-Hellman assumption it might not be possible for the adversary to compute something interesting about g^{xy} given g^x and g^y. This can be defined more precisely by considering an experiment $\mathbf{Exp}_{g,\mathbb{G}}^{cdh}(\mathcal{A})$, in which we select two values x and y in Z_q, compute $X = g^x$, and $Y = g^y$, and then give both X and Y to an adversary $\mathcal{A}$. Let Z be the output of $\mathcal{A}$. Then, the experiment $\mathbf{Exp}_{g,\mathbb{G}}^{cdh}(\mathcal{A})$ outputs 1 if $Z = g^{xy}$ and 0 otherwise. Then, we define advantage of $\mathcal{A}$ in violating the CDH assumption as $Adv_{g,\mathbb{G}}^{cdh}(\mathcal{A}) = Pr[\mathbf{Exp}_{g,\mathbb{G}}^{cdh}(\mathcal{A}) = 1]$ and the advantage function of the group $Adv_{g,\mathbb{G}}^{cdh}(t)$, as the maximum value of $Adv_{g,\mathbb{G}}^{cdh}(\mathcal{A})$ over all $\mathcal{A}$ with time-complexity at most t.

3.2   Security of Message Authentication Scheme

A message authentication scheme is a pair of polynomial algorithms (MAC,VF). The function MAC takes a message m and a key k, and it produces a "message authentication code" (tag) $\mu = \mathrm{MAC}_k(m)$. The function VF takes a message m, a tag μ and a key k, and it returns a bit $\mathrm{VF}_k(m,\mu)$, with 1 standing for accept and 0 for reject. We require that for any m output with positive probability by its tag μ, it is the case that $\mathrm{VF}_k(m,\mu)$.

For the security of the underlying message authentication scheme $\mathcal{MAC}$, we consider the classical definition of existential unforgeability under chosen-message attack (CMA) due to Goldwasser et al. [27]. By definition, the security level for $\mathcal{MAC}$ is to prevent existential forgeries, even for an adversary which has access to the tag generation and verification oracles. We define the advantage of $\mathcal{A}$ in violating the security of $\mathcal{MAC}$ with security parameter l as $Adv_{\mathcal{MAC}}^{euf-cma}(\mathcal{A}) = Pr[k \leftarrow \{0,1\}^l, (m, \mu) \leftarrow \mathcal{A}^{\mathrm{MAC}_k(\cdot), \mathrm{VF}_k(\cdot;\cdot)}() : \mathrm{VF}_k(m; \mu) = 1]$, and the advantage function of $\mathcal{MAC}$, $Adv_{\mathcal{MAC}}^{euf-cma}(t)$ as the maximum value of the advantage $Adv_{\mathcal{MAC}}^{euf-cma}(\mathcal{A})$ over all $\mathcal{A}$ with time-complexity at most t. Note that $\mathcal{A}$ wins the above experiment only if it outputs a new valid authenticator.

4 Our Password-Based Protocol

In this section, we introduce our protocol and provide a rigorous proof of security for it based on the hardness of the CDH problem and the security of the underlying primitives. The security proof is in the random oracle model. It assumes that two clients willing to establish a common secret session key are in two different Kerberos realms and hence share passwords with two respective servers (the latter are connected with a symmetric key). As in [18], we trust as little as possible the third party and assume that the servers are honest but curious, which roughly means that, even though the servers' help is required to establish a session key between two users in the system, the servers should not be able to gain any information on the value of that session key.

4.1 Description

Our scheme is based on a 2-party password-based key exchange protocols in [5]. It runs between two clients A, B and two servers S_A, S_B. The client A (resp. B) and server S_A(resp. S_B) initially share a low-quality password PW_A(resp. PW_B), uniformly drawn from the dictionary $\mathcal{DC}$. The two server are connected with a symmetric key, i.e. the MAC key K. The description is given in Fig.1, where $(\mathbb{G}, g, q)$ is the represented group; l is a security parameter; $\mathcal{H}_i \colon \{0,1\}^\star \to \{0,1\}^l$ is a random oracle, for $i = 0, 1, 2$. In Fig.1, by $U_2 \xleftarrow[send]{message} U_1$ we mean that user U_1 sends $message$ to user U_2.

At first, the client may send a request to the server to start the protocol(e.g. the client sends hello information to the server in the TLS (Transport Layer Security) protocol at the beginning). Then the protocol runs as follows.

1. The server S_A(resp. S_B) chooses an ephemeral public key by choosing a random element t_A(resp. t_B) in Z_q and raising g to that power, encrypts it as T_A(resp. T_B) using the corresponding password PW_A(resp. PW_B), and sends this value to the client A(resp. B) and the other server along with its identity S_A(resp. S_B) and the two clients' identity. Upon receiving a message from the server S_A(resp. S_B), the client A(resp. B) decrypts T_A(resp. T_B) to

Public information: $\mathbb{G}, q, \mathcal{H}_i$
Secret information: $PW_A, PW_B \in \mathbb{G}, K$

Client A	Server S_A	Server S_B	Client B

$$t_A \xleftarrow{R} Z_q \ \ t_B \xleftarrow{R} Z_q$$
$$T_A \leftarrow g^{t_A} \times PW_A \ \ T_B \leftarrow g^{t_B} \times PW_B$$

$$A \xleftarrow[\text{send}]{A,B,S_A,T_A} S_A \xrightarrow[\text{send}]{A,B,S_A,T_A} S_B \ \ S_A \xleftarrow[\text{send}]{A,B,S_B,T_B} S_B \xrightarrow[\text{send}]{A,B,S_B,T_B} B$$

$$x \xleftarrow{R} Z_q, X \leftarrow g^x \qquad\qquad\qquad y \xleftarrow{R} Z_q, Y \leftarrow g^y$$
$$K_{AS} \leftarrow (T_A/PW_A)^x \qquad\qquad\qquad K_{BS} \leftarrow (T_B/PW_B)^y$$
$$\text{Auth1}_A \leftarrow \mathcal{H}_1(ID_{AS}, K_{AS}) \qquad\qquad\qquad \text{Auth1}_B \leftarrow \mathcal{H}_1(ID_{BS}, K_{BS})$$

$$A \xrightarrow[\text{send}]{X, \text{Auth1}_A} S_B \qquad\qquad\qquad S_A \xleftarrow[\text{send}]{Y, \text{Auth1}_B} B$$

$$K_{AS} \leftarrow X^{t_A} \ \ K_{BS} \leftarrow Y^{t_B}$$

$$\text{Auth1}_A \overset{?}{=} \mathcal{H}_1(ID_{AS}, K_{AS}) \ \ \text{Auth1}_B \overset{?}{=} \mathcal{H}_1(ID_{BS}, K_{BS})$$
$$\textit{if false, terminates, terminates}$$
$$\alpha \leftarrow \text{MAC}_K(A, B, S_A, S_B, T_A, T_B, X) \ \ \beta \leftarrow \text{MAC}_K(A, B, S_A, S_B, T_A, T_B, Y)$$

$$S_A \xrightarrow[\text{send}]{S_A, X, \alpha} B \ \ A \xleftarrow[\text{send}]{S_B, Y, \beta} S_B$$

$$\beta \overset{?}{=} \text{MAC}_K(A, B, S_A, S_B, T_A, T_B, Y) \ \ \alpha \overset{?}{=} \text{MAC}_K(A, B, S_A, S_B, T_A, T_B, X)$$
$$\textit{if false, terminates, terminates}$$
$$\text{Auth2}_A \leftarrow \mathcal{H}_2(ID_{AS}, Y, K_{AS}) \ \ \text{Auth2}_B \leftarrow \mathcal{H}_2(ID_{BS}, X, K_{BS})$$

$$A \xleftarrow[\text{send}]{Y, \text{Auth2}_A} S_A \ \ S_B \xrightarrow[\text{send}]{X, \text{Auth2}_B} B$$

$$\textit{terminates and accepts terminates and accepts}$$

$$\text{Auth2}_A \overset{?}{=} \mathcal{H}_2(ID_{AS}, Y, K_{AS}) \qquad\qquad\qquad \text{Auth2}_B \overset{?}{=} \mathcal{H}_2(ID_{BS}, X, K_{BS})$$
$$\textit{if false, terminates} \qquad\qquad\qquad \textit{if false, terminates}$$
$$K \leftarrow Y^x \qquad\qquad\qquad K \leftarrow X^y$$
$$sk \leftarrow \mathcal{H}_0(ID, K) \qquad\qquad\qquad sk \leftarrow \mathcal{H}_0(ID, K)$$
$$\textit{terminates and accepts} \qquad\qquad\qquad \textit{terminates and accepts}$$

Fig. 1. Our password-based authenticated key exchange protocol

recover the server's ephemeral public key, chooses a random index x(resp. y) in Z_q, exponentiates it to that power as the Diffie-Hellman keys K_{AS}(resp. K_{BS}), and at the same time also raises g to the that power as his ephemeral public key X(resp. Y). Then the client computes the authenticators Auth1_A (resp. Auth1_B) via a hash function $\mathcal{H}_1$ so that he can send X (resp. Y)to the server S_A(resp. S_B) in an authenticated way. For simplicity, ID_{AS} and ID_{BS} represent $(A, B, S_A, T_A, X, PW_A)$ and $(A, B, S_B, T_B, Y, PW_B)$ respectively.

2. Upon receiving the messages from both the client A(resp. B) and the other server, the server S_A(resp. S_B) exponentiates the client's ephemeral public key to the t_A-th (resp. t_B-th) power as the Diffie-Hellman keys K_{AS}(resp. K_{BS}). Then the server computes the MAC tag α (resp. β) with the symmetric key K so that he can transfer X (resp. Y)to the other server S_B(resp. S_A) in a secure way. Upon receiving this messages, the server S_A(resp. S_B) first checks the MAC tag β (resp. α) is valid. If it is valid, the server will proceed to compute the authenticators Auth2_A (resp. Auth2_B) via a hash function $\mathcal{H}_2$ so that he can forward Y (resp. X) to he client A(resp. B) in an authenticated way.

3. Upon receiving Y (resp. X) from the server, the client A(resp. B) first checks the authenticators Auth2_A (resp. Auth2_B) is valid. If it is valid, he computes the Diffie-Hellman key K and then uses this value to derive the session key sk via a hash function $\mathcal{H}_0$. In the end, he accepts and terminates the execution of the protocol. For simplicity, ID represents (A, B, X, Y).

All throughout the course, if any participant receives an invalid authenticator, he simply abolishes and terminates the execution of the protocol.

How the Password Becomes an element in $\mathbb{G}$. Since the password PW appears as an element of $\mathbb{G}$ in the computations for our scheme, some additional function is needed to obtain this element from the password string. In the protocol description, we do not care about details of the function and simply use the result PW (in group $\mathbb{G}$) as the "effective password" instead: anyone knowing PW is actually able to impersonate the client or the server, and the security proof shows that attacking the protocol reduces to finding PW. In other words, at the protocol level, PW is the password needed for authentication and password is just a way to remember it.

NOTES. One should remark that K is long-lived key. And thus a nonce is necessarily included in computing α and β in order to prevent replay attacks. To do so, each server also sends to another server its ephemeral public key, which will be included in computing the MAC tag as its nonce.

Efficiency. Our protocol is quite efficient, only requiring a small amount of computation by each user. In what concerns MAC computations and hash computations, each client only has to perform 3 hash computations; and each server only has to perform 2 MAC computation and 2 hash computations. All these can be done efficiently and their computational complexity can be neglected. The most expensive part of our protocol is the number of exponentiation, which entails the highest computational complexity. Since each participant needs to perform 2 exponentiations, our protocol has a per-user computational cost that is comparable to that of the underlying two-party encrypted key exchange.

In addition, from the view of the client side, our protocol is very similar to a 2PAKE with explicit mutual authentication. If the client computes his session key using $sk = \mathcal{H}_1(A, \cdots, S_A, T_A, X, \cdots, K_{AS})$ instead, it shifts to run a 2PAKE protocol with the server. Thus we do not need two separate programme codes to support client-server and client-client PAKE respectively. Instead we can use a common programme to support both them, which saves storage resources. This is very attractive in resource constrained environments.

4.2   Security

As the following theorem states, our proposal is a provably secure password-based key exchange protocol as long as the CDH problem is hard in $\mathbb{G}$ and the underlying message authentication scheme is secure. The specification of this protocol is found on Fig.1.

Theorem 1. *Let $\mathcal{DC}$ be a uniformly distributed dictionary of size $|\mathcal{DC}|$, and $\mathcal{MAC}$ be a message authentication scheme. Let $\mathcal{P}$ describe the password-based authenticated key exchange protocol associated with these primitives as defined in Fig.1. Then $Adv_{\mathcal{P},\mathcal{DC}}^{ake}(\mathcal{A}) \leq \frac{(2q_p+q_s)^2}{q} + \frac{q_h^2+2q_s}{2^l} + \frac{6q_s}{|\mathcal{DC}|} + 2q_s Adv_{\mathcal{MAC}}^{euf-cma}(t) + 4q_h^2 Adv_{g,\mathbb{G}}^{cdh}(q_h, t + 2\tau)$, where q_s denotes the number of active interactions with the parties (Send-queries); q_p denotes the number of passive eavesdroppings*

(Execute-queries); q_h denotes the number of hash queries to $\mathcal{H}_i$; and τ denotes the computational time for an exponentiation in $\mathbb{G}$.

Due to the limitation of the paper length, the complete proof of Theorem 1 is to be included in the full version of this paper.

Finally, we come to consider key privacy with respect to the servers. Since a server is unable to deduce the Diffie-Hellman key K from the clients' ephemeral public keys X and Y (due to computational Diffie-Hellman assumption), he will be unable to retrieve any information about the session key sk between the two clients. Thus, we have

Theorem 2. *Our password-based authenticated key exchange protocol described in Fig.1 has key privacy with respect to the servers as long as the CDH assumption holds in $\mathbb{G}$.*

5   Conclusion

We have presented the new PAKE protocol in a cross-realm setting and proved the security for it in the random-oracle model. Our protocol has several attractive features. In our protocol, any honest server is unable to gain any information on the value of that session key. Moreover, our scheme is reasonably efficient and has a per-user computational cost that is comparable to that of the underlying two-party encrypted key exchange. In addition, from the view of the client side, our protocol is very similar to a 2PAKE with explicit mutual authentication. We can thus use a common programme to support both client-server and client-client applications, which saves storage resources. This is very attractive in resource constrained environments.

References

1. Bellovin, S.M., Merritt, M.: Encrypted key exchange: password-based protocols secure against dictionary attacks. In: Proceedings of the 1992 IEEE Computer Society Symposium on Research in security and Privacy, Oakland, California,USA, pp. 72–84. IEEE Computer Society Press, Washington (1992)
2. Boyko, V., MacKenzie, P., Patel, S.: Provably secure password authenticated key exchange using diffie-hellman. In: Preneel, B. (ed.) EUROCRYPT 2000. LNCS, vol. 1807, pp. 156–171. Springer, Heidelberg (2000)
3. Bellare, M., Pointcheval, D., Rogaway, P.: Authenticated key exchange secure against dictionary attacks. In: Preneel, B. (ed.) EUROCRYPT 2000. LNCS, vol. 1807, pp. 139–155. Springer, Heidelberg (2000)
4. Boyko, V., MacKenzie, P.D., Patel, S.: Provably secure password-authenticated key exchange using Diffie-Hellman. In: Preneel, B. (ed.) EUROCRYPT 2000. LNCS, vol. 1807, pp. 156–171. Springer, Heidelberg (2000)
5. Bresson, E., Chevassut, O., Pointcheval, D.: New security results on encrypted key exchange. In: Bao, F., Deng, R., Zhou, J. (eds.) PKC 2004. LNCS, vol. 2947, pp. 145–158. Springer, Heidelberg (2004)

6. Gennaro, R., Lindell, Y.: A framework for password-based authenticated key exchange. In: Proceedings of the 2003 Advances in Cryptology (EUROCRYPT 2003), Warsaw, Poland, pp. 524–543. Springer, Berlin (2003)

7. Goldreich, O., Lindell, Y.: Session-key generation using human passwords only. In: Kilian, J. (ed.) CRYPTO 2001. LNCS, vol. 2139, pp. 408–432. Springer, Heidelberg (2001)

8. Abdalla, M., Pointcheval, D.: Simple Password-Based Encrypted Key Exchange Protocols. In: Menezes, A. (ed.) CT-RSA 2005. LNCS, vol. 3376, pp. 191–208. Springer, Heidelberg (2005)

9. Abdalla, M., Chevassut, O., Pointcheval, D.: One-time verifier-based encrypted key exchange. In: Vaudenay, S. (ed.) PKC 2005. LNCS, vol. 3386, pp. 47–64. Springer, Heidelberg (2005)

10. Varadharajan, V., Mu, Y.: On the Design of Security Protocols for Mobile Communications. In: Proceedings of Twelfth Annual Computer Security Applications Conference, pp. 78–87. IEEE Computer Society Press, Los Alamitos (1996)

11. Bellare, M., Rogaway, P.: The AuthA protocol for password-based authenticated key exchange. Contributions to IEEE P1363 (March 2000)

12. MacKenzie, P.D.: The PAK suite: Protocols for password-authenticated key exchange. Contributions to IEEE P1363.2 (2002)

13. Boyd, C., Mathuria, A.: Key establishment protocols for secure mobile communications: A selective survey. In: Boyd, C., Dawson, E. (eds.) ACISP 1998. LNCS, vol. 1438, pp. 344–355. Springer, Heidelberg (1998)

14. Byun, J.W., Jeong, I.R., Lee, D.H., Park, C.-S.: Password-authenticated key exchange between clients with different passwords. In: Deng, R.H., Qing, S., Bao, F., Zhou, J. (eds.) ICICS 2002. LNCS, vol. 2513, pp. 134–146. Springer, Heidelberg (2002)

15. Wen, H.-A., Lee, T.-F., Hwang, T.: Provably secure three-party password-based authenticated key exchange protocol using Weil pairing. IEE Proceedings — Communications 152(2), 138–143 (2005)

16. Lin, C.-L., Sun, H.-M., Hwang, T.: Three-party encrypted key exchange: Attacks and a solution. ACM SIGOPS Operating Systems Review 34(4), 12–20 (2000)

17. Yeh, H.-T., Sun, H.-M., Hwang, T.: Efficient three-party authentication and key agreement protocols resistant to password guessing attacks. Journal of Information Science and Engineering 19(6), 1059–1070 (2003)

18. Abdalla, M., Fouque, P.-A., Pointcheval, D.: Password-based authenticated key exchange in the three-party setting. In: Vaudenay, S. (ed.) PKC 2005. LNCS, vol. 3386, pp. 65–84. Springer, Heidelberg (2005)

19. Abdalla, M., Pointcheval, D.: Interactive Diffie-Hellman Assumptions with Applications to Password-based Authentication. In: Patrick, S., Yung, A. (eds.) FC 2005. LNCS, vol. 3570, pp. 341–356. Springer, Heidelberg (2005)

20. Steiner, J.G., Newman, B.C., Schiller, J.I.: Kerberos: An Authentication Service for Open Network Systems. In: USENIX Conference Proceedings, February, 1988, pp. 191–202 (1988)

21. Jaspan, B.: Dual-workfactor Encrypted Key Exchange: Efficiently Preventing Password Chaining and Dictionary Attacks. In: Proceedings of the 6th Annual USENIX Security Conference, July 1996, pp. 43–50 (1996)

22. Shuhong, W., Jie, W., Maozhi, X.: Weaknesses of a password-authenticated key exchange protocol between clients with different password. In: Proceedings of the 2nd International Conference on Applied Cryptography and Network Security (ACNS 2004), Yellow Mountain, China, pp. 414–425. Springer, Berlin (2004)

23. Abdalla, M., Bellare, M., Rogaway, P.: The oracle Diffie-Hellman assumptions and an analysis of DHIES. In: Naccache, D. (ed.) CT-RSA 2001. LNCS, vol. 2020, pp. 143–158. Springer, Heidelberg (2001)

24. Yin, Y., Bao, L.: Secure Cross-Realm C2C-PAKE Protocol. In: Batten, L.M., Safavi-Naini, R. (eds.) ACISP 2006. LNCS, vol. 4058, pp. 395–406. Springer, Heidelberg (2006)

25. Byun, J.W., Lee, D.H., Lim, J.: Efficient and Provably Secure Client-to-Client Password-Based Key Exchange Protocol. In: Zhou, X., Li, J., Shen, H.T., Kitsuregawa, M., Zhang, Y. (eds.) APWeb 2006. LNCS, vol. 3841, pp. 830–836. Springer, Heidelberg (2006)

26. Phan, R.C.-W., Goi, B.: Cryptanalysis of two provably secure C2C-PAKE protocols. In: Barua, R., Lange, T. (eds.) INDOCRYPT 2006. LNCS, vol. 4329, pp. 104–117. Springer, Heidelberg (2006)

27. Goldwasser, S., Micali, S., Rivest, R.L.: A Digital Signature Scheme Secure Against Adaptive Chosen-Message Attacks. SIAM Journal on Computing 17(2), 281–308 (1988)

Forward Secure Password-Based Authenticated Key Distribution in the Three-Party Setting*

Shuhua Wu and Yuefei Zhu

Department of Networks Engineering,
Zhengzhou Information Science Technology Institute,
Zhengzhou 450002, China
wushuhua726@sina.com.cn

Abstract. Key establishment protocols are used for distributing shared keying material in a secure manner. In 1995, Bellare and Rogaway presented a three-party server-based key distribution (3PKD) protocol. But the protocol was recently found insecure and then was fixed by Raymond Choo et al.. But forward-secrecy is not considered in the revised protocol. In this paper, we demonstrate that it is not forward secure indeed. We then revise the protocol to be a password-based authenticated key distribution in the three-party setting and prove our protocol is forward secure in the random-oracle and ideal-cipher models under the Password-based Chosen-basis Gap Diffie-Hellman assumption. Our protocol is quite simple and elegant, and rather efficient when compared to previous solutions.

Keywords: password, forward-secure, three-party.

1 Introduction

The need for authentication is obvious when two entities communicate on the Internet. The password-based mechanism is useful for user authentication in computer network systems. It allows users to be authenticated by remote computer systems via easily memorable passwords and in the absence of public-key infrastructures or pre-distributed symmetric keys. However, since people like to choose simply-guessed strings (e.g. personal identity, nickname, birth day, etc.) as their passwords, many password-based systems are vulnerable to replay attack or dictionary attacks [1]. Designing a secure password-based system is a precise task that has attracted many cryptographers. Bellovin and Merritt [1] proposed the encrypted key exchange (EKE) protocol in 1992. The EKE protocol enables two communication entities to authenticate each other and to establish a session key for securing later transmissions via a weak password. Since then, numerous two-party password-based authenticated key exchange (2PAKE) protocols have been proposed to improve security and performance. However, only a few take

* This work was partially supported by a grant from the National High Technology Research and Development Program of China (863 Program) (No. 2007AA01Z471).

J. Cao et al. (Eds.): NPC 2008, LNCS 5245, pp. 105–115, 2008.

into account the 3-party scenario, e.g., [2,3,4,5,6,7,8], where each communication entity shares a password with a trusted server and any two communication entities can be achieved mutual authentication and secure communication through the server's assistance. Moreover, to the best of our knowledge, with the exception of the protocols proposed in [6,7,8], none of the proposed the three-party password-based authenticated key exchange(3PAKE) enjoys provable security. However, the protocols in [7,8] were subsequently shown insecure in [9] and [10] respectively. As for the protocol proposed in [6], the security was proved in a model with no *Corrupt* oracle and thus the forward security for it was still unknown. Other protocols, such as the symmetric-key-based key distribution scheme of Bellare and Rogaway [11], do consider the 3-party setting, but not in the password-based scenario. Recently, the protocol [11] was found insecure and fixed by by Raymond Choo et al. in [12]. Yet, forward-secrecy is not considered in the revised protocol.

In this paper, we demonstrate that it is not forward secure indeed. We then revise the protocol to be a password-based authenticated key distribution in the three-party setting. One should remark that adding authentication services to a key establishment protocol is a not trivial since redundancy in the flows of the protocol can open the door to different forms of attacks [13]. Fortunately, we can prove our protocol is forward secure in the random-oracle [14] and ideal-cipher models [15] under the Password-based Chosen-basis Gap Diffie-Hellman assumption (see section 4). Our protocol is quite simple and elegant and rather efficient when compared to previous solutions. In particular, the costs for each participant of the new 3-party protocol are comparable to those of a 2-party password-based key exchange protocol. Besides, a three party password-based key distribution protocol is the underlying primitive of the generic construction in [6]. We hope one will leverage our work to obtain tighter and more meaningful security measurements for the forward-secrecy of the protocol.

The remainder of this paper is organized as follows. In Section 2, we introduce the formal model of security for for 3-party key exchange. Next, in Section 3, we recall the computational assumptions upon which the security of our protocol is based upon. Section 4 describes the 3PKD revised by Raymond Choo et al. and demonstrates that the revised protocol is not forward secure indeed. Section 5 then presents the improved protocol— our 3-party password-based key distribution protocol— along with its security claims and rigorous proof. In the last section, We conclude this paper.

2   Security Model for Three-Party Key Exchange

In this section, we introduce the formal security models which will be used in next section when we show that our protocol is secure in the random-oracle model. The model was proposed in 2000 by Bellare, Pointcheval and Rogaway [15], hereafter referred to as the BPR2000 model.

2.1   The Security Model

The interaction between an adversary $\mathcal{A}$ and the protocol participants occurs only via oracle queries, which model the adversary capabilities in a real attack (see literature for more details [15,16].) The types of oracles available to the adversary are as follows:

- $Execute(U_1^{i_1}, S^j, U_2^{i_2})$: This query models passive attacks in which the attacker eavesdrops on honest executions among the client instances $U_1^{i_1}$ and $U_2^{i_2}$ and trusted server instance S^j . The output of this query consists of the messages that were exchanged during the honest execution of the protocol.
- $SendClient(U^i, m)$: This query models an active attack, in which the adversary may intercept a message and then modify it, create a new one, or simply forward it to the intended client. The output of this query is the message that client instance U^i would generate upon receipt of message m.
- $SendServer(S^j, m)$: This query models an active attack against a server. It outputs the message that server instance S^j would generate upon receipt of message m.
- $Reveal(U^i)$: If a session key is not defined for instance U^i or if a Test query was asked to either U^i or to its partner, then return $\perp$. Otherwise, return the session key held by the instance U^i.

2.2   Security Notions

In order to define a notion of security for the key exchange protocol, we consider a game in which the protocol $\mathcal{P}$ is executed in the presence of the adversary $\mathcal{A}$. In this game, we first choose the long-lived keys for each participant, provide coin tosses and oracles to $\mathcal{A}$, and then run the adversary, letting it ask any number of queries as described above, in any order.

Forward Security. In order to model the forward secrecy (semantic security) of the session key, we consider a game $Game^{ake-fs}(\mathcal{A}, \mathcal{P})$, in which two additional oracles are available to the adversary: the $Test(U^i)$ and $Corrupt(U)$: oracle.

- $Test(U^i)$: This query tries to capture the adversary's ability to tell apart a real session key from a random one. In order to answer it, we first flip a (private) coin b and then forward to the adversary either the session key sk held by U^i (i.e., the value that a query $Reveal(U^i)$ would output) if $b = 1$ or a random key of the same size if $b = 0$.
- $Corrupt(U)$: This query returns to the adversary the long-lived key (e.g. passwords pw_U in the password-based scenario) for participant U. As in [15], we assume the weak corruption model in which the internal states of all instances of that user are not returned to the adversary.

The $Test$-oracle can be queried at most once by the adversary $\mathcal{A}$ and is only available to $\mathcal{A}$ if the attacked instance U^i is FS-Fresh, which is defined to avoid cases in which adversary can trivially break the security of the scheme. In this setting, we say that a session key sk is FS-Fresh if all of the following hold:

(1) the instance holding sk has accepted, (2) no *Corrupt*-query has been asked since the beginning of the experiment; and (3) no *Reveal*-query has been asked to the instance holding sk or to its partner (defined according to the session identification). In other words, the adversary can only ask *Test*-queries to instances which had accepted before the *Corrupt* query is asked. Let **Succ** denote the event in which the adversary successfully guesses the hidden bit b used by *Test* oracle. The FS-AKE advantage of an adversary $\mathcal{A}$ is then defined as $Adv_{\mathcal{P}}^{ake-fs}(\mathcal{A}) = 2Pr[\textbf{Succ}] - 1$. The protocol $\mathcal{P}$ is said to be (t, ε)-FS-AKE-secure if $\mathcal{A}$'s advantage is smaller than ε for any adversary $\mathcal{A}$ running with time t. The definition of time-complexity that we use henceforth is the usual one, which includes the maximum of all execution times in the experiments defining the security plus the code size [17].

In the password-based scenario, key exchange protocols are said to be secure against *dictionary attacks* if the advantage of an attacker in distinguishing a real session key from a random key is less than $O(n/|\mathcal{D}|) + \epsilon(k)$ where $|\mathcal{D}|$ is the size of the dictionary $\mathcal{D}$, n is the number of active sessions and $\epsilon(k)$ is a negligible function depending on the security parameter k.

Note 1. In the original security models, $\mathcal{A}$ was required to output the guess bit of b immediately after making a *Test* query. However, such a requirement is not strong enough to guarantee security for certain applications(see section 4). Therefore, this restriction has been removed in the current models.

3   Algorithmic Assumptions

The arithmetic is in a finite cyclic group $G = \langle P \rangle$ of order a k-bit prime number q, where the operation is denoted addictively.

3.1   GDH-Assumption

A $(t, \varepsilon) - CDH_{P,G}$ attacker, in a finite cyclic group G of prime order q with P as a generator, is a probabilistic machine Δ running in time t such that its success probability $\textbf{Succ}_{P,G}^{cdh}(\mathcal{A})$, given random elements xP and yP to output xyP, is greater than ε:

$$\textbf{Succ}_{P,G}^{cdh}(\mathcal{A}) = Pr[\Delta(xP, yP) = xyP] \geq \varepsilon.$$

We denote by $\textbf{Succ}_{P,G}^{cdh}(t)$ the maximal success probability over every adversaries running within time t. The CDH-Assumption states that $\textbf{Succ}_{P,G}^{cdh}(t) \geq \varepsilon$ for any t/ε not too large.

A $(t, n, \varepsilon) - GDH_{P,G}$ attacker is a $(t, \varepsilon) - CDH_{P,G}$ attacker, with access to an additional oracle: a DDH-oracle, which on any input (xP, yP, zP) answers whether $z = xy \mod q$. Its number of queries is limited to n. As usual, we denote by $\textbf{Succ}_{P,G}^{gdh}(n, t)$ the maximal success probability over every adversaries running within time t. The GDH-Assumption states that $\textbf{Succ}_{P,G}^{gdh}(n, t) \geq \varepsilon$ for any t/ε not too large [18].

3.2 PCGDH-Assumption

The so-called Password-based Chosen-basis CDH (PCCDH) problem is a variation of the computational Diffie-Hellman that is more appropriate to the password-based setting: Let $\mathcal{D} = \{1, \cdots, |\mathcal{D}|\}$ be a dictionary containing $|\mathcal{D}|$ equally likely password values. Now let us consider an adversary $\mathcal{A}$ that runs in two stages. In the first stage, the adversary is given as input two random elements U and V in G as well as the dictionary $\mathcal{D}$ and it outputs an element M in G (the chosen-basis). Next, we choose a password $pw \in \mathcal{D}$ randomly and give it to the adversary. The goal of the adversary in this second stage is to output $K = CDH(M + pwU, V)$. We denote by $\mathbf{Succ}_{P,G,\mathcal{D}}^{pccdh}(t)$ the maximal success probability over every adversaries $\mathcal{A}$ running within time t. An $(t, \varepsilon) - PCCDH_{P,G,\mathcal{D}}$ attacker is a probabilistic machine running in time t such that its success probability $\mathbf{Succ}_{P,G,\mathcal{D}}^{pccdh}(\mathcal{A})$ is greater than $1/|\mathcal{D}| + \varepsilon$. The PCCDH-Assumption states that $\mathbf{Succ}_{P,G,\mathcal{D}}^{pccdh}(t) \geq 1/|\mathcal{D}| + \varepsilon$ for any t/ε not too large. Fortunately, the new assumption is not stronger than the CDH-Assumption [19,20]. Similarly, we can define the PCGDH-Assumption.

4   Rmarks on Raymond Choo's protocol

In this section, we revisit Raymond Choo's protocol and demonstrate that the revised protocol is not forward secure indeed.

1. $A \longrightarrow B : R_A$
2. $B \longrightarrow S : R_A, R_B$
3a. $S \longrightarrow A : \{SK_{AB}\}_{K_{AS}^{enc}}, [A, B, R_A, R_B, \{SK_{AB}\}_{K_{AS}^{enc}}]_{K_{AS}^{MAC}}, R_B$
3b. $S \longrightarrow B : \{SK_{AB}\}_{K_{BS}^{enc}}, [A, B, R_A, R_B, \{SK_{AB}\}_{K_{BS}^{enc}}]_{K_{BS}^{MAC}}$

Fig. 1. An execution of Raymond Choo's protocol

As illustrated in Fig.1., Raymond Choo's protocol involves three parties, a trusted server S and two principals A and B who wish to establish communication. The security goal of this protocol is to distribute a session key between two communication principals (i.e. the key establishment goal), which is suitable for establishing a secure session. In the protocol, the notation $\{message\}_{K_{AS}^{enc}}$ denotes the encryption of some message under the encryption key K_{AS}^{enc} and the notation $[message]_{K_{AS}^{MAC}}$ denotes the computation of MAC digest of some message under the MAC key K_{AS}^{MAC}. K_{AS}^{enc} is the encryption key shared between A and B, and K_{AS}^{MAC} is the MAC key shared between A and B. Both keys, K_{AS}^{enc} and K_{AS}^{MAC}, are independent of each other.

The protocol begins by having A randomly select a k-bit challenge R_A and send it to the B with whom she desires to communicate. Upon receiving the message R_A from A, B also randomly selects a k-bit challenge R_B and sends R_B together with R_A as a message (R_A, R_B) to the server S. S, upon receiving the message (R_A, R_B)

from B, runs the session key generator to obtain a session key SK_{AB}, which has not been used before. S then encrypts SK_{AB} with K_{AS}^{enc} and K_{BS}^{enc} to obtain ciphertexts α_A and α_B, and computes the MAC digests β_A and β_B of the strings $(A, B, R_A, R_B, \{SK_{AB}\}_{K_{AS}^{enc}})$ and $(A, B, R_A, R_B, \{SK_{AB}\}_{K_{BS}^{enc}})$ under the keys K_{AS}^{MAC} and K_{BS}^{MAC} respectively. S then sends messages (α_A, β_A, R_B) and (α_B, β_B) to A and B respectively in Steps 3a and 3b of the protocol.

Unfortunately, forward-secrecy is not considered in the protocol. Indeed the revised protocol is not forward secure since any adversary who knows the long-lived encryption keys K_{AS}^{enc} or K_{BS}^{enc} certainly can obtain the session key by decrypting α_A and α_B respectively. Now we describe the attack in the BPR2000 mode and illustrate that it is wrong to make the restriction that the $Test$ query be the adversary's last. It is especially important to understand the security proof in Section 5.2. We assume a malicious adversary $\mathcal{A}$ runs the game simulation $Game$ as follows. As a preliminary step, $\mathcal{A}$ eavesdrops on honest executions among the client instances $U_1^{i_1}$ and $U_2^{i_2}$ and trusted server instance S^j and obtains the messages α_A, α_B. When the session is accepted, $\mathcal{A}$ makes a $Test$ oracle query to the client instance $U_1^{i_1}$ or $U_2^{i_2}$. We should note that the session is still fresh at this moment. $\mathcal{A}$ continues making a $Corrupt$ oracle query to the principal and knows its long-lived key K_{AS}^{enc} or K_{BS}^{enc} and thus the session key and the bit b involved in the $Test$ oracle. Eventually, $\mathcal{A}$ terminates the game simulation and outputs the value of b correctly. Our attack demonstrates that the protocol is not forward secure in the BPR2000 model. However, if $\mathcal{A}$ was required to output the guess bit of b immediately after making a $Test$ query, the attack described above would have not been captured. Therefore, removal of this restriction is quite important to guarantee security.

5   Our Three-Party Password-Based Protocol

As we mentioned in Section 1, the original key distribution scheme of Raymond Choo et al. [12] is not in the password-based scenario. In this section, we revised it to be a password-based authenticated key distribution protocol and provide the rigorous proof of forward-security for it based on the hardness of the Password-based Chosen-basis Gap Diffie-Hellman problem. The security proof is in the random oracle model and the ideal-cipher model. It assumes that the clients willing to establish a common secret session key share passwords with a common server and the latter is a trusted server.

5.1   Description

As illustrated on Fig.2. (with an honest execution of the 3PAKD protocol), the protocol runs between two clients A, B and a server S, and the session-key sk is a random value chosen by S and distributed to the clients. Client and server initially share a low-quality password PW, uniformly drawn from the dictionary $\mathcal{D}$. In Fig.2, by $U_2 \xleftarrow[send]{message} U_1$ we mean that user U_1 sends $message$ to user

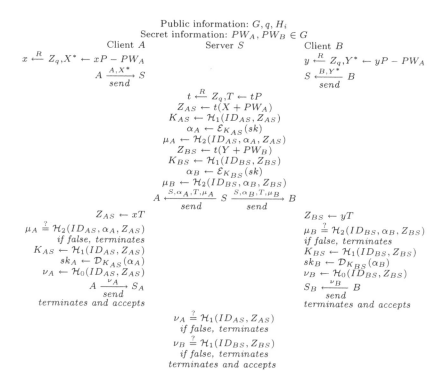

Fig. 2. The password-based authenticated key distribution

U_2. Hash functions from $\{0,1\}^*$ to $\{0,1\}^l$ are denoted $\mathcal{H}_i$ for $i = 0, 1, 2$. A block cipher is denoted $(\mathcal{E}_K, \mathcal{D}_K)$ where K is its private key.

The protocol consists of three flows. First, each client chooses an ephemeral public key by choosing a random element in Z_q and raising P to the that power, encrypts it using his password, and sends it to the server. Upon receiving a message from each client, the server decrypts these messages to recover each client's ephemeral public key, chooses a random index $t \in Z_q$, exponentiates each of the ephemeral public keys to the t-th power as the Diffie-Hellman keys Z, and at the same time raises P to the that power as his ephemeral public key. Then the server computes the private keys K for the block cipher via a hash function H_0 using as input ID and Z, and encrypts the session key sk to be distributed subsequently as the encrypted value α using the block cipher $\mathcal{E}$ with private key K. In the end, the server computes the authenticators μ via a hash function H_1 using as input ID, α and Z. Here, ID represents the string consisting of the transcript of the conversation among the clients and the server and the password. More specifically, ID_{AS} is A, B, S, PW_A, X^*, T and ID_{BS} is A, B, S, PW_B, Y^*, T. This is just for simplicity.

In the second round of messages, the server sends to each client his identity S, the encrypted values α, his ephemeral public key T and the authenticators μ. Upon receiving a message from the server, each client computes the

Diffie-Hellman key Z, and the authenticators μ. Then he checks the authenticator received is valid. If it is invalid, he simply abolishes and terminates the execution of the protocol. Otherwise, he proceeds to compute the private keys K for the block cipher and to recover the session key sk. In addition, he also computes his authenticator ν via a hash function $\mathcal{H}_2$.

In the third round of messages, the client sends his authenticator ν to the server S and accepts and terminates the execution of the protocol. Upon receiving the authenticator from the two clients, the server S checks the authenticators received —ν_A and ν_B— are valid. If both of them are valid, accepts and terminates the execution of the protocol.

Note 2. One should remark that the last round of messages is necessarily included so that the servers can detect online dictionary attacks as pointed out in [21]. For 3-party PAKE protocols, only adding mutual authentication between two communicating clients in the end can not enhance those protocols to be resistant to undetectable on-line dictionary attacks. Unlike 2-party protocols, malicious attacker can play the legal role of client users and interacts with trusted servers to guess the value of passwords.

Our protocol is quite efficient, only requiring a small amount of computation by each user. In what concerns block cipher computations, hash computations, each client only has to perform 1 block cipher computation, and 3 hash computations; and the server only has to perform 2 block cipher computations, and 6 hash computations. All these can be done efficiently and their computational complexity can be neglected. The most expensive part of our protocol is the number of scalar multiplication, which entails the highest computational complexity. Since each client needs to perform 2 scalar multiplications and the server 3 scalar multiplications, our protocol has a per-user computational cost that is comparable to that of the underlying two-party encrypted key exchange. When compared to previous solution in [6], our protocol requires at least one less scalar multiplication for each participant and thus certainly more efficient.

5.2   Security

As the following theorem states, our 3PAKD is a forward-secure 3-party password-based key distribution protocol as long as the Password-based Chosen-basis Gap Diffie-Hellman problem is hard in G . The specification of this protocol is found on Fig.2.

Theorem 1. *Let $\mathcal{D}$ be a uniformly distributed dictionary of size $|\mathcal{D}|$. Let $\mathcal{P}$ describe the 3-party password-based authenticated key distribution protocol associated with these primitives as defined in Fig.2. Then,*

$$Adv_{\mathcal{P}}^{ake-fs}(\mathcal{A}) \leq \frac{(2q_p+q_s)^2}{q} + \frac{2q_{\mathcal{E}}^2}{q} + \frac{q_h^2}{2^l} + \frac{2q_s}{|\mathcal{D}|} + \frac{4q_s+2q_p}{2^l} + 4\boldsymbol{Succ}_{P,G,\mathcal{D}}^{pcgdh}(q_h, t+2\tau),$$

where q_s denotes the number of active interactions with the parties (Send-queries); q_p denotes the number of passive eavesdroppings (Execute-queries);

q_h *denotes the number of hash queries to* $\mathcal{H}_i$*;* $q_{\mathcal{E}}$ *denotes the number of encryption/decryption queries; and* τ *denotes the computational time for an exponentiation in* G.

Due to the limitation of the paper length, the complete proof is to be included in the full version of this paper.

Note 3. The ideal-cipher model is very strong (even stronger than the ideal-hash model) and yet there are natural and apparently-good ways to instantiate an ideal cipher for use in practical protocols (see [22]). Working in this model does not render trivial the goals that this paper is interested in, and it helps make for protocols that achieve provably forward security. We can only prove the proposed scheme is sematic secure but forward secure if we do not assume ideal cipher model. There seems to be some collisions with some technique that is used in our proof when we attempts to reduce an adversary against forward security of the protocol to an adversary against the classical security definition of the encryption scheme.

Rationale for the scheme. At first thought, you may wonder how we can make the original protocol forward-secure by adding password-authentication services. Now let us reconsider the attack in the section 4. In that case, the adversary $\mathcal{A}$ that eavesdrops on honest executions and then corrupts any player of the target session can compute the ephemeral public keys but should not be able to compute the Diffie-Hellman key and thus the private key and the session key. Therefore,we can prove our protocol is forward-secure in the BRP2000 model.

6   Conclusion

We have shown Raymond Choo's protocol is not forward-secure in the BPR2000 model. Following that, we have presented a 3-party password-based authenticated key distribution protocol by adding password-authenti- cation services to Raymond Choo's protocol. Furthermore, we have proved the forward-security for our protocol under the Password-based Chosen-basis Gap Diffie-Hellman assumption in the BPR2000 model. When compared with previous solutions in the password-based scenario, our protocol is efficient. The costs for each participant of the new 3-party protocol are comparable to those of a 2-party encrypted key exchange protocol.

References

1. Bellovin, S.M., Merritt, M.: Encrypted key exchange: password-based protocols secure against dictionary attacks. In: Proc. 1992 IEEE Computer Society Symp. on Research in security and Privacy, May 1992, pp. 72–84 (1992)
2. Byun, J.W., Jeong, I.R., Lee, D.H., Park, C.-S.: Password-authenticated key exchange between clients with different passwords. In: Deng, R.H., Qing, S., Bao, F., Zhou, J. (eds.) ICICS 2002. LNCS, vol. 2513, pp. 134–146. Springer, Heidelberg (2002)

3. Lin, C.-L., Sun, H.-M., Hwang, T.: Three-party encrypted key exchange: Attacks and a solution. ACM SIGOPS Operating Systems Review 34(4), 12–20 (2000)
4. Wang, S., Wang, J., Xu, M.: Weaknesses of a password-authenticated key exchange protocol between clients with different passwords. In: Jakobsson, M., Yung, M., Zhou, J. (eds.) ACNS 2004. LNCS, vol. 3089, pp. 414–425. Springer, Heidelberg (2004)
5. Yeh, H.-T., Sun, H.-M., Hwang, T.: Efficient three-party authentication and key agreement protocols resistant to password guessing attacks. Journal of Information Science and Engineering 19(6), 1059–1070 (2003)
6. Abdalla, M., Fouque, P.-A., Pointcheval, D.: Password-based authenticated key exchange in the three-party setting. In: Vaudenay, S. (ed.) PKC 2005. LNCS, vol. 3386, pp. 65–84. Springer, Heidelberg (2005)
7. Abdalla, M., Pointcheval, D.: Interactive Diffie-Hellman Assumptions with Applications to Password-based Authentication. In: Patrick, S., Yung, A. (eds.) FC 2005. LNCS, vol. 3570, pp. 341–356. Springer, Heidelberg (2005), http://www.di.ens.fr/~pointche/pub.php
8. Wen, H.-A., Lee, T.-F., Hwang, T.: Provably secure three-party password-based authenticated key exchange protocol using Weil pairing. IEE Proceedings — Communications 152(2), 138–143 (2005)
9. Nam, J., Kim, S., Won, D.: Security Weakness in a Three-Party Password-Based Key Exchange Protocol Using Weil Pairing. In: Cryptology ePrint Archive, Report (2005), http://eprint.iacr.org/2005/269.ps
10. Choo, K.-K.R., Boyd, C., Hitchcock, Y.: Examining Indistinguishability-Based Proof Models for Key Establishment Protocols. In: Roy, B. (ed.) ASIACRYPT 2005. LNCS, vol. 3788, pp. 585–604. Springer, Heidelberg (2005)
11. Bellare, M., Rogaway, P.: Provably Secure Session Key Distribution: The Three Party Case. In: 27th ACM Symposium on the Theory of Computing, pp. 57–66. ACM Press, New York (1995)
12. Choo, K.-K.R., Boyd, C., Hitchcock, Y., Maitland, G.: On Session Identifiers in Provably Secure Protocols—The Bellare-Rogaway Three-Party Key Distribution Protocol Revisited. In: Blundo, C., Cimato, S. (eds.) SCN 2004. LNCS, vol. 3352, pp. 352–367. Springer, Heidelberg (2005)
13. Abdalla, M., Bresson, E., Chevassut, O., Pointcheval, D.: Password-based Group Key Exchange in a Constant Number of Rounds. In: Yung, M., Dodis, Y., Kiayias, A., Malkin, T. (eds.) PKC 2006. LNCS, vol. 3958, pp. 427–442. Springer, Heidelberg (2006)
14. Bellare, M., Rogaway, P.: Optimal asymmetric encryption: How to encrypt with RSA. In: De Santis, A. (ed.) EUROCRYPT 1994. LNCS, vol. 950, pp. 92–111. Springer, Heidelberg (1995), http://www-cse.ucsd.edu/users/mihir
15. Bellare, M., Pointcheval, D., Rogaway, P.: Authenticated Key Exchange Secure Against Dictionary Attacks. In: Preneel, B. (ed.) EUROCRYPT 2000. LNCS, vol. 1807, pp. 139–155. Springer, Heidelberg (2000)
16. Bresson, E., Chevassut, O., Pointcheval, D.: New security results on encrypted key exchange. In: Bao, F., Deng, R., Zhou, J. (eds.) PKC 2004. LNCS, vol. 2947, pp. 145–158. Springer, Heidelberg (2004)
17. Abdalla, M., Bellare, M., Rogaway, P.: The oracle Diffie-Hellman assumptions and an analysis of DHIES. In: Naccache, D. (ed.) CT-RSA 2001. LNCS, vol. 2020, pp. 143–158. Springer, Heidelberg (2001)
18. Okamoto, T., Pointcheval, D.: The Gap-Problems: a New Class of Problems for the Security of Cryptographic Schemes. In: Kim, K.-c. (ed.) PKC 2001. LNCS, vol. 1992. Springer, Heidelberg (2001)

19. Abdalla, M., Pointcheval, D.: Simple Password-Based Encrypted Key Exchange Protocols. In: Menezes, A. (ed.) CT-RSA 2005. LNCS, vol. 3376, pp. 191–208. Springer, Heidelberg (2005)
20. Abdalla, M., Bresson, E., Chevassut, O., Möller, B., Pointcheval, D.: Provably Secure Password-Based Authentication in TLS. In: Proc. of at AsiaCCS 2006, Taipei, Taiwan, March 21-24 (2006)
21. Ding, Y., Horster, P.: Undetectable On-line Password Guessing Attacks. ACM Operating Systems Review 29(4), 77–86 (1995)
22. Black, J., Rogaway, P.: Ciphers with Arbitrary Finite Domains (manuscript, 2000)

Key Management Using Certificateless Public Key Cryptography in Ad Hoc Networks

Fagen Li[1,2,3], Masaaki Shirase[1], and Tsuyoshi Takagi[1]

[1] School of Systems Information Science,
Future University-Hakodate, Hakodate 041-8655, Japan
[2] School of Computer Science and Engineering,
University of Electronic Science and Technology of China, Chengdu 610054, China
[3] Key Laboratory of Computer Networks and Information Security,
Xidian University, Xi'an 710071, China
fagenli@uestc.edu.cn

Abstract. As various applications of wireless ad hoc network have been proposed, security has become one of the big research challenges and is receiving increasing attention. In this paper, we propose a distributed key management approach by using the recently developed concepts of certificateless public key cryptography and threshold secret sharing schemes. Without any assumption of prefixed trust relationship between nodes, the ad hoc network works in a self-organizing way to provide the key generation and key management services using threshold secret sharing schemes, which effectively solves the problem of single point of failure. Certificateless public key cryptography is applied here not only to eliminate the need for certificates, but also to retain the desirable properties of identity-based key management approaches without the inherent key escrow problem.

Keywords: Ad hoc network, network security, key management, certificateless public key cryptography.

1 Introduction

An ad hoc network is a collection of autonomous nodes that communicate with each other by forming a multi-hop wireless network. The property of not relying on the support from any fixed infrastructure makes it useful for a wide range of applications, such as instant consultation between mobile users in the battlefields, emergency, and disaster situations, where geographical or terrestrial constraints demand totally distributed networks. While ad hoc network provides a great flexibility for establishing communications, it also brings a lot of research challenges. One of the important issues is the security due to all the characteristics of these networks, such as the vulnerability of the wireless links, the limited physical protection of each node and the dynamically changing topology. Key management service is a crucial security issue because it is the essential assumption of many other security services. For instance, many secure routing protocols,

J. Cao et al. (Eds.): NPC 2008, LNCS 5245, pp. 116–126, 2008.

such as ARAN [1] and SRP [2], assume that a pair of private and public keys and a certificate signed by a trusted third party have been assigned to nodes.

Because ad hoc networks are highly vulnerable to various security threats due to its inherent characteristics, such as open medium, absence of fixed central structure, dynamically changing topology and constrained resource, traditional key management approaches based on public key infrastructure (PKI) is not directly applicable to ad hoc networks. Designing an efficient key management solution should satisfy following characteristics:

Lightweight: Solutions must minimize the amount of computation and communication required to ensure the security services to accommodate the limited energy and computational resources of nodes.

Decentralized: Like ad hoc networks themselves, attempts to secure them must be ad hoc way: they must establish security without a priori knowledge to centralized or persistent entities. Instead, security solutions must utilize the cooperation of all trustworthy nodes in the network.

Reactive: Ad hoc networks are dynamic: nodes may enter and leave the network spontaneously and unannounced. Security solutions must react to changes in network state; they must seek to detect compromises and vulnerabilities.

Fault-Tolerant: Wireless transfer mediums are known to be unreliable; nodes are likely to leave or be compromised without warning. The security solutions should be designed with such faults in mind; they must not rely on message delivery or ordering.

Current research works in key management are mainly based on traditional PKI [3,4,5,6] and identity-based public key cryptography (ID-PKC) [7,8,9]. These approaches based on traditional PKI use a partially distributed or a fully distributed certificate authority (CA) to issue and manage public key certificates. However, the resource-constrained ad hoc networks might be unable to afford the rather complicated certificate management, including revocation, storage and distribution, and the computational costs of certificate verification. ID-PKC get rid of the public key certificates by allowing allowing the user's public key to be any binary string, such as an email address, IP address that can identify the user. ID-PKC have an advantage in the aspect of the key management compared with the traditional PKI. However, ID-PKC needs a trusted private key generator (PKG) which generates the private keys of the entities using their public keys and a master secret key. Therefore, the dependence on the PKG who know all user's private keys inevitably causes the key escrow problem to the ID-PKC systems. For example, the PKG can decrypt any ciphertext in an identity-based public key encryption scheme. Equally problematical, the PKG could forge any entity's signatures in an identity-based signature scheme.

In this paper, we propose a novel key management approach using certificateless public key cryptography (CL-PKC) [10]. The CL-PKC does not require the use of certificates and yet does not have the built-in key escrow feature of ID-PKC. It is a model for the use of public key cryptography that is intermediate between traditional PKI and ID-PKC. A CL-PKC system still makes use of a trusted third party which is called the key generating center (KGC). By way of contrast to the PKG in ID-PKC, the KGC does not have access to the user's private key. Instead, the KGC supplies a user with a partial private key that the KGC computes from the user's identity and a master key. The user then combines the partial private key with some secret information to generate the actual private key. The system is not identity-based, because the public key is no longer computable from a user identity. When Alice wants to send a message to Bob in a CL-PKC system, she must obtain Bob's public key. However, no authentication of Bob's public key is necessary and no certificate is required.

The rest of this paper is organized as follows. In Section 2, we study the related work in the literature. Some preliminary works are given in Section 3. Our proposed key management approach is detailed described in Section 4. Finally, the conclusions are given in Section 5.

2   Related Work

In [3], Zhou and Haas focused on how to establish a secure key management service in an ad hoc networking environment. They proposed to apply the secret sharing technique [11] to distribute the CA's private key among a pre-selected subset of nodes, called servers. Then any combination of t servers can jointly issue public key certificates to mobile nodes. The focus of their work is to maximize the security of the shared secret in the presence of possible compromises of the secret share holders. It assumes a small group of servers with rich connectivity. Therefore, it is not suitable for purely ad hoc environments. [4] and [5] make an extension of [3] and provide a fully distributed CA scheme. In other words, each node holds a secret share, and k or more nodes in a local neighborhood jointly provide complete services. This solution has a good availability since all nodes are part of the CA service, it is easier for a node to locate k neighbor nodes and request the CA service. In [6], Hubaux et al. proposed a self-organized certificate chaining key management approach, which has similarity with PGP "web of trust" concept. Unlike the above publications, it does not require a trusted authority or any special nodes; instead, each node issues its own certificates to other nodes. Key authentication is performed via chains of certificates. Certificate chaining fits naturally with ad hoc networks where there is no physical infrastructure, relying on each mobile node to issue certificates to other nodes at their own discretion. However, certificate chaining requires a warm-up period to populate the certification graph, which completely depends on the individual node's behavior and mobility. Additionally, the validity of a certificate chain depends on the trustworthiness of all the mobile nodes in the chain, which may not be easy to ensure in open networks.

In [7], Khalili et al. provide a key distribution mechanism combining the use of ID-PKC and threshold cryptography. Their scheme avoids the need for users to generate their own public keys and distribute these keys throughout the network, since the user's identity acts as her public key. Besides that, users only need to propagate their identities instead of the certificates. This can lead to huge savings in bandwidth. However, the usage of ID-PKC instead of certificates also results in a few weaknesses. One major weakness is that the key escrow problem since distributed PKG know all user's private keys. The compromise of the PKG's master key could be disastrous in an ID-PKC system, and usually more severe than the compromise of a CA's signing key in a traditional public key cryptography. For these reasons, it seems that the use of ID-PKC may be restricted to small, closed groups or to applications with limited security requirements.

3   Preliminaries

3.1   Certificateless Public Key Cryptography

The idea of CL-PKC is proposed by Al-Riyami and Peterson [10] with the original motivation of eliminating the inherent key escrow problem of ID-PKC. Since then, different encryption and signature schemes were suggested [12,13,14]. In CL-PKC, the KGC supplies an user with a partial secret key which the KGC computes from the user's identity and a master key, and then the user combines its partial secret key and the KGC's public parameters with some secret information to generate its actual secret key and public key respectively. In this way, an user's secret key is not available to the KGC.

In more detail, an certificateless public key encryption scheme consists of the following algorithms:

- Setup: This algorithm takes security parameter k and returns the system parameters *params* and *master-key*. The system parameters includes a description of the message space $\mathcal{M}$ and ciphertext space $\mathcal{C}$. Usually, this algorithm is run by the KGC. The KGC publishes system parameters *params* and keeps the *master-key* secret.
- Partial-Private-Key-Extract: This algorithm takes *params*, *master-key* and an identity for entity A, $ID_A \in \{0,1\}^*$, as input. It returns a partial private key D_A. Usually this algorithm is run by the KGC and its output is transported to entity A over a confidential and authentic channel.
- Set-Secret-Value: This algorithm takes as inputs *params* and an entity A's identity ID_A as inputs and outputs A's secret value x_A.
- Set-Private-Key: This algorithm takes *params*, an entity A's partial private key D_A and A's secret value x_A as input. The value x_A is used to transform D_A into the (full) private key S_A. The algorithm returns S_A.
- Set-Public-Key: This algorithm takes *params* and entity A's secret value x_A as input and from these constructs the public key P_A for entity A.
- Encrypt: This algorithm takes as inputs *params*, a message $m \in \mathcal{M}$, and the public key P_A and identity ID_A of an entity A. It returns either a ciphertext $c \in \mathcal{C}$ or the null symbol $\perp$ indicating an encryption failure.
- Decrypt: This algorithm takes as inputs *params*, $c \in \mathcal{C}$, and a private key S_A. It returns a message $m \in \mathcal{M}$ or a message $\perp$ indicating a decryption failure.

3.2   Threshold Secret Sharing

Secret sharing allows a secret to be shared among a group of users (also called shareholders) in such a way that no single user can deduce the secret from his share alone. To construct the secret, one needs to combine a sufficient number of shares. (k, n) threshold secret sharing represents that the secret is distributed to n shareholders, and any k or more users can reconstruct the secret from their shares, but $k - 1$ or fewer users cannot get any information about the secret. Here, k is the threshold parameter such that $1 \leq k \leq n$. The first threshold secret sharing scheme was proposed by Shamir [11] in 1979, which is based on polynomial interpolation. To distribute a secret S among n users, a trusted authority chooses a large prime q, and randomly selects a polynomial

$$f(x) = S + a_1 x + \cdots + a_{k-1} x^{k-1} (\text{mod } q),$$

where $a_1, \ldots a_{k-1} \in Z_q$. The trusted authority computes each user's share by $S_i = f(i)$ and securely sends the share S_i to user i. Then any k users can reconstruct the secret by computing

$$S = \sum_{i=1}^{k} S_i L_i (\text{mod } q),$$

where

$$L_i = \prod_{j=1, j \neq i}^{k} -j/(i - j)(\text{mod } q).$$

There are two weaknesses in the Shamir secret sharing scheme. On the one hand, his scheme does not detect the trusted authority distributes erroneous shares to some users and does not detect some compromised users provide false shares; on the other hand, his scheme needs a trusted authority to distribute a secret to users. To detect incorrect shares, a few verifiable secret sharing (VSS) schemes was proposed in [15,16,17]. A VSS scheme generates extra public information for each share using a one-way function. The public information can testify the correctness of the corresponding shares without disclosing them. To solve the second weakness of the Shamir secret sharing scheme, Pedersen [19] proposed a secret sharing scheme without having a trusted authority, which selects the secret and distributes it to users. In stead, these users choose the secret and distribute it among themselves.

In the secret sharing schemes described above, the secret is protected by distributing it among several users. However, given sufficiently long time an attacker could compromise k users and obtain their shares, thereby allowing him to reconstruct the secret. To defend against such attackers, proactive secret sharing schemes [18] use share refreshing, which enables users to compute new shares from old ones in collaboration without disclosing the shared secret to any user. The new shares constitute a new (k, n) sharing of the secret. After refreshing, users remove the old shares and only keep the new ones. Because the new shares are independent of the old ones, the adversary cannot combine old shares with new shares to recover the secret. Thus, the attacker is challenged to compromise k users between periodic refreshing.

4   Proposed Security Solution

In this section, we first describe our assumptions about the network, and then give an overview of our key management approach using the threshold secret sharing schemes and certificateless public key cryptography. Finally, we describe our approach in detail.

4.1   Assumptions

Our key management approach does not rely on any assumption of underlying key management subsystem. That is, there is no trusted authority to generate and distribute the public/private keys and there is no pre-built trust association between nodes in the network. All the keys used are generated and maintained in a self-organizing way within the network.

We assume that each mobile node carries an IP address or an identity, which is unique and unchanged during its lifetime in the ad hoc network. The IP address or identity can be obtained through some dynamic address allocation and auto-configuration, only if the address is selected without any conflict with other nodes in the network. We also assume that each mobile node has a mechanism to discover its one-hop neighborhood and to get the identities of other nodes in the network.

4.2   Proposed Security Scheme

4.2.1 Overview

Consider that an ad hoc network has n nodes in the initial phase. The network has a public/private key pair, called master key $\langle PK, SK \rangle$, which is used to provide key generation service to all the nodes in the network. The master key pair is generated in such a manner that the master public key PK is well known to all the nodes in the network, and the master private key SK is shared by all the nodes in a (k, n) threshold fashion. Any k or more nodes can reconstruct the master private key SK from their shares, but $k - 1$ or fewer nodes cannot get any information about the SK. Before utilizing any network service, each node will have to obtain its partial private key corresponding to its identity and distribute its public key throughout the network. This partial private key can be computed by obtaining k shares of its key from the original nodes in the network. Note that the distributed key generation service in a (k, n) threshold fashion requires an adversary to corrupt at least k nodes in order to obtain a user's partial private key. Furthermore, honest nodes need only contact any k nodes in order to obtain their own partial private keys, thus making the protocol resilient to temporary loss of connectivity with other nodes in the network.

Our solution has the following good characteristics: (i) It does not need a trusted authority to select and to distribute the master private key to nodes. Nodes choose the secret and distributes it among themselves. (ii) It does not need public key certificates, saving network bandwidth and computational power of nodes. (iii) The using of the CL-PKC make our solution eliminate the key escrow problem of the ID-PKC key management approaches [7,8,9].

In the following, we describe the basic operations of our key management approach: master public/private key generation, partial private key generation service, key agreement, new master private key share creation, and master private key share refreshing of nodes.

4.2.2   Master Key Generation

Our master key generation mechanism uses the Pedersen's threshold secret sharing scheme without a trusted authority [19]. Therefore, our approach does not need the support of the trusted authority to compute a master private key, separate it into multiple shares and then distribute the shares to shareholders. Instead, the master key pair is computed collaboratively by the initial network nodes. The detailed scheme is as follows.

1. Each node C_i randomly chooses a secret x_i and a polynomial $f_i(x)$ over Z_q of degree $k - 1$ such that $f_i(0) = x_i$. Let

$$f_i(x) = a_{i0} + a_{i1}x + \cdots + a_{i,k-1}x^{k-1},$$

   where $a_{i0} = x_i$.
2. Each node C_i computes $w_{ij} = g^{a_{ij}}$ for $j = 0, \ldots, k - 1$ and broadcasts $\{w_{ij}\}_{j=0,\ldots,k-1}$.
3. When everybody has sent these $k - 1$ values, C_i sends $s_{ij} = f_i(j)$ securely to C_j for $j = 1, \ldots, n$ (in particular C_i keeps s_{ii}).
4. C_i verifies the correctness of s_{ji} from C_j by checking

$$g^{s_{ji}} = \prod_{l=0}^{k-1} w_{jl}^{i^l}.$$

   If this fails, C_i broadcasts that an error has been found, publishes s_{ji} and then stops.
5. C_i can compute its share of master private key as $S_i = \sum_{j=1}^{n} s_{ji}$. That is, the master private key share of node C_i is combined by the subshares from all the nodes, and each of them contributes one piece of that information.
6. Any coalition of k shareholders can jointly recover the secret as in basic secret sharing by computing $\sum_{i=1}^{k} S_i L_i \pmod{q}$, where

$$L_i = \prod_{l=1, l \neq i}^{k} -l/(i - l) \pmod{q}.$$

It is easy to see that the jointly generated master private key

$$SK = \sum_{i=1}^{n} x_i = \sum_{i=1}^{n} f_i(0).$$

Then, the master public key can be computed as

$$PK = SKP = \sum_{i=1}^{k} S_i L_i P,$$

where P is a common parameter used by the certificateless encryption scheme [10].

4.2.3 Distributed Partial Private Key Generation Service

Suppose that an entity A with identity ID_A needs to obtain its public key and corresponding private key. A choose a secret value x_A and set its public key as $P_A = \langle X_A, Y_A \rangle$, where $X_A = x_A P$ and $Y_A = x_A PK$. Then, A make its public key P_A is well known to all the nodes in the network. To obtain the private key, A contacts at least k neighbor nodes, present the identity and request partial private key generation service. These nodes that hold the master private key share can be the KGC service nodes. In our scheme, all the network nodes share the master private key, thus each of them can be the KGC service node. Each of the k KGC service nodes generates a secret share of the partial private key D_A and sends to A. To make sure the generated shares are securely transmitted, each of the KGC service nodes sends encrypted share to the node A using A's public key P_A. The process of generation of a share of the partial private key D_A can be represented by $D_{A_i} = S_i H_1(ID_A)$, where $S_i (i = 1, \ldots, k)$ is the share of the master private key of the KGC node, H_1 is a hash function used by the certificateless encryption scheme [10], and D_{A_i} is the generated partial private key share for the node A. A can verify the correctness of D_{A_i} by checking

$$\hat{e}(D_{A_i}, P) = \hat{e}(H_1(ID_A), W_i),$$

where $\hat{e}$ is a bilinear map defined in [10] and $W_i = S_i P$ is the i-th KGC's share commitments. If this fails, A broadcasts that an error has been found, publishes D_{A_i} and then stops. After obtaining k valid partial private key share, A calculate the complete partial private key as $D_A = D_{A_i} L_i$, where

$$L_i = \prod_{l=1, l \neq i}^{k} -l/(i-l) (\text{mod } q).$$

Then, A can sets its (full) private key $S_A = x_A D_A$.

4.2.4 Key Agreement

Suppose that entity A has its (full) private key S_A and corresponding public key $P_A = \langle X_A, Y_A \rangle$. Entity B has its (full) private key S_B and corresponding public key $P_B = \langle X_B, Y_B \rangle$. If they want to set up a session key, A chooses a random values $a \in Z_q^*$ and sends $T_A = aP$ to B. B chooses a random values $b \in Z_q^*$ and sends $T_B = bP$ to A. After the above messages are exchanged, both entities check the validity of each other's public keys (A checks $\hat{e}(X_B, PK) = \hat{e}(Y_B, P)$ and B checks $\hat{e}(X_A, PK) = \hat{e}(Y_A, P)$). Then A computes

$$K_A = \hat{e}(H_1(ID_B), Y_B)^a \hat{e}(S_A, T_B)$$

and B computes

$$K_B = \hat{e}(H_1(ID_A), Y_A)^b \hat{e}(S_B, T_A).$$

It is easy to see that $K = K_A = K_B$ is a shared session key between A and B.

4.2.5 New Master Private Key Share Creation

When a new node C_p joins a network, it presents its identity, public key, and some other required physical proof to k neighbor nodes and requests the master public key and his share of the master private key. Each node in the coalition verifies the validity of the identity of the new node C_p. If the verification succeeds, the C_p's private key can be generated using the above method. To initialize the share of master private key for the requesting node, each coalition node C_i generates the partial share $s_{ip} = S_i L_i(p)$ for node C_p. Here, $L_i(p)$ is the Lagrange coefficient. It encrypts the partial share using C_p's public key and sends it to C_p. Node C_p obtains its new share by adding the partial shares as

$$S_p = \sum_{j=1}^{k} s_{p,j}.$$

Note that the partial shares may be shuffled before being sent to the joining node to protect the secrecy of the coalition nodes' secret shares [4]. After obtaining the share of the master private key, the new joining node is available to provide KGC service to other joining nodes.

4.2.6 Master Private Key Share Refreshing of Nodes

To protect against attackers that might compromise k or more nodes if there is enough time, a proactive secret sharing scheme is used to enable nodes of a region to compute new shares from old ones in collaboration without disclosing the master private key of the region. It relies on the homomorphic property. We notice that it is unnecessary to require all the nodes involved in the master private key share refreshing process. Instead, the task can be done by only k nodes, since we assume that, between any consecutive secret share updates, the number of adversaries who hold secret shares originated from the same secret key is less than k. To detect those incorrect subshares, the VSS scheme [15,16,17] is employed.

Details are shown as follows. To renew the master private key shares of all the n nodes in a region, k nodes are chosen from this region. Each node $C_i (1 \leq i \leq k)$ randomly generates $(S_{i1}, S_{i2}, \ldots, S_{in})$, a (k, n) sharing of 0. Then, every subshares $S_{ij} (1 \leq j \leq n)$ is distributed to node C_j. When node C_j gets the subshares $S_{1j}, S_{2j}, \ldots, S_{kj}$, it can compute a new share from these subshares and its old share $(S'_j = S_j + \sum_{i=1}^{k} S_{ij})$. The new shares constitute a new (k, n) sharing of the master private key. After refreshing, nodes remove the old shares and use the new ones to provide the partial private key generation service. Because the new shares are independent of the old ones, the adversary cannot combine old shares with new shares to recover the master private key. Thus, the adversary is challenged to compromise k nodes in the same region between periodic refreshing.

5   Conclusions

Ad hoc networks are new paradigm in networking technologies. Key management is one of the most crucial technologies for security of ad hoc networks. This paper presents a new approach for key management using certificateless public key cryptography and threshold secret sharing schemes. Certificateless public key cryptography is applied here not only to eliminate the need for certificates, but also to retain the desirable properties of identity-based key management approaches without the inherent key escrow problem. In addition, we completely avoid a centralized certification authority or trusted third party to distribute the public keys and the certificates, thus enhance the tolerance of the network to compromised nodes and also efficiently save network bandwidth.

Acknowledgements

We would like to thank the anonymous reviewers for their valuable comments and suggestions. This work is supported by the National Natural Science Foundation of China (60673075), the National High Technology Research and Development Program of China (2006AA01Z428), the Key Laboratory of Computer Networks and Information Security of Xidian University (2008CNIS-02), and Youth Science and Technology Foundation of UESTC. Fagen Li is supported by the JSPS postdoctoral fellowship for research in Japan.

References

1. Sanzgiri, K., Dahill, B., Levine, B.N., Shields, C., Belding-Royer, E.M.: A secure routing protocol for ad hoc networks. In: Proceedings of 10th IEEE International Conference on Network Protocols, Paris, France, pp. 78–87 (2002)
2. Papadimitratos, P., Haas, Z.J.: Secure routing for mobile ad hoc networks. In: Proceedings of SCS Communication Networks and Distributed Systems Modeling and Simulation Conference (CNDS 2002), San Antonio, TX, January 27–31 (2002)
3. Zhou, L., Haas, Z.J.: Securing ad hoc networks. IEEE Network 13(6), 24–30 (1999)

4. Kong, J., Zerfos, P., Luo, H., Lu, S., Zhang, L.: Providing robust and ubiquitous security support for mobile ad hoc networks. In: Proceedings of 2001 International Conference on Network Protocols, Riverside, USA, pp. 251–260 (2001)
5. Luo, H., Kong, J., Zerfos, P., Lu, S., Zhang, L.: Self-securing ad hoc wireless networks. In: Proceedings of Seventh IEEE Symposium on Computers and Communications, Taormina-Giardini Naxos, Italy, pp. 567–574 (2002)
6. Hubaux, J.P., Buttyan, L., Capkun, S.: Self-organized public-key management for mobile ad hoc networks. IEEE Transactions on Mobile Computing 2(1), 52–64 (2003)
7. Khalili, A., Katz, J., Arbaugh, W.A.: Toward secure key distribution in truly ad hoc networks. In: Proceedings of 2003 Symposium on Applications and the Internet Workshops, Orlando, FL, USA, pp. 342–364 (2003)
8. Deng, H., Mukherjee, A., Agrawal, D.: Threshold and identity-based key management and authentication for wireless ad hoc networks. In: Proceedings of International Conference on Information Technology: Coding and Computing, Las Vegas, NV, USA, pp. 107–111 (2004)
9. Deng, H., Agrawal, D.: TIDS: threshold and identity-based security scheme for wireless ad hoc networks. Ad Hoc Networks 2(3), 291–307 (2004)
10. Al-Riyami, S.S., Peterson, K.G.: Certificateless public key cryptography. In: Laih, C.-S. (ed.) ASIACRYPT 2003. LNCS, vol. 2894, pp. 452–474. Springer, Heidelberg (2003)
11. Shamir, A.: How to Share a Secret. Communications of the ACM 22(11), 612–613 (1979)
12. Yum, D.H., Lee, P.J.: Generic construction of certificateless encryption. In: Laganá, A., Gavrilova, M.L., Kumar, V., Mun, Y., Tan, C.J.K., Gervasi, O. (eds.) ICCSA 2004. LNCS, vol. 3043, pp. 802–811. Springer, Heidelberg (2004)
13. Yum, D.H., Lee, P.J.: Generic construction of certificateless signature. In: Wang, H., Pieprzyk, J., Varadharajan, V. (eds.) ACISP 2004. LNCS, vol. 3108, pp. 200–211. Springer, Heidelberg (2004)
14. Al-Riyami, S.S., Peterson, K.G.: CBE from CL-PKE: a generic construction and efficient schemes. In: Vaudenay, S. (ed.) PKC 2005. LNCS, vol. 3386, pp. 398–415. Springer, Heidelberg (2005)
15. Chor, B., Goldwasser, S., Micali, S., Awerbuch, B.: Verifiable secret sharing and achieving simultaneity in the presence of faults. In: Proceedings of 26th IEEE Symposium on Foundations of Computer Science, Portland, OR, USA, pp. 151–160 (1985)
16. Feldman, P.: A practical scheme for non-interactive verifiable secret sharing. In: Proceedings of 28th IEEE Symposium on Foundations of Computer Science, Los Angeles, CA, USA, pp. 427–437 (1987)
17. Pedersen, T.: Non-interactive and information-theoretic secure verifiable secret sharing. In: Feigenbaum, J. (ed.) CRYPTO 1991. LNCS, vol. 576, pp. 129–140. Springer, Heidelberg (1992)
18. Herzberg, A., Jarecki, S., Krawczyk, H., Yung, M.: Proactive secret sharing or: how to cope with perpetual leakage. In: Coppersmith, D. (ed.) CRYPTO 1995. LNCS, vol. 963, pp. 457–469. Springer, Heidelberg (1995)
19. Pedersen, T.: A threshold cryptosystem without a trusted party. In: Davies, D.W. (ed.) EUROCRYPT 1991. LNCS, vol. 547, pp. 522–526. Springer, Heidelberg (1991)

A Data Storage Mechanism for P2P VoD Based on Multi-channel Overlay*

Xiaofei Liao, Hao Wang, Song Wu, and Hai Jin

Services Computing Technology and System Lab
Cluster and Grid Computing Lab
School of Computer Science and Technology
Huazhong University of Science and Technology, Wuhan, 430074, China
{xfliao,wusong,hjin}@hust.edu.cn

Abstract. It is a big challenge to provide Video-on-Demand streaming services over Internet in a scalable way. Currently, many researchers use a single channel overlay to implement the scalability of on-demand streaming services. However, in a real application environment, various channels in a P2P VOD system have different popularities, which probably cause the imbalance of data storage-capability of the whole system. It results in a problem that a mass of unpopular channels' caching capability can not be used to satisfy the data requirements of the whole system. In order to solve the problem, this paper proposes a new data-storage mechanism, which constructs a multi-channel overlay to optimize the whole system's caching-capability and greatly improves unpopular channel's caching efficiency. The experimental results show that this mechanism can achieve significant effects.

1 Introduction

When designing a P2P streaming media system, the basic principle is to organize the nodes watching or serving the same program as a single channel overlay, no matter it is tree [1, 2, 3, 4] or mesh topology [5, 6, 7, 8]. Nodes in a single channel overlay store media data to construct P2P network storage. Nodes request and gain media from neighbor peers while they are playing media, in order to reduce the pressure of source server. When the scale of a single channel overlay grows up to a certain size, the P2P network can store most of data to meet all the requirements, minimize direct data requests to the source server.

Based on the analysis of existing P2P Video-on-Demand system, called GridCast [9], the study found that different channels' network scale meet the Zipf distribution. Some popular channels can assemble a large amount of nodes, and P2P network's data storage capability can meet the data request. But most P2P network channels'

* This work was supported in part by China National Natural Science Foundation (NSFC) grants No.60703050, No.60673174, No.60433040, No.60731160630, the Research Fund for the Doctoral Program of Higher Education grants No.20050487040, Wuhan Chengguang Plan with No.200850731350 and Program for New Century Excellent Talents in University under Grant NCET-07-0334.

J. Cao et al. (Eds.): NPC 2008, LNCS 5245, pp. 127–137, 2008.

sizes are small, the single channel overlay only store part of the channel's media, this channel still causes a lot of data sources requests. To effectively improve the load capacity of the entire P2P VoD system, to solve the insufficient data storage capability problem of most unpopular P2P network channels, is particularly important to reduce the pressure on the data source server.

Based on the above analysis, this paper presents a data storage mechanism based on multi-channel overlay, improving unpopular channels' data storage when popular channels' nodes joining unpopular ones. The simulation result proves that this approach can greatly improve the system load capacity.

The rest of paper is organized as follows. Section 2 describes the system architecture. In section 3, how to organize the multi-channel overlay is presented. Section 4 gives the experiments and results. In section 5, related works are described. Section 6 concludes this paper.

2   System Overview

Just like other P2P content distribution systems, GridCast uses a set of source servers to release media files to participating peers, who asynchronously are playing the files while exchanging data among themselves. Unlike file downloading and live streaming, a node is more *selfish* in the sense that it only cares about contents after its current playing position, which is often different from other nodes. Most of the time, a node's downloading targets are those whose playback positions are ahead, and it can only help those that are behind. However, a node can also change its playing position at any time. These characteristics make a VoD system harder to optimize, rendering globally optimal strategies such as *rarest first* employed in BitTorrent [14] inapplicable.

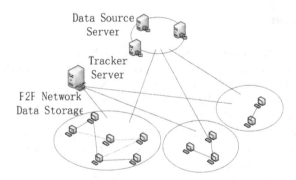

Fig. 1. Architecture overview

To cope with the above problem, the node of GridCast maintains a routing table, which consists of nodes placed in a set of concentric rings with power law distribution distanced using relative playback positions, and uses gossips to keep the routing table up-to-date. This architecture allows a node to find a new group of position-close partners in logarithmic steps after it seeks to a new playing position. The tracker can be considered as a stationary node whose playback position stays fixed at time zero.

The tracker's job is to keep track of its membership view, which bootstraps any new nodes.

3 Multi-channel Overlay

3.1 Network Scale Distribution

In P2P VoD System (Gridcast [9]) based on single channel overlay, each channel's data storage consists of two parts: the P2P network data storage and data server. After one VoD node joins P2P network, it connects with other P2P nodes which are watching the same program to construct a single channel overlay, and exchanges stored data information using Gossip [11] protocol. When the node requests media data, it checks if other nodes in the single channel have stored the data first. If so, it directs request data from the P2P network, and stores data in local cache. Assume that the total media playing time is T, each node stores data with length of time t in local cache. A single channel overlay at least needs T/t nodes to completely stores media data.

The popularities of different programs meet the Zipf distribution [12]. Assuming that the system has n program channels, the probability of user options listed $S1$, $S2$,... Sn, its choice of probability $pi= P\{X=Si\}$ $(i = 1, 2,... n)$, $\{p1, p2,.... pn\}$ with Zipf distribution, $P_i = \frac{1}{i^{1-\theta}} / \sum_{j=1}^{n} (\frac{1}{j^{1-\theta}})$ (θ is the Zipf constant). The collected log data of GridCast shows that θ closes to 0.25. During normal system runtime, the system distributed more than 50% of overall nodes in 20% of the most popular channels, but most channels' network scale fail to achieve stable size. In popular channels, because of the large scale P2P networks, program data stored in the P2P networks are more than data needs. Correspondingly, there are fewer nodes in the unpopular channels; the data storage capability is unable to meet the data needs. There still are a lot of data requests to the data source server.

3.2 Data Storage Status Maintenance

GridCast system uses tracker server to maintain the data storage status of whole P2P network. It keeps track on all of the nodes currently joined GridCast system. A node has been represented as an item that holds nodes GUID, address, port, bandwidth, playing time and so on. In order to maintain the information of all nodes, the tracker needs to update the playing position of each node. Each node will send one UDP message to synchronize its buffer status in every minute.

Tracker server uses a hash table to index one channel's storage status. The length of this hash table is the duration of this channel. Every element of this hash table is a double-link list and it maintains information of each node who has stored the corresponding media data. Figure 2 gives a sketch map of the tracker server. When a P2P node requests data status from tracker server, it sends the ID of requested channel and the playing time of the requested data. Tracker server searches the channel's corresponding hash table and acquires the related nodes' information.

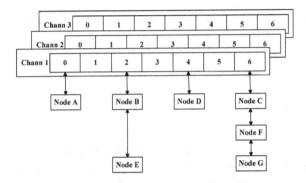

Fig. 2. Data structure of tracker server

P2P node uses a host-list to maintain data storage status of known nodes. The host-list is divided into two levels: neighbors list and nodes list. The neighbors list maintains information of neighbor nodes which are connected with local nodes, and neighbor nodes use directional gossip protocol to exchange information of data storage status. The basic idea of directional gossip protocol is that every node just forwards gossip messages to the neighbors which can retrieve data from source node or send data to source node. Suppose the playing time of one message from some sources is t_{source} and the current playing time of traversed nodes is $t_{forward}$, then we have the following formula: $t_{source}-m{\leq}t_{forward}{\leq}t_{source}+m$, here m represents the total time length in caches.

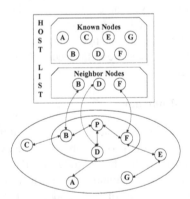

Fig. 3. Host list

3.3 Multi-channel overlay

This paper presents the data storage mechanism from the two areas: 1) constructing a multi-channel overlay network to balance data storage capability between the different kinds of channels; 2) improving utility efficiency of each node's data cache and using idle data storage capacity to raise unpopular channels' data storage capability.

The multi-channel overlay network (Figure 4) is constructed on single channel mesh topology. Compared with the traditional single channel overlay, node can join two kinds of channels in multi-channel overlay: the main channel and the service channel. One node in the main channel plays media, stores data and serves other nodes, and in service channel one node only stores data and serves other nodes. Each node has only one main channel and can choose several service channels. In Figure 4, node K's main channel is channel A, and service channels are channel B and channel C. Node M's main channel is channel A and service channel is channel B. Node L's main channel is channel B, and have no service channel.

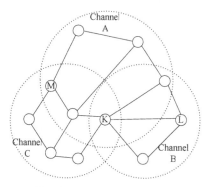

Fig. 4. Multi-channel overlay

Media data will be divided into L data blocks according to granularity τ. Assuming that the total program's duration time is T, The value of L is $\lceil T/\tau \rceil$. Data of playing-time T_i will be classified into $\lceil T_i/\tau \rceil$ data block, and uses a serial number $\lceil T_i/\tau \rceil$ to identify the data blocks. The data storage capability of a node can be described as the ability to store several pieces of data blocks: $N = \lfloor D/(k \times \tau) \rfloor$ (D is the node physical storage capability; k is the encoding rate of media file).

When nodes join the system, in accordance with its own storage capabilities and channel's network scale. The node will decide the number of data blocks stored of the main channel. If it still has idle data blocks, the newly joined node chooses channels that cause the most data source server request, and joins them as its own service channels. The node provides data storage capacity and stores service channels' program data. Throughout the process of accession, node use caching optimization strategy (see section 3.4) to determine the number of data blocks stored in the main channel and service channels.

After joining into the network, the node maintains its data store and elutriation according to program playing process or data storage state of the whole channel's P2P network. The data storage state of one node in one channel can be described as a state of the attribute set $Sp=(Cid, Pc, Np)$. Cid is the channel's identifier. Pc is the initial location of data blocks. Np is the number of data blocks stored locally. Nodes in its main channels choose the starting block $Pc=\lceil pos/\tau \rceil$. Pos is the program playing time. The node in its service channels uses neighborhood nodes' data storage state to maintain its own data in local cache. Nodes exchange data storage state information through gossip protocol. The node can gather data storage information of neighborhood nodes as a set $\pi(P^1, P^2, P^3, ...P^N)$, calculate amount N_1 of nodes which have store data block Pc and amount N_2 of nodes which have store data block $Pc+Np$. If $N_1>N_2$, it means the data stored of other nodes in P2P network are sliding forward. So the node must slide forward its own data blocks.

3.4 Optimization strategy

In a stable P2P VoD system, after nodes join the P2P network, it can not change the data block number of its own data storage. Otherwise, when node's data block number decreases, it will cause the whole P2P networks' data loss. So each node in the main channel of P2P network should determine its number of data blocks according to the node status and channel's data storage state, and optimize the number of data blocks in the storage of the node to optimize whole channel's data storage capability.

The data storage status of a channel can be described as a set $\Omega(C_1, C_2, C_3, ...C_L)$. L means total data blocks of the program. C_i ($i=1, 2, 3......L$) means the number of nodes which store data block i.

When a node joins its main channel, it requests channel's data storage status Ω, and calculates the data blocks number Np that should be stored, according to the data storage status Ω, node's maximum data storage capability N and program's playing time P. The algorithm is as follow:

```
Input: Data storage status Ω, maximum data storage ca-
pability N, playing time P

Output: Data blocks number Np

for i = 0 to N do

  CurrentPos = N+P;

  SelectPos=i+P;

  if CCurrentPos < CSelectPos

  then Np = i;

  end if;

end for i;
```

After a node joins its main channel, if it finds still has idle data blocks, the node distributes the idle data blocks to unpopular channels, according to the data requests of data source server. Distribution conforms to the following principles: a) priority to store data blocks that requesting more data at data source server to reduce system load; b) to reduce the possibility of the same data storage duplication between nodes.

The requesting status of one data block can be described as attribute set $Q=(Cid, Pos, Req)$, Cid is the channel identifier, Pos is the location of data block, Req is the current data request number at data source server.

The distribution process of node P is as follow:

Step1: Node P acquires systems current requesting data blocks set $\Psi(Q^1, Q^2, Q^3, \ldots Q^M)$ at data source server from tracker server;

Step2: Node P sorts set Ψ according to the requesting number Req, and get a new set Ψ;

Step3: In order to avoid conflict between nodes choice, node P sets a selection probability α to choose data block. Sequence checks data blocks in set Ψ, and uses selection probability α to choose whether select or not. When a data block is selected, go to next step;

Step4: Choose channel according to the information of selected data block. Set the selected data block as node P's initialize position of data storage, archive channel's data storage status S from tracker server;

Step5: Calculate data block number Np using the same method as above;

Step6: Node P joins the selected channel, and sets it at node P's service channel.

4 Performance Measurement and Analysis

4.1 Simulation Environment

Simulation programs use GT-ITM [13] topology generator to create a network based on transit-stub model. The network consists of 5 transit domains, each with 20 transit nodes and one transit node connects to 10 stub domains, each with 10 stub nodes. Each stub node offers 35MB physical data storage capability. Set program video's encoding rate to 480kbps. Stub node is able to store 10 minutes of program data. Set system total channel count as 100, with each channel duration 90 minutes. Set granularity size as one minute. We divide program data into 90 data blocks. According to Zipf distribution, set the Zipf constant of the network scale distribution of channels as 0.25. The simulation program test duration is 300 minutes, the start time of nodes in the same channel in accordance with the Poisson distribution. By comparing the simulation based on single channel overlay data storage and multi-channel overlay data storage, we analyze the network scale difference and directly data source requests of the two data storage models, and analyze new multi-channel overlay data storage mechanism performance.

4.2 Network Scale Difference

As showed in Figure 5, in single channel overlay, more than 80% of the total channels' nodes number is below 100. We classify channels of this type as unpopular channels, and classify the opposite 20% channels as popular channels. By building multi-channel overlay network, the network scale of most unpopular channels is upgraded. The node number of smallest channel is 74 nodes. 80% channels' node number of entire system are more than 100, 70% channels' node number of entire system are between 100 and 200. We can see that by building a multi-channel overlay network, unpopular channels' network scale are greatly upgraded, the entire system's nodes distribution is more balanced than single channel overlay.

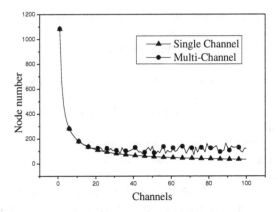

Fig. 5. Node number per channel

4.3 System Performance

By observing the requests number of data source server during the test period, we analyze the performance difference of single channel overlays and multi-channel network. Figure 6 gives each channel's data source server request number during test period. In single channel network, the direct data source server request number of unpopular are more than 600 in general, the average number of data source server request is 890, and the maximum is 1236. The average number of popular channels' data source server request is 442.4. In multi-channel overlay network, the average direct data source server request number of unpopular is 476.1, a decrease of 46.5%, the maximum is 1236, a decrease of 37.5%. The average number of popular channels' data source server request is 403.8, a decrease of 8.7%. We can see that providing some popular channels' idle data storage ability to store unpopular channels' program data can substantially reduce direct requests to data source server. Meanwhile, the reasonably decrease of popular channels' data storage capability does not cause the increase of direct data source server request, but cause the decrease of direct data source server request by decreasing duplicate data request to source server.

Figure 7 gives source server request per minute during test period. We can observe that in the initial period, compared with single channel overlay networks. The source server request pressure is increasing because the number of nodes joining unpopular channels in multi-channel overlay network is larger than that of single channel overlay. After the multi-channel overlay network is built stably, the unpopular channels in multi-channel overlay have more nodes than that of single channel overlay. The data storage capability is improved, and direct data source server request is substantially reduced. From 0 minute to 50 minute, data request per minute to data source server in single-channel P2P network is 206.5, and in multi-channel overlay network is 212.8, request number in multi-channel overlay increases 3.1% than that in single channel overlay. From 51 minute to 300 minute, data request per minute to data source server in single-channel P2P network is 278.3, and in multi-channel overlay network is 174.3, request number in multi-channel overlay decreases 37.3% than that in single channel overlay. In the whole test period, data request per minute to data source server in single-channel P2P network is 266.3, and in multi-channel overlay network is 180.9, request number in multi-channel overlay decreases 32.1% than that in single channel overlay. Although in the early stage of building a multi-channel overlay network will increase data source server requests to a certain extent, but if the entire system's P2P overlay is built stably, multi-channel overlay network can substantially reduce data request to data source server, and impressive upgrade the entire system performance.

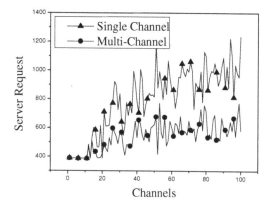

Fig. 6. Server request per channel

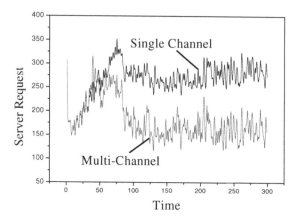

Fig. 7. Server request per minute

5 Related Work

In order to provide a large-scale on-demand streaming service over Internet, several techniques have been proposed to increase the scalability of on-demand streaming by adopting peer-to-peer methods. However, most of them try to use a tree-based overlay to build their logical topology, such as P2Cast [1], P2VoD [2], DirectStream [3],

MetaStream [4]. Compared with the traditional methods, i.e. CDN, proxy, and patching, they achieve better scalability. But for these systems, the greatest challenge is to accommodate the dynamic change and to mask the impact of node joining or leaving frequently. Their drawbacks include the following respects. On the one hand, tree maintenance is always very complicated in order to avoid the impact because of the silent departure of several key parent nodes. On the other hand, each peer depends on only one data supplier. This will lead to inefficient resource utilization and increase the load of the central source server. There are other kinds of streaming systems based on unstructured overlay, such as SplitStream [6], CoolStreaming [7], GNUStream [10], PROMISE [8]. However, all of them focus on the streaming overlay constructions for single channel, not for multiple channels.

6 Conclusions

In order to solve the data storage unbalance problem among channels in P2P VoD system, this paper presents a data storage mechanism based on multi-channel overlay. In the proposed overlay, nodes of popular channels will join unpopular channels' P2P overlays to construct a multi-channel overlay, and use data storage optimization strategy to improve node's data store ability. This mechanism can effective balance node distribution among different channels, and improve the storage capability of the entire system. The experiment results prove the idea.

References

[1] Guo, Y., Suh, K., Kurose, J.: P2Cast: Peer-to-peer Patching Scheme for VoD Service. In: Proceedings of the 12th World Wide Web Conference (WWW 2003), Budapest, Hungary (May 2003)

[2] Do, T., Hua, K.A., Tantaoui, M.: P2VoD: providing fault tolerant video-on-demand streaming in peer-to-peer environment. In: Proceedings of IEEE ICC 2004, Paris, France (June 2004)

[3] Guo, Y., Suh, K., Kurose, J., Towsley, D.: A Peer-to-Peer On-demand Streaming Service and Its Performance Evaluation. In: Proceedings of 2003 IEEE International Conference on Multimedia & Expo (ICME 2003), Baltimore, MD (July 2003)

[4] Zhang, R.M., Butt, A.R., Hu, Y.C.: Topology-Aware Peer-to-Peer On-demand streaming. In: Proceedings of 2005 IFIP Networking Conference (Networking 2005), Waterloo, Canada (May 2005)

[5] Chu, Y.-H., Rao, S.G., Zhang, H.: A case for end system multicast. In: Proceedings of SIGMETRICS 2000, Santa Clara, CA, USA (June 2000)

[6] Castro, M., Druschel, P., Kermarrec, A.M., Nandi, A., Rowstron, A., Singh, A.: SplitStream: High-Bandwidth Content Distribution in Cooperative Environments. In: Proceedings of ACM SOSP 2003 (October 2003)

[7] Zhang, X., Liu, J., Li, B., Yum, T.-S.P.: Data-Driven Overlay Streaming: Design, Implementation, and Experience. In: Proceedings of IEEE INFOCOM 2005, Miami, USA (2005)

[8] Heffeeda, M., Habib, A., Botev, B., Xu, D., Bhargava, B.: PROMISE: peer-to-peer media streaming using CollectCast. In: Proceedings of ACM Multimedia (MM 2003), Berkeley, CA (November 2003)

[9] Cheng, B., Stein, L., Jin, H., Zhang, Z.: GridCast: Providing Peer-to-Peer On-Demand Streaming Service Based On Unstructured Overlay. In: Proceedings of Eurosys. 2008 (2008)

[10] Jiang, X., Dong, Y., Xu, D., Bhargava, B.: GnuStream: a P2P Media Streaming System Prototype. In: Proceedings of International Conferences on Multimedia & Expo (ICME 2003), Maryland, USA (2003)

[11] Sun, Q., Sturman, D.: A Gossip-Based Reliable Multicast for Large-Scale High-Throughput Applications. In: Proceedings of the Int'l Conf Dependable Systems and Networks (DSN 2000) (2000)

[12] Hou, M., Lu, X., Zhou, X., Zhang, C.: Study on Replication in Unstructured P2P System. MINI-MICRO SYSTEMS 26(11), 1903–1906 (2005)

[13] Zegura, E., Calvert, K., Bhattachajee, S.: How to model an Internetwork. In: Proceedings of INFOCOM 1996 (1996)

[14] Guo, L., Chen, S., Xiao, Z., Tan, E., Ding, X., Zhang, X.: Measurements, Analysis, and Modeling of Bit Torrent-like Systems. In: Proceedings of ACM IMC 2005, Berkeley, CA, USA (October 2005)

HTL: A Locality Bounded Flat Hash Location Service*

Ruonan Rao, Shuying Liang, and Jinyuan You

Department of Computer Science and Engineering
Shanghai Jiaotong University Shanghai, China 200030
rao-ruonan@cs.sjtu.edu.cn,liangsy@sjtu.edu.cn,you-jy@cs.sjtu.edu.cn

Abstract. Many location services have been proposed, but some challenges remain. In this paper, we present a new location service, named HTL (Hash Table Localized) to solve the locality problem, that in a location service, the location information can be stored potentially far away from both the source and destination nodes, even when the source and destination nodes are close. As a result, it causes high overhead in update and query. HTL uses a double index hash function to map a node to a location in the network area called the virtual coordination of that node. Then, a novel method is employed to divide the physical space into lattices. The publish and query algorithms are designed based on this division. In HTL, when the distance between the source and destination nodes is l, the cost of query is $O(l^2)$. We define this property as n^2-locality bounded. HTL is the location service that achieves this property with the least storage and network overhead. Both analysis and experiment results are presented in this paper concerned with the cost, the locality bounded property and the scalability.

1 Introduction

A mobile ad hoc network (MANET) is a network formed by a collection of mobile wireless nodes without any perviously deployed infrastructure. Due to the lack of infrastructure support, each node in MANET should act not only as an end system but also as a router at the same time.

A fundamental challenge in MANETs research is the design and implementation of scalable and robust routing protocols. The current routing protocols can be roughly divided into two categories: Topology-based routing and Geographic-based routing. The former is based on the knowledge of the whole network's topological information while the latter on the knowledge of each node's position. Intuitionally, compared with topological-based routing, geographic-based routing incurs less communication overhead. However, geographic-based routing also faces two challenges:

1. How to deliver a packet to destination when the position of destination node is known? This is called as the forwarding strategy.

---

* This paper is supported by the Defense Pre-Research Foundation of China under Grant No.513150302

J. Cao et al. (Eds.): NPC 2008, LNCS 5245, pp. 138–149, 2008.

2. How to let the source node know the position of the destination node? This is called as the location service.

The first one is almost solved by several proposed algorithms, especially GPSR[1] [2]. Whereas, some problems remain in the second one, though many location service algorithms have been proposed. One of them is called locality problem, i.e. the corresponding location information may be stored far away from both the source and destination nodes, but the source and destination may be close. As a result, update and query operations cause high overhead. This problem is more serious in a location service without any hierarchy architecture, which we called, the flat location service. Compared with hierarchy approach, a flat location service avoids the complexity of maintaining the hierarchy structure, but introducing the locality problem. In this paper, we try to solve this problem.

HTL is a flat hash based location service, which means that HTL uses hash functions to determine where to store the nodes location information, and no hierarchy in HTL. A hash based approach uses hash functions to map a node to a location or a region in the network area, then stores the corresponding location information near or in such location or region. HTL is designed to cooperate with GPSR to support geographic based routing. With a novel method to divide the geographic area into lattices, HTL guarantees that when the distance between the source and destination nodes is l, the query takes at most $O(l^2)$ to finish. HTL is the best one we have known that takes the least cost to achieve such a property.Some simulation experiments are used to verify HTL.

This paper has 7 sections. It starts with an overview of related works in section 2. In section 3, we state the locality problem of location services in MANET. In section 4 and section 5, details of HTL and some mathematical analysis are given. The experiments results are presented in section 6. Section 7 is a short conclusion with discussion on future works.

2   Related Works

Many location service algorithms have been proposed. Surveys on some of the algorithms can be found in [3], [4] [5] [6] and [7], but not all of them are hash based. The following are some typical algorithms proposed related to location service.

GLS [7] is a location service with a hierarchy of square regions. A node belongs to only one square in each order in the hierarchy. It stores its location information on 3 nodes in each square containing it. If two nodes are close enough, they will be in the same square area with a low order and need not travel a long distance to exchange the location information. However, the cost of maintaining such a hierarchy structure is expensive. The work in [8] shows some similar results. In addition, GLS has not been proved that it has an upper bound of query cost. LLS[9] is the first location service that takes locality into account. It uses a recursive approach that promulgates the location information to the nodes 2^i away in ith step, with a similar query method. It has been proved that it is d^2 locality bounded. However, the cost of publishing location information and storing the location information is relatively high. GHLS protocol proposed in [10] is a simple flat hash based location service. In this paper, the authors have mentioned the locality issues, and tried to solve those problems by a method called α-scaled region– a hash function that maps a node to a location only in a region called **scaled location server region** which is similar to the whole area and located in the center. Intuitively, this approach can reduce the cost of query when the source and destination nodes are all near the center, but its effect is limited in other situations. In addition, GHLS does not possess the locality bounded property, either. GHT[11] is designed for data-centric storage in sensornets. One can consider location information as a specifical data in sensornets, and augments of GHT can also be used as a location service. Although GHLS and our work share some characteristics with GHT, GHT can not be effectively used as a location service in MANET. The design objectives in GHT are fundamentally different from location services. An analysis on GHT in MANET can be found in [12].

3   Locality Problem in Flat Hash Based Location Services

A location service is a service that provides the corresponding location information according to a node's unique identifer. Its main functionality is to support geographic based routing, when it also can be used to support location related applications.

In a typical flat hash based location service, a hash function is used to map each nodes unique identifier to a home region. However, the cost of underlying routing can be surprisingly high if the source and destination nodes are close, when the home region is far away. To formally evaluate this problem, following definition is given.

Definition 1 (Locality Bounded). *A location service is called **locality bounded**, if the distance between the source node S and the destination node D is l, and the cost of query the location of D by S is at most $f(l)$. We call such a location service is f-Locality Bounded.*

4   HTL: A Hash Table Localized

In this section, we present the details of HTL. HTL is built on the top of GPSR, and it cooperates with GPSR to provide geographic based routing. We first study some properties of GPSR, then some concepts of HTL are introduced, followed with a novel method by which HTL uses to divide the physical space being presented. Finally,the publish and query algorithms are illustrated.

4.1   Map to Physical Space

As stated before, a flat hash based location service will map a node's identifer to a region named home region using a hash function. HTL uses the same approach with a little modification. The hash function used in HTL is a double index hash function $H(N.id) = (h1(N.id), h2(N.id))$ that maps node N's identifier $N.id$ to a coordination $(h1(N.id), h2(N.id))$ inside the area of the network. We call the associated coordination $(h1(N.id), h2(N.id))$ of node N N's virtual coordination. The definition is given in definition 2.

Definition 2 (Virtual coordination). *A Node N with unique identifer $N.id$, its virtual coordination is $H(N.id) = (h1(N.id), h2(N.id))$, where $h1$, $h2$ is hash functions.*

The major difference between typical flat hash based location services and HTL is that HTL pushes the concept of home region to the extreme: the home region becomes a single point in this area.

4.2   Divide the Physical Space

With node N's identifier $N.id$, one can find the virtual coordination $H(N.id)$. We define a parameter d named lattice length. After finding the virtual coordination, HTL divides the physical space into lattices using the virtual coordination as the original point according to the following rules:

- Make circles C_i with radius $r_i = d * i, i = 0, 1, \ldots$[1] with the same center $H(N.id)$. We call these circles **lattice circles**.
- For a circle C_i, $(i = 1, 2, \ldots)$, let $j = \lceil \log_2 i \rceil$, then divide C_i into 2^{j+2} with equal angle, starting from the x axis. We denote the lines used to divide the circle as $l_m^{2^{j+2}}, m = 0, 1, \ldots, 2^j - 1$, and call them **lattice lines**. These lines intersect the circles $C_k, k = 2^j, 2^j + 1, \ldots, i$ with points P_m^k, which are named **lattice points**.
- For each 4 points, P_k^m, P_k^{m+1}[2], P_{k+1}^m, P_{k+1}^{m+1}, $(m = 0, 1, \ldots, 2^j - 1, k = 2^j, 2^j + 1, \ldots, i - 1)$, form a **lattice corner**, dedicated by LC_k^m.
- The area enclosed by lattice corner LC_k^m and the corresponding line and circle is called a **lattice**, denoted as L_k^m.

4.3   Location Servers Selection and Location Information Update

Unlike other typical flat hash based location service, HTL stores the location information not only in the home region, but also stores on the way to the home region. For a node N, assuming its current location is $N.loc$, and its virtual coordination is $H(N.id)$. Obviously, a short path that travels along the lattice lines exits between $N.loc$ and $H(N.id)$. The path can be found based on following steps:

1. First, determine the lattice $L(N.loc)$ where N is based on N's current location $N.loc$:

---

[1] When $i = 0$, the circle becames the point $H(N.id)$.
[2] Here, $m+1$ means $m+1 mod 2^{j+2}$. In this paper, we use m_n to denote such situations when it is not ambiguous.

(a) Calculate the distance $dist$ between $N.loc$ and $H(N.id)$. Let $k = \lfloor dist/d \rfloor$ and $j = \lceil \log_2 i \rceil$.

(b) Calculate the angle α from vector $\overrightarrow{(1,0)}$ to vector $\overrightarrow{(N.loc, H(N.id))}$ in anticlockwise direction. Let $m = \lfloor \frac{\alpha}{\frac{2\pi}{2^{j+2}}} \rfloor = \lfloor 2^{j+1} \frac{\alpha}{\pi} \rfloor$.

(c) Then node N is located lattice $L(k)^m$. Two corresponding lattice lines are $l_m^{2^{j+2}}$, $l_{m+1}^{2^{j+2}}$.

2. One of the lattice lines $l_m^{2^{j+2}}$, $l_{m+1}^{2^{j+2}}$ is closer to N than another [3]. The location information will be sent along this line.

3. When the path comes to the circle C_{2^j-1}, the lattice line chosen will terminate. However, it may not arrive the virtual coordination $H(N.id)$. Then a new lattice line should be chosen. If the current lattice line is $l_{m'}^{2^{j'}}$, the next lattice to travel is chosen based on the following rule:

  - If m' is an even number, the next lattice line is $l_{m'/2}^{2^{j'-1}}$

  - If m' is an odd number, the next lattice line is $l_{(m'-1)/2}^{2^{j'-1}}$

This rule can be not only applied when the first lattice line is terminated, but also suitable for the next lattice line and next's next lattice line.

The shortest path to the virtual coordination can be found. But where the location information will be stored? In each lattice line along the path found, there are several lattice points, called **server coordinations**. The location servers are the nodes nearest to these server coordinations. The location information of N will be stored on these nodes.

Then another problem arises—how to deliver the packet to the nodes that are nearest to the server coordinations? We use GPSR routing to solve this problem. Some properties of GPSR can help to decide when and who will consume the packet for location disseminating. Thus a location server can be easily found during the routing process. The next question to answer is when should a node publish its location information into HTL, and how?

When Node N moves from location x to location y, it performs the publish as following:

  - If $LN(x) = LN(y)$, new location information is published to the same servers.
  - Else, node N first issues a packet to infor the servers that store the old location information to erase the information. Then it publishes the new location information.

Another parameter d_u is defined to indicate the distance a node can move before it do a update. Generally speaking, when a node move from one lattice to another, it must perform an update. As a result, d_u should not be larger than $d/2$, where d is the lattice parameter defined above.

---

[3] If the distances from N to the two lines are equal, $l_m^{2^{j+2}}$ is chosen.

4.4 Perform Query

When node S wants to know where D is, it performs a query operation. The query operation performs in tow modes: extension mode and non-extension mode. In extension mode, the query will goes to the servers located on the adjacent lattice lines, when in non-extension mode, the query is limited to current lattice lines. The query process try to cover the area that may intersect with the path where D puts its location information as soon as possible. The details of the query process is described bellow.

1. In step 1, S calculates which lattice of D it is in using the method given in previous section. We denote this lattice as L_k^m. Node S first query the location servers whose location server coordination are P_k^m and P_k^{m+1} in **extension mode**(P_k^m left-extension and P_k^{m+1} right-extension).

2. In step i $(i = 1, 2, 3, \ldots, k-1)$, location servers $P_{k-i+1}^{m'}$ [4] will get the query. It process the query based on the following situations:

   – It knows where D is, then it answer this query, and informs other location server in the same iterative level to terminate this query.
   – It dose not know the answer.
     • The query is in non-extension mode.
       * $k - i + 1 == 2^j$, no future action is needed.
       * $k - i + 1! = 2^j$, forward the query to $P_{k-i}^{m'}$ in non-extension mode.
     • The query is in extension mode. We only discuss the left-extension case. The right-extension case is similar.
       * $k - i + 1 == 2^j$ and m' is an odd number. Deliver a query to $P_{k-i}^{\frac{m'-1}{2}}$ in left-extension mode.
       * $k - i + 1 == 2^j$ and m' is an even number. Deliver a query to $P_{k-i}^{\frac{m'}{2}-1}$ in left-extension mode and a query to $P_{k-i}^{\frac{m'}{2}}$ in non-extension mode.
       * $k - i + 1! = 2^j$, Deliver a query to $P_{k-i}^{m'-1}$ in left-extension mode and a query to $P_{k-i}^{m'}$ in non-extension mode.

3. In step k, the query arrives $H(D.id)$. If the location server knows where D is, then it reply the answer, otherwise it will tell S the location of D is not known.

Figure 1 gives an example of query in HTL. Node S wants to know where D is. It calculates the lattice of D where it is in. In the example, S is in L_6^{19}, it deliver queries to P_6^{19} in left-extension mode and to P_6^{20} in right-extension mode. We trace the thick line in figure 1 to explain the query process in detail. In the first iterative step, P_6^{19}, 6 is not the power of 2. P_5^{18} (left extension mode), P_5^{19} (non-extension mode) will get the query. Then, P_4^{17} (left extension mode), P_4^{18} (non-extension mode), P_4^{19} (non-extension mode). Here, $4 = 2^2$, and 17 is an odd number. Then, P_4^{17} deliver query to P_3^8. The process will go on until a server replies or the query arrives $H(D.id)$.

---

[4] We use the location server coordination to denote location server, when there is no ambiguousness.

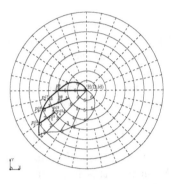

Fig. 1. An Example of Query in HTL

4.5 Location Servers Maintain

Due to the node mobility, location information stored on one location server may need to be migrated to other nodes that become closer to the server coordination. As in GHLS[10], every node acts as a location server to check whether there is a neighbor node closer to the server coordination when it receives a beacon packet from another node. GPSR uses beacon to construct the location information about its neighbor nodes. HTL uses this facility of GPSR to maintain the location servers.

5   Analysis on HTL

Due to space limitation, we omit some properties of HTL here, but remain the most important one, the Locality Bounded Property. A further analysis for this property is also shown.

Query Cost and Locality Bounded Property: As stated before, the most remarkable feature of HTL is that HTL is l^2 locality bounded.

Theorem 1. *HTL is l^2 locality bounded.*

The proof is not presented here due to the limitation of space.

A brief Comparison: Table 1 gives a brief comparison between HTL and other location service related in section 2. For detailed analysis, please refer [12],[10] and [13]. From the table, we can conclude that only LLS and HTL bear the property of locality bounded. Yet compared with LLS, HTL is with less network and storage overhead.

6   Experiments

In this section, we present the experiments results on HTL. The experiments are concerned with the performance of HTL in static network, and in mobile network and with the issue of scalability.

Table 1. A brief Comparison

	GLS	GHLS	GHT	LLS	HTL
Cost of publish	$O(h^2)$	$O(\sqrt{N})$	$O(\sqrt{N})$	$O(u^2)$	$O(\sqrt{N})$
Cost of Storage	$O(h)$	$O(1)$	$O(Dens)$	$O(u^2)$	$O(\sqrt{N})$
Server Maintaining	$O(2^h)$	$O(1)$	$O(N)$	N/A	$O(1)$
Locality Bounded	N/A	N/A	N/A	$O(l^2)$	$O(l^2)$

In GLS the height of grid is set to h, and in LLS the unit length is u. N is the number of nodes in the network.

6.1   Experiment Method and Metrics

We have implemented HTL in ns2[14]. In all experiments, we use a 802.11 radio model with a nominal bit-rate of 11Mbps and a transmission range of 250m. The discrete metrics are listed in table 2. The experiments on static and mobile networks run 300s, and the experiments on scalability run 150s.

Table 2. Metrics used for evaluating HTL

Metric	Description
P_n	The number of packets used to publish location information. We call such packets PUT packets.
P_r	The average hops a PUT packet travels.
R_n	The number of packets used to erase location information. We call such packets REMOVE packets.
R_r	The average hops a REMOVE packet travels.
U_n	The number of packets used to migrate location information to another node. We call such packets UPDATE packets.
U_r	The average hops a UPDATE packet travels.
LN_{max}	The maximum number of location information entries a node stored.
LN_{min}	The maximum number of location information entries a node stored.
LN_{ave}	The average number of location information entries a node stored.
RQS	The ratio of query success.

All experiments are performed as following:

- In the first a few second (30s), all nodes publish their location information into HTL.
- Then, each node chooses a destination randomly and independently, and queries its location.

Concerned with static networks, the topology scenarios are generated using the following model:

1. Uniform and Random Network. If there are N nodes in the network, then we divide the whole area of the network into N parts with equal area. Each node is placed randomly in each divided part.

In each topology, we vary the node densities and the value of lattice parameter d. The node densities are varied among $5625m^2/node$, $10000m^2/node$, and $22500m^2/node$. d are varied among $100m$, $150m$, $200m$, $250m$, and $300m$.

Concerned with mobile networks, we use random way point mobility model (RWP) for evaluating HTL in an entity mobility model and reference point group mobility model (RPGM) for evaluating HTL in a group mobility model. We use IMPORTANT[15] to generate the mobile scenarios. Concerned with the scalability issue, we study the performance of HTL in both static and mobile network by varying the number of nodes.In static network, the uniform and random topology is chosen, when in mobile network, the RPW mobility model is chosen.

6.2 Results on Static Network

Table 3 gives the results of experiments on static networks.Based on the results shown above, we can verify the analytical results in the previous section. For example, in the case where the density of nodes is $10000m^2$ and d is $250m$, the distance between a node N and its virtual coordination $H(N.id)$ is among $[0, 1000\sqrt{2}]$. If the hash function distributes uniformity, then the average distance is about $700m$. The average store cost should be $700/250 \approx 3$, and the experiment result is 3.3. A little higher than theory result, but in a reasonable range. Concerned with the locality bounded property, in the random destination chosen model we used, the distance between the source and destination nodes is also approximately $700m$. Without locality, the cost for query should approximately equal to the cost of publish. In the result, the Q_r is smaller than P_r, which means that with locality, distances of a query packet travels decreases.

Table 3. Experiment results in static network

Density($m^2/node$)	$d(m)$	P_n	P_r	R_n	R_r	U_n	U_r	Q_r	LN_{min}	LN_{max}	LN_{ave}	QSR
5625	100	100	4.3	0	-	0	-	3.4	0	13	2.4	100%
5625	150	100	3.7	0	-	0	-	3.1	0	14	2.5	100%
5625	200	100	3.1	0	-	0	-	3.2	0	17	2.4	100%
10000	150	100	5.2	0	-	0	-	3.7	0	11	3.0	100%
10000	200	100	4.9	0	-	0	-	3.3	0	11	2.9	100%
10000	250	100	4.7	0	-	0	-	3.0	0	13	3.3	100%
22500	200	100	6.3	0	-	0	-	4.2	0	12	3.7	100%
22500	250	100	6.2	0	-	0	-	4.1	0	12	3.5	100%
22500	300	100	6.7	0	-	0	-	3.9	0	13	3.6	100%

6.3 Results on Mobile Network

Results on RWP: Figures 2(a), 2(c), 2(b), 2(d), 2(e), 2(f), 2(g), and 2(h) give the results of experiments on RWP. The conclusions can be drawn are:

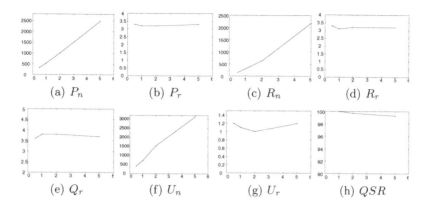

Fig. 2. Results of RWP

- The QSR decreases when the speed increases. This is also a problem in all current available location services as shown in [10] and [8]. In mobility situations, this occurs when the destination node is reachable, but the links to location servers are broken. Unlike other similar approaches, the location servers in HTL are not concentrated near the home region (or virtual coordination). Thus, the chances that all location servers are not reachable decreases, and the QSR is higher than other approaches.
- The results also show the locality property of HTL, Q_r is almost constant when the speed varies.

Results on RPGM: The experiment results on RPGM are given in table 4. The performance in RPGM is better than RWP in the case with comparable parameters, expecting that the P_r is higher in RPGM than that in RWP. The better performance is due to consistent of nodes movement in RPGM. The higher P_r is because in a group mobility mode, all nodes may be concentrated in a small area, where some virtual coordination are outside. Then a long routing path may be needed to find the corresponding location server.

Table 4. Experiment results on RPGM

P_n	P_r	R_n	R_r	U_n	U_r	Q_r	S_q	Loc_{max}	Loc_{ave}
1789	7.4	1543	6	2145	1.3	4.1	100%	29	4.7

6.4   Results on Scalability

The results of the experiments on the issue of scalability of HTL are given in figure 3 and figure 4. Note that not all metrics defined in section 6.1 are used to evaluate the scalability of HTL. It is not only because the space limitation, but also because other metrics are not related to the issue of scalability.

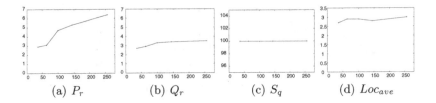

(a) P_r (b) Q_r (c) S_q (d) Loc_{ave}

Fig. 3. Scalability of HTL in static networks

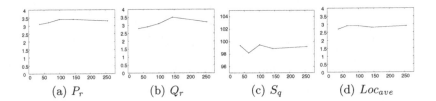

(a) P_r (b) Q_r (c) S_q (d) Loc_{ave}

Fig. 4. Scalability of HTL in mobile networks

7   Conclusion

In this paper we present a new location service named HTL, which possesses
the property of locality bounded. The most remarkable of HTL is that HTL is
the best one of so many location services proposed incorporating locality with
minimal cost introduced. HTL employs a novel method to divide the physical
space into lattices. The publish and query algorithms are based on this division.
HTL is l^2 locality bounded, which means the cost of query is at most l^2, when
the distance between the source and destination node is l. We give the analytical
and simulation results in details in this paper.

Although HTL gives promising results both on theoretical analysis and sim-
ulative experiments. Some issues are worth future studying.

The first one is on the low bound of the locality bounded property. In both
LLS and HTL, the result is $O(l^2)$. We doubt it is the best answer. If it is not, then
what is the lower bound of locality a location service can achieve? Intuitively,
$O(l^2)$ may be the final answer. Think about a node who knows the destination is
at most l away, but do not know the exact location. It should reach all possible
locations, which is $O(l^2)$.

The second one is about HTL itself. Compared with other similar approaches,
HTL needs more computing capability. In HTL, types of computing include
computing on trigonometric function, manipulation on vectors and so on, all of
which do not appear in other location services. Although the computing power
of mobile devices are continuing increasing, reduce the complexity of HTL is still
worth future investigating.

References

1. Karp, B.N.: Geographic routing for wireless networks. Ph.D. dissertation, Harvard Universtiy (2000)
2. Karp, B.N., Kung, H.T.: Greedy perimeter stateless routing for wireless networks. In: Proc. of the 6th Annual ACM/IEEE International Conference on Mobile Computing and Networking (MobiCom 2000), August 2000, pp. 253–254 (2000)
3. Bae, I.-H., Liu, H.: FHLS: Fuzzy Hierarchical Location Service for Mobile Ad Hoc Networks. In: Fuzzy Systems Conference FUZZ-IEEE (July 2007)
4. Chang, Y.-J., Shih, T.L.: Intersection location service and performance comparison of three location service algorithms for vehicular ad hoc networks in city environments. In: 3rd International Symposium on Wireless Pervasive Computing (May 2008)
5. Camp, T., Boleng, J., Wilcox, L.: Location Information Services in Mobile Ad Hoc Networks. In: Proc. of the IEEE International Conference on Communications (ICC) (2002)
6. Mauve, H.H.M., Widmer, J.: A survey on position-based routing in mobile ad hoc networks. IEEE Network (2001)
7. Li, J., Jannotti, J., Couto, D.S.J.D., Karger, D.R., Morris, R.: A scalable location service for geographic ad hoc routing. In: ACM MobiCom (August 2000)
8. Kasemann, M., Hartenstein, H., Fuber, H., Mauve, M.: Analysis of a location service for position-based routing in mobile ad hoc networks. In: Proc. of the 1st German Workshop on Mobile Ad-hoc Networking (WMAN 2002) (March 2002)
9. Abraham, I., Dolev, D., Malkhi, D.: Lls: a locality aware location service for mobile ad hoc networks. In: Proc. of the 2004 Joint Workshop on Foundations of Mobile Computing(DIALM-POM) (2004)
10. Saumitra, H.P., Das, M., Hu, Y.C.: Performance comparison of scalable location services for geographic ad hoc routing. In: 24th Annual Joint Conference of the IEEE Computer and Communications Societies (INFOCOM 2005) (2005)
11. Ratnasamy, S., Karp, B., Estrin, D., Govindan, R., Shenker, S.: Ght: A geographic hash-table for data-centric storage in sensornets. In: The First ACM International Workshop on Wireless Sensor Networks and Applications (WSNA 2002), Atlanta, GA (September 2002)
12. Liu, F., Rao, R.: Analysis of ght in mobile ad hoc network. In: The Proceeding of Third International Symposium on Parallel and Distributed Processing and Applications (ISPA 2005), Nanjing, China (November 2005)
13. Liu, F.: Research on location services in mobile ad hoc network, Masters thesis, Shanghai Jiaotong University (2005)
14. The network simulator - ns-2, http://www.isi.edu/nsnam/ns/
15. Helmy, F.B.N.S.A.: The important framework for analyzing the impact of mobility on performance of routing for ad hoc networks. Ad Hoc Networks Journal 1(4), 383–403 (2003)

Accelerating the Propagation of Active Worms by Employing Multiple Target Discovery Techniques

Xiang Fan and Yang Xiang

School of Management and Information Systems
Centre for Intelligent and Networked Systems
Central Queensland University
North Rockhampton, Queensland 4701 Australia
{x.fan2,y.xiang}@cqu.edu.au

Abstract. Recently, active worms have done significant damage due to their rapid propagation over the Internet. We studied propagation mechanisms of active worms employing single target discovery technique and various combinations of two or three different target discovery techniques from attackers' perspective. We performed a series of simulation experiments to investigate their propagation characteristics under various scenarios. We found uniform scanning to be an indispensable elementary target discovery technique of active worms. Our major contributions in this paper are first, we proposed the discrete time deterministic Compensation Factor Adjusted Propagation (CFAP) model of active worms; and second, we suggested the combination of target discovery techniques that can best accelerate propagation of active worms discovered from results of the comprehensive simulations. The significance of this paper lies in it being very beneficial to understanding of propagation mechanisms of active worms, and thus building effective and efficient defense systems against their propagation.

Keywords: Network Security; Invasive Software; Worms; Propagation; Modeling.

1 Introduction

Kienzle and Elder defined a worm as 'malicious code (standalone or file-infecting) that propagates over a network, with or without human assistance' [1]. Weaver et al. defined a computer worm as 'a program that self-propagates across a network exploiting security or policy flaws in widely-used services' [2]. In this paper, we define active worms as those which actively self-propagate across a network exploiting security or policy flaws in widely-used services by employing scanning, pre-generated target list, or internally generated target lists (target lists for short) as their target discovery technique. The Code Red worms of 2001 (Code-RedI v1, Code-RedI v2, and CodeRedII) employed various types of scanning as their target discovery techniques [3]. The Slammer (sometimes called Sapphire) worm of 2003 employed uniform scanning as its target discovery technique [4]. The most recent Witty worm of 2004 employed scanning as its target discovery technique as well [5]. If IP addresses of

J. Cao et al. (Eds.): NPC 2008, LNCS 5245, pp. 150–161, 2008.

vulnerable hosts could be obtained in advance, there exists an opportunity to employ pre-generated target list as a worm's target discovery technique. Pre-generated target list is also termed as 'hit-list' [6]. Internally generated target lists are lists found on infected hosts which contain information about other potential vulnerable hosts. The Morris Internet Worm of 1988 employed internally generated target lists as its target discovery technique [7].

Recently, active worms have done significant damage due to their rapid propagation over the Internet. For example, the Code Red worm caused about $2.6 billion financial loss in July and August 2001 alone [8]. The situation of worm defenders will be worsened if worms stop propagation by using some self-stopping mechanisms [9] after they have successfully infected nearly all vulnerable hosts. For example [3], the Code Red worms propagated for a time, then stopped propagating, and then focused all of its intention on executing a Distributed Denial of Service (DDoS) [10] attack on a specific host.

According to Xiang et al. [11], an active worm is not limited to employing single target discovery technique only, and thus future active worms could employ multiple target discovery techniques simultaneously in an attempt to accelerate their propagation. To find an effective countermeasure against this sort of future worms, we studied propagation mechanisms of active worms employing single target discovery technique only, and a combination of two or three different target discovery techniques from attackers' perspective. We also performed a series of simulation experiments to investigate their propagation characteristics under various scenarios.

2 Related Work

Life cycle of a worm from when it is released to when it finishes infecting vulnerable hosts, consists of the initialization phase, the network propagation phase, and the payload activation phase [12]. In the network propagation phase, a worm attempts to infect its target hosts by performing a sequence of actions including target acquisition, network reconnaissance, attack, and infection. Since target acquisition and network reconnaissance together essentially dictate target discovery technique(s) employed by a worm, we derived the significance of target discovery techniques in shaping a worm's propagation characteristics from its life cycle in [11].

Scanning could be implemented differently, which leads to several different types such as uniform scanning, preferential scanning, sequential scanning [13], routable scanning [14], selective scanning [14], or importance scanning [15]. In the case where the distribution of vulnerable hosts is not available in advance, self-learning that information will be incorporated into the implementation of importance scanning [16]. An incomplete hit-list could be used to increase the number of initially infected hosts and thus accelerate a worm's propagation. A complete hit-list creates a 'flash' worm [17], capable of infecting all vulnerable hosts extremely rapidly. An active worm attacking a flaw in peer-to-peer applications could easily get lists of peers from their victims and use those peers as the basis of their attack, which gives an example of employing the internally generated target lists as one's target discovery technique.

We summarized the factor(s) improved by active worms employing the various target discovery techniques to accelerate their propagation in [11].

Mathematical models developed to model propagation of infectious diseases have been adapted to model propagation of computer worms [13]. In epidemiology area, both deterministic and stochastic models exist for modeling the spreading of infectious diseases [14-17]. In network security area, both deterministic and stochastic models of active worms based on their respective counterpart in epidemiology area have emerged. Deterministic models of active worms could be further divided into two categories: continuous time and discrete time.

For a finite population of size N, the classical simple epidemic model [13-16] could be defined by the following single differential equation:

$$\frac{dI(t)}{dt} = \beta I(t)[N - I(t)], \tag{1}$$

where $I(t)$ denotes the number of infectious hosts at time t; and β stands for the pairwise rate of infection in epidemiology studies [17]. Let $i(t)$ stand for the fraction of the population that are infectious at time t, the following differential equation could be derived:

$$\frac{di(t)}{dt} = N\beta i(t)[1 - i(t)]. \tag{2}$$

Differential equation (2) has the following general analytical solution:

$$i(t) = \frac{e^{N\beta(t-T)}}{1 + e^{N\beta(t-T)}}, \tag{3}$$

which is the logistic equation. A particular analytical solution of differential equation (2) given its initial condition $i(0) = I(0) / N$ is as follows:

$$i(t) = \frac{I(0)}{I(0) + [N - I(0)]e^{-N\beta t}}. \tag{4}$$

The classical general epidemic model (Kermack-McKendrick model) [13-16] improves the classical simple epidemic model by considering removal of infectious hosts due to patching. The two-factor worm model [18] extends the classical general epidemic model by accounting for removal of susceptible hosts due to patching and considering the pairwise rate of infection as a variable rather than a constant. The Analytical Active Worm Propagation (AAWP) model [19] takes into account the time an infectious host takes to infect other hosts. The time to infect a host is an important factor for the spread of active worms [20]. Since propagation of active worms is a discrete event process, the discrete time deterministic model of active worms (the AAWP model) given above is more accurate than its continuous time counterparts in the deterministic regime.

Rohloff and Basar presented a stochastic density-dependent Markov jump process propagation model [21] for active worms employing the uniform scanning approach drawn from the field of epidemiology [14, 17]. Sellke et al. presented a stochastic Galton-Watson Markov branching process model [22] to characterize the propagation of active worms employing the uniform scanning approach.

3 Mathematical Analysis and the Proposed Model

For the classical simple epidemic model (1) given in the last section, Fig. 1 shows the dynamics of I_t -- denoted by $I(t)$ in equation (1) -- as time goes on for a certain set of parameters [23].

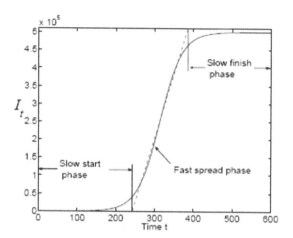

Fig. 1. Classical simple epidemic model

According to Fig. 1, we can roughly partition a worm's propagation into three phases: the slow start phase, the fast spread phase, and the slow finish phase. During the slow start phase, since $I_t \ll N$, model (1) becomes:

$$\frac{dI_t}{dt} \approx N\beta I_t ,$$ (5)

which means that the number of infectious hosts increases exponentially approximately. After a certain number of susceptible hosts are infected and then participate in infecting others, the worm enters its fast spread phase where susceptible hosts are infected at a fast, nearly constant rate. When most susceptible hosts have been infected, the worm enters its slow finish phase because the few susceptible hosts left-over are difficult for the worm to find.

According to equation (4),

$$i_t = \frac{I_0}{I_0 + (N - I_0)e^{-N\beta t}} .$$ (6)

Letting $a = I_0$, $b = N - I_0$, and $c = -N\beta$ will transform equation (3.2) to:

$$i_t = \frac{a}{a + be^{ct}} .$$ (7)

The first derivative of is worked out and shown as follows:

$$\frac{di_t}{dt} = \frac{-abce^{ct}}{(a+be^{ct})^2}.$$ (8)

We can then work out the second derivative of and let it equal to 0:

$$\frac{d^2 i_t}{dt^2} = 0.$$ (9)

This will lead to $i_t = 50\%$. In other words, the maximum rate at which susceptible hosts are infected is achieved at the moment when 50% of susceptible hosts are infected.

We define fast spread as that with a rate not less than half of the maximum rate, which will lead to $i_t \approx 15\%$ and 85%. In other words, according to our definition of fast spread, when less than 15% of susceptible hosts are infected, the worm is in its slow start phase; when more than 85% of susceptible hosts are infected, the worm is in its slow finish phase; in between, the worm is in its fast spread phase.

It is obvious that in order to accelerate a worm's propagation, we must try to let the worm infect the first 15% susceptible hosts and enter its fast spread phase as soon as possible. On the other hand, the last 15% susceptible hosts leftover are not important for attackers if infection of 85% susceptible hosts will serve their purposes, which is usually the case.

Next, we present our proposed discrete time deterministic Compensation Factor Adjusted Propagation (CFAP) model of active worms employing uniform scanning as their target discovery technique. Let η and Ω stand for a worm's scanning rate and scanning space, respectively. Assume at time t, there exist I_t infectious hosts. Then at time $t + 1/\eta$, by assuming the probability of different infectious hosts hitting the same susceptible host to be 0, there will be $I_{t+1} = I_t + \Delta I_t$ infectious hosts, where

$$\Delta I_t = \frac{I_t(N-I_t)}{\Omega}.$$ (10)

During the process that more and more susceptible hosts are infected and then participate in infecting others, the probability of different infectious hosts hitting the same susceptible host is not a constant. Therefore, the actual number of newly infected hosts is less than that predicted by equation (10). Here, we introduce a compensation factor denoted by to account for the difference between them, which varies as time goes on. Therefore, our discrete time deterministic CFAP model could be described by the following difference equation:

$$I_{t+1} = I_t + \frac{I_t(N-I_t)}{\Omega} - C_t.$$ (11)

There exist two methods to determine C_t, which are mathematical analysis or simulation. To predict C_t in a closed form (i.e., with no or very little iteration), mathematical analysis is usually employed. However, in some situations it could be very difficult, if not impossible, to derive a formula of C_t as a function of t. Then, we have to perform simulation experiments to find approximate value of C_t at each time t.

4 Simulation Experiments

There are four different ways to study the characteristics of a piece of self-propagating code, which are using test beds, performing real world experiments, creating mathematical models, and performing simulation experiments [24]. Among them, simulation experiments are often very effective tools to understand complex processes.

We systematically examined propagation characteristics of active worms employing single target discovery technique only, and a combination of two or three different target discovery techniques by conducting a series of simulation experiments under various scenarios. In order to reduce simulation time, we performed our simulation experiments in a class A /8 subnet. In other words, we used scale-down by a factor of $1/2^8$ to explore worm dynamics. According to Weaver et al. [25], scale-down introduces two notable artifacts: a bias towards more rapid propagation (propagation curve being shifted to the left due to scale-up of the density of initially infected hosts), and an increase in stochastic effects. Although these artifacts are significant, scale-down can still capture general behavior as long as the scale-down factor is not too extreme [25]. Therefore, scale-down is an efficient way to understand complex processes if the scale-down factor is appropriately chosen.

Our simulation experiments were based on the assumption that susceptible hosts are uniformly distributed in the above address space with vulnerability density approximately equivalent to that of the Slammer worm. We also assumed average worm scanning rate to be equivalent to the Slammer's as well. All simulations started with only 1 initially infected host, which is equivalent to 2^8 initially infected hosts in the Slammer's case.

In order to eliminate variation in results from different simulation runs for each certain scenario, we performed 10 simulation runs for each scenario using the simulator implemented in C programming language custom made for our simulation experiments. Results from all simulation runs are then averaged to produce final result for each scenario. We repeated our simulation experiments and got exactly the same average results, which indicated that stochastic effects could be eliminated, and the scale-down factor chosen was appropriate.

4.1 Simple Scenarios

Before we studied propagation characteristics of active worms employing a combination of two or three different target discovery techniques, we had studied propagation characteristics of active worms employing only one of the following target discovery techniques: uniform scanning; a complete hit-list; or internally generated target lists.

The above three kinds of active worms became the first 3 scenarios to be simulated, which are summarized in Table 1. Propagation rate of active worms employing uniform scanning only was our baseline to be compared to. Since an incomplete hit-list only cannot let a worm infect more hosts than those in the list, in practice it must be combined with other target discovery technique(s). Therefore, we chose a complete hit-list as one of the above 3 fundamental target discovery techniques. Average size of internally generated target lists was a candidate factor whose influence on a worm's propagation characteristics was to be investigated.

Table 1. A summary of the 3 simple scenarios simulated

Scenario Type	Scenario Code	Target Discovery Technique Employed
Simple	U	Uniform Scanning Only
Simple	H100%	A Complete Hit-list Only
Simple	I1	Internally Generated Target Lists Only with Average Size of 1
Simple	I2	Internally Generated Target Lists Only with Average Size of 2
Simple	I3	Internally Generated Target Lists Only with Average Size of 3

Table 2. A summary of simulation results of the 3 simple scenarios

Scenario Type	Scenario Code	Average Time (in seconds) to Infect 99% Susceptible Hosts
Simple	U	142
Simple	H100%	1
Simple	I1	Indefinite (maximum infection rate 7% achieved in 1 second)
Simple	I2	Indefinite (maximum infection rate 79% achieved in 1 second)
Simple	I3	Indefinite (maximum infection rate 94% achieved in 1 second)

According to the results (Table 2) from our simulation experiments, a complete hit-list makes a worm propagate extremely rapidly. However, the feasibility of this approach is discounted by the extreme difficulties that will be encountered by attackers in gathering such a list. Due to their exactly same propagation mechanism, an incomplete hit-list lets a worm infect all susceptible hosts in the list as soon as a complete hit-list does. Therefore, an incomplete hit-list is a more feasible approach. It is obvious that active worms only employing internally generated target lists with average size not greater than 3 cannot achieve infection of over 99% susceptible hosts. An explanation to this phenomenon could be that less than 99% of all susceptible hosts are in the combined internally generated target lists of all susceptible hosts infected. However, average size of internally generated target lists has a great influence on the maximum infection rate (maximum percentage of susceptible hosts

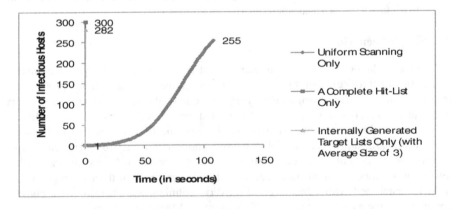

Fig. 2. A comparison of propagation curves of the 3 simple scenarios

a worm can infect). A slight increase in average size from 1 to 3 leads to a dramatic increase in the maximum infection rate. Furthermore, maximum infection rates are achieved in 1 second for all average sizes (1, 2, or 3). As we mentioned earlier in this paper, infection of 85% susceptible hosts would usually serve attackers' purposes. Therefore, internally generated target lists with average size of 3 (with maximum infection rate of 94%) could be employed by active worms to accelerate their propagation. A comparison of propagation curves of the 3 simple scenarios is illustrated by Fig. 2.

4.2 Scenarios with Moderate Complexity

Then, propagation characteristics of active worms employing a combination of two different target discovery techniques formed the focus of our research. As we mentioned earlier in this paper, in order to accelerate a worm's propagation, we must try to let the worm infect the first susceptible hosts and enter its fast spread phase as soon as possible. According to our simulation results of the above 3 simple scenarios, both an incomplete hit-list and internally generated target lists can let a worm infect a certain percentage of susceptible hosts in just one second. Therefore, each of these two target discovery techniques could be followed by uniform scanning to let the worm infect those susceptible hosts leftover. In our simulation experiments, active worms employing an incomplete hit-list followed by uniform scanning as their target discovery techniques would sequentially probe all those hosts in the hit-list prior to employing uniform scanning. Active worms employing internally generated target lists followed by uniform scanning would sequentially probe all those hosts in the target lists generated in process prior to employing uniform scanning.

The above two kinds of active worms formed the basis of our 6 scenarios with moderate complexity to be simulated, which are summarized in Table 3. Since we intended to shorten a worm's slow start phase, in which less than of susceptible hosts are infected, an incomplete hit-list with size up to 15% of the number of all susceptible hosts was employed. Both size of incomplete hit-list and average size of internally generated target lists were candidate factors whose influences on a worm's propagation characteristics were to be investigated. We have simulated a limited number of scenarios. More scenarios could be investigated to determine the relationship between average time to infect 99% susceptible hosts and size of hit-list, and the relationship between average time to infect 99% susceptible hosts and average size of internally generated target lists.

According to the results (Table 4) from our simulation experiments, an incomplete hit-list with size of 5% of the number of all susceptible hosts followed by uniform scanning accelerates a worm's propagation dramatically. However, this approach's capability to accelerate active worms' propagation is diminishing while size of the hit-list is increasing. Active worms employing internally generated target lists followed by uniform scanning performed especially well under all average sizes (1, 2, or 3) of the target lists. Here, average size of the target lists has a great influence on a worm's propagation rate. The larger the average size becomes, the faster the worm propagates.

Table 3. A summary of the 6 simulated scenarios with moderate complexity

Scenario Type	Scenario Code	Target Discovery Techniques Employed
Moderate	H5%+U	An Incomplete Hit-list with Size = 5% of the Number of All Susceptible Hosts; Followed by Uniform Scanning
Moderate	H10%+U	An Incomplete Hit-list with Size = 10% of the Number of All Susceptible Hosts; Followed by Uniform Scanning
Moderate	H15%+U	An Incomplete Hit-list with Size = 15% of the Number of All Susceptible Hosts; Followed by Uniform Scanning
Moderate	I1+U	Internally Generated Target Lists with Average Size of 1; Followed by Uniform Scanning
Moderate	I2+U	Internally Generated Target Lists with Average Size of 2; Followed by Uniform Scanning
Moderate	I3+U	Internally Generated Target Lists with Average Size of 3; Followed by Uniform Scanning

Table 4. A summary of simulation results of the 6 scenarios with moderate complexity

Scenario Type	Scenario Code	Average Time (in seconds) to Infect 99% Susceptible Hosts
Moderate	H5%+U	99
Moderate	H10%+U	89
Moderate	H15%+U	85
Moderate	I1+U	60
Moderate	I2+U	36
Moderate	I3+U	21

We have also investigated propagation characteristics of active worms employing both an incomplete hit-list and internally generated target lists as their target discovery techniques. According to our simulation results of the 3 simple scenarios, an incomplete hit-list ought to be employed prior to internally generated target lists because generally the former is more effective to boost the number of initially infected hosts. Therefore, in our simulation experiments, active worms employing both an incomplete hit-list and internally generated target lists as their target discovery techniques would sequentially probe all those hosts in the hit-list prior to sequentially probing all those hosts in the target lists generated in process. Our simulation results show that active worms employing internally generated target lists with average size not greater than 3 cannot achieve infection of over 99% susceptible hosts, even if the number of initially infected hosts is boosted by an incomplete hit-list of size up to 15% of the number of all susceptible hosts. A simple and efficient way to infect those leftover susceptible hosts is by uniform scanning. Therefore, we believe uniform scanning is an indispensable elementary target discovery technique of active worms.

4.3 Complex Scenarios

Finally, propagation characteristics of active worms employing a combination of three different target discovery techniques were examined. In our simulation experiments, active worms employing an incomplete hit-list followed by internally generated target lists followed by uniform scanning as their target discovery techniques would sequentially probe all those hosts in the hit-list prior to prior to sequentially probing all those hosts in the target lists generated in process. Once those lists were exhausted, they would start uniform scanning.

The above kind of active worm formed the basis of our 9 complex scenarios to be simulated, which are summarized in Table 5. Both size of incomplete hit-list and average size of internally generated target lists were candidate factors whose influences on a worm's propagation characteristics were to be investigated. We have simulated a limited number of scenarios. More scenarios could be investigated to determine the relationship between average time to infect 99% susceptible hosts and size of hit-list and average size of internally generated target lists.

Table 5. A summary of the 9 complex scenarios simulated

Scenario Type	Scenario Code	Target Discovery Technique(s) Employed
Complex	H5%+I1+U H5%+I2+U H5%+I3+U	An Incomplete Hit-list with Size = 5% of the Number of All Susceptible Hosts; Followed by Internally Generated Target Lists with Average Size of 1, 2, or 3; Followed by Uniform Scanning
Complex	H10%+I1+U H10%+I2+U H10%+I3+U	An Incomplete Hit-list with Size = 10% of the Number of All Susceptible Hosts; Followed by Internally Generated Target Lists with Average Size of 1, 2, or 3; Followed by Uniform Scanning
Complex	H15%+I1+U H15%+I2+U H15%+I3+U	An Incomplete Hit-list with Size = 15% of the Number of All Susceptible Hosts; Followed by Internally Generated Target Lists with Average Size of 1, 2, or 3; Followed by Uniform Scanning

Table 6. A summary of simulation results of the 9 complex scenarios

Scenario Type	Scenario Code	Average Time (in seconds) to Infect 99% Susceptible Hosts
Complex	H5%+I1+U	54
Complex	H5%+I2+U	34
Complex	H5%+I3+U	18
Complex	H10%+I1+U	55
Complex	H10%+I2+U	36
Complex	H10%+I3+U	19
Complex	H15%+I1+U	53
Complex	H15%+I2+U	35
Complex	H15%+I3+U	18

According to the results (Table 6) from our simulation experiments, an additional incomplete hit-list only accelerates a worm's propagation slightly, compared to the results of the last 3 scenarios in Table 4. Increasing size of the hit-list has little effect on a worm's rate of propagation. However, average size of internally generated target lists has a great influence on a worm's rate of propagation. The larger the average size becomes, the faster the worm propagates. In other words, the results indicate the combination of the three different target discovery techniques is not the best for attackers taking into account the added effort they have to make to build the worm. We suggest internally generated target lists with average size of 3 followed by uniform scanning is the most effective and efficient among all approaches examined in this paper to accelerate propagation of active worms.

5   Conclusions and Future Work

This paper provides a reasonably comprehensive but not exhaustive coverage of various target discovery techniques that future active worms might employ to accelerate their propagation. We derived from mathematical analysis that in order to accelerate a worm's propagation, we must try to let the worm infect the first 15% susceptible hosts and enter its fast spread phase as soon as possible.

A hit-list lets a worm infect all susceptible hosts in the list in an extremely short period. When followed by uniform scanning, an incomplete hit-list's capability to accelerate a worm's propagation is diminishing while size of the hit-list is increasing. When not followed by uniform scanning, internally generated target lists with average size not greater than 3 cannot let a worm achieve infection of over 99% susceptible hosts, no matter the number of initially infected hosts is boosted by an incomplete hit-list of size up to 15% of the number of all susceptible hosts or not. However, when followed by uniform scanning, internally generated target lists performed especially well. The larger the average size becomes, the faster the worm propagates. An additional incomplete hit-list only accelerates the worm's propagation slightly.

Our major contributions in this paper are first, we proposed a new discrete time deterministic model of active worms; and second, we suggested the combination of target discovery techniques that can best accelerate propagation of active worms discovered from results of the comprehensive simulations. The research is from attackers' perspective. We believe it can be very beneficial to understanding of propagation mechanisms of active worms, and thus building effective and efficient defense systems against their propagation.

In order to counter super fast propagation of future active worms employing the various combinations of multiple target discovery techniques, novel mechanisms need to be discovered since current ones, due to their inherent drawbacks, respond too slowly compared to propagation of even active worms employing single target discovery technique.

References

1. Kienzle, D.M., Elder, M.C.: Recent Worms: A Survey and Trends. In: WORM 2003, Washington D.C., USA, pp. 1–10 (2003)
2. Weaver, N., Paxson, V., Staniford, S., Cunningham, R.: A Taxonomy of Computer Worms. In: WORM 2003, Washington D.C., USA, pp. 11–18 (2003)
3. Moore, D., Shannon, C., Brown, J.: Code-Red: A Case Study on the Spread and Victims of an Internet Worm. In: IMW 2002, Marseille, France, pp. 273–284 (2002)
4. Moore, D., Paxson, V., Savage, S., Shannon, C., Staniford, S., Weaver, N.: Inside the Slammer Worm. IEEE Security & Privacy 1, 33–39 (2003)
5. Shannon, C., Moore, D.: The Spread of the Witty Worm. IEEE Security & Privacy 2, 46–50 (2004)
6. Staniford, S., Paxson, V., Weaver, N.: How to Own the Internet in Your Spare Time. In: Security 2002, San Francisco, CA, USA, pp. 149–167 (2002)
7. Spafford, E.H.: The Internet Worm Program: An Analysis. ACM SIGCOMM Computer Communication Review 19, 17–57 (1989)

8. Berghel, H.: The Code Red Worm: Malicious Software Knows No Bounds. Communications of the ACM 44, 15–19 (2001)
9. Ma, J., Voelker, G.M., Savage, S.: Self-Stopping Worms. In: WORM 2005, Fairfax, VA, USA, pp. 12–21 (2005)
10. Xiang, Y., Zhou, W., Chowdhury, M.: A Survey of Active and Passive Defence Mechanisms against DDoS Attacks (Technical Report), TR C04/02, School of In-formation Technology, Deakin University, Australia (2004)
11. Xiang, Y., Fan, X., Zhu, W.: Propagation of Active Worms: A Survey. International Journal of Computer Systems Science and Engineering (accepted, 2008)
12. Ellis, D.: Worm Anatomy and Model. In: WORM 2003, Washington D.C., USA, pp. 42–50 (2003)
13. Anderson, R.M., May, R.M.: Infectious Diseases of Humans: Dynamics and Control. Oxford University Press, Oxford (1991)
14. Andersson, H., Britton, T.: Stochastic Epidemic Models and Their Statistical Analysis. Springer, New York (2000)
15. Bailey, N.T.: The Mathematical Theory of Infectious Diseases and Its Applications. Hafner Press, New York (1975)
16. Frauenthal, J.C.: Mathematical Modeling in Epidemiology. Springer, New York (1980)
17. Daley, D.J., Gani, J.: Epidemic Modelling: An Introduction. Cambridge University Press, Cambridge (1999)
18. Zou, C.C., Gong, W., Towsley, D.: Code Red Worm Propagation Modeling and Analysis. In: CCS 2002, Washington D.C., USA, pp. 138–147 (2002)
19. Chen, Z., Gao, L., Kwiat, K.: Modeling the Spread of Active Worms. In: IEEE INFOCOM, pp. 1890–1900 (2003)
20. Wang, Y., Wang, C.: Modeling the Effects of Timing Parameters on Virus Propagation. In: WORM 2003, Washington D.C., USA, pp. 61–66 (2003)
21. Rohloff, K., Basar, T.: Stochastic Behavior of Random Constant Scanning Worms. In: 14th ICCCN, San Diego, CA, USA, pp. 339–344 (2005)
22. Sellke, S., Shroff, N.B., Bagchi, S.: Modeling and Automated Containment of Worms. In: DSN 2005, pp. 528–537 (2005)
23. Zou, C.C., Towsley, D., Gong, W.: On the Performance of Internet Worm Scanning Strategies. University of Massachusetts (2003)
24. Wagner, A., Dubendorfer, T.: Experiences with Worm Propagation Simulations. In: WORM 2003, Washington D.C., USA, pp. 34–41 (2003)

Online Accumulation: Reconstruction of Worm Propagation Path*

Yang Xiang, Qiang Li**, and Dong Guo

College of Computer Science and Technology, JiLin University
ChangChun, JiLin 130012, China
sharang@yahoo.cn, li_qiang@jlu.edu.cn, guodong@jlu.edu.cn

Abstract. Knowledge of the worm origin is necessary to forensic analysis, and knowledge of the initial causal flows supports diagnosis of how network defenses were breached. Fast and accurate online tracing network worm during its propagation, help to detect worm origin and the earliest infected nodes, and is essential for large-scale worm containment. This paper introduces the Accumulation Algorithm which can efficiently tracing worm origin and the initial propagation paths, and presents an improved online Accumulation Algorithm using sliding detection windows. We also analyzes and verifies their detection accuracy and containment efficacy through simulation experiments in large scale network. Results indicate that the online Accumulation Algorithm can accurately tracing worms and efficiently containing their propagation in an approximately real-time manner.

Keywords: Worm, Propagation path, Online tracing, Containment.

1 Introduction

Network worms allow attackers to control thousands of hosts in a short time, launch DDoS attacks, steal security information, and destroy critical data. Since 2001, Slammer and other network worms[1,2] have brought unprecedented threat and damage to the Internet. There is increasing threat of network worms against computer system security and network security.

Tracing worm's attack paths (i.e., obtaining the propagation paths of network worm) [3,5,6] can dig out the initial victims and the infect sequence of hosts. Even if only partial path can be obtained, it still has significance in worm containment, evidence collecting and investigating.

Worm containment works by detecting that a worm is operating in the network and then blocking the infected machines from contacting further hosts. A key problem in containment of scanning worms is efficiently detecting and suppressing the scanning. Since containment blocks suspicious machines, it is critical that the false positive rate be very low[14].

In addition, the overwhelming majority of the attack traffic originates from victims of the attack, as opposed to the true source of the attack. While network terminals

---

* Supported by NSFC (60703023).

** Corresponding author.

deploy corresponding defense gradually, the infected hosts may no longer participate in the following attack. In contrast, worm source and the initial infected hosts may be artificially controlled, these hosts are more danger, and can not be easily detected or recovered. So, reconstruct worm source and the initial causal flows, makes worm containment more effective.

However, the reaction time of efficient worm containment could be less than a few hours or even minutes[12]. For example, Code-Red II worms infected more than 359,000 computers on the Internet in less than 14 hours[2]. Slammer worms probed all four billion IPv4 Internet addresses for potential victims in less than 10 minutes[1]. Therefore, it is necessary to do research on online worm tracing approaches in complex network environments, to trace network worm origins in a real-time manner.

In order to achieve online tracing, the following issues must be resolved: (1) shorten the time required for reconstructing worm propagation paths in order to reduce computation complexity; and (2) guarantee reconstruction of paths continuously.

Contribution of this paper includes: (1) introduction of the *Accumulation Algorithm* for reconstructing worm propagation paths, which can fleetly and efficiently trace worm attacking origins and initial propagation paths; (2) introduction of the online *Accumulation Algorithm* using sliding windows, which can obtain worm origin and tracing initial attack edges at the early days of worm propagating; and (3) deployment of a simulation environment for worm propagation in large scale network, verify the performance of our algorithm.

This paper is organized as follows. Section 2 introduces the related work of worm detection and containment; section 3 gives some definitions and assumptions of the following analysis; section 4 proposes the *Accumulation Algorithm* and prove its feasibility through theoretical analysis; section 5 introduces the online *Accumulation Algorithm*; section 6 verify the accuracy and efficiency of our algorithm through simulation experiments in large scale network; finally section 7 gives a conclusion.

2   Related Work

Worm containment has been studied in previous work. Network-based worm containment techniques can be classified into two major categories, that is, address blacklisting and signature-based filtering. Besides network-based techniques, Vigilante et al.[15] employs the collaboration among end hosts to contain worms by using self-certified alerts. Shield et al.[16] installs host-based network filters that are vulnerability specific and exploit generic once a vulnerability is discovered and before a patch is applied. DOMINO et al.[7] builds an overlay network among active-sink nodes to distribute alert information by hashing the source IP addresses. Worminator et al.[13] summarizes portscan alerts in Bloom filters and disseminates them among collaborating peers. Our work is focus on online tracing worm origin and initial propagation paths, help to quickly and effectively deploy worm containment.

To date, merely a few approaches for offline tracing the sequence of hosts infected by a worm are proposed. Xie et al.[5,11] offered a randomized approach that traces the origin of a worm attack by performing a random walk over the hosts contact graph, which is generated by collecting flow rates between potential victims during the worm's propagation. Besides, aiming at the flow characteristics of mobile worm in wireless networks, Sarat et al.[9] improved random moonwalk algorithm so that the algorithm tends to be effective continuously. Rajab et al.[3] presented a simple technique that uses the history data acquired through a network telescope to infer the actual sequence of host infections. A different approach was proposed by Kumar et al.[6] where a Witty worm was reversely engineered to recover the random scanning algorithm and corresponding initial seeds. Finally, using protocol graph, Collins et al.[8] detect hit-list worm and identify attack origin through monitoring the abnormal changes in various of protocol graphs.

3   Problem Formulation

We consult some definitions in [5]: the host communications in network is defined as a directed graph $G =< V, E >$, called *host contact graph*. Nodes of G is a tuple set $V = H \times T$, where H is all hosts in the network and T is time. The set of edges E is a subset of $V \times V$. Each direct edge $e =< u, t^s, v, t^e >$ in the *host contact graph* represents a network flow, where $< u, t^s >\in H \times T$ represents source host and start time, $< v, t^e >\in H \times T$ represents destination host and finish time. An edge is defined as an *attack edge* if it carries attack traffic, whether or not it is successful in infecting the destination host. An *attack edge* is defined as a *causal edge* if it corresponds to a flow that successfully infects a normal host. All other edges in G besides *attack edges* are called *normal edge*.

If two edges $e_1 =< u_1, t_1^s, v_1, t_1^e >$, $e_2 =< u_2, t_2^s, v_2, t_2^e >$ in G satisfy the condition $u_2 = v_1$ and $t_1^e < t_2^s < t_1^e + \Delta t$ (Δt is a pre-determined time interval parameters), then e_2 is called e_1's *successor*, e_1 is called e_2's *precursor*. All e's *precursors* represent as: $e_{pre}^1, \cdots,$ $e_{pre}^j, \cdots, e_{pre}^{PRE(e)}$, $PRE(e)$ is the total number of e's *precursor*. Similarly, all e's *successors* represent as: $e_{suc}^1, \cdots, e_{suc}^j, \cdots, e_{suc}^{SUC(e)}$, $SUC(e)$ is the total number of e's *successor*. *Precursor* and *successor* describe the relationships between the neighbor edges.

Under normal circumstances, we assume that there is only one worm origin in the network, so the worm's propagation process forms a tree (defined as *causal tree*). A path in *causal tree* from the root to one of the leaves called a *causal chain*. *Causal tree* is formed by all *causal edges* in G. The root of *causal tree* denotes the worm attack origin, while *causal edges* from levels higher up in the *causal tree* denote the initial attack sequences. Reconstructing worm origin and the initial attack sequences has significance in restraining evolution of worm in investigating and collecting evidence. After we know *host contact graph* G, our algorithm identifies a set of edges that, with high probability, are edges from the top levels of the *causal tree* (i.e., initial attack sequences after worm breaks out).

4   Accumulation Algorithm

Network worms can infect a large number of hosts in a very short period of time. This requires worm tracing algorithms be able to obtain propagation path as soon as possible in order to reduce loss. At the same time, traffic data in the network are generated very fast, usually occupying a large portion of bandwidth. Consequently, it requires that the time and space complexity of the algorithm to be near-linear. We use dynamic programming to optimize the implementation of our *Accumulation Algorithm*. With even millions of input size, the algorithm is able to complete in a very short time, implying more time for the deployment of defense against possible future attacks for the same worm.

4.1 Algorithm Specification

In order to continuously infect other hosts, after a host has been infected, it usually sends more flows compare to former, while there is no significant increase in the number of received flows[5]. Compare to a *normal edge*, a *causal edge* has more *successors* while the number of *precursor* is similar on average. Motivated on this difference, we propose a worm propagation path reconstruction method - *Accumulation Algorithm*. First of all, we assign each edge with the same weight; then after K iterations of weight's 'aggregation - cumulation' (*accumulation process*), more weights tend to aggregate to *causal edges*; finally we pick out top Z edges (*TOP-Z*) which have the largest weight to trace initial propagation paths and reconstruct top levels of *causal tree*.

We define $p(e, i)$ as the *weight increment* in the i-th *accumulation process*, then when the algorithm is complete e has its total weight value $p(e) = \sum_{i=1}^{K} p(e, i)$. In fact each *accumulation process* is a redistribution of the previous *weight increment*. Specifically, each accumulation process evenly distributes the previous *weight increment* $p(e, i-1)$ to e's every *precursors* $e_{pre}^1, \cdots, e_{pre}^j, \cdots, e_{pre}^{PRE(e)}$, counting as a faction of the current weight increment for each of the precursors. After K iterations, each edge's *weight increment* is continuously distributed to their *precursors*. In fact, the redistribution process of *weight increment* is a weight accumulates process performed along the reverse *causal chain*. The following snapshot illustrates the *Accumulation Algorithm*:

STEP 1: $i = 0$; $p(e) = 0.0$; $p(e, 0) = 1.0$;
STEP 2: $i = i + 1$;

$$p(e, i) = \sum_{j=1}^{SUC(e)} \frac{p(e_{suc}^j, i - 1)}{PRE(e_{suc}^j)}; \tag{1}$$

$p(e) = p(e) + p(e, i)$;
STEP 3: If $i \le K$ goto STEP 2, else goto STEP 4;
STEP 4: Pick out TOP-Z, Reconstruct top levels of causal tree.

Adjust of the *weight increment* can be treated as a redistribution process, no additional weight is generated. The redistribution process of *weight increment* is called 'aggregation', and adding one's *weight increment* to its total weight is called 'cumulation'. In the *accumulation process*, a weight value aggregates to the top levels of *causal tree* along reverse *causal chain*. This becomes our primary evidence used to discover the initial attack sequences.

During the K iterations, one can completely generates the $(i+1)$-th weight increment according to the i-th value. That is, the 'future' weight increment relies on only the 'current' weight, instead of the 'past' weight. So we can use dynamic programming method gradually calculate all the $p(e, i)$ ($e \in E, 1 <= i <= K$). Therefore, the time and space complexity of weight redistribution is $O(|E|)$. *Accumulation Algorithm* has K iterations of weight redistribution, thus the total time complexity is $O(K \times |E|)$. Experiments show that ideal accuracy can be achieved even if K is very small. Therefore, it is roughly the case that *Accumulation Algorithm* has a linear time complexity and space complexity.

4.2 Analysis and Prove

Accumulation Algorithm tries to identify initial *causal edges* with high accuracy and reconstruct the *causal tree*. To illustrate the accuracy and feasibility of our algorithm, we need to model the traffic data and worm attack. Suppose a normal host sends A flows in Δt seconds, and an infected host sends B flows in Δt seconds, including A normal flows and $B - A$ attack flows (clearly there is $B > A$). For an aggressive worm, the number of sending flows increase significantly after a host is infected (i.e., $B >> A$). But before and after infection, the number of flows a host received in Δt seconds remains almost unchanged (defined as C).

We define an edge $e =< u, t^s, v, t^e >$ as a *malicious-destination edge* if host v is infected at (or before) time t^e, marked as e_m. Other edges is called *normal-destination edge*, marked as e_n. Every *normal-destination edge* is a *normal edge*, but *malicious-destination edges* include all *causal edges*, some *normal edges* and a part of non-causal *attack edges* (v has been infected before time t^e). Assume that, on average, x *normal edges* sent by a host in Δt seconds are *malicious-destination edges*.

Next we prove that $p(e_m, i) > p(e_n, i)$ for all $1 <= i <= K, e_m, e_n \in E$.

Proof. Using Mathematical Induction:

1. First, prove that $p(e_m, 1) > p(e_n, 1)$:

$$p(e_m, 1) = \sum_{j=1}^{SUC(e_m)} \frac{p((e_m)^j_{suc}, 0)}{PRE((e_m)^j_{suc})} \approx \frac{B}{C}, \quad p(e_n, 1) = \sum_{j=1}^{SUC(e_n)} \frac{p((e_n)^j_{suc}, 0)}{PRE((e_n)^j_{suc})} \approx \frac{A}{C},$$

$\because p(e_m, 1) - p(e_n, 1) \approx \frac{B-A}{C} > 0, \quad \therefore p(e_m, 1) > p(e_n, 1)$.

2. Assume $p(e_m, i) > p(e_n, i)$ when $0 < i < K$, prove that $p(e_m, i + 1) > p(e_n, i + 1)$:

$$p(e_m, i + 1) = \sum_{j=1}^{SUC(e_m)} \frac{p((e_m)^j_{suc}, i)}{PRE((e_m)^j_{suc})} \approx \frac{A-x}{C} \cdot \overline{p(e_n, i)} + \frac{B-A+x}{C} \cdot \overline{p(e_m, i)},$$

$$p(e_n, i + 1) = \sum_{j=1}^{SUC(e_n)} \frac{p((e_n)^j_{suc}, i)}{PRE((e_n)^j_{suc})} \approx \frac{A-x}{C} \cdot \overline{p(e_n, i)} + \frac{x}{C} \cdot \overline{p(e_m, i)},$$

Thereinto $\overline{p(e_m, i)} = \frac{\sum_{e \in E} p(e_m, i)}{\sum_{e \in E} 1}, \quad \overline{p(e_n, i)} = \frac{\sum_{e \in E} p(e_n, i)}{\sum_{e \in E} 1}$.

$\because p(e_m, i + 1) - p(e_n, i + 1) \approx \frac{B-A}{C} \cdot \overline{p(e_m, i)} > 0, \quad \therefore p(e_m, i + 1) > p(e_n, i + 1)$.

So we have proved that $p(e_m, i) > p(e_n, i)$ for all $1 <= i <= K, e_m, e_n \in E$.

From the above proof, we can get that $p(e_m, i) - p(e_n, i)$ is proportional to $B - A$. For aggressive worm $p(e_m, i) >> p(e_n, i)$ because of $B >> A$. While the *accumulation process* is proceeding, $p(e_m, i) - p(e_n, i)$ increases gradually, and the weight advantage of *malicious-destination edges* grows. Furthermore, because the *accumulation process* follows the reverse order of *causal chain*, initial *causal edge* will get more weight. Thus these early propagation paths can be highlighted from all the edges.

However, *malicious-destination edges* include not only *causal edge*, but also some of the *normal edge* and non-causal *attack edge*. In the early phase of worm propagation, there is not much infected host, so the vast majority of *malicious-destination edges* are *causal edges*. In the late phase, almost all the vulnerable hosts in the network have been infected – the result being that the amount of *normal edges* and non-causal *attack edges* in all *malicious-destination edge* increase. Therefore, tracing worm in the early phase has a lower false negative rate, and thus is helpful for detecting worm as soon as possible, saving more time for defense against continues spread of the worm.

5   Online Accumulation Algorithm

With online tracing, propagation paths can be detected in the initial phase (e.g. 30 minutes) after the worm breaks out. As a result, inhibition and defense can be launched in the earlier stage, reducing some loss otherwise.

In the related works, we mention that enabling a detection algorithm to execute in real-time usually exploits sliding windows [4,17]. The *Accumulation Algorithm* is able to promptly obtain the detection results and thus provides an ameliorate condition for online tracing. Based on the offline *Accumulation Algorithm*, we propose an online tracing algorithm also based on sliding window, as follow:

STEP 1. $i = 0$;
STEP 2. Collect traffic date within recent S seconds, construct the host contact graph G_i using these traffic data;
STEP 3. Execute the Accumulation Algorithm in G_i, obtain top-z_i;
STEP 4. Compose TOP-Z_i by extracting Z edges with the highest weight values from top-z_i $\cup$ TOP-Z_{i-1}. Reconstruct current causal tree via TOP-Z_i;
STEP 5. $i = i + 1$, iterate again from STEP 2 after R seconds.

This algorithm has many advantages: First, it is triggered every R seconds, thus worm can be detected as soon as possible. Second, each run needs to collect traffic data only within the recent S seconds – a large amount of overhead is avoided and improves its efficiency. One disadvantage of this algorithm is relatively low detection accuracy cased by the fact that it relies on only partial data.

6   Simulation Experiments

This section is constructed as follows. Section 6.1 gives the performance metrics; section 6.2 figure out our simulation methodology; section 6.3 discuss the parameters' influence on the performance of *Accumulation Algorithm*; section 6.4 discuss the parameters' influence on the performance of the online *Accumulation Algorithm*; section 6.5 illustrate effect of worm containment by the online *Accumulation Algorithm*.

6.1   Evaluation Methodology

To quantitatively evaluate the performance of *Accumulation Algorithm*, first we consider the following two metrics:

$$\text{Attack edge Accuracy } (AA) = \frac{\text{\# attack edge in TOP-Z}}{Z};$$

$$\text{Causal edge Accuracy } (CA) = \frac{\text{\# causal edge in TOP-Z}}{Z};$$

Further more, *Accumulation Algorithm* is designed to identify worms initial attack sequences. In the following experiments the earliest 10% *causal edges* (defined as *INIT-10%*) are considered as 'initial attack sequence'. Then there are two more metrics to evaluate the ability of tracing initial causal edges:

$$\text{False Negative } (FN) = \frac{\text{\# edge in INIT-10\% but not in TOP-Z}}{\text{\# causal edge}};$$

$$\text{False Positive } (FP) = \frac{\text{\# edge in TOP-Z but not in INIT-10\%}}{\text{\# non-causal edge}};$$

6.2   Simulation Methodology

In the worm detection works, experimental data usually produced by mixing real-world network traffic and man-made worm propagation flows [5,8,9]. Using pre-captured real network flows as the background traffic makes repeating experiments more convenient. Background flows often captured from main switches or routers. Worm attack flows are added artificially base on the real-world background data.

We use a part of NZIX II[10] trace from WAND as our background traffic data. This is a 9000 seconds long GPS-synchronized IP header traces captured at the New Zealand Internet Exchange, including exchange flows between 6 intranets, involving a total of 0.1 million hosts and 3 million flows. These flows are captured through the SPAN port of router, only containing summary information of every flow, but not including the specific contents of packages. Traces contain TCP, UDP and ICMP flows, being anonymized by mapping the IP addresses into network 10.X.X.X.

We let the worm break out at second 900. After a host has been infected, it sends an attack flow to a randomly chosen host every 30 seconds. A destination host will be infected if it is a vulnerable host, otherwise it won't. In the following experiments, we choose *0.1* as the fraction of vulnerable hosts in the network. Some information of experimental data is shown in Table 1. From Table 1 and Fig. 1 we can seen that, all the vulnerable hosts have been infected after 5000 seconds, and 41% of flows are attack flows.

Table 1. Three different worm scanning rates

Total flows (million)	5.08
Fraction of attack edges	0.41
Fraction of causal edges	0.0024
Fraction of vulnerable hosts	0.1
Fraction of infected hosts	0.100

When considering given parameter's effect to the algorithm performance, we only allow the corresponding parameter to change. Without special note, the initial values of the parameters in the experiment are shown in Table 2.

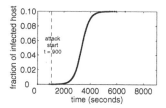

Fig. 1. Fraction of infected host along with time

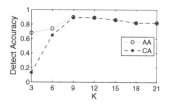

Fig. 2. K vs. AA, CA

Table 2. The initial values of parameters

Number of *accumulation process*: K	10
Time interval on the definition of precursor: Δt (seconds)	1000
Number of edges in the result set: Z	100
Running duration of online algorithm: R (seconds)	480
Size of sliding window: S (seconds)	2400

6.3 Preferences of Accumulation Algorithm

Parameter K. Fig. 2 shows the impact of K on AA and CA. Algorithm performs the best when $K=9$, while AA and CA are both the highest. From this we can see that a good result only requires a few number of *accumulation process*. From Fig. 2 we also find that when K continuous increases, its accuracy declines a little. Because while accumulating along the reverse order of *causal chain*, excessive iterations of *accumulation process* makes the weight more likely to be aggregated to some normal edges before the worm breaks out, then more non-causal *malicious-destination edge* will enter *TOP-Z*.

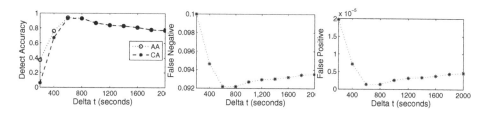

Fig. 3. Δt vs. AA, CA **Fig. 4.** Δt vs. FN **Fig. 5.** Δt vs. FP

Parameter Δt. Fig. 3 shows the impact of Δt on AA and CA. When Δt is increasing, detection accuracy climbs up but finally drops slightly. The accuracy is very low when Δt is very small, because reverse accumulation is more likely to arrive at a host that has no precursor in the previous Δt seconds, making some weights lost, reducing the possibility of pooling the weight into the top levels of *causal tree*.

Larger Δt makes the weight have more chance to accumulate to the top levels of *causal tree*, so detection accuracy will increase along with Δt. But *AA* and *CA* both lowered down when continuous increase Δt. This is because a wider Δt indicates more *precursors* – weight has higher possibility to be aggregated to some *normal edges* before the worm breaks out. We can also discover this from Fig. 4 and Fig. 5. The *FP* and *FN* are both increasing along with Δt, because of more *normal edges* are selected into *TOP-Z*.

From Fig. 2 and Fig. 3 we can see that, *CA* is usually very close to *AA*. This is because as the *accumulation process* proceeds, weights gradually accumulate to the initial *malicious-destination edges*. While at the initial phase of worm breaks out, there is not many infected host, the vast majority of *malicious-destination edge* are *causal edges*.

6.4   Preferences of Online Accumulation Algorithm

For an online algorithm, we hope its detect duration can be very short, so that worm propagation can be detected as soon as possible. Fig. 6 and Fig. 7 shows the impact of window size S and running duration R on detection accuracy. Using only partial data is not only an inevitable demand and benefits (reducing running time and memory consume) but also is a shortage (lower accuracy rate) for the online algorithm. As can be seen in Fig. 6 and Fig. 7, a bigger size of window leads to a higher detection accuracy, but there is only a little difference between the accuracy of $S=2400$ and $S=3600$. Increasing the running duration enables the algorithm accuracy to be increased. This is because when merging two trees form adjacent slide windows, more edges in the overlapping time interval will cause more conflict edges. Yet the change of accuracy with running duration is gentle, launching the *Accumulation Algorithm* every 60 seconds can achieve 70% accuracy.

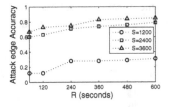

Fig. 6. R, S vs. *AA*

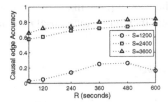

Fig. 7. R, S vs. *CA*

6.5   Effect of Containment

Fast and accurate tracing worm source and initial propagation paths is essential to contain worms at the Internet scale. From Fig. 7 we can see that, when the parameters' value of online *Accumulation Algorithm* are $R = 120$, $S = 2400$, $Z = 100$, *CA* is at least 60%. To illustrate the effects of worm containment, we conduct the following simulation experiments.

We add h infected hosts to the blacklist every 120 seconds ($h = minimal \{60, total\times 0.002\}$). Which '*total*' is the amount of infected hosts (excluding hosts already in the

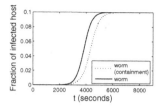

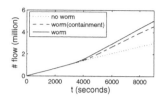

Fig. 8. Fraction of infected host at time t **Fig. 9.** Total number of flows before time t

blacklist), '*minimal*$\{x, y\}$' return the smaller numerical value of x and y. Fig. 8 and Fig. 9 shows the simulation result. We can see thus containment delays worm spread about 500 seconds, while it reduces the network traffic by 10%.

7   Conclusions

Online tracing the evolution of a worm outbreak reconstructs not only patient zero (i.e., the initial victim), but also the infection node list in evolution process. Even if the proportion trails can be captured, it has significance in restraining evolution of worm in investigating and collecting evidence.

Tracing network worm propagation from the initial attack can inhibit continuous spread of the worm, ensuring that no more hosts is infected by the worm, and providing basis for the determination of worm attack origins. Experiment results indicate that the *Accumulation Algorithm* can achieve 90% detection accuracy.

References

1. Moore, D., Paxson, V., Savage, S., Shannon, C., Staniford, S., Weaver, N.: Inside the Slammer Worm. IEEE Security and Privacy (August 2003)
2. Moore, D., Shannon, C., Claffy, K.: Code-Red: A Case Study on the Spread and Victims of an Internet Worm. In: Proceedings of Second ACM SIGCOMM Workshop Internet Measurement, pp. 273–284 (2002)
3. Rajab, M.A., Monrose, F., Terzis, A.: Worm evolution tracking via timing analysis. In: Proceedings of the 2005 ACM Workshop on Rapid Malcode, WORM 2005, November 11, 2005, pp. 52–59. ACM Press, New York (2005)
4. Peng, P., Ning, P., Reeves, D.S., Wang, X.: Active Timing-Based Correlation of Perturbed Traffic Flows with Chaff Packets. In: ICDCS Workshops 2005, pp. 107–113 (2005)
5. Xie, Y., Sckar, V., Maltz, D.A., Reiter, M.K., Zhan, H.: Worm Origin Identification Using Random Moonwalks. In: Proceedings of IEEE Symposium on Security and Privacy, May 2005, pp. 242–256 (2005)
6. Kumar, A., Paxson, V., Weaver, N.: Exploiting Underlying Structure for Detailed Reconstruction of an Internet Scale Event. In: Proceedings of ACM IMC (October 2005)
7. Yegneswaran, V., Barford, P., Jha, S.: Global Intrusion Detection in the DOMINO Overlay System. In: Proceedings of Network and Distributed System Security Symp (NDSS) (2004)
8. Collins, M.P., Reiter, M.K.: Hit-list worm detection and bot identification in large networks using protocol graphs. In: Kruegel, C., Lippmann, R., Clark, A. (eds.) RAID 2007. LNCS, vol. 4637, pp. 276–295. Springer, Heidelberg (2007)

 9. Sarat, S., Terzis, A.: On the detection and origin identification of mobile worms. In: Proceedings of the 2007 ACM Workshop on Recurring Malcode, WORM 2007, Alexandria, Virginia, USA, November 02, 2007, pp. 54–60. ACM, New York (2007)
10. WAND Network Research Group. 2000 WAND WITS: NZIX-II trace data (July 2000), http://wand.cs.waikato.ac.nz/wits/nzix/2/nzix-ii.php
11. Xie, Y., Sekar, V., Reiter, M.K., Zhang, H.: Forensic Analysis for Epidemic Attacks in Federated Networks. In: Proceedings of the IEEE International Conference on Network Protocols (October 2006)
12. Moore, D., Shannon, C., Voelker, G.M., Savage, S.: Internet Quarantine: Requirements for Containing Self-Propagating Code. In: Proceedings of 22nd Conf. Computer Comm. (2003)
13. Locasto, M.E., Parekh, J., Keromytis, A.D., Stolfo, S.: Towards Collaborative Security and P2P Intrusion Detection. In: Proceedings of Sixth Ann. IEEE SMC Information Assurance Workshop (IAW), June 2005, pp. 333–339 (2005)
14. Weaver, N., Staniford, S., Paxson, V.: Very Fast Containment of Scanning Worms. In: Proceedings of Usenix Security Symp., pp. 29–44 (2004)
15. Costa, M., Crowcroft, J., Castro, M., Rowstron, A., Zhou, L., Zhang, L., Barham, P.: Vigilante: End-to-End Containment of Internet Worms. In: Proceedings of 20th ACM Symp. Operating Systems Principles (SOSP) (October 2005)
16. Wang, H.J., Guo, C., Simon, D.R., Zugenmaier, A.: Shield: Vulnerability-Driven Network Filters for Preventing Known Vulnerability Exploits. In: Proceedings of 2004 ACM Conf. Applications, Technologies, Architectures, and Protocols for Computer Comm (SIGCOMM), pp. 193–204 (2004)
17. Stafford, S., Li, J., Ehrenkranz, T.: Enhancing SWORD to detect 0-day-worm-infected hosts. SIMULATION: Transactions of the Society for Modeling and Simulation International 83(2), 199–212 (2007)

HRS: A Hybrid Replication Strategy for Exhaustive P2P Search

Hanhua Chen[1], Hai Jin[1], Xucheng Luo[2], and Zhiguang Qin[2]

[1] Huazhong University of Science and Technology, Wuhan, 430074, China
[2] University of Electronic Science and Technology of China, Chengdu, 6110054, China
hjin@hust.edu.cn

Abstract. Successful search and versatile query support are two important requirements for peer-to-peer (P2P) search applications. Replication strategy is an effective approach to improve the search performance of unstructured P2P systems. However, existing replication strategies either adapt only to popular queries or incur excessive replication cost for unpopular queries. In this work, we propose HRS, a hybrid replication strategy to improve the search performance of unstructured P2P networks. By combining a query popularity independent strategy with the square-root strategy, HRS can effectively and efficiently handle both kind of queries, popular or not. We evaluate this design through mathematical proof and comprehensive simulations. Results show that HRS outperforms existing replication-based search paradigms in terms of search performance and resource consummation.

1 Introduction

Since the emergence of peer-to-peer (P2P) [1,2,3] file sharing systems, such as Napster [4] and Gnutella [5], millions of users started to harness the desired data on the Internet with P2P tools. Recently, large scale P2P information sharing applications such as DistriWiki [6], Decentralized Wiki engine [7], and Peer-to-Peer Web [8,9] have attracted much attention. For this kind of application, both successful search and versatile query language support are important requirements. To guarantee successful search, unstructured P2P systems need exhaustive search techniques, where each $< item, query >$ (In this paper, we use "item", "data", "file", and "file metadata" interchangeably) pair can be evaluated with high probability and at low cost. Since network items can be in a heterogeneous format, such as html, XML, and other complex web objects, versatile query styles, such as keyword matching and XQuery [10], are preferable for a system design.

Current P2P systems mainly use three search schemes: flooding-based searching [11,1], Distributed Hash Table (DHT) looking up [12,13,14], and hybrid P2P searching [15,16,17]. In the first scheme, queries are flooded into an unstructured P2P network, suffering from excessive network traffic. DHT maintains a global index for item locating, guaranteeing a perfect successful rate while suffering from the problem of "exact match". Although some extensions based on

J. Cao et al. (Eds.): NPC 2008, LNCS 5245, pp. 173–184, 2008.

DHT are proposed to support complex queries, existing schemes incur unacceptable communication overheads [18]. Based on the observation that flooding is efficient for popular items while DHT is more suitable for rare items, Hybrid P2P [15,16,17] search schemes are proposed. A hybrid P2P network combines the unstructured protocol with the DHT global index, and performs a query by either flooding or DHT looking up according to the item's popularity.

Unstructured P2Ps are naturally the best candidate for supporting versatile queries because the matching operations can be evaluated at the nodes that store the relevant items. The first unstructured P2P protocol, Gnutella, is not scalable due to the adoption of flooding query scheme. An efficient approach to improve the search performance of unstructured P2Ps is to utilize replication strategies. The existing replication strategies can be divided into two categories. The first type is the query popularity aware strategies. The number of replicas is determined by the query's popularity. Existing research [11] claimed that the square-root replication strategy has the optimal expected search size (ESS), which is the average number of random probes required to solve a query. However, this strategy is inefficient for solving "insoluble queries", the queries for rare and non-existent items. For non-existent items, the query stop rule is crucial for reducing the search cost. Obviously, it can not guarantee the query to be searched exhaustively. The second type is independent of the popularity of a query, such as RWPS [19], Bubblestorm [20], and RandRep [21]. This kind of strategy deploys an optimal number of item replicas randomly in a P2P network to achieve probabilistically exhaustive search, without exploiting the query's popularity to reduce the query overhead. For example, in Bubblestorm, each item, popular or not, has the same number of replicas, which is determined by the network size.

The key issues for replication-based probabilistically exhaustive search in unstructured P2P networks is how to estimate the optimal number of replicas and disseminating the replicas optimally throughout the network. In this paper, we propose HRS, a hybrid replication strategy to improve the search performance of unstructured P2P networks. By combining a query popularity independent strategy with the square-root strategy, HRS can effectively handle queries for both popular and rare items. We conduct comprehensive simulations to evaluate this design. Results show that HRS outperforms existing techniques in terms of search performance and search cost.

The remainder of the paper is organized as follows. In Section 2, we review related work. The model and the problem statement are given in Section 3. Section 4 presents the design of HRS. We evaluate the performance of HRS in Section 5. We conclude in Section 6.

2   Related Work

Without centralized index servers, nodes in a decentralized P2P system have to cooperate with each other to perform a search for desired data items. Existing systems utilize replication strategies to improve the search performance. Existing replication strategies in unstructured P2P networks can be divided into two categories, the query popularity aware replication approach and the query popularity independent replication strategy.

2.1   Query Popularity Aware Replication

In this kind of strategy, the number of replicas is related to the query rates. Let r_i denote the number of replicas of item i. The sum of the replica amounts is $R = \sum_{i=1}^{m} r_i$. Let q_i denote the query rate of item i, which is the fraction of all queries that are issued for item i. The number of replicas in this strategy is $r_i = f(q_i)$. Two natural strategies among existing schemes are uniform and proportional strategies, while in the uniform replication strategy, all items are equally replicated, that is $r_i = R/m$. In the proportional replication strategy, the number of replicas is proportional to the query rates, that is $r_i = R \times q_i$. Cohen et al. [11] have studied the two query-rate based strategies. Their analysis results show that the above two strategies are not optimal as to the expected number of random probes (ESS). Another result is that the above two strategies have the same ESS and any strategies between them are better than them as to the ESS. Cohen et al. then propose the square-root replication (SRR), where the number of replicas is proportional to the square-root of the query rates. In SRR, the number of replicas is $r_i = \lambda\sqrt{q_i}$, where $\lambda = R/\sum_{i=1}^{m} \sqrt{q_i}$. They also prove that SRR is optimal as to ESS. In short, as to the expected search size, uniform strategy is the same as proportional strategy. The square-root replication strategy achieves optimal expected search size. The average search size of uniform replication strategy and proportional replication strategy is given by

$$E\left[T_{uniform}\right] = E\left[T_{proportional}\right] = \frac{Nm}{R} \tag{1}$$

The ESS of SRR is given by

$$E\left[T_{optimal}\right] = \frac{R}{N}\left(\sum_{i=1}^{m} \sqrt{q_i}\right)^2 \tag{2}$$

Although square-root replication can achieve optimal expected search size, it is only practical for "soluble queries". In SRR, the "soluble queries" are queries which can be solved within the given maximum search size. However, defining the maximum search size is not easy. For items with a small number of replicas, to guarantee exhaustive search, the number of random probes is very big. SRR refers to queries for these kinds of items as "insoluble queries", which can not be solved efficiently by SRR. Furthermore, how to divide popular and unpopular queries is also not clear. Thus, exhaustive search can not be guaranteed with high probability at low cost in this scheme.

2.2   Query Popularity Independent Replication

Recently, the query popularity independent replication strategy has attracted much attention. All items are equally replicated regardless of the popularity of the related queries. For file search, queries are replicated to some random nodes. The well-chosen parameters guarantee the collision of item replica and query with high probability. This idea is inspired by the birthday paradox [22]. However, since item and query replications are two independent processes, the birthday paradox can not be directly used to design the related parameters.

RWPS [19] firstly propose this kind of replication in a Gnutella network. To implement the installation of replicas, RWPS employs random walk to sample some random nodes. RWPS can guarantee exhaustive search with high probability. However, random walk is not fault-tolerant, a failed node in the path could reduce replica amount. Thus, the search success probability can not be guaranteed. On the other hand, random walk has long latency.

To overcome the shortcoming of RWPS, Terpstra et al. propose Bubblestorm [20] to achieve probabilistic and exhaustive search. Bubblestorm employs random multi-graph to connect peers. The related joining and leaving protocols are designed to keep the attributes of random multi-graph. To improve the performance of message propagating, they also design a new algorithm-bubblecast to distribute replicas and queries, which is the combination of both random walk and flooding.

RandRep [21] is another implementation of query rate independent replication. In this scheme, a lightweight DHT is employed to support network size estimation and random node selection. All items have equal numbers of replicas. To guarantee the search success with high probability, the number of replicas is carefully determined. Let r and q denote the numbers of item replicas and query replicas, respectively. If $rq \geq N\left((1 + \varepsilon \ln N) + \sqrt{(1 + \varepsilon \ln N)^2 - 1}\right)$, the probability of two kinds of replicas encountering in at least one node is $P \geq 1 - N^{-\varepsilon}$, where $\varepsilon > 0$ is a constant. For current P2P network size, it is suitable that the value of rq is $N(2 + \ln N)$. If the traffic of each query and item replica is the same, the value of r and q is $\sqrt{N(2 + \varepsilon \ln N)}$, that is to say $r = q = O(\sqrt{N \ln N})$.

Query popularity independent strategy can achieve exhaustive search with high probability. Since the query popularity is not considered in this strategy, it is not optimal for popular queries in terms of search cost. The drawback of such strategy is very clear. Uniformly replicating all items including the infrequently queried ones, is inefficient. On the contrary, for the popular queried items, a small number of query replicas can efficiently reduce the overall cost of the search system.

3   System Model and Problem Statement

The model is related to the overlay network, item replicas, and queries. The network is composed of N nodes. Several approaches for obtaining the network size N have been proposed, for example [23,24]. There are m items shared in the network. Each item, i, is replicated at r_i sites. The vector of replica amounts is $(r_1, r_2, \ldots, r_m)$. The sum of the replica amounts is $R = \sum_{i=1}^{m} r_i$. The query rate vector for items is $(q_1, q_2, \ldots, q_m)$, where q_i is the query-rate for item i, which

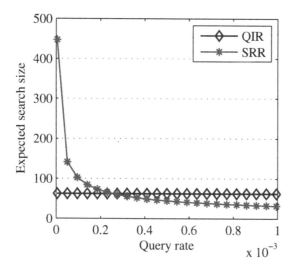

Fig. 1. Search size comparison for QIR and SRR

is the fraction of all queries issued for item i. The rate q_i is normalized, that is $\sum_{i=1}^{m} q_i = 1$. If all items are equally replicated, the number of replicas is denoted as r. Correspondingly the query amounts for specific items are equal, which is denoted as q. In this kind of P2P sharing network, we consider the random search method adopted in [11]. This random search method sends query messages to random nodes in the network until the query is answered or the search reaches the maximum size. There are several approaches to achieve the random nodes, for example, the combination of random multi-graph with bubblecast in Bubblestorm [20] and the RandRep scheme which combines a lightweight DHT with an unstructured P2P overlay to address random peer sampling [21].

In this paper, we propose HRS, a hybrid replication strategy to improve the search performance of unstructured P2P networks. HRS performs an exhaustive search, which probabilistically guarantees that the application's query evaluator runs on a peer containing a replica of the related item. By combining a query popularity independent strategy with the square-root strategy, HRS can effectively handle queries for items, popular or not. We address the following problem. What is the efficient and practical replication strategy for a query issued in unstructured P2P networks regardless of how popular it is?

4   HRS Replication

For real systems, popular queries, unpopular queries, and even queries for non existent items should all be considered. Square-root replication strategy is just practical for popular queries. As for unpopular queries and queries for non existent items, query rate independent replication (QIR) strategy is better than square-root replication strategy. Figure 1 illustrates the search size comparison of QIR and SRR in a 50,000 node network. At the query rate about 0.27, QIR and SRR have the same search size. Prior to that, QIR has a smaller search size. After that, SRR performs better. Therefore, it would be reasonable to combine SRR and QIR to meet the requirements of real systems. Based on the observation, we propose HRS, which is a combination of SRR and QIR. The challenge here is how to implement the effects of both SRR and QIR.

4.1 HRS Strategy

Replication strategy is an allocation of replicas for each item. The objective is to improve the related performance metrics. In order to consider both query and item popularity, the following allocation function is given.

$$r_i = f(N, q_i) \tag{3}$$

For an item with very small q_i, to guarantee exhaustive search, the fraction of all nodes which have a replica of item i should be bigger than a given threshold. Under this condition, this item can be searched within a given maximum search size with high probability. If the maximum search size is reached while the item is not found, it is the case that there are no such item in the network with high probability. In the QIR strategies, each item has an equal number of replicas to guarantee the exhaustive search. Thus, this value can be treated as the minimization of the number of replicas in HRS. That is given by

$$r_{min} = \sqrt{N\left(2 + \ln N\right)} \tag{4}$$

On the other hand, the query rate should be considered. Obviously, we should incorporate the square-root strategy in HRS. There is a critical point of the query rate. At this point, we have the below equation.

$$\sqrt{N\left(2 + \ln N\right)} = \frac{R \times \sqrt{q_i}}{\sum_{j=1}^{m} \sqrt{q_j}} \tag{5}$$

Then, the critical point of the query rate is

$$q_c = \frac{N(2 + \ln N)(\sum_{j=1}^{m} \sqrt{q_j})^2}{R^2} \tag{6}$$

Therefore, for items with query rate bigger than q_c, the square-root strategy is employed. Other items should have r_{min} replicas.

According to above analysis, the HRS replica allocation function is given by

$$r_i = \begin{cases} \sqrt{N(2 + \ln N)} & \text{where } q_i < q_c \\ \frac{R \times \sqrt{q_i}}{\sum_{j=1}^{m} \sqrt{q_j}} & \text{where } q_i \geq q_c \end{cases} \tag{7}$$

4.2 Implementation of HRS

HRS employs reactive operations to replicate items. Two actions trigger the replication operation. The first action is node joining. At this point, there are no replicas of items shared by this node. The corresponding query rates are zero, which is obviously smaller than the critical point p_c. Therefore, a minimum number of replicas should be distributed in the network. The new node replicate their items to r_{min} random nodes. This operation guarantees an exhaustive search with high probability. The second action is item querying. A query to item F may succeed or fail. If $s \leq \sqrt{N(2 + \ln N)}$ probes are required to get the answer, s replicas of item F are added into the network after the search. Otherwise, the query fails, which implies that the queried item is non existent. This operation is used to maintain the square-root replication strategy.

We adopt random walk to implement HRS. Random walk is an efficient approach to solve problems in random networks, for example, resource search [25], overlay construction [26]. Another important functionality of random walk is random node sampling which is the base for random replication. As to the sampling efficiency, it is optimal for sampling r random nodes at the cost of r messages. Unstructured P2P networks have two important attributes related to node sampling. The first is that the topology is modeled as a random graph. Usually, the Poisson random graph and power-law random graph [27] are used to model unstructured P2P networks. The second attribute is that P2P systems are dynamic system. Nodes can only maintain their neighborhood information efficiently. Due to the two attributes, random walk is a reasonable approach for sampling random node subset. HRS employs random walk to implement optimal random node subset sampling.

For arbitrary node $v_i \in V$, $\Gamma(v_i)$ is the set of nodes which connect to node v_i and $d_i = |\Gamma(v_i)|$ is the degree of node v_i. Random walk on a graph is a sequence of nodes, for example $v_0, v_1, \cdots, v_i, v_j, \cdots$. If the position is v_i at time t, the probability of reach vertex v_j at time $t + 1$ is:

$$p_{ij} = \begin{cases} 1/d_i & \text{if } i \neq j \text{ and } j \in \Gamma(v_i) \\ 0 & \text{otherwise} \end{cases} \tag{8}$$

Random walk on a graph is a Markov chain. The corresponding probability transition matrix is $P = \{p_{ij}\}$. The initial distribution is denoted as $\pi(0)$. The distribution at time t is $\pi(t)$. If the Markov chain is irreducible, finite, and aperiodic, this Markov chain has unique stationary distribution [28]. Random walk on P2P networks is corresponding to this kind of Markov chain. If the graph is regular, random walk reaches each node with equal probability after the Markov chain converging. However, P2P networks are not regular graph, simple random walk can not obtain uniform sampling. Two alternatives are proposed to address uniform sampling in non-regular graph. The first is the Maximum Degree random walk (MD), in which the graph is converted to regular graph by adding self-loop to low degree nodes. The second is the Metropolis-Hasting random walk (MH). The transition probability of MH is given by

$$p_{ij} = \begin{cases} 1/\max(d_i, d_j) & \text{if } i \neq j \text{ and } j \in \Gamma(i) \\ 1 - \sum_{j \in \Gamma(i)} p_{ij} & \text{if } i = j \\ 0 & \text{otherwise} \end{cases} \tag{9}$$

In HRS, MH is used to sample nodes. The time from the initial distribution to the stationary distribution is called mixing time. Although MD is very simple, its mixing time is bigger than that of MH [29]. The existing random walk based node sampling algorithms are one random node each time. For sampling a random subset, it is straightforward to sample multiple times. Due to excessive message overhead and big latency, however, this strategy is not practical. According to recently research results, we find that the efficiency of random walk-based sampling can be improved. For MH random walk on a random graph, continuous s steps obtain s random nodes. After random walk on a random graph converges, the successive s steps obtain s random nodes [26]. For random walk start from node A, it reaches node B after convergence. As to A, B is a random node. According to the reverse random walk path principle [30], A is also a random node for B. Since s step random walk from B is a sampling of s random nodes, s step random walk from A is also a sampling of s random nodes. That is to say, s step random walk from arbitrary node obtains s random nodes.

HRS can efficiently solve queries for any items. In HRS, the baseline of the replica amount for any item is r. This setting guarantees all queries can be solved or ended with at most $\left\lceil \sqrt{N(2 + \ln N)} \right\rceil$ probes. For popular queries, the reactive replication operation inserts additional replicas into the network. As the replica amount increases, the search size decreases. However, the search cost for each query does not increase.

5   Performance Evaluation

In this section, we present the performance metrics, experimental setup, and performance evaluation in our simulations.

5.1   Simulation Methodology

Many metrics are related to the search performance, for example, search success probability, search size, search traffic, search cost, and query delay. In HRS, the replica amount guarantees the search success with high probability. As for queries for non existent items, the search stop rule is the maximum search size. Therefore, it is not necessary to measure the search success probability. In the design, the random probe is used to search items, which is also adopted in the square-root replication strategy [11]. In the evaluation of HRS, we are mainly concerned with search size and search cost. The search size is the number of random probes until the termination of the search. The search cost is averaged. For some item, the number of replicas is x. The number of queries for this item is y. If the sum of probes is p, the search cost is $(x + p)/y$.

In the simulation, networks with 10,000, 300,000, 500,000, 700,000, 900,000, and 110,000 nodes are constructed. Initially, each item is treated as a new item and uniformly replicated at $\left\lceil \sqrt{N(2 + \ln N)} \right\rceil$ random nodes. Queries for these items are put into the network to trigger the replication. The measurements of real P2P systems show that the popularity of queries follow a Zipf-like distribution [31]. For a query with popularity rank i, the number of this query is proportional to $i^{-\alpha}$. In the simulation, the parameter α is 0.6 according to the measurements. We generate the queries according to the Zipf distribution and insert these queries into the networks.

5.2   Results

Firstly, we implement the QIR strategy. Each item is equally replicated, then, different queries are issued. Each query is repeated 10,000 times and the averages are calculated. The result is illustrated in Fig. 2. Compared with the network size, the number of replicated items is small. The average number of probes for search success is also very small. For a network with 110,000 nodes, this value is about 100.

The search performance of HRS is shown in Fig. 3. The results from 50,000, 70,000, and 90,000 node networks are illustrated. In the simulation, each query is repeated 10,000 times and the average is calculated. As the number of queries increases, the number of probes decreases rapidly. This distribution shows that the query popularity can be exploited to reduce the search size.

Figure 4 is the search cost comparison of HRS and QIR. The network size is 100,000. When the query is not popular, HRS and QIR have almost the same search cost. As the query popularity increases, the search cost gap of HRS and QIR becomes larger. Furthermore, we study the sum of search cost under Zipf query popularity distribution. The results are illustrated in Fig. 5 in which the parameter α is 0.6. The search cost of HRS is less than that of QIR.

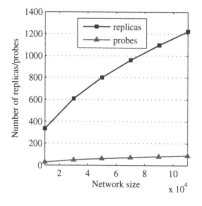 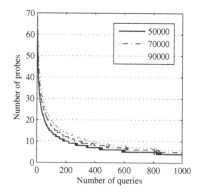

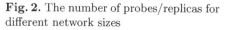

Fig. 2. The number of probes/replicas for different network sizes

Fig. 3. The search size of HRS in networks with different sizes

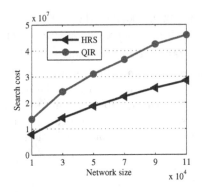 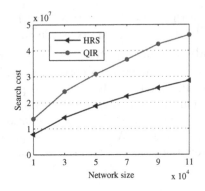

Fig. 4. The search cost comparison of HRS and QIR

Fig. 5. The search cost comparison with Zipf query popularity distribution ($\alpha = 0.6$)

6   Conclusions

To address the issue of exhaustive search in unstructured P2P networks, we propose HRS, a hybrid replication strategy to improve the search performance of unstructured P2P networks. By combining a query popularity independent strategy with the square-root strategy, HRS can effectively handle queries, popular or not. We evaluate this design through mathematical proof and comprehensive simulations. Results show that HRS can achieve a small search size at a reasonable search cost. Therefore, HRS is a practical replication strategy for real P2P systems.

Acknowledgements

This work was supported by National Science Foundation of China (NSFC) under grants No.60433040 and No. 60473090, NSFC/RGC Joint Research Foundation under grant No.60731160630, and National 973 Key Basic Research Program under grant No.2003CB317003.

References

1. Liu, Y., Liu, X., Xiao, L., Ni, L.M., Zhang, X.: Location-aware topology matching in p2p systems. In: Proceedings of IEEE INFOCOM 2004, Hong Kong, China. IEEE, Los Alamitos (2004)
2. Cao, J., Liu, F.B., Xu, C.Z.: P2pgrid: integrating p2p networks into the grid environment. Concurr. Comput. Pract. Exper. 19(7), 1023–1046 (2007)
3. Li, M., Lee, W.C., Sivasubramaniam, A.: Semantic small world: An overlay network for peer-to-peer search. In: Proceedings of IEEE ICNP 2004, Washington, DC, USA, pp. 228–238. IEEE Computer Society Press, Los Alamitos (2004)
4. Saroiu, S., Gummadi, K., Gribble, S.: Measuring and analyzing the characteristics of napster and gnutella hosts. Multimedia Systems Journal 9(2), 170–184 (2003)

5. Chawathe, Y., Ratnasamy, S., Breslau, L., Lanham, N., Shenker, S.: Making gnutella-like p2p systems scalable. In: Proceedings of ACM SIGCOMM 2003, Karlsruhe, Germany, pp. 407–418. ACM, New York (2003)
6. Morris, J.C.: Distriwiki: a distributed peer-to-peer wiki network. In: Proceedings of ACM ISW 2007, Quebec, Canada, pp. 69–74. ACM, New York (2007)
7. Urdaneta, G., Pierre, G., Steen, M.v.: A decentralized wiki engine for collaborative wikipedia hosting. In: Proceedings of WEBIST 2007, Barcelona, Spain, pp. 855–858. Springer, Heidelberg (2007)
8. Chen, H., Jin, H., Wang, J., Liu, Y., Ni, L.M.: Efficient multi-keyword search over p2p web. In: Proceedings of ACM WWW 2008, Beijing, China, pp. 989–997. ACM, New York (2008)
9. Deshpande, M., Amit, A., Chang, M., Venkatasubramanian, N., Mehrotra, S.: Flashback: A peer-to-peer web server for flash crowds. In: Proceedings of IEEE ICDCS 2007, Toronto, Ontario, Canada, p. 15. IEEE, Los Alamitos (2007)
10. Chamberlin, D.: Xquery: a query language for XML. In: Proceedings of ACM SIGMOD 2003, San Diego, California, USA, p. 682. ACM, New York (2003)
11. Cohen, E., Shenker, S.: Replication strategies in unstructured peer-to-peer networks. In: Proceedings of ACM SIGCOMM 2002, Pittsburgh, PA, USA, pp. 177–190. ACM, New York (2002)
12. Stoica, I., Morris, R., Karger, D., Kaashoek, M.F., Balakrishnan, H.: Chord: a scalable peer-to-peer lookup service for internet applications. In: Proceedings of ACM SIGCOMM 2001, San Diego, California, USA, pp. 149–160. ACM, New York (2001)
13. Ratnasamy, S., Francis, P., Handley, M., Karp, R., Schenker, S.: A scalable content-addressable network. In: Proceedings of ACM SIGCOMM 2001, San Francisco, California, USA, pp. 161–172. ACM, New York (2001)
14. Zhao, B.Y., Huang, L., Stribling, J., Rhea, S.C., Joseph, A.D., Kubiatowicz, J.D.: Tapestry: a resilient global-scale overlay for service deployment. IEEE Journal on Selected Areas in Communications 22(1), 41–53 (2004)
15. Loo, B.T., Huebsch, R., Stoica, I., Hellerstein, J.M.: The case for a hybrid p2p search infrastructure. In: Voelker, G.M., Shenker, S. (eds.) IPTPS 2004. LNCS, vol. 3279, pp. 141–150. Springer, Heidelberg (2005)
16. Chen, H., Jin, H., Liu, Y., Ni, L.M.: Difficulty-aware hybrid search in peer-to-peer networks. IEEE Transactions on Parallel and Distributed Systems (TPDS) (2008)
17. Zaharia, M., Keshav, S.: Gossip-based search selection in hybrid peer-to-peer networks. In: Proceedings of IPTPS 2006, Santa Barbara, CA, USA (2006)
18. Li, J., Loo, B.T., Hellerstein, J., Kaashoek, F., Karger, D.R., Morris, R.: On the feasibility of peer-to-peer web indexing and search. In: Kaashoek, M.F., Stoica, I. (eds.) IPTPS 2003. LNCS, vol. 2735, pp. 207–215. Springer, Heidelberg (2003)
19. Ferreira, R.A., Ramanathan, M.K., Awan, A., Grama, A., Jagannathan, S.: Search with probabilistic guarantees in unstructured peer-to-peer networks. In: Proceedings of P2P 2005, Konstanz, Germany, pp. 165–172. IEEE, Los Alamitos (2005)
20. Terpstra, W.W., Kangasharju, J., Leng, C., Buchmann, A.P.: Bubblestorm: Resilient, probabilistic, and exhaustive peer-to-peer search. In: Proceedings of ACM SIGCOMM 2007, Kyoto, Japan, pp. 49–60. ACM, New York (2007)
21. Luo, X., Qin, Z., Han, J., Chen, H.: Dht-assisted probabilistic exhaustive search in unstructured p2p networks. In: Proceedings of IEEE IPDPS 2008, Miami, Florida, USA. IEEE, Los Alamitos (2008)
22. Motwani, R., Raghavan, P.: Randomized Algorithms. Cambridge University Press, Cambridge (1995)

23. Massouli, L., Le Merrer, E., Kermarrec, A.M., Ganesh, A.: Peer counting and sampling in overlay networks: Random walk methods. In: Proceedings of ACM PODC 2006, Denver, CO, USA, pp. 123–132. ACM, New York (2006)

24. Kostoulas, D., Psaltoulis, D., Gupta, I., Birman, K., Demers, A.: Decentralized schemes for size estimation in large and dynamic groups. In: Proceedings of IEEE NCA 2005, Cambridge, MA, USA, pp. 41–48. IEEE, Los Alamitos (2005)

25. Lv, Q., Cao, P., Cohen, E., Li, K., Shenker, S.: Search and replication in unstructured peer-to-peer networks. In: Proceedings of ACM ICS 2002, pp. 84–95. ACM, New York (2002)

26. Gkantsidis, C., Mihail, M., Saberi, A.: Random walks in peer-to-peer networks. In: Proceedings of IEEE INFOCOM 2004, Hong Kong, China. IEEE, Los Alamitos (2004)

27. Barabasi, A.L., Albert, R.: Emergence of scaling in random networks. Science 286, 509 (1999)

28. Lovasz, L.: Combinatorics. Paul Erdos is Eighty 2(2), 353–398 (1996)

29. Awan, A., Ferreira, R.A., Jagannathan, S., Grama, A.: Distributed uniform sampling in unstructured peer-to-peer networks. In: Proceedings of HICSS 2006, Washington, DC, USA, p. 223.3. IEEE, Los Alamitos (2006)

30. Bar-Yossef, Z., Friedman, R., Kliot, G.: Rawms - random walk based lightweight membership service for wireless ad hoc networks. ACM Trans. Comput. Syst. 26(2), 1–66 (2008)

31. Sripanidkulchai, K.: The popularity of gnutella queries and its implications on scalability. In: Oram, A. (ed.) The O'Reilly Peer-to-Peer and Web Services Conference. O'Reilly, Sebastopol (2001)

ResourceDog: A Trusted Resource Discovery and Automatic Invocation P2P Framework

Bowei Yang, Guanghua Song, and Yao Zheng

College of Computer Science, and Center for Engineering and Scientific Computation,
Zhejiang University, Hangzhou, 310027, P.R. China
boweiy@zju.edu.cn, ghsong@cs.zju.edu.cn, yao.zheng@zju.edu.cn

Abstract. In this paper we propose a trusted resource discovery and automatic invocation P2P framework. It provides a series of amazing features to overcome the drawbacks of existing P2P frameworks, such as totally decentralized structured and semantic searchable topology based on dual level DHT network hierarchy, distributed metadata storage, unified resource abstraction and trusted recommendation system based on statistic model of reputation. The Resource-Dog framework provides a mechanism to discovery resources by tags, prepare runtime environment for resources automatically, gather and model out rank of rating for resources. The results demonstrate that the ResourceDog framework provides convenient, powerful and trusted resources for general users in P2P environment.

Keywords: P2P, dual level DHT, resource abstraction, reputation system.

1 Introduction

1.1 Motivation

In the recent years, Peer-to-Peer (P2P) computing has gained a lot of popularity in many distributed applications over the Internet. These include distributed file sharing [5, 6], high performance computing [19] and so on.

In this paper we discuss a framework, called ResourceDog, for unifying the most important features of grid computing and P2P computing into a common computing framework.

Currently, grid computing is mainly providing services for scientific computing, and grid frameworks usually focus on providing highly reliable services on small scale but stable infrastructures [20]. On the contrary, P2P frameworks manage larger scale but not so devoted nodes. Not only scientific computing but also general computing needs a relatively unified, stable, flexible, reliable and high-powered framework. However most of existing popular P2P systems only cover file sharing and all of them are obsessed with single point of failure, non-supported to various resources or unable to identify malicious nodes. Original Bittorrent [5] or Emule [6] needs a central server for seeds storing, Bittorrent protocol with DHT [1, 2, 3, 4] technology can't support searching for resources, none of them implement service oriented architecture. Since all of the control information of the P2P network is stored in the central

J. Cao et al. (Eds.): NPC 2008, LNCS 5245, pp. 185–195, 2008.
© IFIP International Federation for Information Processing 2008

server, all of the services will be down if the central server is down. The ResourceDog framework enables the automatically computing services invocation based on P2P architecture. Furthermore, statistical recommendation feature is included to resist malicious behaviors and to encourage contribution behaviors.

The presented P2P framework includes resource discovery algorithm, resource utilize architecture and recommendation model based on reputation and ranking. The three main parts will be covered in this paper respectively.

1.2 Solution Overview

Axis [7] is introduced as the main engine of ResourceDog to take advantage of standard web services, thus all language compatible with standard WSDL [8] will be accepted as the compatible service provider language. Dual level DHT mapping combined with word splitting method is adopted to provide the classical DHT topology with semantic search feature. Semantic Web service [9] and ontology is pulled in for service automatic invocation, and an innovational positive feedback statistic model is drawn out to support recommendation which tries to simulate the scenario in our social network.

2 Design

First we describe our ResourceDog P2P framework in its most basic form, in the below subsections we present the details.

In a P2P environment, node A may interact with any nodes in the same network, we represent the transaction from node A to B as $T_{a,b}(TN)$, where node A is the initiator and node B is acceptor, TN refers the name for the resource on node B. Two types of transaction are included in the P2P environment, the first is control transaction, and the second is functional transaction. Control transaction exists for maintaining P2P structure, notifying newly added nodes, reputation rating storage and retrieval and so on; Functional transaction is customized by resource providers of ResourceDog, which includes but not limited to file sharing, scientific computing, image processing and instant chat. In addition, after every transaction $T_{a,b}(TN)$, node A should provides a rating for this transaction denoted by $R_{a,b}(TN)$. This rating is maintained by several nodes in the dual level DHT network. Before every transaction starts, the recommendation rating worked out by modeling all the ratings for a resource TN on target node X $R_x(TN)$ will be presented to the initiator to assist in making decision.

2.1 Routing and Searching in the ResourceDog Framework

A ResourceDog node maintains a coordinate routing table that holds the IP address, last visit time (LVT), and the unique identifier (UID) for every node that has contacted with itself or obtained from its neighbors. All of the routing data is stored in the Derby [10] embedded database, with index key UID for fast accessing and retrieving. Compared with the improvement to speed up resource searching, lots of rare occupied coefficient routing data is meritorious, so the routing data purging process could be started with a long period. In our approach, the expression of UID for node A listened on IP AA.BB.CC.DD is:

$$UID(N_a) = (AA << 24) \mid (BB << 16) \mid (CC << 8) \mid DD \tag{1}$$

In ResourceDog, every resource such as files or services will be described with a short phrase stored in the metadata of this resource. During the resource publish process, ResourceDog will split words of the phrase, filter them and publish all of the meaningful words to remote nodes, the same as what the general search engine does.

Our example framework is implemented with Java, however, the method java.lang.String.hashCode() is too simple to generate a random and well-proportioned distributed hash code, Algorithm 1 presents a proved suitable enough method to achieve this goal in our environment.

Algo. 1. The hashcode generate procedure.

```
A = SUM((Integer)(every four bytes of input word))
B = 16807 * (A % 127773) - 2836 * (A / 127773)
IF B > 0 THEN:
    Return B
ELSE
    Return B + 2147483647
ENDIF
```

In addition, the distance D_{ar} between one node N_a with $UID(N_a)$ and one resource R_r with hash code HashCode(R_r) is:

$$D_{ar} = ABS(UID(N_a) - HashCode(R_r)) \tag{2}$$

In the resource publish process, ResourceDog will filter all the index words, and publish them to the M most nearest nodes as the 1st DHT indexes for searching to every word respectively. And N copies of metadata for the resource should be published to network as the 2nd DHT indexes for reputation integrity checking, too. Here, M and N are the parameters to balance the robustness and overhead of ResourceDog P2P framework.

Figure 1 shows an example scenario. Node G is the provider of resource "calcPI", and "calc(ln(x))" is provided by node H, G published 3 copies of 1st DHT layer indexes, "calc", "calculate" and "PI" to node B, node D and node C respectively according to the most nearest publishing algorithm, 2 copy of 2nd DHT layer index , "calcPI" to node F and itself, also node H published 3 copies of 1st DHT layer indexes, "calc", "calculate" and "ln(x)" to node B, node D and node E. As a client, node A provides "calculate" as the search key word, it checks its own nodes cache, and select M most nearest nodes to HashCode("calculate"), node D is one of them. Node D will transfer to node A a list of resources which provide "calculate" as the 1st DHT layer search key word. In the demo shown in Figure 1, both of "calcPI" and

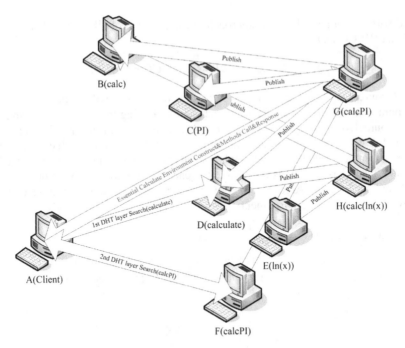

Fig. 1. An example of resource discovery

"calc(ln(x))" provide "calculate" as the 1st DHT layer search key word, so "calcPI" and "calc(ln(x))" will be returned to node A, node A may select node F or node G for the details of "calcPI". Then node A will compare the rating provided by node F with that provided by node G to check whether node G has been increased the rating by itself. If the rating on most of 2nd DHT layer nodes (says node F) linked with "calcPI" is different with that provided by the servant (says node G), the servant will be marked as cheating. At last node A get the host information (node G) of "calcPI", and requests details from node G.

As shown in Figure 1, the reason that Node F holds "calcPI" as the 2nd DHT layer index is not only accelerating the search process, but also checking the integrity and authenticity of metadata for resources, for all of the recommendation data can be accessed by clients.

After every transaction, the two nodes will exchange their own nodes cache, and every node in the network will check their own cached resource indexes periodically, if one of the resources is invalid or the entry is idle for some times, the index entry will be deleted. After every changing to the cache of a resource provider, it will calculate the remapping of the resource, if modification is required, it will republish the index of resource to network.

To a totally new participator, a list of bootstrap nodes is essential to join the P2P network. The functioning of ResourceDog framework doesn't depend on the details how this is done, but we adopt JXTA [11] as our bootstrap mechanism in the demonstration. The detailed demonstration will be shown in section 3.

2.2 Automatic Invocation

The ResourceDog framework provides a mechanism to access resources without any manual intervention. A resource will be defined as a mixture of file transfers and several remote method calls, simplified ontology is adopted to describe the structure of calling stubs. ResourceDog framework provides a session-like status machine routine to check whether the necessary precondition is satisfied. Lots of security mechanisms are implemented to enhance the framework, such as RSA asymmetric encryption and three-way handshake just like the same in TCP/IP protocol. All of the public keys will be treated as normal resources, they're stored and accessed by the same routine introduced in section 2.1.

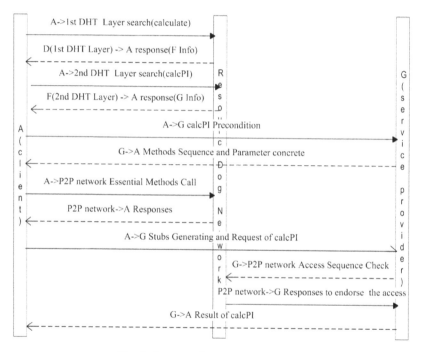

Fig. 2. An example resource automaton

A simplified resource call sequence demonstrated in Figure 1 is shown in Figure 2. All of the background transactions will be transparent to the end user.

2.3 Reputation and Recommendation

Currently, lots of P2P systems are receiving accusations that malicious nodes, free-ride [12] and bad behaviors are flooding over them, so security, trust, ranking and recommendation mechanism is urgently required by P2P systems. Various models [13, 14] are proposed to add rating or ranking feature to P2P systems, but few of them adopt statistical model to generate a recommendation rating for later comers to simulate the scenario in our social network.

Rating for transactions is widely used in modern auction websites, Ebay [15] will ask the clients to vote for the transaction they participated, 1 for "Positive", 0 for "Neutral" and -1 for "Negative", so that the later comers will know the ratios for all of "Positive", "Neutral" and "Negative".

ResourceDog will refine the result of the voting for resources. A statistic modeling will take all of the voting data as input and generate a recommendation ratio for later comers.

In our voting system, all of the voters will vote for a certain resource in their own ways. The vote rating will follow the Gaussian distribution as the voting goes on, since the voting behaviors are independent of each other. Figure 3 will show several probability and cumulative distributions for Gaussian distribution.

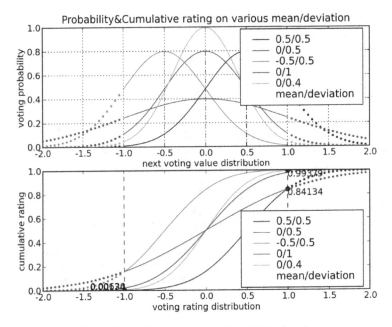

Fig. 3. Probability and cumulative distribution chart

The cumulative distribution function (*cdf*) can be formulated by an airy function called "Error Function" (*erf*).

Error function is used widely in probability, statistics, partial differential equations, and denoise-smoothing communication.

$$cdf(x) = \frac{1}{2}\left(1 + erf\left(\frac{x-\mu}{\sigma\sqrt{2}}\right)\right) \qquad (3)$$

$$erf(x) = \frac{2}{\sqrt{\pi}} \int_0^x e^{-t^2} dt \qquad (4)$$

ResourceDog framework generates the recommendation rating for a certain resource using cumulative function denoted by error function.

The recommendation rating (RRR) for a certain resource t with total cumulative rating ($\sum_0^n R(TN_{x,t})$) will be:

$$RRR_x(\sum_0^n R(TN_{x,t})) = erf(coefficient * \frac{\sum_0^n R(TN_{x,t})}{n}) \tag{5}$$

After a voting of Z with voting rating for this transaction ($R(TN_{z,t}')$), RRR' will be:

$$RRR_x' = erf(coefficient * \sum_0^{n+1} R(TN_{x,t}))$$

$$= coefficient * cdf'(x)$$

$$= coefficient * \frac{1}{2} * (1 + erf(\frac{\frac{\sum_0^n R(TN_{x,t}) + R(TN_{z,t}')}{n+1}}{\sigma'\sqrt{2}})) \tag{6}$$

ResourceDog will store every $R(TN_{x,t})$ of TN_t on the 2nd layer DHT network, since every 2nd layer DHT nodes is determinate by well-known Hashing algorithm, so that clients are able to check the integrity of recommendation of resources with different 2nd layer DHT nodes. Malicious nodes will be detected easily by the routine illuminated in figure 1.

3   Experiments

3.1   Routing and Searching

In order to demonstrate the usage of this framework and to evaluate the performance, we will give out several demos.

We built a local area network comprised of 30 PCs, all the PCs run different operating systems including Linux and Windows. They are divided into 4 100M based fast ethernet network segments. All nodes are configured with a stable enough initializing seeding node.

A node in the network will collect neighbor nodes information every 5 minutes from all the known neighbors or exchange with buddies after every transaction. A node in figure 4 received a notification of neighbor changing at 47 minutes for a transaction occurred at that point.

The first demo we present is a simple numeric computing Message Passing Interface (MPI) [16] parallel routine, a general LAM-MPI [17] parallel process will be invoked by ResourceDog framework.

The numeration integration of Π can be presented by:

$$\Pi = \int_0^1 \frac{4}{1+x^2} dx \tag{7}$$

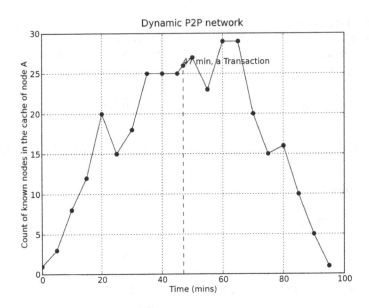

Fig. 4. Demonstrating for dynamic changing of our P2P network

Π equals the area surround by the curve and x-axis on [0, 1], so the area can be approximately calculated by lots of rectangles, in our demo, we divide [0, 1] into 1,000,000,000 intervals, and accumulate all of their areas. The execution time comparison of pure LAM-MPI and LAM-MPI on the ResourceDog framework using variant number of nodes in a cluster is listed in Table 1.

Table 1. Execution time(s) comparison

Test platform	1 node	2 nodes	4 nodes	8 nodes	16 nodes
Pure LAM-MPI	50.921	25.461	12.748	6.388	3.204
Resource Dog	52.114	26.701	13.904	7.572	4.331

According to Table 1, Resource Dog P2P framework takes about one second to prepare the environment for MPI execution such as authentication and remote process calling in our demo.

3.2 Resource Automatic Invocation

Web service based on HTTP protocol is connectionless oriented, so real time resources can't be built on traditional web service platform. The second demo will introduce a new architecture for real time resources on ResourceDog. An Internet Relay

Chat (IRC) [18] like chatting service has been implemented on our ResourceDog connectionless oriented framework.

In the chat service, nodes is grouped by the topic servers, ResourceDog servers can setup a topic service and publish the metadata to the DHT network as the way JXTA [11] publishes pipeline advertisements, others interested with the topic can join the channel, two actions will be taken during the joining process. First, the client create a socket with the local ResourceDog server, second, the local ResourceDog server registers itself to the topic server. After every receiving of messages, the topic server will scan the registered local servers list, and send the message to them one by one, then the local server will send the message to its client in time via local connection oriented socket. No connections will be established between topic server and the local servers. Thus real-time chatting is achieved on the connectionless framework.

3.3 Reputation and Recommendation Simulation

In this section, we will show the experimental result by a simulated demonstration.

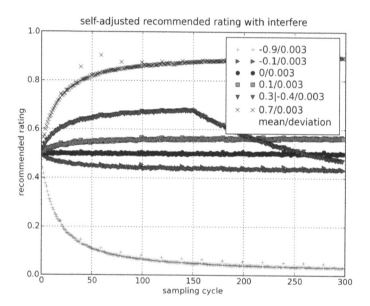

Fig. 5. Recommended rating after every voting

As shown in Figure 5, we simulate 300 users to rate for 6 resources respectively. Every user will vote for a resource at a normal distribution with certain mean value and standard deviation, also an interferential voting is included every 20 cycles. The simulated result shows a good-fit chart for true situation, since the recommendation rating accurately shows the cumulative effect of ratings and can be self-adjusted to anti-interference as the voting going on, moreover the resource will never be totally opponent or recommended.

4 Related Works

There have been some researches focusing on various aspects of P2P framework. Some interesting models and frameworks have been proposed. Here we describe a few related examples from two aspects, resource discovery and trust computing.

JXTA [11] community sponsored by Sun micro system mainly aims to build a wide area P2P network composed of all of smart devices. It provides a convenience and platform independent routine to organize all of nodes and access the demanded resource. However, as the core conception of JXTA framework, advertisements can't support semantic search, so JXTA framework does not overcome the search problems. Also JXTA framework never refers to reputation problems of nodes in the network.

In trust computing area, some researches just focus on the hierarchy of reputation system and reputation data storage strategy [21].

EigenTrust [22] only worked out the global reputation rating for nodes, but ignored ratings of resources, also it doesn't simulate the real society network to give out the recommendation rating based on statistical models.

In [23], Damiani et al. propose a distributed reputation sharing and assessing model, based on Gnutella. They developed a protocol for Gnutella to enhancement the security and reliability of nodes and resources in Gnutella by assigning, sharing, and combining reputations on servants and resources.

5 Conclusions and Future Work

In this paper, we discussed the architecture and algorithm of the ResourceDog P2P framework. ResourceDog provides a complete discovery, invocation and recommendation P2P platform that caters scientific computing, flexible computing and trusted computing. The experimental results show that ResourceDog is more stable, flexible and secure than most of existing P2P platforms. Applications on the Internet, such as file sharing, real-time chatting, and format transformation can be managed and rated properly under the framework. Therefore, we can utilize variant applications in one-stop framework and defend the malicious behaviors.

At present, only some typical types of resources have been tested on ResourceDog, we will try to deploy more types of resources in the framework. Furthermore, smarter searching with Semantic Web services and optimized routing algorithms will be adopted to adapt for the complex real-network.

References

[1] Ratnasamy, S., Francis, P., Handley, M., Karp, R., Shenker, S.: A scalable contentaddressable network. In: Proceedings of the ACM SIGCOMM, San Diego, CA, August 2001, pp. 161–172 (2001)
[2] Stoica, I., Morris, R., Karger, D., Kaashoek, F., Balakrishnan, H.: Chord: A scalable PeerToPeer lookup service for internet applications. In: Proceedings of the ACM SIGCOMM, pp. 149–160 (2001)

[3] Druschel, P., Rowstron, A.: Pastry: Scalable, distributed object location and routing for largescale peertopeer systems. In: Proc. of the 18th IFIP/ACM International Conference on Distributed Systems Platforms(Middleware 2001) (November 2001)

[4] Zhao, B., Kubiatowicz, J., Joseph, A.: Tapestry: An infrastructure for faulttolerant widearea location and routing. University of California at Berkeley, Computer Science Department, Tech. Rep. UCB/CSD011141 (2001)

[5] Bittorrent, http://www.bittorrent.org

[6] Emule, http://www.emule-project.net

[7] AXIS, http://ws.apache.org/axis

[8] Christensen, E., Curbera, F., Meredith, G., Weerawarana, S.: Web services description language (wsdl) 1.1 Technical report (2001), http://www.w3.org/TR/wsdl/

[9] Rahm, E., Bernsteindoi, P.A.: A survey of approaches to automatic schema matching. The International Journal on Very Large Data Bases, 334–350 (2001)

[10] Apache Derby, http://db.apache.org/derby

[11] Gong, L.: JXTA: a network programming environment. Internet Computing, 88–95 (2001)

[12] Adar, E., Huberman, B.A.: Free Riding on Gnutella, Technical report, Xerox PARC (2000)

[13] Aberer, K., Despotovic, Z.: Managing trust in a peer-2-peer information system. In: Proceedings of the international conference on Information and knowledge management, pp. 310–317 (2001)

[14] Emekci, F., Sahin, O.D., Agrawal, D., El Abbadi, A.: A peer-to-peer framework for Web service discovery with ranking. In: Proceedings of IEEE International Conference Web Services, pp. 192–199 (2004)

[15] Ebay, http://www.ebay.com

[16] Message Passing Interface Forum, MPI: A Message-Passing Interface Standard (1994)

[17] Burns, G., Daoud, R., Vaigl, J.: Lam: An open cluster environment for mpi. In: Proceedings of Supercomputing Symposium, pp. 379–386 (1994)

[18] Oikarinen, J., Reed, D.: Internet Relay Chat Protocol (1993), http://tools.ietf.org/html/rfc1459

[19] Abramson, D., Sosic, R., Giddy, J., Hall, B.: Nimrod: A Tool for Performing Parameterised Simulations Using Distributed Workstations. In: Proceedings of 4th IEEE Symp. on High Performance Distributed Computing, pp. 112–121 (1995)

[20] Foster, I., Iamnichi, A.: On Death, Taxes, and Convergence of P2P and Grid Computing. In: Proceedings of the 2nd Int'l Workshop on Peer-to-Peer Systems (IPTP3 2003), pp. 118–128 (2003)

[21] Dutta, D., Goel, A., Govindan, R., Zhang, H.: The Design of a Distributed Rating Scheme for Peer-to-Peer Systems. In: 1st Workshop on Economic Issues in P2P Systems (2003)

[22] Kamvar, S., Schlosser, M., Garcia-Molina, H.: The Eigentrust Algorithm for Reputation Management in P2P Networks. In: Proceedings of 12th ACM World Wide Web (ACM WWW), pp. 640–651 (2003)

[23] Damiani, E., Paraboschi, S., Samarati, P., Violante, F.: A reputation-based approach for choosing reliable resources in peer-to-peer networks. In: Proceedings of the 9th ACM conference on Computer and communications security, pp. 207–216 (2002

A Novel Approach to Manage Asymmetric Traffic Flows for Secure Network Proxies

Qing Li

Blue Coat Systems, Inc., 420 N. Mary Ave., Sunnyvale, CA 94085-4121, USA
Qing.Li@BlueCoat.com

Abstract. A transparent secure network proxy intercepts web traffic such as HTTP requests and applies access policies to the intercepted traffic. The proxy will reinitiate a request on behalf of the client when policies permit. Depending on policy configuration, this proxy may masquerade as the client when generating the request. The response from the server may reach the client instead of the proxy due to asymmetric routing, and if so, would be rejected by the client as an invalid response. Consequently the proxy can not complete the original request. This paper presents a new protocol and a comprehensive mechanism that facilitates the formation of a cluster comprised of multiple proxies. This proxy cluster can cover a network that spans a large geographical area, and collaboratively discover and redirect asymmetrically routed traffic flows towards the appropriate member proxy. The protocol and the algorithms presented in this paper can operate in both IPv4 and IPv6 [1] networks.[1]

1 Background and Motivation

Secure network proxies play an essential role in today's enterprise networks. These proxies can enforce access policies, conduct traffic monitoring, and perform content delivery acceleration through caching and WAN optimization. The various security requirements combined with reliability requirements present complex network architectures in which proxies cannot be deployed due to application breakage. The deploy-ability of a secure network proxy is measured by the types of policies the proxy can enforce without impeding applications. In other words, applications must continue to function even when application traffic is subject to processing at the proxy. This section provides a general introduction to the concept of a secure network proxy followed by descriptions of example problems challenging the proxy deployment.

1.1 Introduction

In this paper, a secure network proxy is an appliance that is situated between network nodes (i.e. clients) that make service and content requests, and network nodes (i.e. servers) that offer those requested services and content. Within the secure network proxy appliance, a set of application proxies operate in concert to classify and process the requests according to specific protocols. Examples of application proxies [2] are

---

[1] This work and its publication are sponsored by Blue Coat Systems Inc., Sunnyvale, CA, USA.

J. Cao et al. (Eds.): NPC 2008, LNCS 5245, pp. 196–209, 2008.
© IFIP International Federation for Information Processing 2008

HTTP proxy, FTP proxy, Streaming Media Proxy, Peer-to-Peer proxy, SSL proxy, MAPI proxy and CIFS proxy. A secure network proxy typically operates at the application layer (layer-7) of the OSI stack [3]. In practice, since a secure network proxy is deployed at the network perimeter to manage traffic flowing between the Intranet and the Internet, a secure network proxy is commonly known as a *gateway proxy*. The most common gateway proxy is a web proxy that specializes in processing HTTP and HTTPS traffic. In this paper the terms secure network proxy, secure web proxy, web proxy and proxy are used interchangeably to simply the discussions.

A web proxy is termed a *transparent* proxy [4] if its presence is not known to the clients and servers. A web proxy is termed an *explicit* proxy when clients are configured to send all requests to that proxy instead of to the servers directly. A web proxy is said to be deployed *inline* if all traffic generated between the clients and the servers always traverse a path through the proxy.

Once a proxy intercepts a request, the access polices installed in the proxy are executed to determine what actions to apply to the request. The most common actions are *intercept* and *bypass*. Bypassed traffic will pass through the proxy without any modification. In this case the proxy acts as either a router or a bridge. Intercepted traffic is subject to further processing within the proxy by one or more application protocol proxies.

Since a web proxy operates at the application layer, the web proxy may initiate a request to the server on behalf of the client. For example, the proxy intercepts a HTTP request by first terminating the associated TCP connection [5], i.e. completing that TCP connection as if the proxy were the server. Then the subsequent HTTP request is transferred to the HTTP application proxy. If the HTTP application proxy decides to grant that request, the HTTP proxy will then initiate an actual request to the origin server on behalf of the client.

In essence, the proxy created two TCP connections for the original client request: one TCP connection is established between the client and the proxy (also known as the *client connection* or *client inbound connection*), and another TCP connection is established between the proxy and the origin server (also known as the *server connection* or *server outbound connection*). The response received on the server connection is then forwarded onto the client connection. Transformations may be applied to the response by the application proxy before it is forwarded to the client. The proxy may also decide to serve the response from its local cache instead of contacting the origin server.

1.2 Problems and Motivation

Since the server may use the client IP address as a means of authentication, the web proxy may masquerade as the client (sometimes known as *client-spoofing*) [6] by using the client's IP address as the source address of the TCP connection that the proxy initiates. In environments where asymmetric routing is a common occurrence, or due to routing policy or traffic engineering, the server response may not reach the proxy but instead reaches the client. Such environments present a challenge to the extent that deploying transparent proxies may be impossible. Consider the example given in Fig. 1.

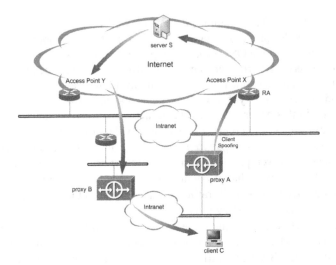

Fig. 1. This figure illustrates a typical asymmetric routing situation in an enterprise network

Fig. 1 illustrates an enterprise network where two access points are available over two different ISPs. In this example, router RA is configured as the default gateway at the client C. Proxy A is inline between C and RA. Proxy A intercepts the request from C, and then initiates another connection to the origin server S. Proxy A exercises client-spoofing because S performs IP address based authentication. This proxy A-to-S connection is through access point X. The return traffic from S to A, however, is routed through access point Y, which traverses proxy B instead of A. The main reason for this asymmetric flow is because which path the server decides to take for reaching the client's IP address (proxy A spoofed that IP address), is determined by the configuration at server S and by the routing policy defined at access point Y. Proxy B may decide to bypass this response because it has no corresponding request state. Client C, however, will reject this response because it does not have an active TCP connection that matches the response from S. More security conscious proxies may decide to reject the response outright by dropping the flow. In either case, the original request will never succeed.

Traffic load balancers and Layer-4 (L4) switches [7] are an integral part of the design in many enterprise networks. The function performed by the load balancer or the L4 switch may impose adverse effects that threaten the effectiveness of a transparent proxy. Consider the example given in Fig. 2. In order to handle a large volume of traffic, a typical design is to deploy a traffic load balancer in front of a farm of proxies that have similar capabilities and processing logics. In this figure, proxy A is called a *downstream proxy* and each proxy in the proxy farm is called an *upstream proxy* [2].

Proxies can operate in conjunction with one another in what is known as *proxy chaining* [2]. This proxy chain performs specialized functions that may require shared state. An example is dictionary compression where two proxies maintain parallel dictionaries generated from traffic passing through this proxy chain. These dictionaries allow the proxies to replace previously seen data sent between them with small tokens. Each token refers to a location in the dictionary where the previously seen data is stored.

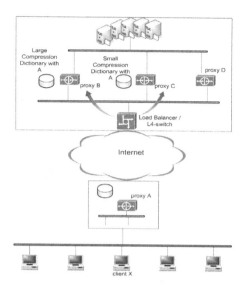

Fig. 2. Load balancers and L4 switches may break upstream and downstream proxy affinity

In this example, a downstream proxy needs to establish a chain with an upstream proxy from the proxy farm when servicing a request. It is preferable the downstream proxy establishes a chain with the same upstream proxy when the downstream proxy services other requests. The goal is to maintain an affinity in the proxy chain so to continue to build that shared state and maximize its usage.

Traffic from the downstream proxy reaches the load balancer first. The load balancer may use the client and server addresses in making its load balancing decision. If the downstream proxy is deployed transparently and exercises client spoofing, then the load balancer will see the client's IP address in the connections initiated by the downstream proxy. Subsequently the load balancer may forward the request to a different upstream proxy. On the other hand, the desired upstream proxy would be chosen correctly without client spoofing because the IP address of the downstream proxy would be visible instead.

Assume in this example that a downstream proxy creates a chain with an upstream proxy to perform dictionary based compression for traffic acceleration. The size and the lifetime of the dictionary are important factors in achieving a good compression ratio. In this example, downstream proxy A and upstream proxy B have built up a large dictionary over time. This dictionary has been consulted each time A serves requests from client X, as such, client X has been enjoying a good response time for its requests. Then at some point in time the server changed its policy to using IP address based authentication. Now proxy A must activate client spoofing resulting in the load balancer deciding to redirect traffic from proxy A to proxy C. Since proxies A and C have had limited exchange, the dictionary constructed thus far is relatively small. Client X would begin to experience a sudden drop in performance that translates into noticeable delays.

1.3 Related Work

Transparent proxies are essentially man-in-the-middle appliances that monitor, log and intercept all traffic flows that traverse through them. The concerns for privacy, copyright and content integrity [4] have only grown in recent years. In the corporate environments, individual user's desire for privacy conflicts with the corporate interests, where visibility and control are the main focuses.

Since the operational goals of the corporate lies in the opposite spectrum of those goals demanded by the users, perhaps for this reason there is a substantive lack of research activities in academia to improve the operational efficiencies and to expand the deployment coverage of these transparent proxies. Yet in the enterprise environments secure gateway proxies are essential and are confronted by numerous challenges presented by the various networks in which these proxies are deployed. Research into the vendor space yields a single vendor product that offers a partial solution, however, that partial solution in terms of algorithms is not disclosed.

The above are the main motivations for this research and the publication of this paper. The goals are to bring these issues to light, and to offer a detailed disclosure on a solution that is fully deployed in production environments in hope to solicit peer reviews, and to invigorate additional research activities in this area.

2 System Architecture

To solve the aforementioned problems, this section presents the details of a protocol that facilitates the formation of a cluster. This cluster is comprised of multiple member proxies that can be multiple hops away from each other. Each member proxy exchanges information about the requests that it has processed with every other member proxy. The clustering protocol is designed to manage the cluster membership as well as to exchange states of processed requests.

2.1 Overview

In the problem illustrated in Fig. 1, if proxy B has the ability to recognize traffic flows that belong to proxy A and can forward to A those traffic flows, then these transparent proxies can be deployed throughout an autonomous system without concerns for asymmetric routing or the presence of load balancers. Proxy A must inform proxy B about the connections that A has processed. Similarly proxy B must inform proxy A of those connections that belong to B. The solution presented in this paper can handle the situation where asymmetrically routed traffic reaches a member proxy before the proxy-to-proxy notification arrives at that member proxy.

The solution is to create a *proxy cluster* that includes A and B and let A and B form a peering relationship. Proxy A and B can signal one another about their respective workload after successfully establishing the peering relationship. Proxies are typically deployed in different subnetworks and these proxies are multiple hops away from each other. The notifications must be delivered reliably. For these reasons proxy peers within the cluster are connected over a full-mesh topology. The connection between any pair of peers is a TCP connection. Fig. 3 visualizes the secure proxy cluster.

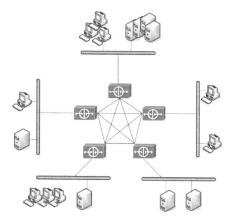

Fig. 3. Member proxies form a cluster with full-mesh TCP connectivities

Section 3 provides additional information on the reasons why the solution is not based on a multicast protocol.

The solution is comprised of the following three main modules:

- cluster control-channel management module
- connection management module
- traffic flow forwarding module

The cluster control-channel management module is responsible for establishing and maintaining peer relationships with every other member in the cluster.

The connection management module is responsible for maintaining the database that describes connections that are processed by local proxy as well as connections that are processed in peer proxies.

The traffic flow forwarding module is responsible for classifying packets against this connection database and forwarding the packets to either local on-box application proxies, or redirecting these packets to peer proxies.

2.2 Cluster Control-Channel Management

In the first implementation of this solution, the cluster membership is statically configured into each proxy. A proxy attempts to establish a TCP connection to every other peer in the membership list. The membership list may be static, but the proxies identified in the list may join and leave the cluster dynamically. A proxy may leave the cluster either voluntarily or involuntarily due to hardware or software failure.

This special peer-to-peer TCP connection is called a *cluster control-channel*, or simply the *control-channel*. A specially chosen TCP port is reserved by the implementation as the service port on which peering requests are made. If successful, the two peers begin to synchronize their respective *connection tables* over the control-channel. In the context of this paper, the connection table includes all of the TCP and UDP connections associated with the requests that have been processed by a proxy.

Note for intercepted requests, the connection table contains both client bound and server bound connections.

The *cluster connection database*, or simply *connection database* is defined as the connection table that contains all of the intercepted and bypassed connections that have been collected from all of the active peers of the cluster. The cluster connection database is described in more detail in Section 2.4.

The types of messages that are exchanged over the control-channel are given in Table 1. The INSTALL_CONNECTION message informs the receiver about those connections that are handled by the sender. The receiver will store these connections in its connection database so that it can recognize packets that are associated with those connections, and forward those packets back to the sender. The REMOVE_CONNECTION message informs the receiver about those connections that have been completed, or those connections that should no longer be bypassed (perhaps due to changes made in the access policy). The receiver will remove those connections from its connection database.

Table 1. Cluster Management Control Connection Message Types

Message Type	Action	Description
INSTALL_CONNECTION	FORWARD	This message installs state about a connection into a peer. Traffic belonging to this connection will be forwarded to the originator of this message.
	BYPASS	This message installs state about a bypassed connection into a peer.
REMOVE_CONNECTION	FORWARD	This message removes state about a forwarded connection from a peer.
	BYPASS	This message removes state about a bypassed connection from a peer.
CLUSTER_PEER_SYNC	PEER_JOIN	This message indicates the sender is in the process of establishing a peering relation with the receiver. This message provides a safeguard against accidental connection being made to the clustering port. This message is also an indication the sender requests a peer to send over its connection table that includes both intercepted and bypassed connections.
	PEER_KEEPALIVE	This message informs a peer the sender is alive.
	PEER_LEAVE	This message informs peers that the sender of this message is exiting the cluster and is no longer an active member of the cluster.
	PEER_REJECT	This message informs a peer that the peering request initiated by the receiver has been denied. This reason for the denial accompanies the PEER_REJECT message.

2.3 Cluster Control-Channel Packet Formats

The control-channel packets have a generic four-byte header, which is shown in Fig. 4. The first two bytes are common, and the content of the subsequent two bytes depends entirely on the message type.

Each packet begins with a *Message Type*. The defined message types are IN-STALL_CONNECTION, REMOVE_CONNECTION, and CLUSTER_PEER_SYNC. The *Action Type* can be one of FORWARD or BYPASS. The *Protocol Family* can be either TCP or UDP, which identifies subsequent connection information as to contain either TCP or UDP connections. The *Address Family* specifies whether the IP addresses of a given connection are IPv4 or IPv6 addresses.

0	7	8	15	16	23	24	31
Message Type		Action Type		Protocol Family		Address Family	
INSTALL_CONNECTION		FORWARD / BYPASS		Protocol Family		Address Family	
REMOVE_CONNECTION		FORWARD / BYPASS		Protocol Family		Address Family	
CLUSTER_PEER_SYNC		PEER_JOIN		Version		(zero)	
CLUSTER_PEER_SYNC		PEER_KEEPALIVE		(zero)		(zero)	
CLUSTER_PEER_SYNC		PEER_LEAVE		Error Code		(zero)	
CLUSTER_PEER_SYNC		PEER_REJECT		Error Code		(zero)	

Fig. 4. Control-Channel packet header format

A proxy that intercepts a client request will issue two FORWARD actions to all of its peers. The first FORWARD action installs the client inbound connection and the second FORWARD action installs the server outbound connection in the peers. All traffic that belongs to these two connections which arrives at any other peer will be forwarded to the intercepting proxy.

The BYPASS action is necessary when one proxy receives a client request and the policy indicates the connection is to be bypassed. In this case, instead of redirecting the return traffic that was asymmetrically routed to the intercepting proxy, the intercepting proxy can ask its cluster peers to bypass the traffic, thus forwarding the traffic toward the requesting client or server directly. This direct bypass approach can be considered as an optimization.

The PEER_JOIN action serves as a safeguard against accidental connection made to the special TCP port reserved for cluster peering requests. Once the TCP connection is successful, the peering initiator must issue the PEER_JOIN action as the first exchange. In return, the peer will respond with a PEER_JOIN message. The peer that is waiting for the peering requests on the special socket [8] will close the control connection if the PEER_JOIN action is not the first exchange. In other words, for both ends of the control-channel, the first bytes exchanged must constitute a PEER_JOIN action and its associated data. The number of connect attempts to be made for establishing peering relation to another cluster member before abandoning that peer is configurable by the administrator. Infinite retries is a configurable option to manage the situation where the peer is down for an extended period of time but will eventually recover.

The packet formats may change depending on the *Version* field. Therefore, at the time of establishing the peering relation the version field must be examined by each peer to determine if the peers are compatible. Incompatible peers will result in the failure of peering establishment. The version field is carried in the PEER_JOIN message only.

The PEER_KEEPALIVE action is necessary when a configured period of time has elapsed and there is no traffic on a control-channel. The PEER_KEEPALIVE is sent to each peer to inform those peers about the liveliness of the sender. A response is not necessary because the control channel operates over TCP, which is reliable. Once a proxy deems its peer unreachable, that proxy will remove all connections (whether bypassed or intercepted) associated with the unreachable peer from its cluster connection database.

A member proxy that voluntarily leaves the cluster issues the PEER_LEAVE action to all other members. The PEER_LEAVE action is a proactive way of informing other peers to immediately remove all connections associated with the sender of the PEER_LEAVE action from their connection databases.

A member proxy transmits the PEER_REJECT action to inform another proxy that its peering request has been denied, for example, because the other proxy is not present in the cluster membership list. The reason for the rejection is included in the PEER_REJECT message.

For the PEER_REJECT message, the *Error Code* field indicates reason for peering failure. Peering failure can occur when a peer is not in the cluster membership list but attempts to connect to other members that are in the list. Another reason for peering rejection is version number mismatch.

After a proxy has established the control channel with another proxy, if an unrecognized message is received on their control-channel, that control-channel will be closed. The main reason is at the point where the bad message is read, the proxy can no longer parse the remaining bytes received on that channel. In this case the proxy will issue a PEER_LEAVE action to its peer with an error code that indicates bad message.

Fig. 5 illustrates an example of a control-channel packet carrying IPv4 connection information, and this connection would be forwarded by the peers. The size of the source and destination ports is fixed. Each INSTALL_CONNECTION and RE-MOVE_CONNECTION will carry only one set of connection information. In other words, if there are two blocks of connection information to be installed, then there will be two INSTALL_CONNECTION messages.

0	7 8	15 16	23 24	31
INSTALL_CONNECTION	FORWARD	IPPROTO_TCP	AF_INET	
Source Port		Destination Port		
Source IPv4 Address				
Destination IPv4 Address				

Fig. 5. This is an example of an IPv4 connection installation packet

As can be seen from Fig. 5, the size of the packet can be derived from the packet header. For example, if the message type is INSTALL_CONNECTION, the protocol is TCP, and the address family is IPv4, then the packet is 16 bytes long. On the other hand, if the address family is IPv6, then the packet is 40 bytes in size (4-byte header, 4 bytes for ports, 16-byte source IPv6 address, and 16-byte destination IPv6 address).

Fig. 6 illustrates the possible usage of these message types. The INIT state is the state where a proxy reads and parses the cluster membership list, and determines which peers it should initiate an active peering request to. In the CONNECT state, the peering request initiator responds with a PEER_JOIN and enters the SYNCHRONIZE state. In the SYNCHRONIZE state, the two peers exchange their respective connection tables. The SYNCHRONIZE state is the same as the ESTABLISHED state if the initiator has an empty connection table.

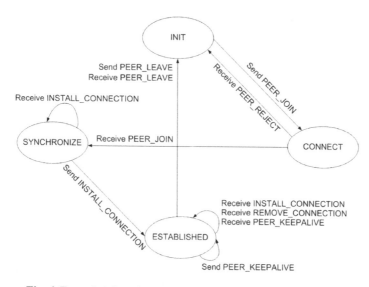

Fig. 6. Example of peering states and associated message exchanges

2.4 Cluster Connection Database Management

At the completion of the cluster establishment, all of the proxies belonging to the same cluster must have the same connection database of all the connections that are intercepted and bypassed by every member proxy. The most efficient way to synchronize the connection table is to exchange local connection table with each peer at the peering time. Once the cluster is fully established, each proxy will maintain a cluster connection database covering all of the active peers. New members can join the cluster and the peer table will be updated accordingly.

Each time a new request is processed by a proxy, that proxy sends the IN-STALL_CONNECTION notification to all its peers before it initiates a connection to the server for that request. This approach will reduce possible memory overhead that may be incurred by a peer if the server response reaches a peer before the notification arrives at that peer.

Each proxy unilaterally sends out PEER_KEEPALIVE messages on its own timer, and the other side of the control channel treats this peer as unresponsive if that side does not hear any traffic after some fixed time interval, for example, 3 times the PEER_KEEPALIVE interval. The connections associated with a peer are removed from the local connection database if the peer becomes non-responsive. The number of probes to send and the probe interval are configurable by the administrator on a per peer basis. A proxy will reset the PEER_KEEPALIVE transmission timer each time a message of INSTALL_CONNECTION or REMOVE_CONNECTION type is received. The periodic timer is also reset when a PEER_KEEPALIVE is triggered.

Table 2 illustrates the structure of the connection table at the intercepting proxy, and the corresponding connection database maintained by the peers.

Table 2. Connection Table and Connection Database

Connection Table of the Intercepting Proxy A

Connection	Direction	Responsible Proxy
< src-A, src-PA, dst-B, dst-PB >	Client to Proxy	Proxy A
< src-C, src-PC, dst-D, dst-PD >	Proxy to Server	Proxy A

Connection Database at Proxy B

Connection Information <source-IP, source-Port, destination-IP, destination-Port>	Protocol	Action	Originating Proxy
< src-A, src-PA, dst-B, dst-PB >	TCP	Forward	IP address X
< src-C, src-PC, dst-D, dst-PD >	TCP	Bypass	IP address X
< src-E, src-PE, dst-F, dst-PF >	UDP	Bypass	IP address Y

2.5 Traffic Flow Forwarding Module

Once the connection database is synchronized among all peers, the traffic flow forwarding module within a proxy can begin processing traffic flows that belong to other member proxies.

The traffic flow module must first act as a packet classifier, i.e. the traffic flow module must examine all traffic received by the proxy and match this traffic against the local connection database. Conceptually the connection database is comprised of all connections that have been processed by all member proxies. In the actual implementation, however, connections local to a proxy are not inserted to that database but are kept in a separate table for performance reasons.

For an input packet that matches a connection in the connection database, i.e. for a packet that belongs to a traffic flow processed by another proxy, the traffic flow module will package this off-box packet and transmit it to the proxy identified by the connection database entry (i.e., to the IP address specified in the connection entry). The off-box packet is encapsulated inside an IP-in-IP frame [9]. The IP-in-IP frame has the address of the local proxy as the source address, and the address of the remote proxy as the destination address. The choice of using IP-in-IP encapsulation for transporting off-box traffic is to take advantage of the existing routing infrastructure, and for ease of implementation.

3 Discussion

The clustering protocol could be built on top of a multicast mechanism because multicasting connection state information to all other members simultaneously is more scalable. IP multicast forwarding is not a mandatory requirement and is by default disabled in the majority of the enterprise routers. The connection state information must be exchanged reliably and in bounded time among the peers. There exists reliable multicast protocols, but those solutions are typically too complex to implement. The solution presented in this paper assumes the number of peers would not exceed 20 proxies for all practical purposes. A reliable multicast clustering protocol would be desirable if the number of peers exceed that limit.

When a proxy first encounters a partial flow, e.g. the proxy receives a TCP <SYN,ACK> packet, or when the proxy receives a TCP packet with only the <ACK> bit set, and the proxy cannot find any connection that matches this packet in either the local connection table or the overall connection database. In this situation, the proxy cannot discard any packet belonging to the partial flow. The reason being another member proxy may have processed that flow, and the notification about that flow is in transit and has not reached the local proxy. The longer a proxy can hold these partial packets, the longer the distance is tolerated between a pair of proxies. In other words, the packet hold time determines the diameter of the cluster. Once the hold time expires, the queued packets are subject to re-classification and can be dropped if a matching connection is still missing.

The solution proposed in this paper can be utilized to build intelligent load balancers. Intelligence comes from the fact that offloading decisions (i.e. connection forwarding) can be made by an external module operating at a layer higher than layer-4. Refer to Fig. 2, consider the scenario where a TCP connection request (e.g. as a result of a HTTP request) is received at a member proxy. This TCP <SYN> packet can be handed to the WAN optimization module. The WAN optimization module examines the client and server addresses, and determines another proxy is best at handling this request because that other proxy has built a better compression dictionary. In this case, the WAN optimization module would instruct the connection management module to install this connection as an off box connection, and then subsequently forward this connection to the chosen member proxy. Such a method is sometimes referred to as *connection handoff*.

The traditional load balancer or L4 switches operate at layer-3 and layer-4 of the OSI stack. The load balancer is typically a single point of failure, and the traffic flow is load balanced in one direction. The full-mesh cluster topology as shown in Fig. 3 enables bidirectional load balancing and provides reliability in the overall solution because if one member proxy is inoperable, only a subnetwork that is covered by that failed proxy would be affected. Traffic is not affected by the failure if the network has built-in redundancy and can re-route the traffic around the failed proxy to another member proxy.

Since the connection database contains all of the requests processed by every member proxy, and because each entry in the database identifies a responsible proxy, an administrator can access any member proxy to gain a complete view of all proxied traffic flowing through the entire network. In other words, the solution proposed can serve as an excellent network troubleshooting tool.

Another observation is each member proxy can enforce both the access policies defined in it, and at the same time enforce policies defined in the other member proxies as well. This solution enables a large amount of security and access policies to be divided into smaller subsets and install each subset into one member proxy to enforce. In other words, this solution allows for the implementation of a distributed policy enforcement mechanism.

In the enterprise environment where the clustering solution is deployed, and accordingly to the appliance capability specification, there are approximately 20,000 simultaneous requests active within the appliance at any given time. At a minimum, each connection state holds the protocol type, the address family, connection 4-tuple <source address, source port, destination address, destination port>, the IP address of the responsible proxy and the action type. For IPv4 each connection state requires roughly 32 bytes, and with a cluster containing 20 member proxies, the size of the connection database is approximately 25.6 MB.

In the same deployment environment, each proxy is subject to approximately 2000 requests per second. Assuming these requests are HTTP requests, each requested object is typically 10K bytes in size, which translates into 20MB per second per link traffic. In other words, the proxy receives 160Mbps from the server and then transfers this same amount of traffic to the client. In the worst situation where all traffic destined to one proxy must always traverse another member proxy, and assume there is a 100ms delay between the two peers, then that other member proxy must buffer 2MB of packets on behalf of its peer.

At 2000 requests per second, approximately 390Mbps is exchanged within the cluster for installing or removing connection states. Each proxy handles roughly 19.5Mbps of cluster protocol exchange in the worst case and with 20 proxies in the cluster.

The solution presented in this paper has been implemented in a system with 4 CPUs, 4GB RAM and multiple Gigabit Ethernet interfaces, which represents a typical high-end appliance. The system memory and network bandwidth requirements in the worst case scenario are easily satisfied.

4 Conclusion and Future Work

In this paper I have described a protocol and system that enable a group of proxies to form a proxy cluster. This cluster can cover a large scale network that can span geographical locations. This proxy cluster acts as a single virtual proxy that can enforce a large distributed set of policies. Without the proposed solution, transparent proxies that perform client spoofing cannot be deployed in environments where asymmetric routing takes place. The solution presented in this paper also enables the construction of better load balancers and application layer switches.

The solution proposed in this paper has been deployed in real-world production environments. Performance measurements were conducted using commercial web performance testing tools against the requirements specification. A formal system performance analysis is in progress.

Acknowledgements. I would like to thank Blue Coat Systems for sponsoring this research work and granting me the permissions for publication. I would like to thank the various reviewers from Blue Coat Systems for their comments and suggestions, in particular Min Hao (Howard) Chen and Yusheng Huang. I would like to thank Ron Frederick for his review and his technical contribution.

References

1. Li, Q., Jinmei, T., Shima, K.: IPv6 Core Protocols Implementation. Morgan Kaufmann, San Francisco (2006)
2. Gourley, D., Totty, B., Sayer, M., Reddy, S., Aggarwal, A.: HTTP The Definitive Guide. O'Reilly, Sebastopol (2002)

3. Tanenbaum, A.S.: Computer Networks, 4th edn. Prentice Hall PTR, Upper Saddle River (2002)
4. Wessels, D.: Web Caching. O'Reilly, Sebastopol (2001)
5. Stevens, W., Wright, G.: TCP/IP Illustrated. The Implementation, vol. 2. Addison-Wesley, Upper Saddle River (1994)
6. Wikipedia, http://en.wikipedia.org/wiki/IP_address_spoofing
7. Syme, M., Goldie, P.: Optimizing Network Performance with Content Switching: Server, Firewall, and Cache Load Balancing. Prentice Hall PTR, Upper Saddle River (2003)
8. Stevens, W.: Unix Network Programming. The Sockets Networking API, 3rd edn., vol. 1. Addison-Wesley, Upper Saddle River (2003)
9. Simpson, W.: RFC 1853, IP in IP Tunneling, IETF (1995)

Automatic Transformation for Overlapping Communication and Computation

Changjun Hu, Yewei Shao, Jue Wang, and Jianjiang Li

School of Information Engineering, University of Science and Technology Beijing
NO.30 Xueyuan Road, Haidian District, Beijing, P.R.China
huchangjun@ies.ustb.edu.cn, yeweishao@gmail.com,
ncepu5@gmail.com, jianjiangli@gmail.com

Abstract. Message-passing is a predominant programming paradigm for distributed memory systems. RDMA networks like infiniBand and Myrinet reduce communication overhead by overlapping communication with computation. For the overlap to be more effective, we propose a source-to-source transformation scheme by automatically restructuring message-passing codes. The extensions to control-flow graph can accurately analyze the message-passing program and help perform data-flow analysis effectively. This analysis identifies the minimal region between producer and consumer, which contains message-passing functional calls. Using inter-procedural data-flow analysis, the transformation scheme enables the overlap of communication with computation. Experiments on the well-known NAS Parallel Benchmarks show that for distributed memory systems, versions employing communication-computation overlap are faster than original programs.

Keywords: Parallel compiling; Communication optimization; Control-flow analysis; Source-to-source transformation.

1 Introduction

Message-passing is widely used in parallel programs and is a standard interface for message-passing parallel programs written in C, C++, or Fortran that supports point-to-point communications (send, receive, isend, ireceive) and collective operations (broadcast, gather, scatter, alltoall, alltoallv). The algorithm presented in this paper is applicable to message-passing codes. Our platform is a set of sixteen processor nodes, connected with an infiniBand switch. Current infiniBand switches have Remote Direct Memory Access (RDMA) capability and support that non-blocking communication can progress concurrently with computation.

The benefit of overlapping communication and computation in parallel computing has been extensively studied in the past decade. We can classify previous works into three kinds. Some of researches are achieved by compiled methods [1, 2, 3, 4, 5]; some of them have been performed in the field of Global Address Space languages [6, 7, 8] or achieved by particular hardware [9, 10, 11]. However, these techniques may be effective for overlapping communication and computation only in a single loop. In

J. Cao et al. (Eds.): NPC 2008, LNCS 5245, pp. 210–220, 2008.

this paper, we present a transformation scheme to overlap communication with computation using inter-procedural data-flow analysis.

Compared with previous researches, our main contributions are as follows:

- Using inter-procedural data-flow analysis to find the minimal region from producer to consumer in context of message-passing programs.
- We propose a transformation scheme to overlap communication with computation.
- We evaluate some NAS benchmarks to validate our transformation.

The rest of this paper is organized as follows. Section 2 gives the algorithm to create the control-flow graph for message-passing programs. Section 3 describes a source-to-source transformation scheme to optimize the parallel programs. Section 4 evaluates the performance of NAS benchmarks using our transformation algorithm. Section 5 places this paper in the context of related work. Section 6 presents conclusions.

2 Control-Flow Graph for Message-Passing Program

The compiler must characterize the control-flow and the data-flow of programs, so that the programs can be optimized in next step. It is regrettable that the previous control-flow graph does not consider the message-passing call, which can result in less precise and even incorrect analysis results. To resolve these problems, Shires et al. [12] give an extension to the control-flow graph called the MPI-CFG. A motivation example will be given in figure1, which is a generic code segment in SPMD (Single Process, Multiple Data) parallel program. The array dum is communicated between statement S1 and S2. In figure 2 MPI-CFG contains control-flow edges represented with solid lines and a communication edges represented with dash lines. This is the start point of our work.

```
     if ( rank == 0 ) then
         do j=jst,jend
             dum(1,j)=g(1,nx,j,k)
             ......
         end do
S1:      MPI_SEND( dum(1,jst), 5*(jend-jst+1), dp_type,
                 south, from_n, MPI_COMM_WORLD,
                 IERROR )
     else
S2:      MPI_RECV( dum1(1,jst), 5*(jend-jst+1), dp_type,
                 north, from_n, MPI_COMM_WORLD,
                 status, IERROR )
         ......
     end if
     ···=dum(1,jst)
```

Fig. 1. A code segment of SPMD program

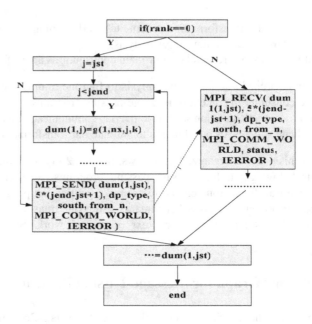

Fig. 2. The MPI-CFG of the code segment presented in Figure1

3 The Overlap of Communication and Computation

There are two challenges involved in data-flow analysis. The first challenge is to identify message-passing variables and characterize corresponding data accesses. The second challenge is that producer-consumer data-flow analysis need to be performed to ensure communication-computation overlap.

3.1 Inter-procedural Data-Flow Analysis for Message-Passing Programs

To characterize and analyze data accesses in message-passing program, we perform the inter-procedural dataflow analysis for message-passing variables. Message-passing variable is defined as data that may be communicated or related to communication data, such as the parameters in message-passing call and the compiler identifies these message-passing variables using the algorithm described in Figure 3. In Figure 3, we first locate communication statements, and then obtain their parameters and functional calls. If the parameters are communicated through communication statement, we add these parameters into our Message-passing Variables list. If the communication statement has function calls, we should go into these functions and get parameters from these calls, and then add these parameters into our list. Finally, our list is a set of variables that may be communicated or related to communication data.

```
Algorithm list_message-passing_variables
Input :
        A - An MPI program.
Output:
        V – A List of Message-passing Variables in A
Begin
(1)  Set V= Φ
(2)  do ∀Comm(L), which is an message passing call in A, L is the
        set of variables in Comm(L)
(3)  do ∀Pr, Pr is a procedure defined within A
(4)     do ∀F, F is function call with Pr
(5)        do ∀Pa, Pa is a parameter of F
(6)           if ( Pa ∈ L)
(7)              Let FP be the procedure that defines F
(8)              Let PA be the procedure parameter of FP
                    corresponding to function parameter Pa
(9)              set V = V ∪ PA
(10)          end if
(11)       end do
(12)    end do
(13)  end do
(14) end do
```

Fig. 3. Algorithm to create list of message-passing variables

```
Algorithm : Find the minimal region from producer to consumer
Input:
              V – A List of Message-passing Variables in A
              MPI control flow graph signed RSD
              Data Dependence
Output:
              PP – the Set of the place that produce variables in V
              PC – the Set of the place that consume variables in V
              Region  –  the Set of region, while Region = {minPlace_P,
              minPlace_Q  minPlace_P ∈ PP, minPlace_Q ∈ PC}
Begin
    (1)    Initialize PP = Φ, PC = Φ,  Region = Φ
    (2)    do ∀ variable L, L ∈ V
    (3)        Set LastDistance = MAX (LastDistance is the Distance
                   between two places that we want to know, MAX is just a single)
    (4)        Set minPlace_P = 0( minPlace_P is the place of producer that
                   the minimal place from producer to communication statement)
    (5)        Set minPlace_Q = 0(minPlace_Q is the place of consumer that
                   the minimal place from communication statement to consumer)
    (6)        Set W(L) = set of produce L
    (7)        do ∀ P, P ∈ W(L)
    (8)            CurrentDistance = getDistance ( P, Comm(L))
                       (Comm(L) is the communication statement about
                           variable L, getDistance(P,Comm(L)) is a function to
                           compute the distance from p to Comm(L))
    (9)            if ( CurrentDistance < LastDistance)
    (10)               LastDistance = CurrentDistance
    (11)               minPlace_P = P
    (12)           PP = PP ∪ minPlace_P
    (13)       end do
    (14)       LastDistance = MAX
    (15)       Set FU(L) = set of future use of L
    (16)       do ∀ Q, Q ∈ FU(L)
    (17)           CurrentDistance = getDistance ( Comm(L), Q)
    (18)           if ( CurrentDistance < LastDistance)
    (19)               LastDistance = CurrentDistance
    (20)               minPlace_Q = Q
    (21)           PC = PC ∪ minPlace_Q
    (22)       end do
    (23)       Region = getRegion ( minPlace_P, minPlace_Q )
    (24)   end do
```

Fig. 4. Algorithm to construct the minimal region from producer to consumer

3.2   Constructing the Minimal Region from the Producer to Consumer

In this section we give producer-consumer relationship analysis which can be applied at any level. If the statement S1 precedes S2 in execution order, then S1 < S2. Dependence between two statements in program is relation that constrains their execution order and control dependence constrain that arises from control-flow graph. Data dependence arises from flow of data. Therefore, we will give the types of producer-consumer dependencies. If S1 < S2, and S1 sets value and later S2 uses it, then call it producer-consumer. If S1 < S2, and S1 uses some variable value and S2 sets it, then call it anti producer-consumer. We treat producer-consumer and anti producer-consumer differently.

To expose the maximum available opportunity for overlapping communication with computation, the algorithm shown in Figure 4 resolves the minimal region from producer to consumer, which contains the communication function calls. Each variable could be produced and be consumed in multi places in the program, and we only pay attention to the minimal region from the producer to the consumer. Getting variable from the Message-passing Variables list which is described in Figure 3, we locate the places that produce this variable and then we select the place called minPlace_P that is the minimal place from the producer to the communication statement which contains variable. Then we choose the place called minPlace_Q that is the nearest place consuming the variable after communication statement. Finally, our minimal region is from minPlace_P to minPlace_Q.

3.3   Transformation Algorithm

We classify the communication patterns into two cases, blocking communication and non-blocking communication. To overlap communication and computation, messages are initiated early using non-blocking sends/receives and completed just before the consumption point at the receiver with a wait.

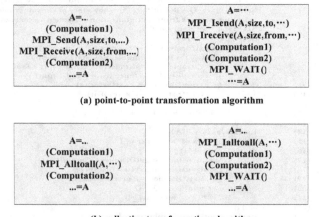

(a) point-to-point transformation algorithm

(b) collective transformation algorithm

Fig. 5. Transformation algorithm for overlapping communication and computation

MPI provides a direct interface to non-blocking point-to-point operations, while non-blocking collective operations to overlap communication and computation are not directly supported by the MPI standard. For blocking communication, we change it into non-blocking communication using the techniques of Hoefler et al [13, 14]. In other words, we change MPI_Send into MPI_Isend, MPI_Receive into MPI_Ireceive, and get the non-blocking communications including MPI_Ibcast, MPI_Igather, MPI_Iscatter, MPI_Ialltoall and MPI_Ialltoallv. Since collective communication and point-to-point communication are used in a different way, they should be considered separately.

We give the transformation algorithm presented in Figure5. The algorithm based on the minimal region from producer to consumer described in Figure5 and guarantee the maximization of overlapping communication and computation.

4 Experimental Results

To evaluate the effect of our strategy, the performance comparisons between the original program and our optimized program using our transformation algorithm. The experimental environment is a set of sixteen processor nodes, connected with a high-performance infiniBand switch. Each node has an Intel Xeon 3.0G processor with 1024KB L2 Cache, and the switch has a Remote Direct Memory Access (RDMA) capability, whereby non-blocking message-passing communication can progress concurrently with computation. The Operating System is RedHat Linux version FC3, with Kernel 2.6.9 and we use MVAPICH2 1.0[15] for communication over Infini-Band. Time is measured by inserting MPI_Wtime() calls before and after the region we want to execute.

To validate the transformation scheme, we design several experiments implementing the algorithm of overlapping communication and computation using data-flow analysis to apply to NAS benchmarks. The NAS parallel benchmarks [16] are a set of programs designed originally to evaluate supercomputers. We use NPB 2.4 [17] implementation written in MPI and give some experiments based on the NAS parallel programs which confirm to our algorithm, such as LU, IS, BT, MG.

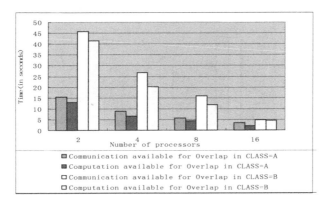

Fig. 6. Performance in LU benchmark

Figure6 shows the performance of LU benchmark before and after optimized program. The transformed program succeeds in tolerating the communication latency and reducing the execution time by almost from 10% to 17% going from two to sixteen nodes both in class A problem size, while reducing time from 5% to 17% in class B problem size.

Figure7 shows the time taken in communication and computation available for overlap both in class A problem size and class B problem size in LU benchmark. The time taken in communication available for overlap is close to the time taken in computation and it occupies a large proportion in the parallel program. Therefore, optimized program of LU benchmark succeeds in reducing the execution time taken in parallel program.

Figure8 shows the performance of MG benchmark while Figure9 shows the communication and computation available for our algorithm. The time taken in communication available for overlap is much larger than the time taken in computation. Although the time spent in communication occupies a large proportion in the parallel program, the actual time spent in overlapping is relatively low. In Figure 8 the transformation algorithm reduces the execution time only from 5% to 8%. Therefore,

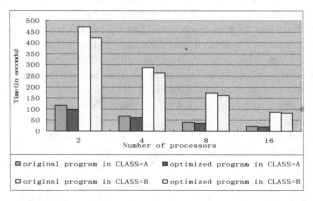

Fig. 7. Communication and computation available for overlapping in class A and class B problem size (LU benchmark)

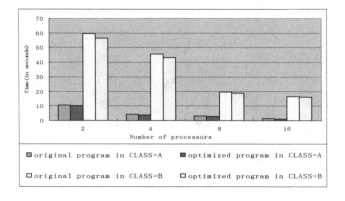

Fig. 8. Performance in MG benchmark

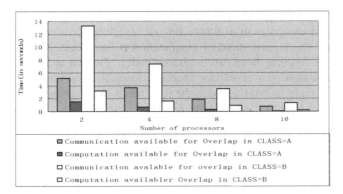

Fig. 9. Communication and computation available for overlapping in class A and class B problem size (MG benchmark)

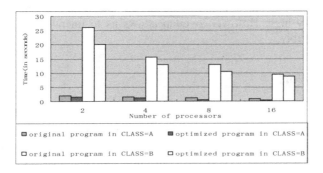

Fig. 10. Performance in IS benchmark

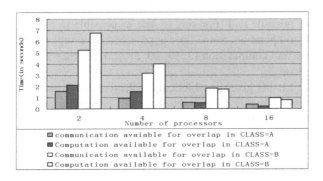

Fig. 11. Communication and computation available for overlapping in class A and class B problem size (IS benchmark)

transformation algorithm achieves good performance only if the time taken in communication available for overlap is close to the time taken in computation. The time taken in available to overlap occupies relatively low in the whole parallel program execution in BT benchmark, so it does not show an obvious result in this benchmark

Figure 10 shows the performance of IS benchmark while Figure 11 shows the communication and computation available for our algorithm. It is obviously seen from Figure 11 that the descent speed of computation is faster than the descent speed of communication in going from two to sixteen nodes. On two to four nodes, the time taken in communication available for overlap is lower than the time taken in computation, while on eight to sixteen nodes the time taken in communication available for overlap is larger than the computation. Since the time taken in communication available for overlap is close to the time taken in computation and the time occupies a large proportion in the parallel program execution, Figure 10 shows that the optimized program can reduce the time from 11% to 39% in class A problem size and from 17% to 22% in class B problem size.

From the above observations, the improvement of performance depends on the following aspects. The first aspect is the proportion of actual time for overlapping occupied in parallel programs. The second one is the time taken in communication should be close to the time taken in computation available for overlap.

Even after our overlap communication and computation, the communication volume is still very high. However, overlap allows us to tolerate the communication latency considerably.

5 Related Work

Control-flow frameworks have been extended by Shires et al. [12], which represents the semantics of message-passing by including communication edges between message-passing procedure calls. This control-flow graph can not describe non-blocking communication accurately. To resolve this problem, our analysis contains inter-procedural in the control-flow graph and inter-procedural in the data-flow graph.

Reducing communication latency using overlap communication and computation has been used in the past decade. HPF compilers [18] proposed a notion of posting of sends as early as possible and receiving as late as possible in order to overlap communication with computation. Some later approaches have suggested the overlapping of communication and computation [2, 19, 20, 21, 22], but they are limited to overlap them in a single loop.

Hoefler et al. [13, 14] gives non-blocking collective operations which are obvious extensions to message-passing. Kennedy et al. [23] presents a communication placement framework that reduces communication latency. The difference between us is that the communication placement can be determined by a sequence of simple unidirectional analyses while we add communication edges and use inter-procedural analysis in control-flow graph. This is the important starting points for our work. In our previous work [24], we pipelined an irregular loop by splitting inspector phase and using corresponding dependence analysis.

To the best of our knowledge, this paper presents the first approach to overlap communication and computation by the inter-procedural analysis of message-passing programs. Algorithm could be used in both point-to-point communications and collective operations.

6 Conclusions

In this paper, we present a transformation scheme to achieve overlapping communication and computation based on inter-procedural data-flow analysis. The data-flow analysis gives the RSD of each variable in message-passing calls and the minimal region from producer to consumer. Finally, we give transformation scheme to accomplish our optimization. To study the impact of our optimization, we give some experiment results to illustrate that our strategy is useful for improving the performance of the message-passing programs.

Acknowledgments

The research is partially supported by the Key Technologies Research and Development Program of China under Grant No.2006038027015, the Hi-Tech Research and Development Program (863) of China under Grant No. 2006AA01Z105 and No. 2008AA01Z109 Natural Science Foundation of China under Grant No.60373008, and by the Key Project of Chinese Ministry of Education under Grant No. 106019 and No.108008.

References

1 Basumallik, A., Eigenmann, R.: Optimizing Irregular Shared-Memory Applications for Distributed-Memory Systems, PPOPP, New York, USA, March 29-31 (2006)
2 Fishgold, L., Danalis, A., Pollock, L., Swany, M.: An automated approach to improve communication-computation overlap in cluster. NIC Series, vol. 33, pp. 481–488. John von Neumann Institute for computing, Julich (2006)
3 Danalis, A., Pollock, L., Swany, M.: Automatic MPI application transformation with AS-PhALT. IEEE, Los Alamitos (2007)
4 Danalis, A., Kim, K.-Y., Pollock, L., Swany, M.: Transformations to Parallel Codes for Communication-computation Overlap. ACM, New York (2005)
5 Kreaseck, B., Carter, L., Casanova, H., Ferrante, J.: On the Interference of Communication on Computation in Java. IEEE, Los Alamitos (2004)
6 El-Ghazawi, T.A., Carlson, W.W., Draper, J.M.: UPC specification, v. 1.1 (2003), http://upc.gwu.edu/documentation
7 Hilfinger, P., Bonachea, D., Gay, D., Graham, S., Liblit, B., Pike, G., Yelick, K.: Titanium language reference manual. tech report ucb/csd-01-1163, u.c. berkeley (November 2001)
8 Numrich, R.W., Reid, J.K.: Co-Array Fortran for parallel programming. ACM FortranForum 17(2), 1–31 (1998)
9 Goumas, G., Sotiropoulos, A., Koziris, N.: Minimizing completion time for loop tiling with computation and communication overlapping. In: Proceedings of the 15th International Parallel and Distributed Processing Symposium (IPDPS 2001), April 23–27, 2001, p. 39. IEEE Computer Society, Los Alamitos (2001)
10 Gupta, S.K.S., Huang, C.-H., Sadayappan, P., Johnson, R.W.: Atechnique for overlapping computation and communication for block recursive algorithms. Concurrency: Practiceand Experience 10(2), 73–90 (1998)

11 Sohn, A., Biswas, R.: Communication studies of dmp and smp machines. Technical Report NAS-97-005,NASA Ames ResearchCenter (March 1997)

12 Shires, D., Pollock, L., Sprenkle, S.: Program Flow Graph Construction for Static Analysis of MPI programs. In: International Conference on Parallel and Distributed Processing Techniques and Applications (PDPTA 1999) (June 1999)

13 Hoefler, T., Lumsdaine, A., Rehm, W.: Implementation and Performance Analysis of Non-Blocking Collective operations for MPI. In: SC 2007, Reno, Nevada, USA, November 10-16 (2007)

14 Hoefler, T., Lumsdaine, A.: Optimizing non-blocking collective operations for infiband (April 2008); Accepted for publication at the CAC 2008 in conjunction with the IDPDS 2008

15 http://mvapich.cse.ohio-state.edu

16 http://www.nas.nasa.gov/software/NPB

17 Bailey, D., Barszcz, E., Barton, J., Browning, D., Carter, R., Dagum, L., Fatoohi, R., Fineberg, S., Frederickson, P., Lasinski, T., Schreiber, R., Simon, H., Venkatakrishnan, V., Weeratunga, S.: The NAS parallel benchmarks, Tech. Rep. RNR-94-007, NASA Ames

18 Gupta, M., Miskiff, S., Schonberg, E., Seshadri, V., Shields, D., Wang, K., Ching, W., Ngo, T.: An HPF compiler for the IBM SP2. In: Proceedings of Supercomputing 1995, San Diego, CA (1995)

19 Ishizaki, K., Komatsu, H., Nakatani, T.: A loop transformation algorithm for communication overlapping. International Journal of Parallel Programming 28(2), 135–154 (2000)

20 Tseng, E.H.Y., Gaudiot, J.L.: Communication generation for aligned and Cyclic(k) distributions using integer lattice. IEEE Transactions on Parallel Distributed Systems 10(2), 136–146 (1999)

21 Lancu, C., Husbands, P., Chen, W.: Message Strip Mining Heuristics for High Speed Networks. In: VECPAR (2004)

22 Bell, C., Bonachea, D., Nishtala, R., Yelich, K.: Optimizing Bandwidth Limited Problems Using One-Side communication and overlap. In: 20th International parallel & Distributed Processing Symposium (IPDPS) (2006)

23 Kennedy, K., Sethi, A.: A Communication Placement Framework with Unified Dependence and Data-flow Analysis. In: Proceeding 3rd International Conference on High Performance Computing, December 19-22, 1996, pp. 201–208 (1996)

24 Hu, C., Yao, G., Wang, J., Li, J.: OpenMP Extensions for Irregular Parallel Applications on Cluster. In: Chapman, B.M., Zheng, W., Gao, G.R., Sato, M., Ayguadé, E., Wang, D. (eds.) IWOMP 2007. LNCS, vol. 4935. Springer, Heidelberg (2008)

Cooperative Communication System for Parallel Computing Agents in Multi-cluster Grid

Chen Qing-Kui and Wei Wang

School of Computer Engineering, University of Shanghai for Science and Technology,
Shanghai 200093, China
chenqingkui@tom.com

Abstract. The idle computational resources of CSCW environment that is composed of computer clusters are mined to construct the multi-cluster grid in order to support the computation-intensive tasks. For fitting the state changes of idle computing resources during the computing process, the techniques of cooperation and migration agents are adopted. Through the concurrent dataflow, the supper element, and the density factor, the dynamic buffer pool (DBP) was built up. By using of the Grid techniques, the cooperative computing agent, the cooperative communication agent, and DBP, a cooperative communication system (CCMS) for parallel computing agent was designed and implemented. The experimental results show that CCMS can increase the speed-up of parallel computing task. It can be fit for the computation in CSCW based on Internet.

Keywords: cooperative communication agent; dynamic buffer pool; multi-cluster grid; parallel computing.

1 Introduction

With the rapid development of information techniques and Internet, the research results based CSCW became the key techniques building enterprise information infrastructure[1].The computer aided design based on cooperative work environments is playing the more and more important role in the business behavior of enterprise today. Especially, CSCW work contains a lot of computation-intensive task to be processed in some high performance computes. On the other hand, Intranet is more and more extended and a great deal of cheap personal computers are distributed everywhere, but the use rate of their resources is very low. The researches of papers [2, 3] point out that many resources is idle in most network environments at a certain time. Even it is the busiest time of a day, still one third of their workstations weren't used completely. So the paper [4] proposed a framework how to min and use the idle computational resources of CSCW environment that composed of multi-clusters connected by Intranet. It uses the idle computer resources in CSCW environment to construct a Visual Computational System (VCE). VCE can support two kinds of migration computations: (1) the Serial Task based on Migration (STM); (2) the Task based on Data Parallel Computation (TDPC). For adapting these heterogeneous and dynamic environments, we use the Grid [5] techniques, multi-agent [6, 7] techniques

J. Cao et al. (Eds.): NPC 2008, LNCS 5245, pp. 221–231, 2008.

and cooperative leaning model of agent [8] and min the idle resource of CSCW environment to construct multi-cluster grid (MCG). Because of the migration of cooperative computing agent in MCG, the communication resources in computing node are changed frequently. So the communication efficiency is decreased gradually along with the increasing of cooperative computing team scale. The study of communication techniques [9~12] becomes very important. Paper [9] proposed a synchronous communication mechanism for parallel computing. Paper [10,11] study the mobile agent communication problem. Paper [12] implements a middleware for agent communication. But all these methods can't satisfy the need of parallel computing in dynamic multi-cluster grid.

This paper proposed a cooperative communication system for parallel computing agents in multi-cluster grid that is composed of many computer-clusters connected by Intranet. By using of dynamic buffer blocks and concurrent dataflow technique, we construct the dynamic buffer pool in every computing node; through the cooperative communication agent, global directory and dynamic buffer pool, we build up a independent cooperative communication system in MCG. This system can support the grid computing and pervasive computing based on task-migratory mechanism, and it can fit the heterogeneous and dynamic network Environment. The experimental results show that this model can increase the speed-up of parallel cooperative computing and use effectively the memory resources for communication buffers.

2 Architecture of MCG

We use of the idle computational resources (e.g. the time that the users take a rest or do the other works and the computer is idle) in CSCW environment, to support the computation-intensive tasks of CSCW. The Computation-Intensive Task is that it needs very long time to run, and it also needs high performance computer to support, such as the finite element analysis. For describing this communication model, we introduce some definitions:

(1) **Computing Node (CN)** is defined as CN (id, CT, A_m, CMA, AS), where id denotes the identifier of CN; CT denotes the type of computing node; A_m denotes the main control agent of CN; CMA is the cooperative communication agent of CN; AS is the set of the control and computing agents running on CN.

(2) **Computer cluster (CC)** is defined as CC (M_a, CS), where M_a denotes the main computer of CC; CS= {CN_1, CN_2...CN_p} denotes the set of all computing nodes which CC includes.

(3) **Computing Agent (CA)** is defined as CA (id, PRG, BDI, KS, CE), where id denotes the identifier of CA; PRG denotes the executable program set of CA; BDI is the description of its BDI; KS is its knowledge set; CE is its configuration environment.

CA is the basic element to execute computation task. If a CA could complete independently the task, we call it as the independent computing agent (ICA). If a CA couldn't complete independently the task, and it must cooperate with others, we call it as the cooperative computing agent (CCA).

(4) Cooperation Computing Team (CCT) is defined as *CCT (id, A_m, CAS, BDI, CKS, CCE)*, where *id* denotes the identifier of *CCT*; A_m denotes the main control agent of *CCT*; *CAS* denotes the set of all cooperative computing agents which *CCT* includes; *BDI* is the description of its *BDI*; *CKS* is its knowledge set. *CCE* is its configuration environment. *CCT* can support the data parallel computation in the logical computer cluster.

(5) Global Computing Group (GCG) is defined as *GCG (id, A_m, ICAS, CCTS, GKS, GCE)*, where *id* denotes the identifier of *GCG*; A_m denotes the main control agent of *GCG*; *ICAS* denotes the set of *ICA* which *GCG* includes; *CCTS* denotes the set of *CCT* which *GCG* includes; *GKS* is its knowledge set. *GCE* is its configuration environment.

Many tasks are executed together in *GCG* during the same time, and the tasks are calculated by a lot of *ICA*s or *CCT*s.

(6) Cooperative Communication Agent (CMA) is defined as *CMA (id, CN, DBP, BDI, CKS, CCE)*, where id denotes the identifier of *CMA*; *CN* denotes the computing node on which *CMA* runs; *DBP* is the dynamic communication buffer pool of *CMA*; BDI is the description of its *BDI*; *CKS* is its knowledge set. *CCE* is its configuration environment. Every a computing node has a *CMA*, and *CMA* do all communication work for computing and control in the computing node.

(7) Cooperative Communication System (CCMS) is defined as *CCMS (CCAS, GD)*, where *CCAS* denotes the set of all *CMA*s in a parallel computing environment composed of many computing node ; *GD* denotes the global directory of *CCMS*.

(8) Multi-cluster Grid (MCG) is defined as *MCG (M_a, CCS, N, R, GCG, CCMS)*, where M_a denotes the master computer of *MCG*; *CCS* denotes the set of all computer clusters which *MCG* includes; *N* is the connection network set of *MCG*; *R* is the rules of connections; *GCG* is the global computing group; *CCMS* is the cooperative communication system.

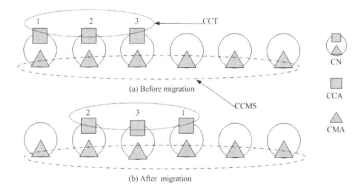

Fig. 1. The example of the relation between CCT and CMAS in MCG

CMA is the only communication component in a computing node and *CMA* is on this computing node forever. During the computing process, the migration component only is the cooperative computing agent. The figure 1 shows that the cooperative computing agent 1 has been migrated from computing node 1 into computing node 4. But the *CMA* of CN_1 is still in CN_1.

3 CCMS Structure

(1) Buffer block (BB) is defined as a communication unit, and it is composed of a certain size memories. Its size be defined as |B|.

(2) Concurrent Dataflow (CDF) There is a communication relation between cooperative computing agent CCA_i and $CCA_j (i \neq j)$, C_i is a *CN* on which CCA_i runs, C_j is a *CN* on which CCA_j runs. CMA_i and CMA_j are two cooperative communication agents which run on C_i and C_j respectively. DF_{ij} is the dataflow from CCA_i to CCA_j, DF_{ji} is the dataflow form CCA_j to CCA_i. During the computing and migration process, there are many dataflow among the computing agents at the same time. These dataflow are call as concurrent dataflow.

A dataflow DF_{ij} is a sequence of buffer blocks, and it has a density factor k ($k \geq 0$) that is the buffer block numbers from CCA_i to CCA_j in a unit time. When k is 0, DF_{ij} is closed.

(3) Dynamic Buffer Pool (DBP) is defined as *DBP* (m, *RM*, *RFC*, w_r, *SM*, *SFC*, w_s), and its main parts are described as follows:

● m is the numbers of cooperative communication agents which communicate with C_i; there are $2m$ data flows for C_i . There are m data flows for sending and m data flows for receiving.

●*RM* is $m \times w_r$ matrix and it is the receiving buffers that store data received from other m concurrent data flows; it is called as receiving buffer matrix. Its matrix element is called as supper element, and it has two formats: ① null; ② compose of k ($k \geq 0$, k is the density factor) buffer blocks that size is |B|; w_r is the numbers of column of *RM*.

Every a row of *RM* is a dataflow that save data received from other cooperative computing agent. So *RM*[i] ($1 \leq i \leq m$) is the ith receiving dataflow.

● *RFC* is m vector and its element is the density factor of dataflow; Namely, *RFC*[i] is the density factor of dataflow *RM*[i].

● *SM* is $m \times w_s$ matrix and it is the sending buffers that store data sent into other m concurrent data flows, and it is called as sending buffer matrix. Its matrix element is also supper element; w_s is the numbers of column of *SM*.

● *SFC* is m vector and its element is the density factor of dataflow; Namely, *SFC*[i] is the density factor of dataflow *SM*[i].

(4) Global Directory (GD) is defined as a relation table *GD* (CCA_{id}, CN_{id}, CCT_{id}, *sta*), where CCA_{id} denotes the identifier of *CCA*; CN_{id} denotes the identifier of computing node on which *CCA* runs; CCT_{id} is the identifier of *CCT* which *CCA* belongs to; *sta* is the state of *CCA*, and *sta* ∈ {'ready', 'computing', 'migration'}.The row numbers of *GD* be written as p and its means is that there are p cooperative computing agents in *MCG* at present.

(5) Buffer Block Set (BBS) is the set of all communication buffer blocks in a computer node, and its size is |B| × N_B.

CCMS structure is shown as the figure 2. There are three cooperative computing agents distributed into three computing nodes. Figure 2 shows that communication method of these cooperative computing agents through CCMS.

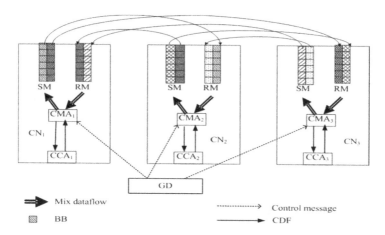

Fig. 2. The structure of CCMS composed of three computing nodes

4 Descriptions of CCMS Process

4.1 CCMS Start-Up

Algorithm 1 (Start-up and Calculation of CCT)

(1) GCG gets a parallel job and constructs a $CCT= \{CCA_1, CCA_2,...,CCA_t\}$;the identifier of CCT is cno;

(2) GCG gets a logical computer cluster $LCC= \{C_1, C_2... C_t\}$ from MCG;

(3) For $1 \leq i \leq t$, GCG do step(4) repeatedly;

(4) send CCA_i into C_i; append a new tuple NT into GD and do as follows: { $NT.CCA_{id}=$ identifier (CCA_i); $NT.CN_{id}=C_i$; $NT.CCT_{id}=cno$; $NT.sta=$'ready';}

(5) GCG send 'initialization' to CMA_i $(1 \leq i \leq t)$, which CMA_i is the cooperative communication agent in computing node C_i;

(6) CMA_i $(1 \leq i \leq t)$ does algorithm 2 in parallel in order to initialize the dynamic buffer pool on computing node C_i;

(7) GCG start all cooperative computing agents $CCA_1, CCA_2,... CCA_t$ to complete the parallel job cooperatively;

(8) If the migrations occur during the computing process, GCG starts migration process [4] and all CMAs do algorithm 3 to adjust CCMS;

(9) Repeat to do step (8) (9) until the parallel job has been finished.

4.2 Operation for CCMS

Algorithm 2 (Initialization of DBP)

$CCT= \{CCA_1, CCA_2...CCA_t\}$ is a cooperative computing team and $LCC= \{C_1, C_2... C_t\}$ is the logical computer cluster which is supporting CCT. GD is global directory.

For initializing the dynamic buffer pools of CCMS, all CMA_i $(1 \leq i \leq t)$ do as follows cooperatively each other.

(1) For $(1 \leq j \leq t \wedge j \neq i)$ do (2)~(5);

(2) CCA_i calculates the data size ds which will be sent into CCA_j;

(3) CCA_i calculates the density factor k_{ij} of dataflow from CCA_i to CCA_j by ds; CMA_i constructs dataflow DF_{ij} (from CCA_i into CCA_j) according to ds and adds DF_{ij} to SM of CMA_i; CMA_i sends ds into CMA_j; CMA_j constructs dataflow DF_{ij} (from CCA_i into CCA_j) according to ds and adds DF_{ij} to RM of CMA_j;

(4) CCA_j calculates the density factor k_{ji} of dataflow from CCA_j to CCA_i by ds; CMA_j constructs dataflow DF_{ji} (from CCA_j into CCA_i) according to ds and adds DF_{ji} to SM of CMA_j; CMA_j sends ds into CMA_i; CMA_i constructs dataflow DF_{ji} (from CCA_j into CCA_i according to ds; CMA_i adds DF_{ji} to RM of CMA_i;

(5) CMA_i gets the tuple NT form GD by CCA_i and inform CCMS to replace $NT.sta$ with 'ready';

(6) End.

Algorithm 3 (Adjustment for CCMS After Migration)

$CCT=\{CCA_1, CCA_2 \ldots CCA_t\}$ is a cooperative computing team and $LCC=\{C_1, C_2 \ldots C_t\}$ is the logical computer cluster which is supporting CCT. GD is global directory. Suppose that $MIG=\{CCA_{m1}, CCA_{m2} \ldots CCA_{mg}\}$ is the subset of CCT and all cooperative computing agents in MIG will be migrated from $LEAVE=\{C_{m1}, C_{m2} \ldots C_{mg}\}$ into new computing node set $NLC=\{NC_{m1}, NC_{m2} \ldots NC_{mg}\}$. There is $LEAVE \subset LCC$. For simple description, suppose that CCA_{mi} $(1 \leq i \leq g)$ will be migrated into computing node NC_{mi}. When all cooperative computing agents in MIG finished their migration process, for adjusting the dynamic buffer pools of CCMS, all CMA_{mi} $(1 \leq i \leq g$, CMA_{mi} is the cooperative communication agent of computing node C_{mi}) do as follows cooperatively each other.

Set $NMIG=CCT-MIG$; /*agent set of no-migration*/

S_{nmig} is the set of cooperative communication agents of computing nodes in LCC-$LEAVE$; S_{mig} is the set of cooperative communication agents of computing nodes in NLC; S_{leave} is the set of cooperative communication agents of computing nodes in $LEAVE$;

/*Delete the old dataflow of migration agents from CCMS*/

(1) For $CMA_j \in S_{leave} \wedge 1 \leq j \leq g$ do (2)(3);

(2) CMA_j gets its CCA_j from MIG and informs CCMS to replace $GD.sta$ (which CCA_j has) with 'migration';

(3) For $CMA_i \in S_{nmig} \wedge 1 \leq i \leq t$-$g$ do $\{CMA_i$ delete the dataflow DF_{ij} from its DBP; CMA_j delete the dataflow DF_{ji} from its DBP; $\}$

/* Construct new dataflow among CCAs in MIG */

(4) For $CMA_i \in S_{mig} \wedge 1 \leq i \leq g$ do (5);

(5) For $CMA_j \in S_{mig} \wedge j \neq i \wedge 1 \leq i \leq g$ do (6) (7);

/* CCA_i is active operator */

(6) CCA_i calculates the data size ds which will be sent into CCA_j; CCA_i calculates the density factor k_{ij} of dataflow from CCA_i to CCA_j by ds; CMA_i constructs dataflow DF_{ij} (from CCA_i into CCA_j) according to ds and adds DF_{ij} to SM of CMA_i; CMA_i

sends ds into CMA_j; CMA_j constructs dataflow DF_{ij} (from CCA_i into CCA_j) according to ds and adds DF_{ij} to RM of CMA_j;

/ * CCA_j is active operator */

(7) CCA_j calculates the density factor k_{ji} of dataflow from CCA_j to CCA_i by ds; CMA_j constructs dataflow DF_{ji} (from CCA_j into CCA_i) according to ds and adds DF_{ji} to SM of CMA_j; CMA_j sends ds into CMA_i; CMA_i constructs dataflow DF_{ji} (from CCA_j into CCA_i) according to ds and adds DF_{ji} to RM of CMA_i; }

/* Construct new dataflow between $NMIG$ and MIG */

(8) For $CMA_i \in S_{mig} \wedge 1 \leq i \leq g$ do (9);

(9) For $CMA_j \in S_{nmig} \wedge 1 \leq i \leq t\text{-}g$ do (10);

(10) CCA_i calculates the data size ds which will be sent into CCA_j ; CCA_i calculates the density factor k_{ij} of dataflow from CCA_i to CCA_j by ds; CMA_i constructs dataflow DF_{ij} (from CCA_i into CCA_j) according to ds and adds DF_{ij} to SM of CMA_i; CMA_i sends ds into CMA_j; CMA_j constructs dataflow DF_{ij} (from CCA_i into CCA_j) according to ds and adds DF_{ij} to RM of CMA_j; CCA_j calculates the density factor k_{ji} of dataflow from CCA_j to CCA_i by ds; CMA_j constructs dataflow DF_{ji} (from CCA_j into CCA_i) according to ds and adds DF_{ji} to SM of CMA_j; CMA_j sends ds into CMA_i; CMA_i constructs dataflow DF_{ji} (from CCA_j into CCA_i) according to ds and adds DF_{ji} to RM of CMA_i;

(11) CMA_i ($CMA_i \in S_{mig} \cup S_{nmig}$) gets the tuple NT form GD by CCA_i and inform CCMS to replace $NT.sta$ with 'computing';

(12) End.

4.3 CCMS Communication Process

$CCT = \{CCA_1, CCA_2 \ldots CCA_t\}$ is a cooperative computing team and $LCC = \{C_1, C_2 \ldots C_t\}$ is the logical computer cluster which is supporting CCT. GD is global directory. CMA_i ($1 \leq i \leq t$) is the cooperative communication agent of computing node C_i. Suppose that CCA_i ($1 \leq i \leq t$) had been allotted on C_i. Set $SCMA = \{CMA_1, CMA_2 \ldots CMA_t\}$.

Algorithm 4 (Sending Data Process)
The sending data process includes two threads: one is the data gather thread (DGT) from local CCA; another is the data sending thread (DST) through network adapter. DGT process is as follows:

(1) Do step (2) (3) repeatedly;

(2) CCA_i does the local computing work and produces dada d; CCA_i transfer d to local cooperative communication agent CMA_i;

(3) CMA_i decides the destination CCA_j ($1 \leq i \leq t$, $j \neq i$) by d and gets k (k is density factor)buffer blocks $B_1, B_2 \ldots B_k$ from BBS ; CMA_i saves d into $B_1, B_2 \ldots B_k$ and builds up a supper elements $B = \{ B_1, B_2 \ldots B_k \}$; CMA_i adds B into dataflow DF_{ij} (that is dataflow from CCA_i to CCA_j);

DST process is as follows:

(1) Do step (2) (3) repeatedly;

(2) Scan all dataflow DF_{ij} ($1 \leq i \leq t$, $1 \leq j \leq t$) of SM in DBP;

(3) If DF_{ij} is not NULL then {get data d from DF_{ij} ; send d into CMA_j which runs on C_j; free the buffer blocks;}

Algorithm 5 (Receiving Data Process)
The receiving data process includes two threads: one is the data receiving thread (DRT) from network; another is the data transfer thread (DTT) that transfer data to local CCA. DRT process is as follows:

(1) Do step (2) ~ (4) repeatedly;

(2) Receive data d from the network adapter;

(3) Decide the data source CCA_j by d;

(4) get the density factor k of dataflow DF_{ji} from CCA_j to CCA_i; get k buffer blocks B_1, B_2...B_k from BBS; Save d into B_1, B_2...B_k and build up a supper elements $B= \{B_1, B_2...B_k\}$; add B into dataflow DF_{ji} of RM;

DTT process is as follows:

(1) Do step (2) (3) repeatedly;

(2) Scan all dataflow DF_{ij} ($1 \leq i \leq t$, $1 \leq j \leq t$) of RM in DBP;

(3) If DF_{ij} is not NULL then { get data d from DF_{ij} and free the buffer blocks which d used; transfer d into CCA_i which runs on C_i;}

4.4 Computation for Density Factor

Suppose that CCA_i and CCA_j is a pair of cooperation computing agents and DF_{ij} is the dataflow from CCA_i to CCA_j. The calculation process for density factor k of DF_{ij} is as follows:

(1) CCA_i estimates the communication data size s from CCA_i to CCA_j per unit time;

(2) $k= \lfloor s/|B| \rfloor +1$.

5 Analysis and Experiments

5.1 Analysis for CCMS

CCMS has many characteristics, they are as follows:

(1) Any a row of the matrix SM and RM of DBP is a concurrent dataflow that is a logical channel between a pair of cooperative computing agents. CCMS use the Matrix SM to implement the one-to-many communication; CCMS use the Matrix RM to receive message from other many cooperative computing agents which runs on other computing node. So CCMS can support the parallel computing.

(2)Every concurrent dataflow has a density factor. The size of density factor is the communication data quantity of concurrent dataflow. We can adjust the value of density factor to control parallel dataflow.

(3)The element of SM and RM is called as the supper element, because it can be composed of k buffer blocks. When $k=0$, the dataflow had been closed.

(4)SM and RM share the BBS space, so it can increase the use rate of memories for buffer blocks.

5.2 Experiments

We built a *MCG* that is composed of 16 computers and 4 computer-clusters that connected by Intranet. The computing tasks provided by *MCG* are the matrix operations and the linear programming. The *CCT* algorithms (Parallel algorithms based on computer cluster) for the matrix operations and the linear programming are given. The intranet clock is synchronous by GTS protocol. In order to make the tasks to migrate as far as possible in the *MCG*, We make use of the random migration function *RandMigration*() and form the migration strategy during the test processes. The description for cooperative rules [8] is given. The experimentation includes seven times, and each time has 12 hours, and the total amount is 84 hours. Through the average values of the test information, we observe the operation results of CCMS. We implement two communication models: One is CCMS which had been implemented according to CCMS; another is BCMS (binding communication system) which communication agent will be migrated with their cooperative computing agent together and it doesn't adopt the DBP technique. The experiment results are as follows:

There are four types of *CCT* scale: (1) *CCT* is composed of 2 *CCA*s; (2) *CCT* is composed of 4 *CCA*s; (3) *CCT* is composed of 8 *CCA*s;(4) *CCT* is composed of 16 *CCA*s.

Experiment 1. The CCMS and BCMS speed-up, which are along with *CCT* scales change, have been tested. The test result is shown as in the figure 3. This test result shows that CCMS keeps linear speed-up and CCMS can support parallel computation effectively.

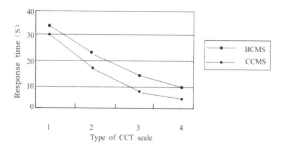

Fig. 3. The speed-up of CCMS and BCMS

Experiment 2. The changes of memory resources for communication buffer in CCMS and BCMS have been tested. The test result is shown as in the figure 4. This test result shows that the numbers of CCMS memory resources become stable when *CCT* scale type is 2. CCMS can increase the use rate of communication buffers.

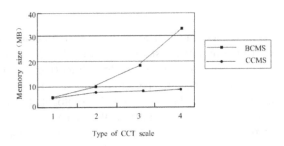

Fig. 4. The memory size for communication buffer in CCMS and BCMS

Experiment 3. The response time along with the changes of density factor k=1, 2, 3, 4 have been tested. There are $|B|$ =1MB. The test result is shown as in the figure 5. This test result shows that CCMS can effectively support the communication work for high density dataflow and it can be implemented by increasing the density factor of dataflow.

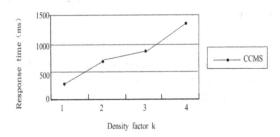

Fig. 5. The changes of response time along with the changes of density factor

6 Analysis and Experiments

Because of the heterogeneous resources, the state changes of idle computing resources during the computing process and the migration of cooperative computing agent, the communication problem of agent become very important. Constructing cooperative communication system, which is independent system from the computing agent system, we can increase the speed-up of parallel computing task and effectively use the memory resources for communication buffer.

Acknowledgement

We would like to thank the support of National Nature Science Foundation of China (No.60573108), Shanghai Leading Academic Discipline Project (No.T0502) and the Innovation Program of Shanghai Municipal Education Commission (No. 08ZZ76, 07ZZ92).

References

1. Raybourn, E.M., Newman, J.: WETICE 2002 Evaluating Collaborative Enterprises Workshop Report. In: Proceeding of the Eleventh IEEE international Workshops on enabling technologies: Infrastructure for Collaborative Enterprises, pp. 11–17. IEEE Press, New York (2002)
2. Markatos, E.P., Dramitions, G.: Implementation of Reliable Remote Memory Pager. In: Proceedings of the 1996 Usenix technical Conference, pp. 177–190 (1996)
3. Acharya, A., Setia, S.: Using Idle Memory for Data-Intensive Computations. In: Proceedings of the 1998 ACM SIGMETRICS Conference on Measurement and Modeling of Computer Systems, pp. 278–279. ACM press, New York (1998)
4. Chen, Q.K., Na, L.: Grid Cooperation Computational System for CSCW. In: Proceedings of the 10th IEEE International Conference on Computer Supported Cooperative Work in Design, pp. 894–899. IEEE Press, New York (2006)
5. Foster, I., Kesselman, C.: The Grid: Blueprint for Future Computing Infrastructure. Morgan Kaufmann Publishers, San Francisco (1999)
6. Osawa, E.: A Scheme for Agent Collaboration in Open MultiAgent Environment. In: Proceeding of IJCAI 1993, August 1993, pp. 352–358 (1993)
7. Wooldridge, M.: An Introduction to Multivalent System. John Wiley & Sons, Chichester (2002)
8. Chen, Q.K.: Cooperation Learning Model of Agents in Multi-cluster grid. In: proceedings of the 11th IEEE International Conference on Computer Supported Cooperative Work in Design (CSCWD 2007), pp. 418–423. IEEE Press, New York (2007)
9. Franke, H., Dangelmaier, W., Klopper, B., Kosters, C.: Synchronous Communicating Agents for Parallel Improvement in Transport Logistics. In: Artificial Intelligence and Applications(AIA 2004), Innsbruck, Austria (2004)
10. Mishra, S., Xie, P.: Interagent Communication and Synchronization Support in the DaAgent Mobile Agent-Based Computing System. IEEE transactions on parallel and distributed system 14(3), 290–306 (2003)
11. Venticinque, S., Di Martino, B., Aversa, R., Vlad, G., Briguglio, S.: Mobile Agents Based Collective Communication: An Application to a Parallel Plasma Simulation. In: Guo, M., Yang, L.T., Di Martino, B., Zima, H.P., Dongarra, J., Tang, F. (eds.) ISPA 2006. LNCS, vol. 4330, pp. 724–733. Springer, Heidelberg (2006)
12. Riley, P.: MPADES: Middleware for Parallel Agent Discrete Event Simulation. In: Kaminka, G.A., Lima, P.U., Rojas, R. (eds.) RoboCup 2002. LNCS (LNAI), vol. 2752, pp. 162–178. Springer, Heidelberg (2003)

CPI: A Novel Three-Phase Algorithm for QoS-Aware Replica Placement Problem*

Wei Fu, Yingjie Zhao, Nong Xiao, and Xicheng Lu

School of Computer, National University of Defense Technology, Changsha, P.R. China
lukeyoyo@tom.com

Abstract. QoS-aware replica placement decides how many replicas are needed and where to deploy them to meet every request from individual clients. In this paper, a novel three-phase algorithm, namely CPI, is proposed. By dividing candidate nodes into proper medium-scale partitions, CPI is capable to handle with large-scale QoS-aware replica placement problem. Pharos-based clustering algorithm obtains ideal grouping, and partition integrating method is developed to obtain final replica policy. Theoretical analysis and experiments show that CPI has lower computation complexity and good scalability. The replicating cost and updating cost remains acceptable under different simulating conditions.

1 Introduction

Replication is the process of sharing resources so as to ensure consistency between redundant copies. These copies are formally called replicas, which usually spread at geographically distributed locations. As a simple but effective technique, replication is widely employed in distributed systems [1-6]. Proper replica mechanism can speedup response time, reduce network traffic, balance overload, as well as enhance data reliability and fault-tolerance. Distributed databases [1], distributed file systems [2], content distributing network [3, 4], P2P systems [5] and Data Grids [6] are some of the most common scenarios to use replicas. Replica placement takes charge of a proper replica policy. It decides how many replicas should be deployed and where to locate them, which is very important to the effectiveness of replication.

Traditional replication researches aimed at optimize the global/average metrics as much as possible. For example, Qiu [7] tried to minimize the average accessing delay, and Cidon [8] aimed to spend the least communication messages. While an average performance measure may be important from the system's point of view, it does not differentiate the various performance requirements of the individuals [9]. With the rapid growth of time-critical applications, some researches [9-12] tried to provide QoS-guaranteed replica service. Instead of only concerning about average metrics, their first and foremost objective is to guarantee that EVERY individual request should meet its QoS requirement, usually response time. They named it as **Q**oS-**A**ware **R**eplica **P**lacement problem (QARP for short), which has been proved to be NP-Complete. Several heuristic algorithms have been presented to solve the problem,

---

* This paper is supported by National 863 High Technology Plan (NO. 2006AA01A118, NO. 2006AA01A106), and Chinese NSF (NO.60573135, NO. 60736013).

J. Cao et al. (Eds.): NPC 2008, LNCS 5245, pp. 232–243, 2008.

including Tang [9], Wang [10] and Fu [12]. However, they are all centralized methods and lack of scalability. Furthermore, the computation complexities are rather high. Theoretically, the time complexities are about $O(|V|^3)$ or even $O(|V|^{2l+2})$ [9-11].

In order to overcome the difficulty, a novel three-phase algorithm CPI is presented to solve large-scale QoS-aware replica placement problem. CPI divides the entire problem into several medium-scaled problems. Then each sub-problem deals with its own placement problem in parallel. Finally, all sub-problem solutions are integrated to form a final solution. The main contributions of the paper are listed as follows:

1. A novel semi-distributed method CPI is proposed to solve large-scale QoS-aware replica placement problem;
2. A pharos-based algorithm are invented for node clustering;
3. A simple but effective integration mechanism is introduced to obtain global placement policy;

2 Related Work

In 2004, Tang and Xu put forward the QARP problem for the first time [9]. They proved the replica-aware QARP to be NP-complete. Meanwhile, two families of heuristic algorithms, named *l-Greedy-Insert* and *l-Greedy-Delete* respectively, are proposed for optimal solution. The selection of *l* reflects a tradeoff between the time complexity and the quality of solution. On the basis of their work, Jeon [11] gave another proof of NP-hard property. He deduced it to be a minimum set cover problem. With the help of matrix, a centralized algorithm based on the approximation algorithm for minimum set cover problem was presented. Wang [10] proposed another heuristic algorithm called *Greedy-Cover* inspired by set operations. Recently, Fu and Xiao et.al [12] utilized vector operations to accelerate computation. The output replica is organized into a ring structure for concurrent updating.

However, all these solutions are classified as centralized algorithms. A dominate node is required to collect communication cost between any two nodes, and the algorithm will be performed in this single node. If the scale of network is small or medium (e.g., < 1000), they work well. However, when the scale is a bit larger, the computation cost and memory cost will both increase sharply [10]. Either the time cost will be so long, or it will cause the out of memory exception. We can confirm this judgment from experimental results in section 6.

Generally speaking, all of them lack of scalability. And the loads are imbalanced. While the dominate node is over-used, all the other nodes are almost idle. The powerful capabilities are not exploited.

3 Replication System Model and QoS-Aware Replica Placement Problem Definition

In this section, a replication system model is introduced. Some servers are selected to hold replicas, which are called replica nodes. The other servers are called non-replica nodes. In this context, the terms "server" and "node" are regarded as the same thing.

Let an undirected graph $G = (V, E)$ represent the server network, where V is the set of servers, $E \subseteq V \times V$ denotes the set of links between these nodes. Each node is identified by a global unique identifier. Without loss of generality, we use integer 0, 1, 2, ..., n, where n = $|V|$−1. A storage function $s(v)$ is assigned to node v, representing for the storage cost when a replica resides on it. Besides, Let $d(u, v)$ denote the communication cost between a pair of nodes u and v. If $(u, v) \in E$, $d(u, v)$ means communication cost of the link between u and v. Otherwise, $d(u, v)$ equals to the smallest cost among all possible path from u to v.

QARP problem is defined on the basis of this model. Given an original data in a source node labeled by s, the objective of QARP is to find a subset of nodes R (i.e., $R \subseteq V - \{s\}$). When each server in R holds a copy from s, any of the other nodes can arrive at a replica node without violating its QoS restriction. At the same time, the replicating cost should be minimized. Figure 1 illustrates a typical graph with communication costs.

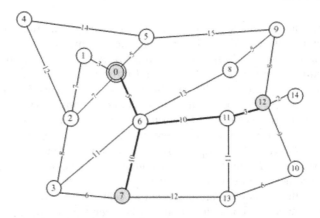

Fig. 1. This is a graph with 15 nodes and 22 edges. Node 0 is the original server, and grey circles are replica nodes. Any node can reach to his nearest replica node within a distance restrict of QoS $\leqslant$ 19. Thick paths show the updating distributing tree rooted by 0, with an updating cost of 5+10+10+3 = 28.

The replicating cost of R is calculated by the following equation:

$$Cost(R) = \lambda \cdot Storage(R) + (1-\lambda) \cdot \mu \cdot Update(R) \tag{1}$$

where λ is a relative weight. Let μ be the update rate of data, $Storage(R)$ and $Update(R)$ are respectively represented by the follows:

$$Storage\ (R) = \sum_{v \in R} s(v) \tag{2}$$

$$Update\ (R) = \sum_{(u, p(u)) \in T} d(u, p(u)) \tag{3}$$

In equation (3), T denotes an update distribution tree [13] rooted by s, and token $(u, p(u)) \in T$ means that u and its parent node $p(u)$ are a pair of successive nodes in the tree T.

4   Three-Phase Placement Algorithm

As discussed above, most of existing algorithms are centralized solutions. The lack of scalability and the rather high computation complexity make them incapable to solve a large-scale QARP problem. In this section, a novel QoS-aware replica placement algorithm CPI is introduced. Namely, the algorithm consists of three phases, illustrated by the pseudo-code in Figure 2.

```
Input:  G = (V, E); QoS; s
Output: Policy P; Update distributing tree T
1   Begin
        //Phrase 1: Node grouping
2       Find 3 pharoses with Pharos Electing Policy;//Sec. 4.2
3       Group all nodes into N Clusters V₁,V₂,…,Vₙ; //Sec. 4.1
        //Phrase 2: Find local replica placement policy
4       For each Cluster Vᵢ
5           Find local replica policy Pᵢ;    //Sec. 4.3
6           Construct local update tree Tᵢ; //Sec. 4.4
7       End for;
        //Phrase 3: Integration of all local policies
8       P = P1∪P₂∪…∪Pₙ;
9       Construct T from T₁,T₂,…,Tₙ;//Sec. 4.4
10      End
```

Fig. 2. The pseudo-code of algorithm CPI: **C**lustering, **P**lacing and **I**ntegrating

4.1   Pharos-Based Clustering Algorithm

To divide all nodes into different clusters, the principle to be followed is that:

- If two nodes are close to each other, they should be in the same cluster;
- If two nodes are far away from each other, they should be in different clusters.

Therefore a technique is urgently needed to distinguish whether two nodes are close to or far away from each other. The idea is inspired by GPS [14]: the Global Positioning System. A typical GPS receiver can easily calculate its 3-D coordinate position using the distances to four or more GPS satellites. In our algorithm, since the graph G is in a 2-D coordinate system, it is easily to understand that 3 "satellites", here we called them pharoses[2], are enough to position a node.

The basic idea of the pharos-based clustering algorithm is to find out which nodes are close to each other, and then classify them into one cluster. As an simple example illustrated by Figure 3.

---

[2] Pharos is a peninsula in the Mediterranean Sea at Alexandria, Egypt. It is the site of an ancient lighthouse. Ancient sailors used it to estimate their positions on the sea.

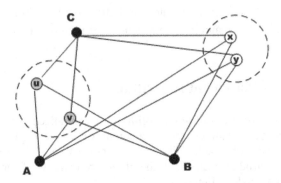

Fig. 3. With the help of 3 pharoses A, B and C, it can be found out that node u is close to v, while x and y are far away from u or v. Thus, four nodes are clustered into two clusters, as the dashed circles shows.

Another important issue is how many clusters should be generated. Let N denote the number of clusters. The choice of N is a tradeoff between local replica placement cost and integrating cost. Generally, we decide N by controlling each cluster's size to be medium-sale. Therefore, N can be calculated by the following expression:

$$N = \lceil |V| / k \rceil \qquad (4)$$

Where k is an integer, equal to the scale we want each cluster to be.

The clustering algorithm is illustrated by the pseudo-code in Figure 4.

```
Input:   G =(V, E); Pharoses set{p1, p2, p3}; # of cluster: N
Output: Subsets V1, V2,···, VN
1.  Begin
        //Initialize N subsets
2.      For each node u, let pha(u)=d(u,p1)²+d(u,p2) ²+d(u,p3) ²;
3.      Sorting  all  pha(u),  then  divide  all  nodes  into  N
        subsets V1,V2,···,VN according to their pha values;
        //Clustering processing
4.      For each node u, do loops:
5.        For each subset Vi, do loops:
6.            Calculate average distances from Vi to pharoses:
7.            d̄ⱼ = ∑(v∈Vi) d(v,pⱼ)/|Vi| ,  j= 1, 2, 3;
8.            diff(u)=(d(u,p1)- d̄₁ )²+(d(u,p2)- d̄₂ )²+(d(u,p3)- d̄₃ )²
9.        End of For each subset
10.       Move n to the Vi which gets the minimal diff(u);
11.    End of For each node
12. End
```

Fig. 4. The pseudo-code of Pharos-based Clustering Algorithm

Finally, N un-intersect subsets $V_1, V_2, \cdots, V_N$ are generated. They meet the following conditions:

$$V_1 \cup V_2 \cup \cdots \cup V_N = V \tag{5}$$

$$\forall\, i, j \in \{1,2,\dots,N\},\ V_1 \cap V_2 = \emptyset \tag{6}$$

4.2 Pharos Determination Policy

In a 2-D coordinate system, 3 different reference points would be enough for positioning an unknown u. This can be easily confirmed by the left part of Figure 5.

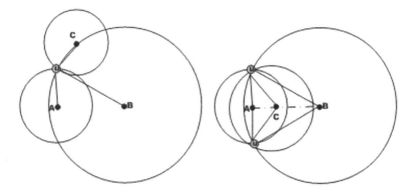

Fig. 5. Left: Let d1, d2 and d3 denote the distances from u to three reference points A, B and C. Regard A as the centre, d1 as the radius, draws a circle Circle(A, d1). Similarly draw Circle(B, d2) and Circle(C, d3). Three circles can only intersect at one single point. Figure 5 Right: If three reference points are on a straight line, the position of u cannot be determinate, because it still has two alternatives.

Feasible pharoses should avoid being on the same line. Furthermore, geometrical theorem reveals that far-away reference points can improve positioning accuracy. Here introduce an elaborate method to meet these two requirements. Firstly, find out the diameter of G, denoted as D. Suppose two end nodes connecting the diameter are p_1 and p_2. Secondly, find out the set of nodes whose distances to p_1 are larger than $2/D$, denoted as Set1. Similarly, find out another set of nodes whose distances to p_2 are larger than $2/D$, denoted as Set2. Finally, let p3 be the node which makes the maximum sum: $d = d(p,p_1) + d(p,p_2),\ p \in \text{Set1} \cap \text{Set2}$. Then $\{p_1,\ p_2,\ p_3\}$ are the selected pharoses. Since $d(p_1,\ p_3) + d(p_2,\ p_3) > D/2 + D/2 = D = d(p_1,p_2)$, it is surely that $p_1,\ p_2$ and p_3 are not on a straight line. Meanwhile, these three nodes are as far away as possible from each other.

4.3 Local Replica Placing Process

After Clustering phase, a large-scale problem is divided into several medium-scale problems. It is noticeable that these problems are completely independent from each other. One cluster's result has none dependence with another's. Obviously, distributed and parallel Placing phrase can provide more scalability and speedup the whole algorithm. In each cluster V_i, any existing algorithm mentioned in section 2 can be applied to obtain local replica policy P_i with much smaller computation and memory overhead.

In order to minimize update cost, a shortest path tree is adopted to act as the update distributing tree T. Every V_i establishes its local tree T_i according to the location of source node s. In cluster V_s which contains the original node s, take s as the root of T_s. In other clusters, a root should be found through the following rule. Let t_i denote the root of T_i. Then it can be picked out by calculate the distance between any node in V_i and original tree T_s. Let $d(u', v')$ denote the smallest one:

$$d(u', v') = \min_{u \in T_i}\{\min_{v \in T_s}\{d(u, v)\}\} \tag{7}$$

Then $t_i = u'$. And v' will be recorded as the attaching point, see Section 4.4.

4.4 Partition Integrating Mechanism

In order to obtain the global policy, every cluster submits its local policy to the original node. It is obviously that the finial replica policy is $P = P_1 \cup P_2 \cup \cdots \cup P_N$.

The last thing remaining is the integrating of update distributing trees. During the Integrating phase, every tree T_i is submitted to s. Then they are attached to T_s one by one, as Figure 6 illustrated. The attaching points also come from (7). This only needs constant time complexity.

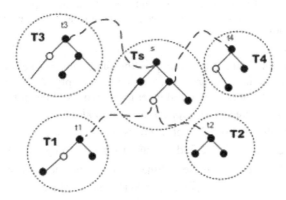

Fig. 6. An example of tree integration during Integrating phase. Black dots represent for replica nodes, while whit dots for non-replica nodes. Four local update distributing trees are grafted to the original tree, thus obtaining the global update distributing tree T.

5 Theoretical Analysis

The philosophical foundation of CPI algorithm is deduction and induction. At the beginning, a large-scale problem is deducted to several small-scale problems with the same essence. On finishing these small problems, all partial results are inducted to generate a complete result. Moreover, CPI is provided with parallel and distributed features in the second phase.

Recall the pseudo-code in Figure 2, we will analyze the time complexity of CPI line by line.

(1) Line 2: the pharos electing algorithm is performed at the time complexity $O(|V|^2)$.

(2) Line 3: the pharos-based clustering process is executed. It contains a sorting process, which has $O(|V|*\log|V|)$ time complexity [15]. About the nested For loops in Figure 4, there are $|V|$ nodes and N clusters, so the complexity is $O(N*|V|)$. Thus the total time complexity of line 3 is $O(|V|*\log|V| + N*|V|)$.

(3) In the For loops from line 4 to line 7, suppose the time complexity of the local replica placement algorithm is typically $O((|V|/N)^3)$, since constructing update distributing tree only needs a complexity of $O((|V|/N)^2)$ [13], so the total time complexity is $O(N*(|V|/N)^3)=O(|V|^3/N^2)$.

(4) Line 8: constant time.

(5) Line 9: according to equation (6), since the average sizes of V_S and V_I are all n/N, so the time complexity is $O(|V|^2/N^2)$.

Therefore, the total time complexity is $O(|V|^3/N^2 + |V|^2)$, depending on the choice of N. For example, in our experiments, let $N=|V|/k$, k is a constant. Then the final time complexity is $O(k^2*|V| + |V|^2) = O(|V|^2)$. It can be concluded that the computation cost is much cheaper than all existing ones.

6   Experiments and Evaluation

With Java language, we developed a simulating test-bed for replica algorithm validating. It consists of 5 parts, listed as follows:

- A famous network topology generator BRITE [16] was imbedded to produce networks graphs. Also corresponding functions were designed to read in BRITE output files and generate all-pairs shortest path matrix.
- A Java GUI graphic tool was developed to show how nodes and replicas are distributed in a square plane.
- A class was implemented to generate a shortest path tree and obtain update cost.
- A library included many existing replica placement algorithms, as well as CPI.
- Other utilities and assistant classes.

The test-bed is running at a personal computer with Intel Pentium M Process 1.7GHz, 1GB memory, 100GB disk and Windows XP OS. For justice, only "pure" costs of algorithms are recorded. For one graph size, BRITE generated 100 graphs to test effects of one algorithm. The result of this algorithm in our record is the average of 100 times of experiments. We chose the Waxman model [16] to generate network topology. The process can be outlined as follows: firstly N nodes are randomly placed into a square plane ordered by HS and LS. Then link is created between each pair of nodes (u, v) with the probability of $p(u, v) = \alpha \cdot e^{-d(u,v)/(\beta \cdot D)}$, where $d(u, v)$ is the Euclidean distance between u and v, D is the diameter of the graph, and α, β are both Waxman parameters. Larger β will generate more edges, and higher α will result more long edge. Finally a bandwidth is set to every edge. In our experiments, HS = 1000, LS = 1000, $\alpha = 0.15$, $\beta = 0.2$. Additionally, the label of original node was generated randomly. Without loss of generality, $s(v) \equiv 1$ and $\lambda \equiv 0.5$.

6.1 The Choice of Parameter N

As we discussed in section 4.1, number of clusters N influences the clustering algorithm so much. In this section, different sizes of k are tested to find the proper rang of N. Let k varies from 100 to 800. At the same time, different sizes of N are tested. Since update cost is consistent with the time cost, we only recorded the time expended. Table 1 shows the influence of k.

Table 1. Time complexity of CPI under different parameter k (unit: second)

N	100	200	400	800	1600	3200
$k=100$	2.47	2.86	23.16	63.03	241.37	328.73
$k=200$	2.14	23.86	24.67	41.93	125.42	245.32
$k=400$	3.03	3.86	11.12	34.17	63.25	183.25
$k=800$	3.39	5.97	33.67	242.27	445.13	456.31

When k is large, the time cost is mainly decided by the local replica algorithm. On the contrary, it is mainly generated from the clustering algorithm. From table 1 we can conclude that $k=400$ is a proper value.

6.2 Time Complexity and Space

Four different algorithms were operated on the test-bed, with the number of nodes growing from 100 to 3200. The QoS is fixed to $0.2 * D$, where D is the diameter of graph G. *0-Greedy-Insert* and *0-Greedy-Delete* are introduced in Tang and Xu's paper [9]. *GC* stands for *Greedy-Cover* algorithm [10]. In CPI algorithm, *0-Greedy-Insert* is adopted to solve cluster replica placing problem. The number of clusters k is set to 400, as discussed in Section 6.1. If $N < 400$, no clustering operation occurs. And the CPI algorithm will be degraded to be a normal *0-Greedy-Insert*. Note: if running time exceeds 2 hours (7200 seconds), it will be marked as the symbol E/T, which means OutOfTime exception. Comparatively, another symbol E/M represents for the OutOfMemory exception.

Table 2 shows how the number of nodes influenced the time complexity of traditional algorithms. As the node number doubled, the time costs of *0-Greedy-Insert*, *0-Greedy-Delete* and *GC* increased by an order of magnitude. *GC* got better results than *0-Greedy-Insert* or *0-Greedy-Delete* because it didn't have to repeat calculating the update cost during placing. The construction of update distributing tree can be finished at the very end of the algorithm.

Only CPI can handle a placement problem with over 3000 nodes. When N is less than 400, time cost of CPI is almost the same with a local algorithm. In this case, CPI is degenerated to a *0-Greedy-Insert* algorithm. When N is larger than 400, the cost of CPI keeps stable at several tens of seconds, which is approximate the cost of *0-Greedy-Insert* handling 400 nodes. Even when $N = 3200$, the cost does not exceed 500 seconds. This result accords with the theoretical analysis in section 5.

Table 2. Time & space costs of different algorithms (unit: second)

# of Nodes	*0-Greedy-Insert*	*0-Greedy-Delete*	*GC*	*CPI*
100	0.19	5.78	0.11	0.35
200	2.78	151.45	0.38	3.66
400	35.78	5285	3.16	37.85
800	542.27	E/T	29.50	42.72
1600	E/T	E/T	259.91	192.65
3200	E/M	E/M	E/M	472.23

6.3 The Effect of Replica Placement

In this section we will compare the effect of different algorithms. Metrics includes the number of replicas and the update costs, and thus the replica cost calculated by the expression (1).

Suppose that CPI still use *0-Greedy-Insert* as the local cluster replica placement solution. From figure 7 we know that CPI needs more replicas than *0-Greedy-Insert* to satisfy all clients' QoS requirements. However, the replica number of CPI is much

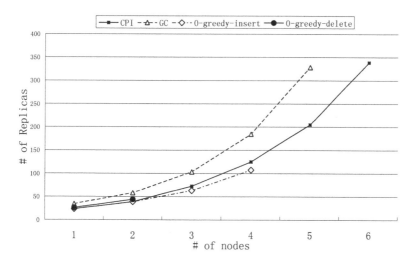

Fig. 7. With the growth of nodes, increments of replica numbers of different algorithms remain stable. The coordinates 1-6 at x- axis stand for 100 nodes, 200 nodes, 400 nodes, 800 nodes, 1600 nodes and 3200 nodes respectively.

less than that of GC. This is because GC only considered the nodes nearby, while CPI will check the whole node sets to find proper clusters. The increment of storage cost is also acceptable. From the experiment we also found that update cost is closely relative with the number of replicas. It has the similar curves as in Figure 7. For the limitations of space, we omitted to describe it.

7 Conclusion

By testing various existing QoS-aware replica placement algorithms on our self-designed test-bed, we found out that they all lacks of scalability and can only handle small-scale and medium-scale QARP problems. In this paper, we propose a novel three-phase algorithm CPI to overcome the embarrassment. The ideal of CPI is to divide a large-scale problem into several medium-scale partial problems with an effective clustering algorithm. After each partial problem is solved, the integration of all partial results will generate the complete result.

There are several original ideas in the algorithm, including the pharos-based clustering methods and the integrating mechanism of multiple update distributing trees. In order to investigate and test different algorithms, we designed and implemented a general-purposed test-bed by ourselves. Elaborate plans and sufficient experiments make our work solid and convincible.

References

1. Patiño-Martinez, M., Jiménez-Peris, R., et al.: MIDDLE-R: Consistent database replication at the middleware level. ACM Transactions on Computer Systems (TOCS) 23(4), 375–423 (2005)
2. Zhang, J., Honeyman, P.: Hierarchical Replication Control in a Global File System. In: Seventh IEEE International Symposium on Cluster Computing and the Grid, CCGRID 2007, pp. 155–162 (2007)
3. Gkantsidis, C., Rodriguez, P.R.: Network coding for large scale content distribution. In: 24th Annual Joint Conference of the IEEE Computer and Communications Societies, vol. 4, pp. 2235–2245 (2005)
4. Krishnamurthy, B., Wills, C., Zhang, Y.: On the use and performance of content distribution networks. In: Proceedings of the 1st ACM SIGCOMM Workshop on Internet Measurement table of contents, pp. 169–182
5. Malkhi, D., Novik, L., Purcell, C.: P2P replica synchronization with vector sets. ACM SIGOPS Operating Systems Review archive 41(2), 68–74 (2007)
6. Ann Chervenak, I.F., Kesselman, C., Salisbury, C., Tuecke, S.: The Data Grid: Towards an Architecture for the Distributed Management and Analysis of Large Scientic Datasets. Journal of Network and Computer Applications 23, 187–200 (2001)
7. Qiu, L., Padmanabhan, V.N., Voelker, G.M.: On the Placement of Web Server Replicas. In: Proc. IEEE INFOCOM 2001, pp. 1587–1596 (2001)
8. Cidon, I., Kutten, S., Soffer, R.: Optimal Allocation of Electronic Content. In: Proc. IEEE INFOCOM 2001, April 2001, pp. 1773–1780 (2001)
9. Tang, X., Xu, J.: Qos-aware replica placement for content distribution. IEEE Transactions on Parallel and Distributed Systems 10, 921–932 (2005)

10. Hsiangkai Wang, P.L., Wu, J.-J.: A QoS-Aware Heuristic Algorithm for Replica Placement. In: Grid Computing Conference 2006 (2006)
11. Won, J., Jeon, I.G., Nahrstedt, K.: QoS-aware Object Replication in Overlay Networks. In: IPTPS 2005 (2005)
12. Fu, W., Xiao, N., Lu, X.: QoS-Guaranteed Ring Replication Management with Strong Consistency. In: ApWeb/WAIM Workshops, Huangshan China (2007)
13. Tao, W., Wei-Sheng, L.: A Fast Low-Cost Shortest Path Tree Algorithm. Journal of Software (China) 15(5), 660–665
14. http://en.wikipedia.org/wiki/Global_Positioning_System (2008)
15. Schnorr, C.P., Shamir, A.: An optimal sorting algorithm for mesh connected computers. In: Proceedings of the eighteenth annual ACM symposium on Theory of computing table of contents, pp. 255–263 (1986)
16. Medina, A., Lakhina, A., Matta, I., Byers, J.: BRITE: an approach to universal topology generation. In: Ninth International Symposium on Modeling, Analysis and Simulation of Computer and Telecommunication Systems, pp. 346–353 (2001)

Online Balancing Two Independent Criteria

Savio S.H. Tse

Department of Computer Engineering,
Bilkent University,
Ankara 06800, Turkey
sshtse@cs.bilkent.edu.tr
http://www.cs.bilkent.edu.tr/~sshtse

Abstract. We study the online bicriteria load balancing problem in this paper. We choose a system of distributed homogeneous file servers located in a cluster as the scenario and propose two online approximate algorithms for balancing their loads and required storage spaces.

We first revisit the best existing solution for document placement, and rewrite it in our first algorithm by imposing some flexibilities. The second algorithm bounds the load and storage space of each server by less than three times of their trivial lower bounds, respectively; and more importantly, for each server, the value of at least one parameter is far from its worst case. The time complexities for both algorithm are $O(\log M)$.

Keywords: Approximate, Distributed, Online algorithm; Load balancing, Scheduling; Distributed file server; Document placement.

1 Introduction

Load balancing is a technique to achieve better coordination between entities such that the load burdened on each entity should not differ too much from that on others. In other words, load balancing is to prevent overwhelming any small subset of entities. The problem becomes NP-hard if we aim at evenly distributing the workload to all entities which provide the same services, or minimizing the difference between them. Therefore, approximate solutions are expected. The load on an entity can be its access rate, the number of execution of some important steps for each access, the number of bits transferred for each request, etc.. There are some different types of approximate solutions for load balancing. A common one is to bound the load of each entity by a limit [4,12,14]. Its variant is to set the limit according to the capacity of each individual entity [3]. In this paper, we choose the first type. In reality, there are often more than one parameter needed to be balanced. For example, execution time and memory utilization are two common parameters requiring simultaneous balancing. In this paper, we address the online bicriteria load balancing problem, and the two criteria are independent. We consider a system of distributed homogeneous file servers in a cluster, and the parameters to be balanced are the load and storage space. Hereafter, the single word "load" is referred to a parameter while "load

J. Cao et al. (Eds.): NPC 2008, LNCS 5245, pp. 244–254, 2008.

balancing" is referred to the classical problem. The load of a document stored in the file server system can be one of the quantities discussed above, and the storage space can be its physical size, or the memory space needed to process the document. The system designer can also take any other reasonable choices.

1.1   Related Works

With applying a limit to a set of homogeneous servers for bounding their loads, the single criterion load balancing problem is basically the NP-hard multiprocessor scheduling problem, which is reduced from the classical problem PARTITION [8]. Many heuristics have been proposed for solving it. The latest result was given by Fleischer and Wahl [7], which is an online $(1+\sqrt{\frac{1+\ln 2}{2}})$-competitive algorithm. (An online algorithm is c-competitive if the parameter needed to be minimized is bounded by c times its optimal values.) It is asymptotically the best known upper bound result. The latest lower bound result is by Rudin et al. [13], which shows that no c-competitive algorithm exists if $c < 1.88$.

For bicriteria load balancing, as there is one more constraint to tackle, higher upper bounds for both load and storage space are expected. In 2001, Chen et al. gave two offline algorithms, and one of them balances both the load and storage space [4]. It bounds the load by $4L$ using at most $4S$ storage space, where L and S (defined in Section 2) are commonly used as the trivial worst case lower bounds for load and storage space, respectively. In 2005, we proposed some algorithms [14], including an $O(\log M)$-time online algorithm which bounds the load and storage space of each server by $k_l L$ and $k_s S$, respectively, where $k_l > 2$, $k_s > 2$, and $\frac{1}{k_l-1} + \frac{1}{k_s-1} \leq 1$. In 2006, Bilò et al. gave a $(\frac{2M-k}{M-k+1}, \frac{M+k-1}{k})$-competitive algorithm [2], where k can be any integer from 1 to M. It bounds the load and storage space by $\frac{2M-k}{M-k+1}L$ and $\frac{M+k-1}{k}S$, respectively. It slightly improves the result for the online algorithm in [14], especially for small values of M. This is the best known result which can be generalized for balancing multi-parameters. Note that $k_l < 3 \Leftrightarrow k_s > 3$, and $\frac{2M-k}{M-k+1} < 3 - \frac{4}{M+1} \Leftrightarrow \frac{M+k-1}{k} > 3 - \frac{4}{M+1}$. Therefore, asymptotically $(M \to \infty)$, there is no result which can bound the load by $h_l L$, and the storage space by $h_s S$, where h_l and h_s are any positive real numbers less than three.

1.2   Our Contribution

By modifying a technique in [14], we improve slightly on their last result in our first algorithm. This result is essentially the same as, but more flexible than, the upper bound result in [2]. The bounds of the load and storage space in our first result are $t_l L$ and $t_s S$, respectively, where $t_l, t_s > 1$ are real numbers satisfying both $\frac{1}{t_l-1} + \frac{1}{t_s-1} \leq 1 + \frac{2}{M-1}$ and $[\frac{M-1}{t_l-1}, \frac{M-1}{t_s-1} \notin I^+] \implies [\lfloor\frac{M-1}{t_l-1}\rfloor + \lfloor\frac{M-1}{t_s-1}\rfloor < M]$. Comparing with the algorithm in [2], practically, the advantage of our algorithm is the flexibility in choosing suitable servers. An example in Section 3.2 shows the possibility of finding a server which can allow us to gain a lot in storage space at the expense of little sacrifice on load. However, we improve the searching algorithm only for bicriteria load balancing, which is a special case for multi-criteria load balancing tackled in [2].

We present our result in two equations, in which we can easily see the tradeoff between the upper bounds of load and storage space, and their symmetry and asymptotic behaviour (as $M \to \infty$). This representation has more theoretical benefit.

The last algorithm bounds the load and storage space of each server by $(3 - \frac{2}{M})L$ and $(3 - \frac{2}{M})S$, respectively, with a feature that dictates if the load is higher than $(\frac{5}{2} - \frac{3}{2M})L$, then the storage space is less than $(\frac{5}{2} - \frac{3}{2M})S$ (and vice versa). In other words, at most one of load and storage space in each server can get close to their upper bounds. It is another style of load balancing, which does not exist in the literature [4,12,14], as far as we know.

2   Definitions and Models

Each document has two fundamental independent attributes, namely load and size. For the convenience of discussion, assume the load of a document to be the product of its access rate and its size plus the number of execution of some specific I/O steps. There are M servers and N documents. The value of N changes accordingly upon each placement and deletion. If server insertion is considered, The value of M will also increase by one on each server insertion. For every $i \in \{1, \ldots, N\}$, the ith document has positive load l_i and size s_i. For convenience, assume the indices of documents will automatically shift up upon each document deletion. The load and storage space of a server is the summation of loads and sizes of all documents stored, respectively. For all $j \in \{1, \ldots, M\}$, the load of the jth server is denoted as $\mathcal{L}_j$ and the storage space as $\mathcal{S}_j$. We do not assume any fixed limit on their values.

Let $\overline{L}$ and $\overline{S}$ be the average load and storage space of all servers in the system. Therefore, $\overline{L} = \frac{\sum_{i \in \{1,\ldots,N\}} l_i}{M}$, and $\overline{S} = \frac{\sum_{i \in \{1,\ldots,N\}} s_i}{M}$. As $\overline{S}$ is highly related to the upper bound of the cost of document recollocation, in order to keep its value reasonably small, M is assumed to be large enough although our algorithms also work for small M. Let L be $\max(\max_{i \in \{1,\ldots,N\}} l_i, \overline{L})$ and S be $\max(\max_{i \in \{1,\ldots,N\}} s_i, \overline{S})$. Note that $\overline{L}$, $\overline{S}$, L and S only depend on the existing documents stored and the number of servers. These algorithm-independent quantities are used in the descriptions of the upper bounds of $\mathcal{L}_j$ and $\mathcal{S}_j$, for all $j \in \{1, \ldots, M\}$, respectively, for all algorithms in this paper. Clearly, L and S are trivial lower bounds on the highest load and storage space of each server, respectively. For completeness, assume $\overline{L} = \overline{S} = 0$ and $L = S = 0$ when there is no document in the server system. We define the capacity index C_j for the jth server to be $\frac{\mathcal{L}_j}{L} + \frac{\mathcal{S}_j}{S}$, for each $j \in \{1, \ldots, M\}$. It is a metric that measures the combined effect of the loads and storage spaces of the servers, and the trivial lower bound of its worst case is obviously two. It is basically the sum of the normalized load and normalized storage space, and therefore, less affected by absolute values of two individual parameters. Obviously, $\sum_{j \in \{1,\ldots,M\}} C_j \leq 2M$.

The purpose of the capacity index is to enhance further balancing among servers. For example, if $\mathcal{L}_j \leq 3L$, $\mathcal{S}_j \leq 3S$, and $C_j < 4$, for all $j \in \{1, \ldots, M\}$, one can conclude that although the worst case of the load and storage space can be three times of L and S, respectively, only of them can be close to its worst case.

Let $t_l, t_s \in (1, M]$ be two real numbers satisfying both

$$\frac{1}{t_l-1} + \frac{1}{t_s-1} \leq 1 + \frac{2}{M-1}, \text{ and} \tag{1}$$

$$[\tfrac{M-1}{t_l-1}, \tfrac{M-1}{t_s-1}] \notin I^+] \Longrightarrow [\lfloor \tfrac{M-1}{t_l-1} \rfloor + \lfloor \tfrac{M-1}{t_s-1} \rfloor < M]. \tag{2}$$

These two values are used throughout the paper to reflect the tradeoff between the bounds of loads and storage spaces for all servers. The relationship between t_l and t_s for all feasible pairs of values and the intuition of these two equations will be discussed later in Section 3.1. Fact 1 below will be used in some proofs in this paper.

Fact 1. *Suppose $x_1, x_2 \in I^+$ such that $x_1 < \frac{M-1}{t_l-1}$ and $x_2 < \frac{M-1}{t_s-1}$. Then, $x_1 + x_2 < M$.*

Proof. If both $\frac{M-1}{t_l-1}$ and $\frac{M-1}{t_s-1}$ are integers, then (let) $y = x_1 + x_2 \leq (\frac{M-1}{t_l-1} - 1) + (\frac{M-1}{t_s-1} - 1) < M$. If the former one (say) is an integer, then $y \leq (\frac{M-1}{t_l-1} - 1) + \lfloor \frac{M-1}{t_s-1} \rfloor = (\frac{M-1}{t_l-1} - 1) + (\lceil \frac{M-1}{t_s-1} \rceil - 1) \leq M + 1 - 2 < M$. If both of them are not integers, then $y \leq \lfloor \frac{M-1}{t_l-1} \rfloor + \lfloor \frac{M-1}{t_s-1} \rfloor < M$.

We apply a tree structure like B^+-tree [11] which is widely employed for storing the information of the servers in this paper. We call it B^0-*tree*, as [14]. A B^0-tree stores a set $\{(l,s)|l, s \in R^+\}$. In each order pair (l, s), l and s are referred to load and storage space of a server, respectively. We assume the elements stored in a B^0-tree are unique. (Precisely, the set can be organized as $(B_1, B_2, \ldots, B_{M'})$, where $B_j = (l, s)$ for some $l, s \in R^+$, $\forall j \in \{1, \ldots, M'\}$, $M' \leq M$.) Like B^+-tree, data (keys) are stored in leaves, and all leaves are located at the bottom level. Except for the root, each internal node has $\frac{K}{2}$ to K children. The root has 1 to K children. Like B^+-tree, the data in the bottom level are sorted according to s-values, and unlike B^+-tree, a parent node stores a copy of one of its children with smallest l-value. If there are two children having the smallest l-value, choose the one with smaller s-value. Hence, the root contains the copy of the data with minimum l-value. The normal operations are similar to those of B^+-tree. To keep the time for maintenance in $O(\log t)$, where t is the number of data stored in the tree, there is an auxiliary B^+-tree for storing the s-values only. For simplicity, we skip the discussion of those necessary but trivial steps for operations, like lookup, insertion and deletion on the data structure.

Let $\mathcal{SEEK}$ be the algorithm for performing searching and updating on a B^0-tree. This algorithm will be used in the following sections. For any input (X, Y), where $X, Y \in R^+$, $\mathcal{SEEK}$ can search an element (l, s) in a B^0-tree and perform updating within $O(\log t)$ time, where s is the smallest possible value such that $l \leq X$. If there are two l's with smallest s-value, choose the smaller one. In the case that $l > X$ for each (l, s) in the tree, $\mathcal{SEEK}$ will output false. The next step is to check $s \leq Y$. If true, output (l, s); otherwise, output false. That means, if output is (l, s), then $l \leq X$ and $s \leq Y$. In other words, $\mathcal{SEEK}$ is used for searching a server with load and storage space inclusively bounded by certain values, respectively, and storage space is as less as possible.

By the similar construction, we can easily obtain an algorithm $\mathcal{SEEK}^*$ such that if output is (l, s), then $l < X$ and $s < Y$. In other words, $\mathcal{SEEK}^*$ is used for searching a server with load and storage space exclusively bounded by certain values, respectively, and storage space is as less as possible.

For conciseness, all B^0-trees used in this paper will be automatically updated and maintained, unless specified.

Let T_A be $\{(\mathcal{L}_j, \mathcal{S}_j) | j \in \{1, \ldots, M\}\}$ which is stored in a B^0-tree. That is, it stores the loads and storage spaces of all servers. The reallocation cost of a document is defined as its size. In particular, if all documents in the ith server are reallocated, the cost will be $\mathcal{S}_i$.

Lastly, our results are for synchronous networks; that is, before the completion of updating the data structures and reallocating the necessary documents for the previous operation, the next operation will not be performed.

3   The First Result

We consider document placement into a distributed file server. Our aim is to bound the loads and storage spaces of all servers by $t_l L$ and $t_s S$, respectively. With smaller values of t_l and t_s, the upper bounds are tightened and imply better balancing on load and storage space, respectively. The bounds are loosened slowly with M according to Equations (1) and (2). This matches with the fact that it is more difficult to coordinate more resources. However, such difficulty is not unlimited, as the bounds asymptotically tend to the result in [14]. We now apply tighter equations for t_l and t_s and analyse on the upper bounds.

Algorithm FIRST:

1.   Upon the arrival of a document d with load l and size s

1.1   Perform $\mathcal{SEEK}$ on T_A with input $(\frac{M}{M-1}(t_l - 1)\overline{L}, \frac{M}{M-1}(t_s - 1)\overline{S})$
         and get output $(\mathcal{L}_j, \mathcal{S}_j)$;

1.2   Place d into the jth server;

1.3   Update $\overline{L}$ and $\overline{S}$;

Theorem 1. *The new document can be placed into a server, and after placement, the load and storage space of the server are no more than $t_l L$ and $t_s S$, respectively.*

Proof. If the server system is initially empty, the algorithm can place the document and give the bounds L and S, respectively.

Assume there are some documents in the server system. Before placing the document d, there are less than $\frac{M-1}{t_l-1}$ servers with load more than $\frac{M}{M-1}(t_l - 1)\overline{L}$, otherwise, the total load will exceed $M\overline{L}$. Similarly, there are less than $\frac{M-1}{t_s-1}$ servers with storage space more than $\frac{M}{M-1}(t_s-1)\overline{S}$. By Fact 1, the number of servers exceeding the load bound or the storage space bound is less than M. Hence, there exists one server with load and storage space at most $\frac{M}{M-1}(t_l-1)\overline{L}$ and $\frac{M}{M-1}(t_s-1)\overline{S}$, respectively, and $\mathcal{SEEK}$ will output such a server as the jth server in Step 1.1.

Suppose that the average load is $\overline{L}'$ after Step 1.2. Then, $\overline{L}' = \overline{L}+\frac{l}{M}$. $\mathcal{L}_j$ is then at most $\frac{M}{M-1}(t_l-1)\overline{L}+l = \frac{M}{M-1}(t_l-1)(\overline{L}'-\frac{l}{M})+l = \frac{M}{M-1}(t_l-1)\overline{L}'+(1-\frac{t_l-1}{M-1})l$. The result for load follows as $\overline{L}'$ and l are no more than the final L. By using similar arguments, the result for storage space follows.

3.1 The Feasible Region for Values of t_l and t_s

We discuss the feasible region for values of t_l and t_s satisfying Equations (1) and (2). The purpose is to provide more information to the system designer to choose values for t_l and t_s for different situations.

For the case that $\frac{1}{t_l-1} + \frac{1}{t_s-1} \le 1+\frac{1}{M-1}$, Equations (1) and (2) are always true. The region for this case is labeled as A in Figure 1.

For the case that $\frac{1}{t_l-1} + \frac{1}{t_s-1} = 1+\frac{2}{M-1}$, if $\frac{M-1}{t_l-1}$ and $\frac{M-1}{t_s-1}$ are non-integers, then $\lfloor\frac{M-1}{t_l-1}\rfloor + \lfloor\frac{M-1}{t_s-1}\rfloor = M$, which implies that Equation (2) is false. Then, we cannot use Fact 1 to guarantee the existence of a server for placement. In order to keep Equation (2) true, one of $\frac{M-1}{t_l-1}$ and $\frac{M-1}{t_s-1}$ must be an integer. As $\frac{M-1}{t_l-1} + \frac{M-1}{t_s-1} = M + 1$, both $\frac{M-1}{t_l-1}$ and $\frac{M-1}{t_s-1}$ are integers between 1 and M, inclusively. In other words, there are M feasible pairs of t_l and t_s on the curve $\frac{1}{t_l-1} + \frac{1}{t_s-1} = 1+\frac{2}{M-1}$, satisfying Equation (2). Let $k = \frac{M-1}{t_s-1}$. Then, $\frac{M-1}{t_l-1} = M - k + 1$. Rewriting the result in Theorem 1 in terms of M and k, our load bound $t_l L = \frac{2M-k}{M-k+1}L$, and storage space bound $t_s S = \frac{M+k-1}{k}S$. This matches exactly with the $(\frac{2M-k}{M-k+1}, \frac{M+k-1}{k})$-competitive algorithm in [2]. In other words, if we equalize the inequality in Equation (1), the algorithm FIRST has identical upper bounds as in [2]. As k is ranged from 1 to M, there are M feasible points for (t_l, t_s) on the curve $\frac{1}{t_l-1} + \frac{1}{t_s-1} = 1+\frac{2}{M-1}$.

Claims 3.1 and 3.1 below investigate the structure for t_l and t_s satisfying $1+\frac{1}{M-1} < \frac{1}{t_l-1} + \frac{1}{t_s-1} < 1+\frac{2}{M-1}$.

Claim. For all $t_l, t_s \in R^+$ satisfying $1+\frac{1}{M-1} < \frac{1}{t_l-1} + \frac{1}{t_s-1} < 1+\frac{2}{M-1}$, Equation (2) is true if and only if there exists a $k \in \{1, 2, \ldots, M\}$ such that $t_s \ge \frac{M+k-1}{k}$ and $t_l \ge \frac{2M-k}{M-k+1}$.

Proof. Suppose Equation (2) is true. If one of $\frac{M-1}{t_l-1}$ and $\frac{M-1}{t_s-1}$ is an integer, without loss of generality, assume that $\frac{M-1}{t_s-1}$ is an integer, and let $k = \frac{M-1}{t_s-1}$. Then $t_s = \frac{M-1}{k} + 1$. As $\frac{M-1}{t_l-1} + \frac{M-1}{t_s-1} < M + 1$, we have $\frac{M-1}{t_l-1} < M + 1 - k$, and result follows. If both $\frac{M-1}{t_l-1}$ and $\frac{M-1}{t_s-1}$ are non-integers, then $\lfloor\frac{M-1}{t_l-1}\rfloor + \lfloor\frac{M-1}{t_s-1}\rfloor < M$. Let $k = \lfloor\frac{M-1}{t_s-1}\rfloor$. Then $\frac{M-1}{t_l-1} - 1 < \lfloor\frac{M-1}{t_l-1}\rfloor < M - k$, and result follows.

Suppose Equation (2) is false. Then, both $\frac{M-1}{t_l-1}$ and $\frac{M-1}{t_s-1}$ are non-integers and $\lfloor\frac{M-1}{t_l-1}\rfloor + \lfloor\frac{M-1}{t_s-1}\rfloor = M$. For all $k \in \{1, 2, \ldots, M\}$, we have $t_s \geq \frac{M+k-1}{k} \Leftrightarrow k \geq \frac{M-1}{t_s-1} > \lfloor\frac{M-1}{t_s-1}\rfloor \Leftrightarrow M-k < \lfloor\frac{M-1}{t_l-1}\rfloor \Leftrightarrow M-k+1 \leq \lfloor\frac{M-1}{t_l-1}\rfloor < \frac{M-1}{t_l-1} \Leftrightarrow t_l < \frac{2M-k}{M-k+1}$. Result follows.

Claim. For all $k \in \{1, 2, \ldots, M-1\}$, the point $(\frac{2M-k-1}{M-k}, \frac{M+k-1}{k})$ is on the curve $\frac{1}{t_l-1} + \frac{1}{t_s-1} = 1 + \frac{1}{M-1}$.

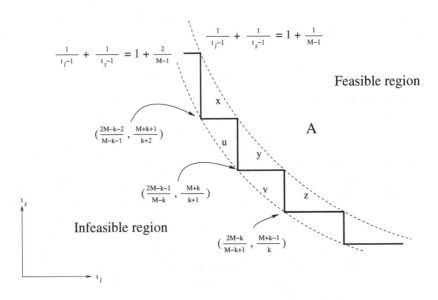

Fig. 1. Feasible Region for values of t_l and t_s

We skip the trivial proof for Claim 3.1. Recalling the M feasible points is on the curve $\frac{1}{t_l-1} + \frac{1}{t_s-1} = 1 + \frac{2}{M-1}$, and together with Claims 3.1 and 3.1, the whole feasible region is now clear and is shown in Figure 1. In the figure, the feasible and infeasible regions are separated by the solid zigzag (-horizontal-vertical-) line which is bounded tightly by two dotted curves $\frac{1}{t_l-1} + \frac{1}{t_s-1} = 1 + \frac{1}{M-1}$ and $\frac{1}{t_l-1} + \frac{1}{t_s-1} = 1 + \frac{2}{M-1}$, and the vertices of the zigzag line touch the curves alternatively. The feasible region is divided into two types of sub-regions. The largest sub-region is the open-ended one bounded below by the upper curve. We label it as A. The sub-regions of the second type, which are disjoint, spread over the gap between two curves. The ones labeled as x, y and z are examples. The values inside the sub-regions of this type satisfy Equation (2). In contrast, the points between two adjacent sub-regions turn Equation (2) false. Examples are u and v in the figure. It is easily seen that the M feasible points in the lower curve are the best in the whole feasible region. Precisely, for every other point in the feasible region, there is a better choice from these M feasible points. Since the two curves will narrow and become one as $M \to \infty$, the sub-regions of the second type diminish with M, and the M best points will coincide with the upper curve.

From the feasible region, we have some suggestions to the system designer. First if M is unchanged, we can use one of the M best points on the lower curve. After the system designer chooses a point, he can proceed to check if both Equations (1) and (2) remain true. If yes, he can apply his values. Otherwise, use binary search to find a point out of the M best points, which is nearest to his original choice. The time needed is $O(\log M)$. Binary search can be used because of the convex nature of the feasible region.

If M can be increased by server insertion, the previous M points may become infeasible as the lower curve shifts upwards. Even when M decreases by server deletion, some points may fall into infeasible region when the two curves shifts down. One can easily see from the figure that there are no two consecutive points staying in the feasible region as M decreases by 1. In order not to put burden on the system maintenance, we suggest to use the points, satisfying $\frac{1}{t_l-1}+\frac{1}{t_s-1} \leq 1$, in the region A, if M can change. These points, used in [14], are independent of M, and is suitable for a system in which the number of servers is changing.

3.2   Remarks on Algorithm FIRST

Comparing Algorithm FIRST with the result in [2], our algorithm has two advantages. First, our upper bounds can spread through the continuous feasible region, not only the M best points. The second advantage comes from the difference of searching algorithms. The algorithm in [2] ignores the servers of the first $M - k$ highest load, $k \in \{1, \ldots, M\}$. In the case that the loads of some of these ignored servers are not very high but the storage spaces of them are very low, our algorithm is beneficial. Take for an example. For all $j \in \{1, \ldots, M-k-1\}$, $\mathcal{L}_j = \overline{L}+\delta$ and $\mathcal{S}_j = \frac{M\overline{S}-\delta}{M-1}$; $\mathcal{L}_{M-k} = \overline{L}$ and $\mathcal{S}_{M-k} = \delta$; and for all $j \in \{M-k+1, \ldots, M\}$, $\mathcal{L}_j = \overline{L} - \frac{M-k-1}{k}\delta$ and $\mathcal{S}_j = \frac{M\overline{S}-\delta}{M-1}$, where δ is extremely small. Then, one of the last k servers will be chosen by the algorithm in [2], but algorithm $\mathcal{SEEK}$ will choose the $(M - k)$th one. The former have little advantage on load but pays much higher price on storage space. Nevertheless, the searching algorithm in [2] can be easily generalized for balancing more than two criteria. Although $\mathcal{SEEK}$ is better, it is designed for two criteria only. Further research can be done on finding better searching algorithms for multi-criteria load balancing problem.

4   The Second Result

In this section, we study the capacity index which measures the integrated effect of load and storage space on each server. Our aim is to bound the load, the storage space and the capacity index of each server by $(3 - \frac{2}{M})L$, $(3 - \frac{2}{M})S$, and $5 - \frac{3}{M}$, respectively, after each document placement.

Consider the algorithm FIRST. We choose $t_l = t_s = 3 - \frac{4}{M+1}$ for odd M. For even M, we choose $t_l = 3 - \frac{2}{M}$, and $t_s = 3 - \frac{6}{M+2}$, or vice versa. Then, a trivial upper bound $6 - \frac{8}{M+1}$ on the capacity index can be obtained immediately. In this section, by using algorithm SECOND, the capacity index is improved to $5 - \frac{3}{M}$, at the expense of a slightly higher upper bound(s) for load and/or storage space, respectively. In other words, if we sacrifice the asymptotically nothing in the upper bounds of load and storage space, respectively, then we gain much more in capacity index in return.

Directly from the definition, the capacity index $5 - \frac{3}{M}$ implies that for each server, at most one of the two parameters, load and storage space, can be close to its upper bound of worst case. For example, if the load in a server gets very close to $(3 - \frac{2}{M})L$, then its storage space keeps a distance of nearly S from the upper bound $(3 - \frac{2}{M})S$. In other words, by using algorithm SECOND, the worst cases of load and storage space are shared by more servers. However, by using algorithm FIRST, the load and storage space can both simultaneously reach their upper bounds, respectively. Therefore, algorithm SECOND beats FIRST when t_l and t_s are chosen close to three.

The improvement in capacity index also gives hope that both parameters could be very close to 2.5 of their trivial lower bounds simultaneously. If succeed, it will then an important step towards the asymptotic latest known upper bound of 1.9201 [7] and the lower bound of 1.88 [13] for balancing a single parameter.

As there always exists a $j \in \{1, \ldots, M\}$ such that $\mathcal{L}_j \leq 2\overline{L}$, $\mathcal{S}_j \leq 2\overline{S}$, and $\overline{C}_j \leq 2$ (otherwise, $\sum_{j=1,\ldots,M} \overline{C}_j > 2M$), an $O(M)$-time algorithm can be applied to search this server in order to obtain a better upper bound on capacity index. For small M, the average storage space is large, and this trivial approach is a better choice. However, when M is large, an $O(\log M)$-time algorithm $CAPACITY$ will be given. Its idea is as follows: Upon the arrival of a new document d, if there is a server in which load and storage space are bounded by $\overline{L}$ and $2\overline{S}$, respectively, Step 1.1 of the algorithm will find it and Step 1.2.1 will place d into it. After placement, the load, the storage space, and the capacity index are kept under the mentioned bounded. The details are shown in Theorem 2. Suppose no such server exists in the system. We aim at a server in which load and storage space are bounded by $2\overline{L}$ and $\overline{S}$, respectively. It such a server exists, Step 1.3.1 will find it out and Step 1.3.2 will place d into it. The correctness proof is based on the observation that if Step 1.1 fails in searching a server, then Step 1.3.1 will succeed.

The algorithm SECOND is given below, and is followed by Theorem 2.

Algorithm SECOND:
1.   Upon the arrival of a document d with load l and size s
1.1   Perform $\mathcal{SEEK}^*$ on T_A with input $(\overline{L}, 2\overline{S})$ and get output;
1.2   If output is $(\mathcal{L}_j, \mathcal{S}_j)$;
1.2.1   Place d into the jth server;
1.3   If output is false
1.3.1   Perform $\mathcal{SEEK}^*$ on T_A with input $(2\overline{L}, \overline{S})$ and get output $(\mathcal{L}_i, \mathcal{S}_i)$;
1.3.2   Place d into the ith server;
1.4   Update $\overline{L}$ and $\overline{S}$;

Theorem 2. *The new document can be placed into a server, and after placement, the load and storage space of the server are less than* $(3 - \frac{2}{M})L$ *and* $(3 - \frac{2}{M})S$, *respectively, and the capacity index less than* $5 - \frac{3}{M}$.

Proof. Assume for contradiction that for all $j \in [1, M]$, $\mathcal{L}_j \geq 2\overline{L}$, $\mathcal{S}_j \geq 2\overline{S}$, or $[\mathcal{L}_j > \overline{L}$ and $\mathcal{S}_j > \overline{S}]$. Suppose there are M_1 servers which loads are at least $2\overline{L}$, M_2 servers which storage spaces are at least $2\overline{S}$, and M_3 servers which loads are more than $\overline{L}$, and storage spaces more than $\overline{S}$. Obviously, $M_1 + M_2 + M_3 \geq M$. If $M_1 = 0$, total storage space will exceed $M\overline{S}$. Hence $M_1 \neq 0$. Similarly, $M_2 \neq 0$. Consider that $M_3 = 0$. Since all servers have positive loads, total load is greater than $2M_1\overline{L}$, which implies $M_1 < M_2$. On the other hand, since all servers have positive storage spaces, total storage space is greater than $2M_1\overline{S}$, which implies $M_2 < M_1$. Hence, $M_3 \neq 0$. Considering $\sum_{j=1}^{M}[\frac{\mathcal{L}_j}{\overline{L}} + \frac{\mathcal{S}_j}{\overline{S}}] > 2M_1 + 2M_2 + 2M_3 \geq 2M$, which is a contradiction. Therefore, there exists a $j \in [1, M]$, such that $\mathcal{L}_j < 2\overline{L}$, $\mathcal{S}_j < 2\overline{S}$, and $[\mathcal{L}_j \leq \overline{L}$ or $\mathcal{S}_j \leq \overline{S}]$. Rewriting it, we have either $[\mathcal{L}_j \leq \overline{L}$ and $\mathcal{S}_j < 2\overline{S}]$ or $[\mathcal{S}_j \leq \overline{S}$ and $\mathcal{L}_j < 2\overline{L}]$. We assume the former case while the argument for the latter one is similar.

After placing d into the server, the average load becomes $\overline{L}' = \overline{L} + \frac{l}{M}$, the average storage space becomes $\overline{S}' = \overline{S} + \frac{s}{M}$, and the values of L and S become L' and S'. Then, $\mathcal{L}_i \leq \overline{L}' - \frac{l}{M} + l = \overline{L}' + (1 - \frac{1}{M})l \leq (2 - \frac{1}{M})L'$. For storage space, $\mathcal{S}_i < 2(\overline{S}' - \frac{s}{M}) + s = 2\overline{S}' + (1 - \frac{2}{M})s \leq (3 - \frac{2}{M})S'$. Hence, $C_i < 5 - \frac{3}{M}$.

References

1. Amita, G.C.: Incremental data allocation and reallocation in distributed database systems. Data warehousing and web engineering, 137–160 (2002)
2. Bilò, V., Flammini, M., Moscardelli, L.: Pareto Approximations for the Bicriteria Scheduling Problem. Journal of Parallel and Distributed Computing 66(3), 393–402 (2006)
3. Brinkmann, A., Salzwedel, K., Scheideler, C.: Compact, Adaptive Placement Schemes for Non-Uniform Requirements. In: Proceedings of ACM Symposium on Parallelism in Algorithms and Architectures (SPAA 2002), Winnipeg, Manitoba, Canada (August 2002)
4. Chen, L.C., Choi, H.A.: Approximation Algorithms for Data Distribution with Load Balancing of Web Servers. In: Proc. of IEEE International Conference on Cluster Computing, Newport Beach, CA, USA, pp. 274–281 (October 2001)
5. Cormen, T.H., Leiserson, C.E., Rivest, R.L., Stein, C.: Introduction to Algorithms, 2nd edn. McGraw-Hill, New York (2001)
6. Fisher, M.L., Hochbaum, D.S.: Database Location in Computer Networks. Journal of ACM 27, 718–735 (1980)
7. Fleischer, R., Wahl, M.: Online scheduling revisited. Journal of Scheduling, Special Issue on Approximation Algorithms for Scheduling Algorithms (part 2) 3(6), 343–353 (2000)
8. Garey, M.R., Johnson, D.S.: Computers and Intractability: A Guide to the Theory of NP-Completeness. W.H. Freeman, New York (1979)
9. Haddad, E.: Runtime reallocation of divisible load under processor execution deadlines. In: Proceedings of the Third Workshop on Parallel and Distributed Real-Time Systems, April 1995, pp. 30–31 (1995)

10. Harada, H., Ishikawa, Y., Hori, A., Tezuka, H., Sumimoto, S., Takahashi, T.: Dynamic home node reallocation on software distributed shared memory. In: Proceedings of the Fourth International Conference/Exhibition on High Performance Computing in the Asia-Pacific Region, May 2000, vol. 1, pp. 158–163 (2000)
11. Knuth, D.E.: The Art of Computer Programming. Sorting and Searching, Section 6.2.4, vol. 3. Addison-Wesley, Reading (1973)
12. Narendran, B., Rangarajan, S., Yajnik, S.: Data Distribution Algorithms for Load Balanced Fault-Tolerant Web Access. In: Proc. of the 16th Symposium on Reliable Distributed Systems, Durham, NC, USA, pp. 97–106 (October 1997)
13. Rudin III, J.F.: Improved bounds for the online scheduling problem. PhD thesis, The University of Texas at Dallas (2001)
14. Tse, S.S.H.: Approximation Algorithms for Document Placement in Distributed Web Servers. IEEE Transactions on Parallel and Distributed Systems 16(6), 489–496 (2005)

Procrastination Scheduling for Fixed-Priority Tasks with Preemption Thresholds

XiaoChuan He and Yan Jia

Institute of Network Technology and Information Security
School of Computer Science
National University of Defense Technology
Changsha, China 410073
XiaoChuanHe@gmail.com

Abstract. Dynamic Voltage Scaling (DVS), which adjusts the clock speed and supply voltage dynamically, is an effective technique in reducing the energy consumption of embedded real-time systems. However, the longer a job executes, the more energy in the leakage current the device/processor consumes for the job. Procrastination scheduling, where task execution can be delayed to maximize the duration of idle intervals by keeping the processor in a sleep/shutdown state even if there are pending tasks within the timing constraints imposed by performance requirements, has been proposed to minimize leakage energy drain. This paper targets energy-efficient fixed-priority with preemption threshold scheduling for periodic real-time tasks on a uniprocessor DVS system with non-negligible leakage power consumption. We propose a two-phase algorithm. In the first phase, the execution speed, i.e., the supply voltage of each task are determined by applying off-line algorithms, and in the second phase, the procrastination length of each task is derived by applying on-line simulated work-demand time analysis, and thus the time moment to turn on/off the system is determined on the fly. A series of simulation experiments was evaluated for the performance of our algorithms. The results show that our proposed algorithms can derive energy-efficient schedules.

1 Introduction

Low power utilization has been an important issue for hardware manufacturing for next-generation portable, scalable, and sophisticated embedded systems. To reduce the power consumption without the sacrifice of performance, architectural techniques have been proposed to dynamically trade the performance and power consumption. Dynamic Voltage Scaling (DVS), which adjusts the supply voltage and its corresponding clock frequency dynamically, is one of the most effective low-power design technique for embedded real-time systems. Since the energy consumption of CMOS circuits has a quadratic dependency on the supply voltage, lowering the supply voltage is one of the most effective ways of reducing the energy consumption.

In many real-time applications, average or worst-case task response time is an important non-functional design requirement of the system. For example, to maintain the system stability, many embedded real-time systems must complete the tasks before

J. Cao et al. (Eds.): NPC 2008, LNCS 5245, pp. 255–265, 2008.

their deadlines. For real-time systems targeting commercial variable voltage micro-processors, since lowering the supply voltage also decreases the maximum achievable clock speed [1], *energy-efficient* task scheduling is to reduce supply voltage dynami-cally to the lowest possible level while satisfying the tasks'timing constraints. In the past decade, energy-efficient task scheduling with various deadline constraints received extensive attention, especially for the minimization of the energy consumption of the dynamic voltage scaling part in a uniprocessor environment [2].

Recently, researchers have started exploring energy-efficient scheduling with the con-siderations of leakage current since the power consumption resulting from leakage current is comparable to the dynamic power dissipation [3]. To reduce the energy consumption resulting from leakage current, a system might be turned off (to enter a *dormant mode*). For periodic real-time tasks, Jejurikar et al. [4] and Lee et al. [5] proposed energy-efficient scheduling on a uniprocessor by procrastination scheduling to decide when to turn off the system. Jejurikar and Gupta [3] then further considered real-time tasks that might com-plete earlier than its worst-case estimation by extending the algorithms presented in [4].

Fixed-priority preemptive (FPP) scheduling algorithms and fixed-priority non-preemptive (FPNP) scheduling algorithms are two important classes of real-time scheduling algorithms. To obtain the benefits of both FPP and FPNP algorithms, there are several other algorithms trying to fill the gap between them. The fixed-priority with preemption threshold (FPPT) scheduling algorithm [6] is one of them. Under FPPT, each task has a pair of priorities: regular priority and preemption threshold, where the preemption threshold of a task is higher than or equal to its regular priority. The pre-emption threshold represents the tasks running-time preemption priority level. It pre-vents the preemption of the task from other tasks, unless the preempting tasks priority is higher than the preemption threshold of the current running task. Saksena and Wang have shown that task sets scheduled with FPPT can have significant schedulability im-provements over task set using fixed priorities [6].

This paper considers energy-efficient FPPT scheduling of periodic real-time tasks on a uniprocessor whose dynamic voltage scaling portion might be turned off for further en-ergy saving. We further combine procrastination scheduling with dynamic voltage scaling to minimize the total static and dynamic energy consumption of the system. An on-line al-gorithm was developed to calculate the respective procrastination interval for each task. A series of simulation experiments was also evaluated for the performance of our algorithms. The results show that our proposed algorithms can derive energy-efficient schedules.

The rest of this paper is organized as follows: Section 2 defines the leakage-aware energy-efficient FPPT scheduling problem in a uniprocessor system. Preliminary results are shown in Section 2. The proposed algorithms are in Section 3. Experimental results for the performance evaluation of the proposed algorithms are presented in Section 4. Section 5 is the conclusion.

2 System Model

2.1 Task Model

This study deals with the fixed priority preemptive scheduling of tasks in a real-time systems with hard constraints, i.e., systems in which the respect of time constraints is mandatory. The activities of the system are modeled by periodic tasks.

The model of the system is defined by a task set $\mathcal{T}$ of cardinality n, $\mathcal{T} = \{\tau_1, \tau_2, ..., \tau_n\}$. The j_{th} job of task τ_i is denoted as $J_{i,j}$. The index, j, for jobs of a task is started from zero. A periodic task τ_i is characterized by a 3-tuple (C_i, T_i, D_i) where each request of τ_i, called instance, has an execution CPU cycles (denoted as C_i), and a relative deadline (denoted as D_i). T_i time units separate two consecutive instances of τ_i (hence T_i is the period of the task). Given a set $\mathcal{T}$ of n tasks, the hyper-period of $\mathcal{T}$, denoted by $\mathcal{L}$, is defined so that $\mathcal{L}/T_i$ is an integer for any task τ_i in $\mathcal{T}$. The number of jobs in the hyper-period of task τ_i is $\mathcal{L}/T_i$. For example, $\mathcal{L}$ is the least common multiple (LCM) of the periods of tasks in $\mathcal{T}$ when the periods of tasks are all integer numbers. We focus on the case that all of the tasks arrive at time 0.

We also associate with each task τ_i a unique priority $\pi_i \in \{1, 2, ..., n\}$ such that contention for resources is resolved in favor of the job with the highest priority that is ready to run.

The analysis presented in section 3 uses the concept of *busy* and *idle periods* [7]. These are defined as follows: A *level-i busy period* is a continuous time interval during which the notional run-queue contains one or more tasks of active priority level π_i or higher. Similarly, a *level-i idle period* is a time interval during which the run-queue is free of level π_i or higher priority tasks. We note that the run queue may become momentarily free of level-i tasks, when one tasks completes and another is released. This appears in our formulation as an idle period of zero length.

2.2 Power Consumption and Execution Models

We explore energy-efficient scheduling on a dynamic voltage scaling (DVS) processor. The power consumption is contributed by the dynamic power consumption resulting from the charging and discharging of gates on the CMOS circuits and the static power consumption resulting from leakage current. The dynamic power consumption P_d of the dynamic voltage scaling part of the processor is a function of the adopted processor speed f:

$$P_d = C_{eff} V_{DD}^2 f \tag{1}$$

$$f = \alpha k' \frac{(V_{DD} - V_{TH})^\alpha}{V_{DD}} \tag{2}$$

where k' is a device related parameter, V_{TH} is the threshold voltage, C_{eff} is the effective switching capacitance per cycle and α ranges from 2 to 1.2 depending on the device technology. Since power varies linearly with the clock speed and the square of the voltage, adjusting both can produce cubic power reductions, at least in theory. The static power consumption P_s of the system comes from the leakage current of the processor, system I/O devices, and RAM. It might be modeled as a nonnegative constant, as in [8], or a linear function of the supply voltage (a sub-linear function of the execution speed) [3], [4],[9], [10].

The power consumption of processor is denoted by P, which is the sum of the dynamic and static power consumption. We consider systems in which $P(f)$ is a convex and increasing function, and $P(f)/f$ is a convex function, similarly to [4],[11].

Recent processors support multiple variable voltage and frequency levels for energy efficient operation of the system. Let the available frequencies be $\{FLK_1, FLK_2, ..., FLK_s\}$ in increasing order of frequency and the corresponding voltage levels be $\{v_1, v_2, ..., v_s\}$. We assume that the CPU speed f_i of task τ_i can be changed between a minimum speed FLK_1 (minimum supply voltage necessary to keep the system functional) and a maximum speed FLK_s. In our framework, the voltage/speed changes take place only at context switch time and while state saving instructions execute. If not negligible, the voltage change overhead can be incorporated into the worst-case workload of each task.

The system could enter the *dormant mode* (or be turned off) whenever needed. The power consumption of the system is treated as 0 when it is in the *dormant mode* [8] by scaling the static power consumption. We consider systems that could be turned on/off at instant. When needed, turning the system off might further reduce the energy consumption. The energy consumption to turn off the system is assumed to be negligible, but it might require additional energy to turn on the system [12]. We denote E_{sw} as the energy of the switching overhead from the dormant mode to the active mode. For the rest of this paper, we say the system is idle at time instant t, if the processor does not execute any task at time instant t. When the system is active and idle, the processor executes NOP instructions and must be at processor speed FLK_1 to minimize the energy consumption. Let P_I be the power consumption when the system is idle and active, where $P_I = P(FLK_1)$.

2.3   Critical Speed

The critical speed $\hat{f}$ is defined as the available speed of the processor to execute a cycle with the minimum energy consumption. Because of the convexity of $P(f)$, executing at a common speed for a CPU cycle minimizes the energy consumption. Hence, the energy consumption to execute a CPU cycle at speed f is $P(f)/f$. Since the power consumption function $P(f)$ is a convex and increasing function, where $P(f)/f$ is merely a convex function. $P(f)/f$ is minimized when f is equal to f^*, with $\frac{d(P(f^*)/f^*)}{df^*} = 0$. As a result, to minimize the execution energy consumption of $\mathcal{T}$, we do not have to consider schedules that execute jobs at any lower speed than f^* since we could execute jobs at speed f^* with lower energy consumption and less execution time. If f^* is between FLK_1 and FLK_s, we know that $\hat{f}$ is f^*. If f^* is less than FLK_1, $\hat{f}$ is set to FLK_1 to satisfy the hardware constraint. Similarly, if f^* is greater than FLK_s, $\hat{f}$ is set to FLK_s, and jobs are executed at FLK_s to minimize the energy consumption. As a result, $\hat{f}$ is $min\{max\{f^*, FLK_1\}, FLK_s\}$. Executing a job of task τ_i at any speed less than $\hat{f}$ would either consume more energy than that at $\hat{f}$ with more execution time or violate the speed constraint. We assume that f^* could be obtained efficiently or pre-determined as a specified parameter in the input.

2.4   Problem definition

The problem considered in this paper is as follows:

Definition 1. (Leakage-Aware Energy-Efficient Scheduling for FPPT, LAEES-FPPT) *Consider a set $\mathcal{T}$ of n independent tasks ready at time 0. Each periodic task $\tau_i \in \mathcal{T}$ is associated with a computation requirement equal to C_i CPU-cycles and its period T_i, where the relative deadline of τ_i is equal to D_i. And each task $\tau_i \in \mathcal{T}$ is assigned with a unique priority $\pi_i \in \{1, 2, ..., n\}$ and a preemption threshold $\gamma_i \in \{1, 2, ..., n\}$ ($\gamma_i \geq \pi_i$), where π_i is used to compete for processor and $gamma_i$ is used to protect τ_i from unnecessary task preemptions after τ_i starts. The power consumption function $P(f)$ is a convex and increasing function, while $P(f)/f$ is merely a convex function. The processor is with a discrete spectrum of the available speeds in $[FLK_1, FLK_s]$. The energy of the switching overhead from the dormant mode to the active mode of a system is E_{sw}, and the power consumption when the system is active and idle is P_I. The problem is to minimize the energy consumption in the hyper-period $\mathcal{L}$ of tasks in $\mathcal{T}$ in the scheduling of fixed-priority tasks with preemption thresholds in $\mathcal{T}$ without missing the timing constraints.* □

A schedule of a task set $\mathcal{T}$ is an assignment of the available processor speeds for each corresponding task execution, where the job arrivals of each task $\tau_i \in \mathcal{T}$ satisfy its timing constraint D_i. A schedule is feasible if no job misses its deadline. A schedule is optimal for the LAEES-FPPT problem, if it is feasible, and its energy consumption is the minimum among all feasible schedules. For the rest of this paper, let S^* be an optimal schedule for $\mathcal{T}$. For a schedule, an idle interval is a maximal interval when the system is idle, while an execution interval is a maximal interval when the processor executes some jobs. The system might be turned off or be at the active mode in an idle interval, while the system is active in an execution interval. For any set X, let $|X|$ be the cardinality of the set. For example, $|I_S|$ is the number of idle intervals in schedule S in $(0, \mathcal{L}]$. If the idle interval is greater than E_{sw}/P_I, turning off the system is worthwhile. Let t_θ be the *threshold idle interval* E_{sw}/P_I. If the idle interval is greater than t_θ, the longer the idle interval is, the more the energy saved by turning off the system.

The energy consumption of a schedule S, denoted as $\mathrm{E}(S)$, consists of two parts: the execution energy consumption $\phi(S)$ and the idle energy consumption $\varepsilon(S)$. The execution energy consumption is the sum of the energy consumption of the executions of jobs in S in the time interval $(0, \mathcal{L}]$. The idle energy consumption is the sum of the energy consumption in the intervals in $(0, \mathcal{L}]$ in which the system does not execute any job. Let $v(t, S)$ be the speed at time instant t in schedule S. The execution energy consumption $\phi(S)$ in $\mathrm{E}(S)$ is $\int_0^{\mathcal{L}} P(v(t, S))dt$. The idle energy consumption $\varepsilon(S)$ in $\mathrm{E}(S)$ is the summation of E_{sw} times the number of instances that the system is turned from the dormant mode to the active mode and P_I times the total interval length that the system is idle and active in $(0, \mathcal{L}]$.

3 Proposed Algorithms

This section presents a two-phase algorithm for periodic real-time tasks. The algorithms determine, in the first phase, the execution speed, i.e., the supply voltage, of each task, and in the second phase the moment to turn on/off the system on the fly.

3.1   An On-Line Procrastination Algorithm to Minimize the Energy Leakage: LA-FPPT

Let S_e be the resulting FPPT schedule by applying some off-line dvs algorithms [13]. For brevity, let C_i be the execution time of a job of task τ_i in S_e, $C_i = C_i / f_i^{opt}$. The first phase of the proposed algorithm [13] decides the execution speed of tasks in T to meet the timing constraints and minimize the execution energy consumption.

The second phase is to reduce the idle energy consumption by turning the system off on the fly. The idea behind scheduling on the fly is to lengthen and aggregate the idle intervals so that the resulting idle time is long enough to turn off the system. The determination of idle intervals can be done by procrastinating the arrival time of the next job to the system, as in [4],[14] for EDF scheduling, and in [9],[11] for fixed-priority scheduling. In [4], [9]procrastination is done by computing the maximum procrastination intervals of all of the tasks in T based on the system utilization, while the idle intervals in [14],[11] are determined by procrastinating the remaining jobs as late as possible.

In this section, we proposes an on-line simulated work-demand analysis approach to the determination of idle intervals. If a job completes at time instant t, and the ready queue is empty, we have to decide whether the system should be turned off or idle. Let $r_i(t)$ be the arrival time of the next job of τ_i for any τ_i in T arrived after time instant t, i.e., $r_i(t) = \left\lceil \frac{t}{T_i} \right\rceil \cdot T_i$. Let $d_i(t)$ be the next deadline on an invocation of task τ_i after time instant t, i.e., $d_i(t) = r_i(t) + D_i$.

Our formulation stems from considering the schedulability of each fixed-priority task with preemption thresholds at time instant t. We focus on finding the maximum amount of idle interval, $S_{\pi_i}^{max}(t)$, which may be stolen at priority level π_i, during the interval $[t, t + d_i(t))$, whilst guaranteeing that task τ_i meets its deadline. (Note, $S_{\pi_i}^{max}(t)$ may not actually be available for idle due to the constraints on hard deadline tasks with priorities lower than π_i. We return to this point later). To guarantee that task τ_i will meet its deadline, we need to analyze the worst case scenario from time t onwards. We therefore assume that all tasks τ_j are re-invoked at their earliest possible next release $r_j(t)$ and subsequently with a period of T_j.

In attempting to determine the maximum guaranteed idle time, $S_{\pi_i}^{max}(t)$, it is instructive to view the interval $[t, t + d_i(t))$ as comprising a number of *level-i* busy and idle periods. Any *level-i idle time* between the completion of task τ_i and its deadline could be swapped for task τ_i's procrastination interval Z_i without causing the deadline to be missed. Hence the maximum procrastination interval Z_i which may be stolen is equal to the total *level-i idle time* in the interval. We use this result to calculate $S_{\pi_i}^{max}(t)$.

We first derive equation 3 using techniques given in [15]. Although the ready queue is empty at time instant t, two components still determine the extent of the busy period under the influence of procrastination scheduling:

1. For the task τ_k with priority $\pi_k < \pi_i < \gamma_k$, τ_k's released workload just before the start of busy period
2. For the task τ_j with priority $\pi_j > \gamma_i$, τ_j's released workload during the busy period

The second component implies a recursive definition. As the processing released increases monotonically with the length of the busy period, a recurrence relation can be used to find $w_i(t)$:

$$w_{\pi_i}^{m+1}(t) = S_{\pi_i}(t) + \max_{\forall k, \pi_k < \pi_i < \gamma_k} C_k + \sum_{\forall j, \pi_j > \pi_i} \left(\left\lceil \frac{w_{\pi_i}^m(t) - x_j(t)}{T_j} \right\rceil \cdot C_j \right) \quad (3)$$

The term $S_{\pi_i}(t)$ represents the beginning of *level-i idle time* from time t.

The recurrence relation begins with $w_{\pi_i}^0(t) = 0$ and ends when $w_{\pi_i}^{m+1}(t) = w_{\pi_i}^m(t)$ or $w_{\pi_i}^{m+1}(t) > d_i(t)$. Proof of convergence follows from analysis of similar recurrence relations by Audsley et al [15]. The final value of $w_{\pi_i}(t)$ defines the length of the busy period. Alternatively, we may view $t + w_{\pi_i}(t)$ as defining the start of a *level-i idle time*.

Given the start of a *level-i idle time*, within the interval $[t, t + d_i(t))$, the end of the idle time, which may be converted to procrastination interval of task τ_i, occurs either at the next release of a task τ_j with priority $\pi_j > \pi_i$ or at the end of the interval. Equation 4 gives the length, $l_i(t, w_{\pi_i}(t))$, of the *level-i idle time*.

$$l_i(t, w_{\pi_i}(t)) = \min \left[\begin{array}{l} d_i(t) - w_i(t), \\ \min_{\forall j, \pi_j \geq \gamma_i} \left(\left\lceil \frac{w_{\pi_i}(t) - r_j(t)}{T_j} \right\rceil \cdot T_j + r_j(t) - w_{\pi_i}(t) \right) \end{array} \right] \quad (4)$$

where the term $d_i(t) - w_{\pi_i}(t)$ means that the end of *level-i idle time* come about at the end of $[t, t + d_i(t))$, the term $\left\lceil \frac{w_{\pi_i}(t) - r_j(t)}{T_j} \right\rceil \cdot T_j + r_j(t)$ describe the workload contributed by task τ_j in the *level-i busy period*, whose length is denoted by $w_{\pi_i}(t)$.

Combining equations 3 and 4, our method for determining the maximum idle time, $S_{\pi_i}^{max}(t)$, proceeds as follows:

1. The idle time which may be derived, $S_{\pi_i}(t)$, is initially set to zero
2. Equation 3 is used to compute the end of a busy period in the interval $[t, t + d_i(t))$
3. The end of the busy period is used as the start of an idle period by equation 4 which returns the length of contiguous idle time.
4. The idle time, $S_{\pi_i}(t)$ is incremented by the amount of idle time found in step 3.
5. If the deadline on task τ_i has been reached, then the maximum idle time which can be derived is given by $S_{\pi_i}(t)$. Otherwise, we repeat steps 2 to 5.

The pseudo-codes of dynamic procrastination algorithm at time instant t when the ready queue is empty, and a job completes are shown in Algorithm 1.

4   Case Studies and Simulations

Section 3 showed that our two-phase algorithm (EE-FPPT [13] + LA-PFFT) will always render the controlled leakage current in CMOS circuits and reduced energy consumptions that will maintain the schedulability of the workload. we use randomly-generated workloads to examine broad trends across a range of design points.

We investigate workload characteristics that affect the energy saving capability attainable through LA-FPPT. We now simulate and analyze randomly generated systems

---

Algorithm 1. On-line Algorithm to Minimize Energy Leakage

1: **procedure** DYNAMIC PROCRASTINATION(t)

                                                        ▷ a job completes at t and the ready queue is empty

2:        sort T by ascending priority order

3:        **for** $(i = 1; i \leq n; i \neq n)$ **do**

4:            $r_i(t) \leftarrow \left\lceil \frac{t}{T_i} \right\rceil \cdot T_i$

5:            $d_i(t) \leftarrow r_i(t) + D_i$

6:            $S_{\pi_i}(t) \leftarrow 0$

7:            $w_{\pi_i}^{m+1}(t) \leftarrow 0$

8:            **while** $(w_{\pi_i}^{m+1}(t) \leq d_i(t))$ **do**

9:               $w_{\pi_i}^m(t) \leftarrow w_{\pi_i}^{m+1}(t)$

10:

$$w_{\pi_i}^{m+1}(t) = S_i(t) + \max_{\forall k, \pi_k < \pi_i < \gamma_k} C_k + \sum_{\forall j, \pi_j \geq \pi_i} \left(\left\lceil \frac{w_{\pi_i}^m(t) - r_j(t)}{T_j} \right\rceil \cdot C_j \right)$$

11:               **if** $(w_{\pi_i}^m(t) = w_{\pi_i}^{m+1}(t))$ **then**

            $S_{\pi_i}(t) \leftarrow S_{\pi_i}(t) + l_i(t, w_{\pi_i}^m(t))$

            $w_{\pi_i}^{m+1}(t) \leftarrow w_{\pi_i}^{m+1}(t) + l_i(t, w_{\pi_i}^m(t))$

12:               **end if**

13:            **end while**

14:            $S_{\pi_i}^{max}(t) \leftarrow S_i(t)$

15:            revise the arrival time $r_i'(t)$ of job $J_{i,t}$ by setting $r_i'(t) \leftarrow r_i(t) + S_{\pi_i}^{max}(t)$

16:        **end for**

17:        **if** $(\min_{\forall \tau_i \in T} r_i'(t) - t > t_\theta)$ **then**

18:            turn the system off at time t and turn on at $\min_{\forall \tau_i \in T} r_i'(t)$

19:        **else**

20:            remain on the active mode

21:        **end if**

22: **end procedure**

---

of tasks to better understand our approaches. The power consumption function of the system speed f was set as $P(f) = f^3 + 3$.

The *normalized total energy* was adopted as the performance metrics. The normalized total energy of an algorithm for an input instance is the energy consumption of the derived solution in $(0, \mathcal{L}]$ divided by the energy consumption by applying the original FPPT scheduling without processor slowdown, procrastination and by turning off the system when the idle interval is long enough.

We tried two different experimental settings. The first experiment investigate separately the effect of the switching overhead E_{sw}, the system utilization on the limited energy consumption achieved by our methods. To cover a wide range of design points, 20,000 real-time task sets with 10 tasks each were randomly generated. These were created so 1000 have a utilization of 50%, 1000 have 52% utilization, and so on up to 90%. For each group of task sets who hold the same utilization, those were created so 20 have a E_{sw} of 0.03, 20 have 0.04, and so on up to 0.53. The second one focused on the impact of the number of tasks and E_{sw} (0.17), another 20,000 real-time task sets with system utilization 67% each were randomly generated too. Those were created so 1000 include 5 independent tasks, 1000 include 6 independent tasks, and so on up to 25 tasks.

Task periods is assigned randomly in the range [1, 100] with a uniform probability distribution function. Moreover, task deadlines were set equal to their respective periods (for simplicity, though not necessary). Tasks' WCETs were set to incur the required overall system utilization. All 40,000 real-time task sets generated were schedulable with a fully preemptive policy.

Using the MPTA, the total energy produced by each system was computed and normalized to the energy required by the original version of the system. The average normalized energy were then plotted as a function of E_{sw}, the system utilization and the number of tasks in turn. The results are shown in figures 1(a), 1(b) and 2(a) respectively.

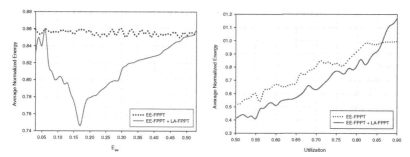

(a) Energy consumption produced for LA-FPPT rises with large E_{sw}, but keep almost constant for EE-FPPT, with system utilization = 0.67

(b) Energy consumption rises with system utilization, but soars up for high-utilization systems.

Fig. 1. Experiment I results for power saving of our approaches

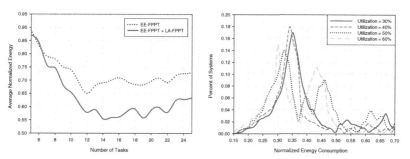

(a) Energy consumption declines with the increment of the number of tasks, on condition that system utilization = 0.67 and $E_{sw} = 0.17$

(b) EE-FPPT + LA-FPPT dramatically accomplishes the energy savings, even for high-utilization systems.

Fig. 2. Experiment II results for power saving of our approaches

In Figure 1(a), the more the switching overhead E_{sw} was, the more the normalized energy consumption was for schedules derived from Algorithms LA-FPPT. When E_{sw} is relatively small ($E_{sw} \leq 0.18$), the energy consumption from leakage current in CMOS circuits still have litter influence on the total energy consumption, thus the more E_{sw}, the less normalized energy consumption.

In Figure 1(b), our algorithms (EE-FPPT + LA-FPPT) outperformed original Algorithm FPPT when the system utilization was greater than 0.87. When the system utilization was large enough, procrastination might create two (or more) idle intervals to turn the system off, but the original FPPT schedule might make the system idle for a short interval and turn the system off for a longer interval. As a result, the energy consumption of procrastination schedules might consume more energy than the original FPPT schedule when the system utilization is large enough. Moreover, when the utilization for task execution is large, the improvement on idle energy consumption is marginal since task execution dominates the total energy consumption.

In Figure 2(a), for all the simulated algorithms, the normalized energy consumption decreased for small number of tasks with $n \leq 12$, and was steady for $n > 12$. This is because the resulting utilization of a task was large when n was small in the experimental setup, and, hence, there was only little room for procrastination to save energy. For task sets with $n > 12$, the maximum procrastination interval was dominated by tasks with small periods, and, hence, the improvement became marginal.

Another interesting property is the distribution of the 20,000 systems of Experiment I among the different normalized power consumption levels. Figure 2(b) show this distribution for the overall system utilization levels of 30%, 40%, 50%, and 60%, respectively. As can be seen, the workloads scheduled with the fixed-priority schemes depend on the system utilization level to some extent.

5 Conclusions

In this paper we discuss the energy-efficient scheduling problem of periodic realtime tasks by applying FPPT policy on a uniprocessor dynamic voltage scaling system that can go into the dormant mode for energy efficiency. We propose a two-phase scheduling algorithm. In the first phase, the execution speed, i.e., the supply voltage, of each task is determined by applying off-line algorithms. In the second phase, the time moment to turn on/off the system is determined on the fly. Theoretical analysis shows that our proposed algorithms could derive scheduling solutions with at most $max\{\frac{1}{(U_{bd})^2}, 2\}$ times of the energy consumption of optimal solutions, where the term U_{bd} represents the *breakdown utilization* [16] of a task set. A series of simulation experiments was evaluated to demonstrate the performance of the proposed algorithms. Our experimental results show that our approaches can accomplish dramatic energy savings as the same time keep the schedulability of task set.

References

1. Takayasu Sakurai, A.R.N.: Alpha-power law mosfet model and its applications to cmos inverterdelay and other formulas. IEEE Journal of Solid-State Circuits 25(2), 584–594 (1990)

2. Padmanabhan Pillai, K.G.S.: Real-time dynamic voltage scaling for low-power embedded operating systems. In: 18th ACM Symposium on Operating System Principles, Chateau Lake Louise, Banff, Alberta, Canada, vol. 35, pp. 89–102. ACM, New York (2001)
3. Ravindra Jejurikar, R.K.G.: Dynamic slack reclamation with procrastination scheduling in real-time embedded systems. In: Joyner Jr., W.H., Martin, G., Kahng, A.B. (eds.) 42nd Design Automation Conference, San Diego, CA, USA, pp. 111–116. ACM Press, New York (2005)
4. Jejurikar, R., Pereira, C., Gupta, R.K.: Leakage aware dynamic voltage scaling for real-time embedded systems. In: Kahng, S.M., Fix, L., Andrew, B. (eds.) 41th Design Automation Conference, San Diego, CA, USA, pp. 275–280. ACM, New York (2004)
5. Lee, Y.-H., Reddy, K.P., Mani Krishna, C.: Scheduling techniques for reducing leakage power in hard real-time systems. In: 15th Euromicro Conference on Real-Time Systems (ECRTS 2003), Porto, Portugal, pp. 105–112. IEEE Computer Society, Los Alamitos (2003)
6. Manas Saksena, Y.W.: Scalable real-time system design using preemption thresholds. In: 21st IEEE Real-Time Systems Symposium, pp. 25–34 (2000)
7. Lehoczky, J.P.: Fixed priority scheduling of periodic task sets with arbitrary deadlines. In: IEEE Real-Time Systems Symposium, Lake Buena Vista, Florida, USA, pp. 201–213. IEEE Computer Society Press, Los Alamitos (1990)
8. Xu, R., Zhu, D., Rusu, C., Chem, R.G.M., Moaaé, D.: Energy-efficient policies for embedded clusters. In: Paek, Y., Gupta, R. (eds.) 2005 ACM SIGPLAN/SIGBED Conference on Languages, Compilers, and Tools for Embedded Systems, Chicago, Illinois, USA. ACM, New York (2005)
9. Ravindra Jejurikar, R.K.G.: Procrastination scheduling in fixed priority real-time systems. In: 2004 ACM SIGPLAN/SIGBED Conference on Languages, Compilers, and Tools for Embedded Systems, Washington, DC, USA, pp. 57–66. ACM, New York (2004)
10. Ravindra Jejurikar, R.K.G.: Dynamic voltage scaling for systemwide energy minimization in real-time embedded systems. In: Roy, R.V.J., Choi, K., Tiwari, V. (eds.) 2004 International Symposium on Low Power Electronics and Design, Newport Beach, California, USA, pp. 78–81. ACM, New York (2004)
11. Quan, G., Niu, L., Hu., X.S., Mochocki, B.: Fixed priority scheduling for reducing overall energy on variable voltage processors. In: 25th IEEE Real-Time Systems Symposium, Lisbon, Portugal, pp. 309–318. IEEE Computer Society, Los Alamitos (2004)
12. Irani, S., Shukla, S.K., Gupta, R.K.: Algorithms for power savings. In: Fourteenth Annual ACM-SIAM Symposium on Discrete Algorithms, pp. 37–46. ACM, New York (2003)
13. XiaoChuan He, Y.J.: Energy-efficient scheduling fixed-priority tasks with preemption thresholds on variable voltage processors. In: Li, K., Jesshope, C., Jin, H., Gaudiot, J.-L. (eds.) NPC 2007. LNCS, vol. 4672, pp. 133–142. Springer, Heidelberg (2007)
14. Linwei Niu, G.Q.: Reducing both dynamic and leakage energy consumption for hard real-time systems. In: Irwin, M.J., Zhao, W., Lavagno, L., Mahlke, S.A. (eds.) 2004 International Conference on Compilers, Architecture, and Synthesis for Embedded Systems, Washington DC, USA, pp. 140–148. ACM, New York (2004)
15. Audsley, N.C., Burns, A., Richardson., M.F., Wellings, A.J.: Applying new scheduling theory to static priority pre-emptive scheduling. Software Engineering Journal 8(5), 284–292 (1993)
16. Lehoczky, J.P., Lui Sha, Y.D.: The rate monotonic scheduling algorithm: Exact characterization and average case behavior. In: IEEE Real-Time Systems Symposium 1989, pp. 166–171 (1989)

Survey on Parallel Programming Model

Henry Kasim[1,2], Verdi March[1,3], Rita Zhang[1], and Simon See[1,2]

[1] Asia-Pacific Science and Technology Center (APSTC), Sun Microsystems
[2] Department of Mechanical & Aerospace Engineering, Nanyang Technological University
[3] Department of Computer Science, National University of Singapore
{henry.kasim,verdi.march,rita.zhang,simon.see}@sun.com

Abstract. The development of microprocessors design has been shifting to multi-core architectures. Therefore, it is expected that parallelism will play a significant role in future generations of applications. Throughout the years, there has been a myriad number of parallel programming models proposed. In choosing a parallel programming model, not only the performance aspect is important, but also qualitative the aspect of how well parallelism is abstracted to developers. A model with a well abstraction of parallelism leads to a higher application-development productivity. In this paper, we propose seven criteria to qualitatively evaluate parallel programming models. Our focus is on how parallelism is abstracted and presented to application developers. As a case study, we use these criteria to investigate six well-known parallel programming models in the HPC community.

Keywords: shared memory, distributed memory, Pthreads, OpenMP, CUDA, MPI, UPC, Fortress.

1 Introduction

The aim of parallel computing is to increase an application's performance by executing the application on multiple processors. While parallel computing has been traditionally associated with the HPC (high performance computing) community, it is becoming more prevalent for the mainstream computing due to the recent development of commodity multi-core architecture. The multi-core architecture, and soon many-core, is a new paradigm in keeping up with the Moore's law. It is motivated by challenges to traditional paradigm of continuously increasing CPU frequency: physical limit of transistors size, power consumption, and heat dissipation [1,2]. Consequently, it is expected that future generations of applications would heavily exploit the parallelism offered by the multi-core architecture.

There are two main approaches to parallelize applications: *auto parallelization* and *parallel programming*; they differ in terms of the achievable application performance and ease of parallelization. The auto-parallelization approach, e.g. ILP (instruction level parallelism) or parallel compilers [3], automatically parallelizes applications that have been developed using sequential programming models.

J. Cao et al. (Eds.): NPC 2008, LNCS 5245, pp. 266–275, 2008.

The advantage of this approach is that existing/legacy applications need not be modified, e.g. applications just need to be recompiled with a parallel compiler. Therefore, programmers need not to learn new programming paradigms. However, this also becomes a limiting factor in exploiting a higher degree of parallelism: it is extremely challenging to automatically transform algorithms with a sequential nature into parallel ones. In contrast to auto parallelization, with the parallel programming approach, applications are specifically developed to exploit parallelism. Generally, developing a parallel application involves partitioning workload into tasks and mapping of tasks into workers. Parallel programming is perceived to result in higher performance gain than auto parallelization, but at the expense of more parallelization efforts.

Throughout the years, there have been a myriad number of parallel programming models proposed. A typical consideration in choosing a model is the performance of the resulted applications. However, it is equally important to also consider qualitative aspects of models. One such qualitative aspect is how parallelism is abstracted and presented to application developers. To evaluate this aspect, we propose that each model is evaluated based on seven criteria: (i) system architecture, (ii) programming methodologies, (iii) worker management, (iv) workload partitioning scheme, (v) task-to-worker mapping, (vi) synchronization, and (vii) communication model. Out list of criteria is inspired by Asanovic et. al. [4].

In this paper, we describe seven qualitative criteria to evaluate parallel programming models. Our goal is to emphasize to people new to parallelism that apart from performance of resulted applications, one should also consider how the chosen programming model affects the productivity of software development. The contributions of this paper are two fold. Firstly, we extend the four criteria in Asanovic et. al. [4] with three new criteria (i.e. system architecture, programming methodologies and worker management). Secondly, we present an investigation of six parallel programming models in the HPC community: three well-established models (i.e. Pthreads [5], OpenMP [6,7], and MPI [8]) and three relatively new models (i.e. UPC [9,10], Fortress [11], and CUDA [12]).

The remainder of this paper is organized as follow. Section 2 defines the seven criteria and Section 3 present a study of six parallel programming models based on the criteria. Finally, Section 4 summarizes this paper.

2   The Seven Criteria

In this section, we describe seven criteria to qualitatively evaluate a parallel programming model.

1. *System Architecture*

   We consider two architectures: *shared memory* and *distributed memory*. Shared memory architecture refers to systems such as an SMP/MPP node whereby all processors share a single address space. With such models, applications can run and utilize only processors within a single node. On the other hand, distributed memory architecture refers to systems such as a cluster of compute nodes whereby there is one address space per node.

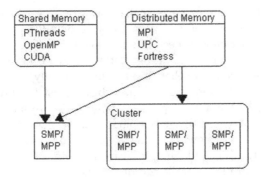

Fig. 1. Six Programming Models and their Supported System Architecture

Fig. 1 illustrates the supported system architecture of the six programming models. As can be seen, Pthreads, OpenMP and CUDA support shared memory architecture, and thus can only run and utilize processors within a single node. On the other hand, MPI, UPC and Fortress also support distributed memory architecture so that applications developed with these model can run on single node (i.e. shared memory architecture) or multiple nodes.

2. *Programming Methodologies*
   We look at how parallelism capabilities are exposed to programmers. For examples, API, special directives, new language specification, etc.

3. *Worker Management*
   This criteria looks at the creation of the unit of worker, threads or processors. Worker management is *implicit* when there is no need for programmers to manage the lifetime of workers. Rather, they need to only specify, for example, the number of unit of workers required or the section of code to be run in parallel. In *explicit* approach, programmer needs to code the creation and destruction of workers.

4. *Workload Partitioning Scheme*
   Worker partitioning defines how the workload are divided into smaller chunks called *tasks*. In *implicit* approach, typically programmers needs to only specify that a workload can be processed in parallel. How the workload is actually partitioned into tasks need not be managed by programmers. In contrast, with the *explicit* approach, programmers need to manually decide how workload is partitioned.

5. *Task-to-Worker Mapping*
   Task-to-worker mapping defines how tasks are map onto workers. In the *implicit* approach, programmers do not need to specify which worker is responsible for a particular task. In contrast, the *explicit* approach requires programmers to manage how tasks are assigned to workers.

6. *Synchronization*
   Synchronization defines the time order in which workers access shared data. In *implicit* synchronization, there is no or little programming effort done

by programmers: either no synchronization constructs are needed or it is sufficient to only specify that a synchronization is needed. In *explicit* synchronization, programmers are required to manage the worker's access to the shared.

7. *Communication Model*

This aspect looks at the communication paradigm used by a model.

3   Parallel Programming Model

In this section, we evaluate six parallel programming models using the criteria presented in Section 2. The overall summary is shown in Table 1.

Table 1. Evaluation of Six Parallel Programming Models

(a) Shared Memory

Criteria	MPI	UPC	Fortress
Unit of Workers	Thread	Thread	Thread
Programming Methodologies	API, C, Fortran	API, C, Fortran	API, Extension to C
Worker Management	Explicit	Implicit	Implicit
Workload Partitioning	Explicit	Implicit	Explicit
Worker Mapping	Explicit	Implicit	Explicit
Synchronization	Explicit	Implicit	Explicit
Communication Model	Shared Address Space	Shared Address Space	Shared Address Space

(b) Distributed Memory

Criteria	MPI	UPC	Fortress
Unit of Workers	Process	Thread	Thread
Programming Methodologies	API, C, Fortran	API, C	New Language
Worker Management	Implicit	Implicit	Implicit/Explicit
Workload Partitioning	Explicit	Implicit/Explicit	Implicit/Explicit
Worker Mapping	Explicit	Implicit/Explicit	Implicit/Explicit
Synchronization	Implicit	Implicit/Explicit	Implicit/Explicit
Communication Model	Message Passing	Partitioned Global Address Space	Global Address Space

3.1   Pthreads

Pthreads or Portable Operating System Interface (POSIX) Threads is a set of C programming language types and procedure calls [5]. Pthreads is implemented as a header (`pthread.h`) and a library for creating and manipulating each of the workers called threads.

Worker management in Pthreads requires programmer to explicitly create and destroy threads by making use of `pthread_create` and `pthread_exit` function. Function `pthread_create` requires four parameters: (i) the thread used to run tasks, (ii) attribute, (iii) tasks to be run by thread in routine call, and (iv) routine argument. The thread created will run the routine until `pthread_exit` function has been called.

Workload partitioning and task mapping are explicitly specified by programmers as arguments to `pthread_create`. The workload partitioning is specified by programmers on the third passing parameter in the form of a routine call, while task mapping is specify on the first passing parameters in the `pthreads_create` function. A thread can join other threads using `pthread_join`. When the function is called, the calling thread will hold its execution until the target thread finish before joining the threads.

When multiple threads access the shared data, programmers have to be aware of data race and deadlocks. To protect critical section, i.e. the portion of code that accesses shared data, Pthreads provides mutex (mutual exclusion) and semaphore [13]. Mutex permits only one thread to enter a critical section at a time, whereas semaphore allows several threads to enter a critical section.

3.2 OpenMP

OpenMP is an open specification for shared memory parallelism [6,7]. It consists of a set of compiler directives, callable runtime library routines and environment variables that extend Fortran, C and C++ programs. OpenMP is portable across the shared memory architecture. The unit of workers in OpenMP is threads.

The worker management is implicit. Special directives are used to specify that a section of code is to be run in parallel. The number of threads to be used is specified using an out-of-band mechanism which is an environment variable. Thus, unlike Pthread, there is no need for programmers to manage the lifetime of threads.

Workload partitioning and task-to-worker mapping require a relatively few programming effort. Programmers just need to specify compiler directives to denote a parallel region, namely (i) `#pragma omp parallel {}` for C/C++, and (ii) `!$omp parallel` and `!$omp end parallel` for Fortran. OpenMP also abstracts away how workload (e.g. an array) is divided into tasks (e.g. sub-arrays) and how tasks are assigned to threads.

OpenMP supports several constructs to support implicit synchronization where programmers specify only where synchronization occurs (Table 2). The actual synchronization mechanism is thus relieved from the programmers' responsibility.

3.3 CUDA

CUDA (Compute Unified Device Architecture) is the extension of C programming language designed to support of parallel processing on Nvidia GPU (Graphics Processing Unit) [12]. CUDA views a parallel system as consisting of a host device (i.e.

Table 2. Synchronization Constructs in OpenMP

Construct	Description
Barrier	Allow synchronization on all threads within the same group
Atomic	Allow all threads execute, but only one of load or store at a time
Ordered	Allow the block of code to be execute sequentially
Flush	Ensure all threads have a consistent view of certain objects in memory

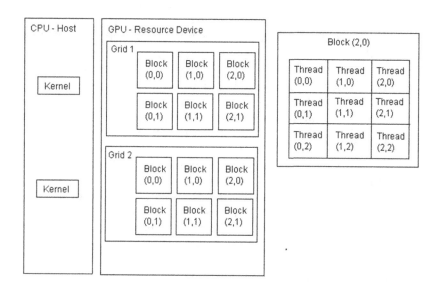

Fig. 2. CUDA Architecture

CPU) and computation resource (i.e. GPU). The computation of tasks is done in GPU by a set of threads that run in parallel. The GPU architecture for threads consist of two-level hierarchy, namely *block* and *grid* (Fig. 2). Block is a set of tightly coupled threads where each thread is identified by a thread ID, while grid is a set of loosely coupled of blocks with similar size and dimension.

Worker management in CUDA is done implicitly; programmers do not manage thread creations and destructions. They just need to specify the dimension of the grid and block required to process a certain task. While workload partitioning and worker mapping in CUDA is done explicitly. Programmers have to define the workload to be run in parallel by using Global_Function<<<dimGrid, dimBlock>>> (Arguments) construct where (i) Global_Function is the global function call to be run in threads, (ii) dimGrid is the dimension and size of the grid, (iii) dimBlock is the dimension and size of each block and (iv) Arguments represent the passing value for the global function. The task to worker mapping of CUDA programming is defined on <<<dimGrid, dimBlock>>> within the command call mentioned before.

Synchronization for all threads in CUDA is done implicitly through function _syncthreads(). This function will coordinate communication among threads of the same block. The function requires a minimum of 4 clock cycles as the overhead, i.e. when no thread is waiting for other threads.

3.4   MPI

Message Passing Interface (MPI) is a specification for message passing operations [8]. It defines each worker as a *process*. MPI is currently the de-facto standard for developing HPC applications on distributed memory architecture. It provides language bindings for C, C++[1], and Fortran. Some of the well-known MPI implementation includes OpenMPI [14], MVAPICH [15], MPICH [16], GridMPI [17], and LAM/MPI [18].

Worker management is done implicitly whereby it is not necessary to code the creation, scheduling, or destruction of processes. Instead, one only needs to use a command-line tool, mpirun, to tell the MPI runtime how many processes are needed, and optionally the mapping of processes to processors. Based on this information, the runtime infrastructure will then carry out the worker management on behalf of users.

Workload partitioning and task mapping have to be done by programmers, similar to Pthread. Programmers have to manage what tasks to be computed by each process. As an example, given a 2-D array (i.e. the workload), one can use a process' identifier (i.e. rank) to determine which sub-array (i.e. a task) the process will compute. Communication among processes adopts the message-passing paradigm where data sharing is done by one process sending the data to other processes. MPI broadly classifies its message-passing operations as *point-to-point* and *collective*. Point-to-point operations such as the MPI_Send/MPI_Recv pair facilitate communications between processes, whereas collective operations such as MPI_Bcast facilitate communications involving more than two processes.

MPI_Barrier is used to specify that a synchronization is needed. The barrier operation blocks each process from continuing its execution until all processes have enter the barrier. A typical usage of barrier is to ensure that global data has been dispersed to appropriate processes.

3.5   UPC

UPC (Unified Parallel C) is a parallel programming language for shared memory architecture and distributed memory architecture [9,10]. Regardless of the system architecture, UPC adopts the concept of partitioned memory. With this concept, programmers view the system as one global address space which is logically partitioned into a number of per-thread address spaces. Each thread has two types of memory accesses: to its own private address space or to other threads' address space. Accesses to both types of per-thread address space use the same syntax. To improve the performance of memory accesses, UPC

---

[1] Supported only on MPI-2.

Table 3. Synchronization Constructs in UPC

Mechanism	Syntax	Implicit/ Explicit	Description
Barrier	upc_barrier expression	Implicit	A blocking synchronization, similar to MPI_Barrier on MPI
Split phase barriers	upc_notify expression upc_wait expression	Implicit	A non-blocking synchronization
Fence	upc_fence	Implicit	Ensure that all shared references is completed before upc_fence
Locks	upc_lock() upc_unlock()	Explicit	Protect the shared data against multiple processors

Memory consistency control	#include <upc_strict.h>
	#include <upc_relaxed.h>
		Explicit	There are two memory consistency models:
			1. *Relaxed*
			   Shared data can be reordered during compile time or runtime
			2. *Strict*
			   Accesses to shared data is serialized

introduces the concept of thread affinity. With this feature, UPC optimizes memory-access performance between a thread and the per-thread address space where the thread has been bound.

In UPC, workload management is implicit, while workload partitioning and worker mapping can be either implicit or explicit. For worker management, programmers just need to specify number of threads required during the call on the command-line tools, upcrun. Implicit workload partitioning and task mapping are supported through an API called upc_forall which is similar to for iteration in C programming, except that the content of the iteration will be run in parallel. When this API is used, there is no need for additional programming effort for programmers to map the task to threads. The explicit approach in UPC for workload partitioning and worker mapping is similar to the one in MPI, where programmers have to specify on what will be run by each threads.

In UPC, communication among threads adopt the *Partitioned Global Address Space* (PGAS) paradigm by making use of *pointers*. There are three types of pointer commonly used in UPC [10]: (i) *private pointer* where the private pointers point to their own private address space, (ii) *private pointer-to-share* where the private pointers point to the shared address space, and (iii) *shared pointer-to-share* where the shared pointers from one address space point to the other shared address space.

UPC provides several synchronization mechanisms [9]. Table 3 briefly describes the synchronization mechanisms available in UPC together with the programming effort require by programmers.

3.6 Fortress

Fortress is a specification programming language designed for High Performance Computing [11]. The unit of worker is threads. Worker management, workload partitioning and worker mapping in Fortress can be implicit or explicit. In the implicitly approach, the iterative for loops is parallel by default. Programmer does not have to specify which threads to be run on each iteration. In the explicit approach, the creation of a thread can be done by using spawn keyword. As an example, in t = spawn Global_Function(Arguments), t denotes the thread created, and Global_Function denotes the tasks to be run by t. Note that apart from a global function call, a task can be an expression as well. Stopping thread t is achieved through t.stop(). The workload partitioning and worker mapping for explicitly spawned threads are similar with in CUDA. One needs to decide how a workload is partitioned into tasks and how tasks are assigned to threads.

To avoid abnormal behavior and data races in one program, programmers have to specify the synchronization constructs explicitly. There are two synchronization constructs called reductions and atomic expression. The use of reduction is to avoid the need for synchronization by performing a computation as local as possible. Second construct, atomic can be used to control the data among the parallel executions. Atomic expression consists of atomic keyword follow by body expression. In body expression, all data reads and writes will appear to occur simultaneously in a single atomic step [11].

4   Summary

Using seven criteria, we have reviewed the qualitative aspects of six representative parallel programming models. Our goal is to provide a basic guideline in evaluating the appropriateness of a programming model in various development environments. The system-architecture aspect indicates the type of computing infrastructure (e.g. single node versus a cluster) supported by each of the programming models. The remaining aspects, which complement the typical performance evaluation, are meant to aid users in evaluating the ease-of-use of models. It should be noted that the seven criteria are by no means exhaustive. Other implementation issues such as debugging support should be considered as well when evaluating a parallel programming models.

References

1. Kish, L.B.: End of Moores̀ Law: Thermal (noise) Death of Integration in Micro and nano electronics. Physics Letters A 305, 144–149 (2002)
2. Kish, L.B.: Moores̀ Law and the Energy Requirement of Computing Versus performance. Circuits, devices and systems 151(2), 190–194 (2004)
3. Sun Studio 12, http://developers.sun.com/sunstudio
4. Asanovic, K., Bodik, R., Catanzaro, B.C., Gebis, J.J., Husbands, P., Keutzer, K., Patterson, D.A., Plishker, W.L., Shalf, J., Williams, S.W., Yelick, K.A.: The Landscape of Parallel Computing Research: a view from Berkeley. Technical Report UCB/EECS-2006-183, Electrical Engineering and Computer Sciences, University of California at Berkeley (December 2006)
5. Butenhof, D.R.: Programming with POSIX Threads. Addison-Wesley, Reading (1997)
6. OpenMP, http://www.openmp.org
7. Chapman, B., Jost, G., Van Der Pas, R.: Using OpenMP: Portable Shared Memory Parallel Programming. MIT Press, Cambridge (2007)
8. Pacheco, P.S.: Parallel Programming with MPI. Morgan Kaufmann, San Francisco (1996)
9. Consortium, U.: UPC Language Specifications, v1.2. Technical report (2005)
10. Husbands, P., Iancu, C., Yelick, K.: A Performance Analysis of the Berkeley UPC Compiler. In: ICS 2003: Proceedings of the 17th annual international conference on Supercomputing, pp. 63–73. ACM, New York (2003)
11. Allen, E., Chase, D., Hallett, J., Luchangco, V., Maessen, J.W., Ryu, S., Steele Jr., G.L., Tobin-Hochstadt, S.: The Fortress Language Specification Version 1.0 beta. Technical report (March 2007)
12. Corporation, N.: NVIDIA CUDA Programming Guide, version 1.1. Technical report (November 2007)
13. Grama, A., Karypis, G., Kumar, V., Gupta, A.: Introduction to Parallel Computing, 2nd edn. Addison-Wesley, Boston (2003)
14. OpenMPI, http://www.open-mpi.org
15. MVAPICH, http://mvapich.cse.ohio-state.edu
16. MPICH, http://www.mcs.anl.gov/research/projects/mpich2
17. GRIDMPI, http://www.gridmpi.org
18. LAM/MPI, http://www.lam-mpi.org

An Integrated Framework for Wireless Sensor Web Service and Its Performance Analysis Based on Queue Theory[*]

Luqun Li[**]

Department of Computer Science of Shanghai Normal University, 100 Guilin Road,
Shanghai, China 200233
liluqun@gmail.com

Abstract. Wireless sensor networks (WSNs) have unlimited and extensive potential application in different areas. Right now, how to integrate WSNs into the web service or grid computing framework is becoming an issue in related research areas. In this paper, we proposed an integrated web service framework for WSNs, and built mobile device hosted web service, moreover we built its corresponding queueing model and gave it performance analysis. Analysis and simulation show that our framework is practical in QoS guaranteed messages transmitting with different priority.

Keywords: web service; wireless sensor networks;QoS; queue theory;Little's Law.

1 Introduction

Right now, wireless sensor networks (WSNs) are currently receiving significant research attention both in theory and application, due to their unlimited and extensive potential application in different areas[1]. WSNs serve as a role that bridges the gap between the physical and logical worlds, by gathering certain useful information from the physical world and transmitting that information to more powerful logical devices that can process it[2]. Each node in WSNs has its unique computing ability in its specific working area, moreover it may own wireless network connection with WLAN or Internet. It can act as a computing nodes in network based computing, such as grid computing and web service computing[1].This seems to be one of the phenomena in Pervasive Computing era[1, 3, 4]. While as for the limited computing ability, storage, battery energy and wireless band width of WSNs, how to efficiently and QoS grantee integrate WSNs with the architecture of current web service or grid service[5, 6]has become an issue in web service integration application. In this paper, firstly, we analysis related research works on this issue then put forward an integrated framework for wireless sensor web service, then we build the differential service queueing model of this framework and give its performance analysis and numeral

---

[*] This work was supported in part by the Shanghai Education Bureau Grant CL200652, SK200709 and PL531.
[**] His main research interests are computer networks, wireless communication and swarm intelligence.

J. Cao et al. (Eds.): NPC 2008, LNCS 5245, pp. 276–285, 2008.

results. Finally, based on the results of performance analysis and numeral result, we give some optimization parameter selection in this framework.

2   Related Work and Challenges

In recent years, there has been a growing interest in sensor data collection and management, with the main focus on integrates WSNs with the current web service architecture framework. Till now, there are many research works on some specific application. These studies[1-11] provide effective techniques for sensor databases and query systems, but their main limitation is the problem scale, being within a single sensor network, besides studies above only give designs of the framework, most of studies did not provide their corresponding mathematics model and performance analysis. Another import fact is in real WSNs, there may exist many different classes users, for example the administrators or common users, different classes users need differential service such as the latency of service. Due to these issues we think the following challenges need to be addressed:

- The framework of integrate WSNs with current web service;
- The mathematics model of the framework;
- How to evaluate the performance of the framework.

To address these key challenges, we have designed the corresponding framework and mathematics model.

3   Proposed Framework

Web service has become an integral part of many web applications in nowadays. Platform-independent, ubiquitous and easy access web services using common standardized protocol SOAP, WSDL, UDDI, have been one of the principal drivers behind this success.

In WSNs, it is impossible for all nodes to be connected with wired network or Internet, usually only the sink nodes in WSNs which have high battery energy will connect with wired network or Internet (See Fig.1).

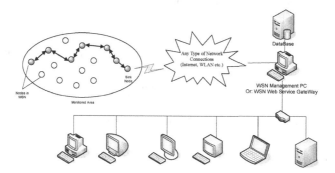

Fig. 1. WSNs Connected With Wired Network

Different from the wired web service provider, web service based on wireless sensor nodes (such as Mica2, Ziggbee etc) which only own constraint computing resources and battery, and very narrow band of wireless network. Moreover, to save the battery, if there is no request for sensor data; nodes in WSNs are usually in battery saving state. Besides these issues, XML and SOAP are not efficient protocol for WSNs nodes to transmit messages, while raw binary code related protocols are still dominated protocols for these devices. Concern on the unique characteristics of WSNs and the standard web service architecture, we prompted the following integrated web service framework for WSNs framework for mobile device hosted web service (See Fig.2).

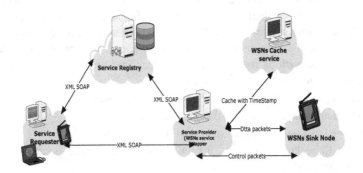

Fig. 2. Integrated Web Service Framework for WSNs

We use the following abbreviation to denote each role in the framework above:

SG : denotes Service Registry; SR : denotes Service Requester;

WSM : denotes WSNs service Mapper;

$WSNd$: denotes the sink node in WSNs;

WCS : denotes WSNs Cache Service.

In this framework, we can see that Service Registry (SG) and Service Requester (SR) are still the traditional roles in web service model. Different from the standard web service model, we introduce a new role which is WSNs service Mapper (WSM). WSM acts as a hybrid role.

From the Service Requester viewpoint, WSM is a standard web service provider, roles on the left side of the framework communicate with each other by SOAP or XML protocol. Though most nodes in WSNs have wireless network connection, they may not own valid IP address; they can not directly provide service just like a server in internet. WSM seems to be one of the most practical approach to solve the problem, it is like a gateway to bridge WSNs and wired network, so WSM is an essential role in this framework.

In our framework above, on the right side, WSM acts as a web service consumer, it can also be taken as a wrapper for sink node in WSNs hosted web service, WSM is usually hosted on a wired computer, it accepts the web service request by standard web service protocol, it requests web service from sink node of WSNs by any proto-cols, we denote it by *WSNd*.

Because each WSN may need to be managed, the user of WSNs may be classified into different privilege levels, to make the problem simple, the users are classified into two classes, or the administrators and the common users. Usually the administra-tors send control packet to sink nodes of WSNs to regulate the states of WSNs, the common user only request for the data from *WSNd*.

Besides, to enhance the throughput of the system and save the battery energy of *WSNd*, we also introduce a web service cache system *WSC* to reduce unneces-sary repeated request to *WSNd*.

As for, in this paper we only focus on the framework and its performance analy-sis, we will not go any further in program coding, you can see the details in program code implementation of our system in [1].

3   Queueing Model for the Framework

To analysis the performance of the integrated web service in Fig.2, we build the fol-lowing queueing mode (See Fig.3)

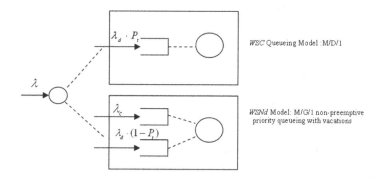

Fig. 3. Queue Model for the Framework

Actually, there are two queues in the queueing model above, and they are:

- Queue.1 The first queue is for *WSC*, the cache system is only for WSNs data packet, WSNs cache system is usually a data search operation, and we use M/D/1 for this queueing model. Web service request messages come to *WSC* queue at the rate of $\lambda_d \cdot P_t$, where λ_d is the rate of data request messages, P_t is probabil-ity of getting data from cache service *WSC*.

- Queue.2 This queue is for *WSNd*. This queue is work for both WSNs control and data packet request, as for the service time of *WSNd* is usually with general distribution and it may be in the state of energy saving (in vacations states), we use M/G/1 non-preemptive priority with vacations for this queueing model.

All $WSNd$ web service request message are firstly sent to WSM. WSM will check the message type and the time stamp to determine which queue the request should be forward to process.

In this model, we assume web service request message types are classified in to n priority classes. Messages of each priority class $i(i = 1, 2, \ldots n)$ arrive according to a Poisson process with rate λ_i and to be served by $WSNd$ with a general service time distribution of mean $\overline{x}_i$ and second moment $\overline{x_i^2}$.

To make the problem simple, we assume there are two priority classes in our model, the first one is control message, which is usually the control message sent by the administrators or some urgent message request, it comes with the rate of λ_c; the second one is data message, it comes with the rate of $\lambda_e = \lambda_d \cdot (1 - P_t)$. The arrival λ_c and λ_d are assumed to be independent of each other and service process. Note that the rate of all messages comes at $\lambda = \lambda_c + \lambda_d$.

λ_c is to be served by $WSNd$ with a general service time distribution of mean $\overline{x}_c$ and second moment $\overline{x_c^2}$.

λ_e is to be served by $WSNd$ with a general service time distribution of mean $\overline{x}_e$ and second moment $\overline{x_e^2}$.

Another import thing to be noted is $WSNd$ may be in energy saving state or so-called a "vacation". In this state $WSNd$ does not process any requests. Assume that $v_1, v_2, \ldots$ are the residual of $WSNd$'s successive vacation time. The mean of vacation time $v_1, v_2, \ldots$ is $\overline{V}$, and the second moment is $\overline{V^2}$.

Then we can summary the parameters and their relationships by the followings:

λ_c: denotes the rate of control messages to $WSNd$;

λ_e: denotes the rate of data messages to $WSNd$

P_t: denotes the probability of data message to WSC

ρ_c: is called the traffic intensity or utilization factor for control message to process;

ρ_e: is called the traffic intensity or utilization factor for data message to process;

ρ: denotes the traffic intensity of the system;

μ_c: denotes the service rate to process control messages;

μ_e: denotes the service rate of to process data messages;

$\overline{x}$: denotes the average service time of the system;

$\overline{x^2}$: denotes the second moment of the system;

$\overline{V}$:denotes the mean of vacation time $v_1, v_2, \ldots$;

$\overline{V^2}$: denotes the second moment of $v_1, v_2, \ldots$.

We can deduce the relationship among these parameters above in the followings:

$$\lambda = \lambda_c + \lambda_d = \lambda_c + \lambda_d \cdot P_t + \lambda_e, \lambda_e = \lambda_d \cdot (1 - P_t) ;$$

$$\rho_c = \lambda_c \cdot \overline{x_c}, \ \rho_e = \lambda_e \cdot \overline{x_e}, \rho = \frac{\lambda}{\mu} = \rho_c + \rho_e ;$$

$$\overline{x} = \frac{\lambda_c}{\lambda} \cdot \overline{x_c} + \frac{\lambda_e}{\lambda} \cdot \overline{x_e}, \ \overline{x^2} = \frac{\lambda_c}{\lambda} \cdot \overline{x_c^2} + \frac{\lambda_e}{\lambda} \cdot \overline{x_e^2}$$

4 Analysis on the Queueing Model

As for Queue.1 above is a $M/D/1$ queueing system, this queue is rather easy, we will not go any further. Now, we will focus on Queue.2.

First, we analysis the residual service time R for all the messages in the system. By Fig.4 we can get that R equals the mean service time of all message with different priority plus the mean service in vocation time ($WSNd$ is in power saving state), we can simple denote it by:

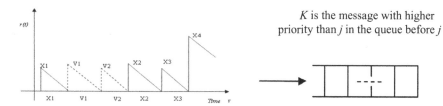

Fig. 4. Residual Service Time for All Messages

K is the message with higher priority than j in the queue before j

Fig. 5. Messages in Queue.2

$$R = \overline{ServiceTime} + \overline{ServiceInVacationTime} ;$$

$$\text{where}, \overline{ServiceTime} = \sum_{k=1}^{n} \rho_k \left(\frac{\overline{x_k^2}}{2\overline{x_k}} \right) = \frac{1}{2} \sum_{k=1}^{n} \lambda_k \overline{x_k^2} ,$$

$$\overline{ServiceInVacationTime} = \frac{\overline{V^2}}{2 \cdot \overline{V}}$$

Where, $\overline{ServiceTime}$ is the system mean service time, $\overline{ServiceInVacationTime}$ is the mean time that $WSNd$ is in power saving state; and j is current message that just is in queue, k is the message with higher priority than j in the queue before j (See Fig.5).

From analysis above, we can directly use the conclusions in $M/G/1$ [12], and arrive at the waiting time of each message with different priority :

$$W_i = \frac{R}{(1-\rho_1-\rho_2-...-\rho_{i-1})(1-1-\rho_1-\rho_2-...-\rho_i)} \tag{1}$$

where W_i is the waiting time of message to $WSNd$ with priority i ,and ρ_i is the traffic intensity or utilization factor for message to $WSNd$ with priority i .

Then from equation (1), according to **Little's Law** in queue theory, we can get the average number of messages N_i with the same priority i in their waiting queue:

$$N_i = \lambda_i \cdot W_i = \frac{\lambda_i \cdot R}{(1-\rho_1-\rho_2-...-\rho_{i-1})(1-1-\rho_1-\rho_2-...-\rho_i)} \tag{2}$$

The total time T_i for each message with priority i spent in Queue.2 is:

$$T_i = W_i + \overline{x_i} = \frac{R}{(1-\rho_1-\rho_2-...-\rho_{i-1})(1-1-\rho_1-\rho_2-...-\rho_i)} + \overline{x_i} \tag{3}$$

The total number of all messages N in Queue.2 is:

$$N = \sum_{k=1}^{n} N_k + \rho = \sum_{k=1}^{n} \left(\frac{\lambda_k \cdot R}{(1-\rho_1-\rho_2-...-\rho_{k-1})(1-1-\rho_1-\rho_2-...-\rho_k)} \right) + \rho \tag{4}$$

In summary, we can evaluate the performance of our framework by W_i, N_i and T_i.

5   Numeral Results and Analysis

To analysis the results that we have deduced above, we give the following initial parameters in the framework:

- The mean data message process time $\overline{x_d} = 0.02$, with variance $\sigma_d^2 = 0.05$ and the second moment $\overline{x_d^2} = \left(\overline{x_d}\right)^2 + \sigma_d^2$;

- The mean control data message process time $\overline{x_c} = 0.002$, with variance $\sigma_c^2 = 0.02$ and the second moment $\overline{x_c^2} = \left(\overline{x_c}\right)^2 + \sigma_c^2$;

- The mean control data message process time $\overline{V} = 0.06$, with variance $\sigma_v^2 = 0.01$ and the second moment $\overline{V^2} = \left(\overline{V}\right)^2 + \sigma_v^2$;to increase the efficiency of system, we change the $\overline{V^2} = \left(\left(\overline{V} \right)^2 + \sigma_v^2 \right) / \lambda$, it means intelligent in power saving state;

• $P_t = 0.1$;

According equation (1)(2)(3)(4), by increase the value of λ, we will also get increased traffic intensity of the system ρ, the we can get the queue size and wait time of each message with different priority, see Fig.6 and Fig.7.

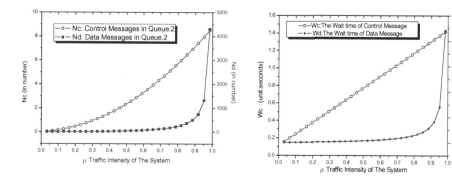

Fig. 6. Queue size of Nc and N_d with ρ **Fig. 7.** Wait time of Wc and W_d with ρ

Fig.6 shows that with the increasing of ρ, N_c will also increase, but the queue size will be below than 9; while N_d will increase very fast, and the queue size nearly 4300;

Fig.7 shows that with the increasing of ρ, W_c will also increase, but the wait time will be below than 1.4 second; while W_d will increase very fast, and the wait time will below 84 second;

We can see that latency of the control message to be processed will be guaranteed.

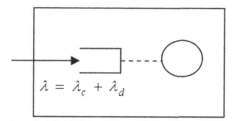

Queueing Model: M/G/1 with vacation without Priority

Fig. 8. Queueing Model M/G/1 with Vacation without Priority

To compare the framework we proposed in Fig.3 with the traditional queueing model M/G/1 with vacation without priority in Fig.8, we run the simulation with the same initial parameters above, then we get Fig.9 and Fig.10.

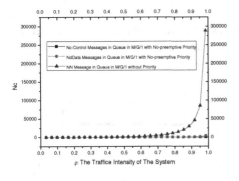
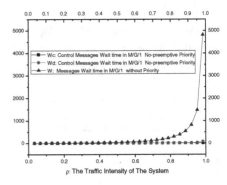

Fig. 9. Queue size in different model with ρ **Fig. 10.** Wait time in different model with ρ

Fig.9 shows that in our framework in Fig.3 with the increasing of ρ, N_c will also increase, but the queue size will be below than 9; while N_d will increase very fast, and the queue size nearly 4300; in the traditional model in Fig.8, the queue size will increase very fast, and the queue size is very large;

Fig.10 shows that with the increasing of ρ, W_c will also increase, but the wait time will be below than 1.4 second; while W_d will increase very fast, and the wait time will below 84 second; in the traditional model in Fig.8, the wait time size will increase to 4800;

With the queueing model in Fig.3 and $WSNd$ is intelligent in power saving state, we can make a conclusion that the performance of the framework we proposed is much better than the traditional queueing model in Fig.8

6   Conclusions

In this paper, we introduced an integrated framework for wireless sensor web service, then, based on queue theory, we give its performance analysis. Analysis and simulation show that our framework is QoS guaranteed for different messages with different priority, and the performance of our is much better than the traditional queueing model in Fig.8.

References

[1] Li, L., Li, M.: The Study on Mobile Web Service Computing for Data Collecting. In: 2004 International Conference on Communications, Circuits and Systems, vol. II, pp. 1497–1501. IEEE, Los Alamitos (2004)

 [2] Yu, Y., Rittle, L.J.: Supporting Concurrent Applications in Wireless Sensor Networks. In: SenSys 2006, Boulder, Colorado, USA, November 1-3, 2006, pp. 139–152 (2006)
 [3] Whitehouse, K., Zhao, F., Liu, J.: Semantic streams: A framework for composable semantic interpretation of sensor data. In: Römer, K., Karl, H., Mattern, F. (eds.) EWSN 2006. LNCS, vol. 3868. Springer, Heidelberg (2006)
 [4] Zhu, F., Mutka, M.W., Ni, L.M.: Service discovery in pervasive computing environments. Pervasive Computing 4(4), 81–90 (2005)
 [5] Delicato, F.C., et al.: A flexible web service based architecture for wireless sensor networks. In: Proceedings of 23rd International Conference on Distributed Computing Systems Workshops, 2003, pp. 730–735 (2003)
 [6] Gaynor, M., Moulton, S.L., Welsh, M.: Integrating Wireless Sensor Networks with the Grid (2004)
 [7] Cardell-Oliver, R., et al.: Field Testing a Wireless Sensor Network for Reactive Environmental Monitoring. In: Proceedings of the International Conference on Intelligent Sensors, Sensor Networks and Information Processing (2004)
 [8] Karl, H., Willig, A.: Protocols and Architectures for Wireless Sensor Networks. Wiley, Chichester (2005)
 [9] Peng, R., Hua, K.A., Hamza-Lup, G.L.: A Web services environment for Internet-scale sensor computing. In: 2004 IEEE International Conference on Services Computing (SCC 2004) Proceedings, pp. 101–108 (2004)
[10] Shi, J., Liu, W.: A service-oriented model for wireless sensor networks with Internet. In: The Fifth International Conference on Computer and Information Technology, 2005. CIT 2005, pp. 1045–1049 (2005)
[11] Woo, A., et al.: A spreadsheet approach to programming and managing sensor networks. In: Proceedings of the fifth international conference on Information processing in sensor networks, pp. 424–431 (2006)
[12] Hock, N.C.: Queueing Modelling Fundamentals. John Wiley & Sons, Chichester (1997)
[13] Broll, G., et al.: Supporting Mobile Service Usage through Physical Mobile Interaction. In: Fifth Annual IEEE International Conference on Pervasive Computing and Communication (PerCom 2007), White Plains, NY, USA (2007)
[14] Dorn, C., Dustdar, S.: Sharing hierarchical context for mobile web services. Distributed and Parallel Databases 21(1), 85–111 (2007)
[15] Phan, K.A., Tari, P., Bertok, P.: A benchmark on soap's transport protocols performance for mobile applications. In: Proceedings of the 2006 ACM symposium on Applied computing 2006 (SESSION: Mobile computing and applications (MCA)), pp. 1139–1144 (2006)
[16] Oh, S., Fox, G.C.: Optimizing Web Service messaging performance in mobile computing. Future Generation Computer Systems 23(4), 623–632 (2007)
[17] Park, Y.H.: Method for supplying a mobile web service by transceiving XML data based an soap and a system therefo, Pantech Co Ltd
[18] Sakkopoulos, E., Lytras, M., Tsakalidis, A.: Adaptive mobile web services facilitate communication and learning Internet technologies. IEEE Transactions on Education 49(2), 208–215 (2006)
[19] Oh, S., Fox, P.C.: Optimizing Web Service messaging performance in mobile computing Future Generation Computer Systems, May 2007, vol. 23(4) (2007)
[20] Srirama, S.N., Jarke, M., Prinz, W.: Mobile Web Service Provisioning. In: Proceedings of the Advanced Int'l Conference on Telecommunications and Int'l Conference on Internet and Web Applications and Services (February 2006)
[21] Srirama, S.N., Jarke, P., Prinz, P.: A Mediation Framework for Mobile Web Service Provisioning. In: Proceedings of the 10th IEEE on International Enterprise Distributed Object Computing Conference Workshops, October 2006, p. 14 (2006) (0-7695-2743-4)

Grid Computing: A Case Study in Hybrid GMRES Method

Ye Zhang, Guy Bergere, and Serge Petiton

Laboratoire d'Informatique Fondamentale de Lille, USTL
59650 Villeneuve D'Ascq, France
{Ye.Zhang,Guy.Bergere,Serge.Petiton}@lifl.fr

Abstract. Grid computing in general is a special type of parallel computing. It intends to deliver high-performance computing over distributed platforms for computation and data-intensive applications by making use of a very large amount of resources. The GMRES method is used widely to solve the large sparse linear systems. In this paper, we present an effective parallel hybrid asynchronous method, which combines the typical parallel GMRES method with the Least Square method that needs some eigenvalues obtained from a parallel Arnoldi process. And we apply it on a Grid Computing platform Grid5000. From the numeric results, we will present that this hybrid method has some advantage for some real or complex systems compared to the general method GMRES.

Keywords: Grid, hybrid, GMRES, complex.

1 Introduction

Iterative methods are a common choice for solving the large linear sparse system of the form Ax=b. A popular class of iterative methods is Krylov subspace methods. The generalized minimum residual algorithm (GMRES) [2] is used widely and it is often referred to as an "optimal" method because it finds the approximate solution in the Krylov subspace that minimaized the 2-norm of the residual. In order to limit both computation and memory requirements, a restarted version is often used. It has been implemented on parallel systems [1], but this method does not always converge very fast. There are some existing modifications to the standard GMRES algorithm. We study a hybrid method [9] which calculates in parallel some eigenvalues by the Arnoldi method [3], [4]. As soon as they are approximated with a sufficient accuracy, the eigenvalues are used to perform some iterations of the Least Squares method [6] for getting a new initial vector for the next GMRES restarts. We have applied it on the supercomputer to solve some small real linear system [9], [15].

We perform our experiments on a Grid system. As known to all, the Grid is well established as a research domain and proposes technologies that are mature enough to be used for real-life applications. It is dedicated to achieve a high performance of large scale computing by using a large amount of unoccupied computing resources.

J. Cao et al. (Eds.): NPC 2008, LNCS 5245, pp. 286–296, 2008.

The Grid5000 project has been launched to provide the community of Grid researchers with an unprecedented large-scale infrastructure to study Grid issues under real experimental conditions. Grid'5000 is a large scale computing tool composed of many clusters distributed in several computing centers in France.

In this paper, we present the distributed hybrid method GMRES(m)/LS-Arnoldi which is well implemented on the GRID system Grid'5000. And we try to apply it on the large linear systems and the complex systems.

This paper is organized as follows. The numerical methods used in our hybrid method will be present in section 2. In section 3, we introduce the implementation on Grid'5000. In section 4, we present the results obtained on the platform Grid'5000. At the same time we sum up the advantages and characteristic and see the effect on complex problem. Finally, in section 5, we present a summary and discuss directions for future research.

2   GMRES(m)/LS-Arnoldi Hybrid Parallel Method

This method aims to accelerate the convergence with the benefit of Arnoldi and Least Square methods. Arnoldi method uses the Gram-Schmidt method to compute the orthonormal basis of the Krylov subspace. It is well-known for approximating eigenvalues of large sparse matrices. Least Square is a polynomial iteration method that can offers us a new initial vector by using the eigenvalues information.

The idea is that during the GMRES iterations, if we can offer more information about the matrix, the efficiency of convergence can be increased. So we use Least Square method to obtain the new initial vector for the next GMRES iterations. And the Arnoldi process is performed in parallel to calculate some eigenvalues with a sufficient accuracy for the Least Square computation.

2.1   GMRES Method

GMRES (Generalized Minimum RESidual) method is one of the iterative methods based on Krylov subspace. Such methods find an approximate solution $x_i \in x_0 + K_i(A, r_0)$, where $K_i(A, r_0) \equiv span\{r_0, Ar_0, ..., A^{i-1}r_0\}$ denotes an i-demensional Krylov subspace, x_0 is the initial guess, and r_0 is the initial residual.

The GMRES method was proposed by Saad and Schultz[2] in 1986. It is used widely to solve non-symmetric linear systems. The mth iterate x_m of GMRES is the solution of the least squares problem: $minimize_{x \in x_0 + K_m(A, r_0)} \| b - Ax \|_2$, where $r_0 = b - Ax_0$ is the residual of the initial solution. The Arnoldi process applied to $K_m(A, r_0)$ builds $V_{m+1} = [V_m, v_{m+1}]$, an orthonormal basis of $K_m(A, r_0)$, the m+1 by m matrix $\overline{H}_m$ and $\beta = \| r_0 \|_2$. These matrices satisfy the relation $AV_m = V_{m+1}\overline{H}_m$. The iterate x_m can be written as $x_m = x_0 + V_m y_m$, where $y_m \in \Re^m$ is the solution of the least squares problem: $minimize_{y \in \Re^m} \| \beta e_1 - \overline{H}_m y \|_2$.

In the GMRES algorithm the number of vectors requiring storage increases with m. In order to limit both computation and memory requirements, a restarted version is often used.

In the algorithm, x_0 denotes an initial guess of the solution, m denotes the size of Krylov subspaces, and ε denotes the tolerance.

```
Algorithm restarted GMRES(m):
1. Initialization
2. r₀ = b - Ax₀
3. Apply Arnoldi process to Kₘ(A,r₀)
4. yₘ = arg min || βe₁ - H̄ₘy ||₂
         y∈ℜᵐ
   xₘ = x₀ + Vₘyₘ, rₘ = b - Axₘ
5. if || rₘ ||₂≤ ε then stop
   else
       x₀ = xₘ, r₀ = rₘ
       goto step3
   end if
```

2.2 The Hybrid Algorithm GMRES(m)/LS(k,l)

The whole process is that we calculate in parallel some eigenvalues by the Arnoldi method [5]. As they will be approximated with a sufficient accuracy, eigenvalues are used to perform some iterations of the Least Squares method [6] in order to obtain a new initial vector for the next GMRES iterations.

The hybrid algorithm GMRES(m)/LS(k,l) can be given as follows. There are some important parameters, m' denotes the size of Krylov subspace for Arnoldi method, k denotes the degree of the least squares polynomial, and l denotes the number of the successive applications of the Least Squares method.

```
Algorithm: GMRES(m)/LS(k,l)
1. Initialization
2. Compute xₘ, the mᵗʰ iterate of GMRES starting with x₀
   if || b - Axₘ ||₂< ε then Stop
   else
       x₀ = xₘ,  r₀ = b - Ax₀
   end if
2'. Perform m' iterations of the Arnoldi process start-
ing with r₀, to Kₘ'(A,v), and compute the eigenvalues of
Hₘ'
2''. Compute the least squares polynomial Pₖ on the
boundary of H, the hull convex enclosing all computed ei-
genvalues.
```

3. Do $j = 1, \cdots, l$

$\quad\quad \tilde{x} = x_0 + P_k(A)r_0$

$\quad\quad x_0 = \tilde{x}, \quad r_0 = b - Ax_0$

$\quad$ end do

4. if $\| r_0 \|_2 < \varepsilon$ then Stop

$\quad$ else goto step 2

$\quad$ end if

In the algorithm, step 2' and 2'' means that these two steps are performed independently of the GMRES iterations, and the step 2'' is performed following the step 2'.

Step 2' is the Arnoldi process. At first we apply Arnoldi process to the krylov subspaces of Arnldi $K_m(A, v)$. Then we calculate the eigenvalues($\lambda_i,\ 1 \le i \le d$) and the associate eigenvectors ($y_i,\ 1 \le i \le d$) of H_m. After that we compute the Ritz vectors $u_i = V_m y_i$, for i=1, $\cdots$, d. Set $v = \sum_{i=1}^{d} Re(u_i)$, and repeat the process above until $\max_{i=1}^{d} |\rho_i| < \varepsilon$, where $\rho_i = \| \lambda_i u_i - A u_i \|_2,\ 1 \le i \le d$.

Step 2'' is the sequential part of Least Square method. For the Least Square method, it can be written as follows: $\tilde{x} = x_0 + P_k(A)r_0$ where x_0 an initial approximation, r_0 its residual, and P_k is a polynomial of degree k-1. Let P_k^l be the set of the real polynomials p of degree k, such that p(0)=1, and define the polynomial $R_k \in P_k^l$ by $R_k(z) = 1 - zP_k(z)$. Then the residual of the iterate $\tilde{x}$ is $\tilde{r} = R_k(A)r_0$.

In general, we do not have the whole spectrum of A, but only some eigenvalue estimates contained in a convex hull H because all eigenvalue calculation will spend a very long time. H is constructed such as it does not contain the origin. Smolarski and Saylor [11] proposed to find R_k minimizing a weighted L_2-norm on the space of real polynomials, with a suitable weight function w, defined on the boundary of H. We obtain the following least squares problem $\min_{R_k \in P_k^l} \| R_k \|_w$.

The obtained polynomial $P_k = \sum_{i=0}^{k-1} \eta_i t_i$ is expressed in the scaled and shifted Chebyshev basis defined by $t_j(\lambda) = T_j\left(\dfrac{\lambda - c}{d} \right) / T_j\left(\dfrac{a}{d} \right)$ j=0,1,... This is the best basis of polynomials on the ellipse $\varepsilon(c, d, a)$ of smallest area enclosing H (see [10] and [5] for an algorithm computing this optimal ellipse). For more details, see [6].

2.3 The Hybrid Method for Complex Problem

In fact, we realize the solution by the prior treatment for the complex matrix. The complex problem $(Ar + Ai)\times(Xr + Xi) = (br + bi)$ can be split into real part and image part:

$$Ar \times Xr - Ai \times Xi = br$$
$$Ar \times Xi + Ai \times Xr = bi$$

So we extend the complex matrix (size N*N) into a real counterpart (size 2N*2N) [7].

$$
\begin{array}{|c|c|}
\hline
Ar & -Ai \\
\hline
Ai & Ar \\
\hline
\end{array}
\times
\begin{array}{|c|}
\hline
Xr \\
\hline
Xi \\
\hline
\end{array}
=
\begin{array}{|c|}
\hline
br \\
\hline
bi \\
\hline
\end{array}
$$

$$ \text{A'} \qquad\qquad \text{X'} \qquad \text{b'} $$

We apply the hybrid method to this new system $A' \times X' = b'$.

3   Implementation on GRID System

Grid'5000 is a Nation Wide Grid environment that is composed of many clusters distributed in 9 computing centers in France. A fast dedicated network interconnects those clusters. It is a highly configurable, controllable and monitorable instrument that can be configured to work as a real Grid. We implement our experiments on Grid5000 because it isolates the perturbations from outside, par example the communication over the Internet and the load of the computing devices. We can devote ourselves to research the algorithm itself and it would help us improve our analysis of more tests on the worldwide platforms in future.

The Grid5000 usage is based on a reservation policy and a deployment mechanism allowing people configuring their own environment. Details can be found on the Grid5000 website [16]. We distribute our application on one or several sites of Grid5000 with the environment MPI.

We reserve most processors to run the algorithm GMRES(m) by the way of the SPMD model, where one act as an administrative process and the other p identical calculation processes play the role of workers. The calculation processors read directly their own data and execute the method GMRES(m), communicating with their brother processes.

The processors dedicated to the parallel package "PARPACK" are in charge of the residuals reception, the Arnoldi projection and the eigenvalues calculation, performing independently of the processes GMRES.

Only one processor is in charge of the sequential part because of the small set of data for calculation. The parameters "Least Square" obtained are then sent to the processors executing the parallel part of LS method and algorithm GMRES(m).

The whole process and the relationship of the communication between the three parts are presented in Fig. 1.

There are two threads for the whole calculation. The first is the GMRES iteration or Least Square iteration. After each iteration, the GMRES(m) process always checks if the LS parameters arrive. In this case, the GMRES algorithm is then suspend, and the processes perform the parallel part of the LS hybridizations. Then GMRES(m) restart with the obtained initial vector.

Another thread is the eigenvalues calculation by Arnoldi method and the coefficients computation by sequential part of Least Square method. These two processes are performed in serial.

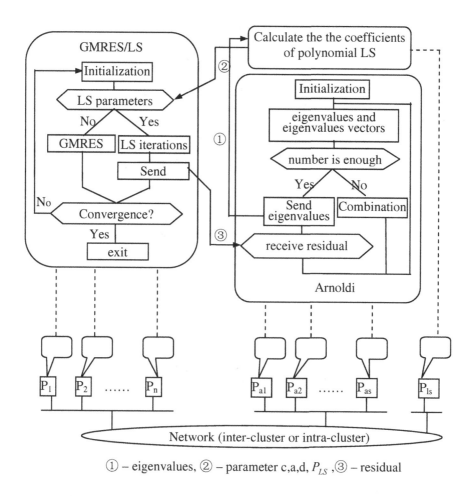

① – eigenvalues, ② – parameter c,a,d, P_{LS} ,③ – residual

Fig. 1. General scheme of asynchronous hybrid GMRES/LS-Arnoldi process

All the processors are interconnected inter-cluster or intra-cluster. Intra-cluster means that the algorithm is performed in one cluster. In other word, the GMRES iteration, the Arnoldi process and LS method are distributed in the nodes of the same cluster. Inter-cluster means that these three components are distributed in different clusters, and each component can be assigned completely in one cluster or be distributed in different clusters.

4   Numeric Results and Analysis

Table 1 shows the excellent network configuration of our experimental platform. The detailed information can be referred to the web site of Grid'5000 [16].

Table 1. Bandwidth and average latency between the clusters of the sites

	Bandwidth	Latency
Inter-Cluster		
Orsay	48.4MB/s	0.11ms
nancy	42.8MB/s	0.09ms
Bordeaux	53.7MB/s	0.086ms
Intra-Cluster		
Orsay – nancy	9.7MB/s	5.7ms
Orsay – Bordeaux	8.1MB/s	7.9ms
Nancy – Bordeaux	4.0MB/s	17ms

All the sparse matrices are stocked in the compressed format CSR (Compress Sparse Row) for saving the memory and reducing the communication on the network. Moreover, in order to be able to verify the results accuracy, we have chosen in all examples the right-hand side so that the solution of the system is $x = (1,1,...,1)^T$. The iteration starts with $x_0 = (0,0,...,0)^T$.

First example (af23560): We experiment some industrial matrices from the site MatrixMarket. In this paper, we present the results obtained with the matrix af23560 (size 23560*23560, 484256 nonzero elements)

Second example: are created by a generator and are block diagonal matrices. (size 17000*17000, 426260 nonzero elements)

Third example: symmetric complex matrix young1c (size 841*841, 4089 nonzero elements). It is from the site MatrixMarket.

Forth example: symmetric complex matrix dwg961b (size 961*961, 10591 nonzero elements).

4.1 Advantages of the Hybrid Method

We can see the first advantage from Fig 2: the high degree of parallelism. GMRES method is a compute-intensive and data parallelism application. During the parallel GMRES processes, there are intensive communication and multiple synchro- nizations. So the parallelism degree is limited. It can't be increased easily. The more processors involve, the more communication spend and the slower the convergence is. In the hybrid method, we add the task parallelism by the participation of Arnoldi process and Least Square method. We use more processors and we accelerate the convergence. In this example, the classic gmres method has an optimal number of processors, 26, and the optimal number for the hybrid method is 34. And we can also remark that the hybrid method spent less time.

The second advantage is the obvious speed up of convergence. The convergence with the hybrid method can be faster, even when it is difficult by using the classic GMRES method (Fig. 3). In this example, we choose a relatively small size of krylov subspace. We can notice a stagnation of convergence for the classic restarted GMRES method. However, for the hybrid method, despite the appearance of many peaks, it converges.

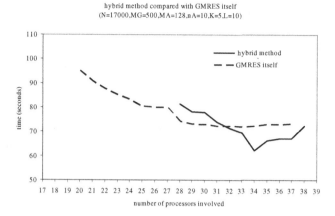

Fig. 2. The comparison of hybrid method and GMRES itself of the matrix (N=17000) with the number of processors

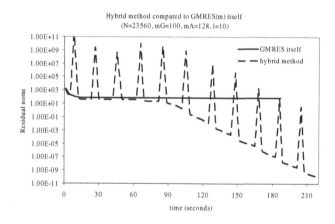

Fig. 3. The comparison of hybrid method and GMRES itself of the matrix (N=23560) in condition of the difficult convergence

The third advantage accompanies the second advantage: low requirement of memory. The use of the restarted GMRES version is because it can limit both computation and memory requirements. The bigger the size of Krylov subspace is, the better the convergence is. However, the bigger size means the more memory requirement. Using the hybrid method, we can realize the convergence by the smaller size of Krylov subspace.

4.2 Characteristics of the Hybrid Method

As the mention in section 4.1, we can obverse some peaks during the convergence of hybrid method (Fig. 3). These peaks appear when the process of hybridization occurs.

The residual increases sharply temporary, however a sharper deduce follows. Overall, the convergence is achieved. Thereby, too many peaks will damage the efficiency, as each hybridization influences many GMRES iterations. When the peaks are high and nearby, divergence may even occur.

Additional, we combine the Arnoldi and Least Square method with the restarted GMRES in order to accelerate the convergence. Although the computation and communication increases, in fact there is almost no influence for the whole performance because these two methods are performed in parallel and the communication between different components is relatively little. Most of their computation time and their communication time can be overlapped. Table 2 illustrates this characteristic.

The symbols (1), (2), (3) correspond to the condition 1, 2, 3.

Condition1: GMRES on Nancy, Anoldi on Nancy, and Least Square on Bordeaux.
Condition2: GMRES on Nancy, Arnoldi on Orsay, and Least Square on Bordeaux
Condition3: GMRES on Nancy and Orsay, Arnoldi on Nancy and Orsay, and Least Square on Bordeaux

The term com1 denotes the communication for GMRES computing like exchange the data with their brother processors. The term com2 denotes the communication between the components, like eigenvalues, LS parameters.

Table 2. Bandwidth and average latency between the clusters of the sites

Time(s)	Intra-cluster (Nancy)	Inter-cluster (Nancy+Orsay)		
		Distribution Inter-component		Distribution Intra-component
		(1)	(2)	(3)
Total time	70.73	71.57	72.69	120.8
Computing	58	58.224	58.358	65.54
Com1	12.42	13.319	14.132	54.42
Com2	0.009	0.024	0.055	0.084
Iteration	10	10	10	10

(2) represents the condition that three different components of the algorithm are distributed respectively in three different clusters. It is obviously that this distribution strategy can't bring much more burden for the communication.

4.3 Complex Problems

Due to the incompatible of the part of hybridization algorithm for the complex elements, the hybrid method is always used to solve the real linear systems. Now we apply the hybrid method on the prior transformed system.

From the experimental results (Fig.4, Fig.5), we can notice that the hybrid method also shows its advantages and characteristic for the solution of complex problem.

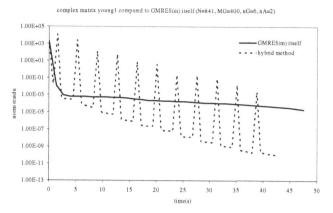

Fig. 4. The comparison of hybrid method and GMRES itself for the complex matrix (N=841)

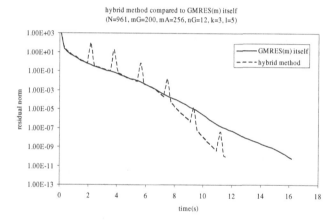

Fig. 5. The comparison of hybrid method and GMRES itself for the complex matrix (N=961)

5   Conclusion

We implemented our algorithm for the hybrid method GMRES(m)/LS-Arnoldi on Grid computing platforms: Grid'5000 with the environment MPI, and applied it to the real problems and the complex problems.

From the experimental results, we sum up the advantages and characteristics of the hybrid method. We obtain very important convergence accelerations, and increase the degree of parallelism.

In future, we will try more complex problems, and extend our method to the scientific problems of larger size.

Moreover, the hybrid method can be improved in many places. We think that it's better to change the parameters dynamically during the solution of the problem. For example, we can decide whether or not to proceed the hybridization of LS according to the speed of the convergence. And we can change the size of Krylov subspaces of

Arnoldi after each LS hybridization to obtain the more important eigenvalues for the next hybridization.

In addition, we will do some tests on the other supercomputers or cluster (i.e. Tsubame in Japon, IBM cell in France) to see the performances. And we will analyze the energy consumption of every component to optimize the implementation in the grid environment.

References

1. Cunha, R.D., Da, H.T.: A Parallel Implementation of the Restarted GMRES Iterative Algorithm for Nonsymmetric Systems of Linear Equations. In: Advances in Computational Mathematics, vol. 2, pp. 261–277. Springer, Heidelberg (1994)
2. Saad, Y., Schultz, M.H.: GMRES: A Generalized GMRES Algorithm for Solving Nonsymmetric Linear Systems. J. SIAM. Sci. Statist. Compt. 7, 856–869 (1986)
3. Edjlali, G., Petiton, S., Emad, N.: Interleaved Parallel Hybrid Arnoldi Method for a Parallel Machine and a Network of Workstations. In: Conference on Information, Systems, Analysis and Synthesis (ISAS 1996), Orlando, pp. 22–26 (1996)
4. Saad, Y.: Variations on Arnoldi's Method for Computing Eigenelements of Large Unsymmetric Matrices. Linear Algebra Appl. 34, 269–295 (1980)
5. Saad, Y.: Numerical Methods for Large Eigenvalue Problems. Manchester University Press, Manchester (1992)
6. Saad, Y.: Least Squares Polynomials in the Complex Plane and their Use for Solving Nonsymmetric Linear Systems. J. SIAM. Sci. Statist. Compt. 7, 155–169 (1987)
7. YinTsung, H., WeiDa, C.: A Low Complexity Complex QR Factorization Design for Signal Detection in MIMO OFDM Systems. In: International Symposium on Circuits and Systems, pp. 932–935. IEEE Press, Seattle (2008)
8. Baker, A.H., Jessup, E.R., Manteuffel, T.: A Technique for Accelerating the Convergence of Restarted GMRES. J. SIAM. MATRIX. Anal. Appl. 26, 962–984 (2005)
9. Essai, A., Bergere, G., Petiton, S.: Heterogeneous Parallel Hybrid GMRES/LS-Arnold Method. In: Ninth SIAM Conference on Parallel Processing for Scientific Computing, Texas (1999)
10. Manteuffel, T.A.: The Tchebychev Iteration for Nonsymmetric Linear Systems. J. Numer. Math. 28, 307–327 (1997)
11. Smolarski, D.C., Saylor, P.E.: An Optimum Iterative Method for Solving any Linear System with a Square Matrix. J. BIT. 28, 163–178 (1988)
12. Georgiou, Y., Richard, O., Neyron, P., Huard, G., Martin, C.: A Batch Scheduler with High Level Components. In: 5th International Symposium on Cluster Computing and the Grid, pp. 2, 776–783. IEEE Press, Cardiff (2005)
13. Franck, C., Eddy, C., Michel, D., Frederic, D., Yvon, J.: Grid'5000: a Large Scale and Highly Reconfigurable Grid Experimental Testbed. International Journal of High Performance Computing Applications 20, 481–494 (2006)
14. Benjamin, Q., Franck, C.: A Survey of Grid Research Tools: Simulators, Emulators and Real Life Platform. In: 17th IMACS World Congress Scientific Computation, Applied Mathematics and Simulation, Paris, France (2005)
15. Ye, Z., Bergere, G., Petiton, S.: A Parallel Hybrid Method of GMRES on GRID System. In: IEEE International Parallel and Distributed Processing Symposium, p. 356. IEEE Press, California (2007)
16. Grid'5000, http://www.grid5000.fr

Towards Resource Reliability Support for Grid Workflows

Jiong Yu[1,2], Guozhong Tian[2], Yuanda Cao[1], and Xianhe Sun[3]

[1] School of Computer, Beijing Institute of Technology
[2] School of Information Science and Engineering, Xinjiang University
[3] Department of Computer Science, Illinois Institute of Technology
yujiong@xju.edu.cn

Abstract. Grid workflow can be defined as an organization of Grid Services into a well-defined flow of operations, and can be thought of as the composition of Grid Services over time on heterogeneous and distributed resources in a well-defined order to accomplish a specific goal. To the time-constrained workflow Scheduling in Grids, we present a scheduling algorithm in terms of the finite-state continuous-time Markov process by selecting a resource combination scheme which has the lowest expenditure under the certain credit level of the resource reliability on the critical path in the DAG-based workflow. The simulation shows the validity of theory analysis.

Keywords: Scheduling Algorithm; Resource Reliability; Grid Workflow.

1 Introduction

In order to support complex scientific experiments, the distributed Grid resources need to be orchestrated while managing the application workflow operations within Grid environments. Correspondingly, workflow systems for Grid Services are evoking a high degree of interest. Workflow scheduling is one of the key issues in the workflow management[1]. A workflow tasks scheduling is a process that maps and manages execution of inter-dependent tasks on distributed resources. It allocates suitable resources to workflow tasks to satisfy objective functions imposed by users. Proper scheduling can have significant impact on the performance of workflow systems. Due to aggregation of geographically distributed autonomous, volatile and heterogeneous resources in Grid environments, the workflow on Grids differs far from the traditional workflow and various workflow Scheduling Algorithms are discussed from different points of view, such as static vs. dynamic policies, objective functions, applications models, QoS constraints, strategies dealing with dynamic behavior of resources, and so on. In general, scheduling workflow applications in a distributed system is an NP-complete problem [2].

A Grid workflow can be represented as a Directed Acyclic Graph (DAG) or a non-DAG[3]. Nowadays, many scheduling algorithms about the DAG-based Grid workflow are developing and are divided into two schemes: OPTIMIST and PESSI-MIST[4]. Time constraints are relaxed in the first scheme, and rigid in the latter. In the Grid workflow of PESSIMIST, it requires overall deadline, expenditure and reliability

J. Cao et al. (Eds.): NPC 2008, LNCS 5245, pp. 297–307, 2008.

constraints for individual tasks, which are explicitly specified by end-users. There are also other constraints, such as network and availability constraints, etc. Here we focus on the overall deadline, expenditure and reliability constraints for QoS requirements within workflows.

The remaining part of the paper is organized as follows: Section 2 introduces the related work in terms of the availability and scheduling scheme. Section 3 then describes the architecture and functionalities of the Grid workflow. Section 4 proposes the algorithm modeling, definition and calculation of the Grid resource reliability within the critical path and illustrates each step through a simple example. Section 5 provides performance evaluations through mathematical analysis and experiments. Section 6 presents the conclusions.

2   Related Works

Prediction-based dynamic scheduling uses dynamic information in conjunction with some results based on prediction. Jin Hyun Son et al.[3] worked out the critical path first, and then used the M/M/c model of Markovian queuing systems to determine the minimum number of parallel Grid resources for tasks so as to cost as low as possible. Rajkumar Buyya[5] proposed a workflow scheduling algorithm that minimizes the cost of execution while meeting the deadline by using Markov Decision Process approach after finding out the critical path in the DAG. Analogously, X.-H.Sun's GHS[6] modeled the resource usage pattern with a M/G/1 queue system to evaluate the impact of resource availability on the performance of a remote task at a certain resource reservation rate, and its goal of scheduling is to minimize the failure-minimization while satisfying the deadline requirement of remote tasks. However, few of them really take account of the volatility of resources. The Grid resources are based on the assumption that the machines on the Grid never break down or never present abnormal performance when workflow tasks are running on them. In fact, the execution time of workflow is affected by 'normal state' and 'abnormal state' of Grid resources occurring in successive turns. As a result, unsuccessful execution of a workflow task at any point will result in the failure of meeting user's deadlines. GHS[6] considered this failure and used a rescheduling trigger system to migrate a task execution to another resource when its initial contract is broken or a better resource is found, but it is difficult to meet the overall deadline finally.

In order to produce a good schedule, estimating the resource scheme reliability (i.e. a probability that all of working resources for workflow tasks are being in the 'normal state') is crucial, especially for constructing a preliminary workflow schedule. By using estimation techniques, it is possible for workflow schedulers to predict how tasks in a workflow or sub-workflow will behave on distributed heterogeneous resources and thus make decisions on how and where to run them.

Overall deadline time is a basic measure for the workflow performance. To model the entire workflow as an optimization problem will produce the larger scheduling overhead. In some literatures (e.g.[5][7][8]), Quite a few algorithms are mainly considered to meet the execution time request of the critical path tasks (activities), because the critical path is a sequence of activities from the beginning to the end of a workflow that has the longest average execution time. The task within the critical path is called the critical task. Similarly, we focus on the resource combination reliability within the critical path. To the critical path task in a DAG, the reliability of Grid resources should be the first consideration which is prior to the expenditure limit, et al, but not to the non-critical path task. There is a simple reason that even if the lower reliability of resources result in unsuccessful execution of a non-critical path task which is relatively short, the task will be rescheduled to prevent the potential performance loss and there is very little probability for failure to recur because of the multiplication of probabilities principle. But we have allowed for another case at the same time: if difference in execution time makespan between tasks on the critical path and tasks on the non-critical path is less than some relative threshold, the question have to be explored further. Under the above-mentioned condition, if we just take into account the reliability of Grid resources within the critical path, the result is nonsense, because importance of the Grid resource reliability within the non-critical path is not less than within the critical path, from another point of view, which is logically equivalent to the reliability of the two-units system in series, and any execution failure of task within the non-critical path will affect the subsequence task within the critical path. Through above analysis, we proposed a stochastic algorithm based on finite-state continuous-time Markov process to solve the problem.

3 Overview of Grid Workflow Management System

Workflow is concerned with the automation of procedures whereby files and data are passed between participants according to a defined set of rules to achieve an overall goal[9]. Fig.1. shows the architecture and functionalities supported by various components of the Grid workflow system based on the workflow reference model proposed by Workflow Management Coalition (WfMC)[10]. At the highest level, functions of Grid workflow management systems could be characterized into build time functions and run time functions. The build-time functions are concerned with defining, and modeling workflow tasks and their dependencies; while the run-time functions are concerned with managing workflow executions and interactions with Grid resources for processing workflow applications. Users interact with workflow modeling tools to generate a workflow specification, which is submitted to a run-time service called the workflow enactment service for execution. Major functions provided by the workflow enactment service are scheduling, fault management and data movement. The workflow enactment service may be built on the top of low level Grid middleware (e.g. Globus toolkit), through which the workflow management system invokes services provided by Grid resources[1]. To ensure workflow management system adopt appropriate scheduling strategy and allocate the corresponding resource to execute task of workflow specification, the information about resources may need to be retrieved through GIS(Grid information services). This information include identifying the list of authorized machines, cost of resource access, keeping track of resource status information, parameters, the historical data related to a particular user's application performance or experience which can also be used in predicting the share of available of resources for user while making scheduling decisions based on QoS constraints. As Grid resources are not dedicated to the owners of the workflow management systems, the Grid workflow management system also needs to identify dynamic information, such as resource accessibility, system workload, and network performance during execution time.

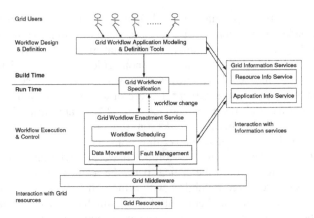

Fig. 1. Grid workflow management systems

4   Description of Algorithm

This section consists of two parts to illustrate our approach. 1st part is the algorithm modeling, which include definition and calculation of reliability of Grid resources within the critical path. 2nd part describes main steps of algorithm.

4.1   The Model

The application can be represented by a directed acyclic graph G(V,E,T) as shown in Fig. 2., where :V(G) ={V1,V2,V3,V4,V5} is the set of v nodes, and each node vi(vi∈ V) represents a task starting point or ending point. Not losing generality, v nodes can be classified as a disunited node (e.g. node v1 in Fig.2.) which have more than one sub-sequence node, simple node(e.g. node v2,v3,v5 in Fig.2.)which have not more than one previous node or subsequence node, united node(e.g. node v4 in Fig.2.) which have more than one previous node, and hybrid node which have both disunited node character and united node character(such node does not appear in our example to simply demonstrate our methodology).

E(G)={e1,e2,e3,e4,e5} is the set of workflow tasks, in which, e1=<V1,V2>, e2 =<V1,V3>, e3=<V2 ,V4>, e4=<V3,V4>, e5=<V4,V5>. The directed edge ei joins two nodes which denote task starting point and ending point respectively.

T(G)={t1,t2,t3,t4,t5}={7, 5, 8, 12, 4} is the set of computation costs in which each ti gives the estimated execution time of related task ei (e.g. t1=7 denotes that estimated execution time of ei is 7 time unit) .

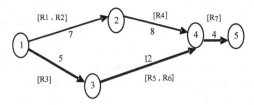

Fig. 2. Task and resource pool of DAG-Grid workflow application

In addition, we can reasonably assume in the Grid environment that the number of Grid resources is very likely more than one and that any of these resources can finish certain task ei within the same time limit. These resources are defined as a resource pool of ei which is denoted by Rei(e.g. Re1= [R1,R2]). Furthermore, the execution time of workflow is affected by 'normal state' and 'abnormal state' of Grid resources occurring in successive turns. As discussed in section2, we assume in this paper that both the 'normal state' and the 'abnormal state' of the Grid resource Ri are exponentially distributed with parameterλRi,μRi, and that resource owners specify their service price and charge users according to the amount of resources they consume. Service price per unit time required by Grid resource Ri is denoted by cRi. Thus, as showed in Fig.2, the number of resource pool is five, i.e. Re1=[R1(λR1,μR1, c R1), R2(λR2,μR2, cR2)]; Re2=[R3(λR3,μR3, cR3)]; Re3=[R4(λR4,μR4, c R4)] ; Re4=[R5(λR5,μR5, cR5), R6(λR6,μR6, cR6)]; Re5=[R7(λR7,μR7, cR7)]. By the way, according to section3, the above information related to resources can be obtained from GIS.

Definition 1. Critical united node is defined as a united node on the critical path in DAG, e.g. node v4 in Fig.2. (It is easy for us to write cp (critical path) out: cp=V1$\rightarrow$V3$\rightarrow$V4$\rightarrow$V5, which is marked out with thick lines)

Definition 2. Critical disunited node is defined as a disunited node on the critical path in DAG, e.g. node v1 in Fig.2.

Definition 3. Critical region denoted by [Vi,Vj] is defined as a region of task between critical united node and critical disunited node in DAG, e.g. [V1,V4] is a critical region in Fig.2.

Definition 4. Set of related tasks within critical region denoted by $E_{[vi,vj]}$ is defined as all of tasks within critical region, which have to satisfy following condition(relative threshold): $t_v > t_r$ (t_v denotes estimated execution time of any task on the non-critical path within [Vi,Vj]; t_r is equal to the difference of total estimated execution time of all tasks between on the critical path and on the non-critical path within [Vi,Vj]). Further, total estimated execution time of $E_{[vi,vj]}$ denoted by $T_{[vi,vj]}$ is equal to the total estimated execution time of all tasks within [Vi,Vj]. For example, owing to t2+t4-t1-t3=t_r=T4=2, t1>t_r, t3>t_r, hence, $E_{[v1,v4]}$= {e1,e2,e3, e4}, $T_{[v1,v4]}$= t2+t4=17. For the sake of simplicity, our example only presented the single non-critical path and the single critical region.

Definition 5. The reliability of single resource denoted by P_{Ri} is defined as absolute probability by which single resource Ri is in 'normal state'.

Definition 6. The reliability of parallel resource group denoted by $P_{<Ri-Ti,Rj-Ti>}$ is defined as following: Clearly, $T_{[vi,vj]}$ can be separated into several phases T1,T2,...Tn (we call them the parallel period of time), and if ei and ej (or a group of tasks)in $E_{[vi,vj]}$ are always being executed at Ri and Rj (or a group of resources) during the phase Ti respectively, we define Ri and Rj as parallel resource group in the phase Ti, denoted by <Ri-Ti, Rj-Ti>; define ei and ej(possibly partial or entire) as the parallel task segment on the phase Ti denoted by <ei-Ti, ej-Ti>; while probability that Ri and Rj are always being in 'normal state' during the phase Ti is called reliability of parallel resource group denoted by $P_{<Ri-Ti,Rj-Ti>}$. Fig.3. can help to comprehend the definition: T[v1,v4] can be separated into 4 phases, T1=5; T2=2; T3=8; T4=2; parallel task segment is, respectively, <e1-T1, e2-T1>, <e1-T2, e4-T2>, <e3-T3, e4-T3>, <0, e4-T4>; if we choose R2 in $R_{e1}=\{R1,R2\}$ as execution resource of e1 and R6 in $R_{e4}=\{R5,R6\}$ as execution resource of e4, parallel resource groups related to above 4 parallel resource group will be <R2-T1,R3-T1>, <R2-T2,R6-T2>, <R4-T3, R6-T3>, <0,R6-T4>, while related 4 reliability of parallel resource groups will be $P_{<R2-T1,R3-T1>}$, $P_{<R2-T2,R6-T2>}$, $P_{<R4-T3,R6-T3>}$, $P_{<0,R6-T4>}$, respectively.

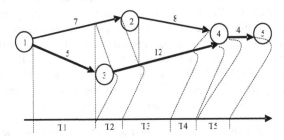

Fig. 3. Parallel execution time of DAG-Grid workflow application

Definition 7. The reliability of critical region denoted by $P_{[Vi,Vj]}$ is defined as a probability that all parallel resource groups are being in the 'normal state' during their respective parallel phase. By multiplication of probabilities principle, We have the following relation: $P_{[Vi,Vj]}=\prod_{T(i=1)}^{n} P_{<Ri-Ti,Rj-Ti>}$; Assume that, in [Vi,Vj], the number of resource combination scheme is m, then the scheme i reliability of critical region is denoted by $P_{[Vi,Vj]-i}$. For example, in Fig.3., there are 4 schemes, i.e. ①{R1,R3,R4,R5}, ②{R1,R3,R4,R6},③{R2,R3,R4, R5},④{R2,R3,R4,R6}, then the 4th scheme reliability of critical region is denoted by $P_{[V1,V4]-4}$, and $P_{[V1,V4]-4}=P_{<R2-T1,R3-T1>}*P_{<R2-T2,R6-T2>}*P_{<R4-T3, R6-T3>}*P_{<0,R6-T4>}$.

Definition 8. The reliability of resource combination on the critical path denoted by P_{cp} is defined as a probability which is equal to the certain scheme reliability of the critical region multiplied by the certain scheme reliability of the non-critical region.

Definition 9. Credit level of reliability of resource denoted by α is defined as a reliability of resource combination on a critical path required by user.

In the following, according to above definition, we derive a mathematic model to ascertain P_{Ri}, $P_{<Ri-Ti,Rj-Ti>}$, $P_{[Vi,Vj]}$ and P_{cp} by computation.

Learning from knowledge of stochastic process, we are able to conclude that the process, in which the 'normal state' and the 'abnormal state' of the Grid resource occur in successive turns and both the 'normal state' and the 'abnormal state' of the Grid resource Ri are exponentially distributed with parameter λ_{Ri}, μ_{Ri} , is a finite-state continuous-time homogeneity Markov process. If 'abnormal state' happened to any resource of <Ri-Ti,Rj-Ti> within Ti, the successor task of [Vi,Vj] would not start at appointed time, it is logically convenient to visualize $P_{<Ri-Ti,Rj-Ti>}$ as reliability of the two-units system in series, as analyzed in section 2. Thus, we can get the two-units system in series models with state space S={0,1,2}, where 0 implies that any resource of <Ri-Ti, Rj-Ti> is in the 'normal state'; 1 implies that the Ri resource of <Ri-Ti,Rj-Ti> is in the 'abnormal state'; 2 implies that the Rj resource of <Ri-Ti,Rj-Ti> is in the 'abnormal state'. Setting N_t, $N_t \in S$, implies the state of the two-units system in series on time t, and the infinitesimal behavior of N_t is governed by the following q-matrix (the infinitesimal generator matrix)[11].

$$Q = \begin{bmatrix} -(\lambda_{Ri} + \lambda_{Rj}) & \lambda_{Ri} & \lambda_{Rj} \\ \mu_{Ri} & -\mu_{Ri} & 0 \\ \mu_{Rj} & 0 & -\mu_{Rj} \end{bmatrix} \tag{1}$$

The q-matrix as in (1) is obviously communicating and is possessed of symmetric properties with symmetric distribution $\alpha = (\alpha_0, \alpha_1, \alpha_2)$, and satisfies $\alpha_0 \lambda_{Ri} = \alpha_1 \mu_{Ri}$, $\alpha_0 \lambda_{Rj} = \alpha_2 \mu_{Rj}$, namely, $\alpha_1 = \dfrac{\lambda_{Ri}}{\mu_{Ri}} \alpha_0$, $\alpha_2 = \dfrac{\lambda_{Rj}}{\mu_{Rj}} \alpha_0$. Setting $\pi = (\pi_0, \pi_1, \pi_2) = (1, \dfrac{\lambda_{Ri}}{\mu_{Ri}}, \dfrac{\lambda_{Rj}}{\mu_{Rj}})(1 + \dfrac{\lambda_{Ri}}{\mu_{Ri}} + \dfrac{\lambda_{Rj}}{\mu_{Rj}})^{-1}$, then it is the reversible distribution of N_t and the reliability of the two-units system in series

$$P_{<Ri-Ti,Rj-Ti>} = \pi_0 = (1 + \frac{\lambda_{Ri}}{\mu_{Ri}} + \frac{\lambda_{Rj}}{\mu_{Rj}})^{-1} \tag{2}$$

By virtue of (2), it can be deduced that reliability of Single resource

$$PRi = \mu Ri/(\lambda Ri + \mu Ri) \tag{3}$$

And it can also extend to reliability of the multi-units system in series[11]. For the simplicity, we just only describe our algorithm through example of the two-unit system in series.

As showed in Fig.3, if we select the 4th resource combination scheme, by virtue of (2), can get results as following:

$$P_{<R2-T1,R3-T1>} = (1 + \frac{\lambda_{R2}}{\mu_{R2}} + \frac{\lambda_{R3}}{\mu_{R3}})^{-1}; \quad P_{<R2-T2,R6-T2>} = (1 + \frac{\lambda_{R2}}{\mu_{R2}} + \frac{\lambda_{R6}}{\mu_{R6}})^{-1};$$

$$P_{<R4-T3,R6-T3>} = (1 + \frac{\lambda_{R4}}{\mu_{R4}} + \frac{\lambda_{R6}}{\mu_{R6}})^{-1}; \quad P_{<0,R6-T4>} = (1 + \frac{\lambda_{R6}}{\mu_{R6}})^{-1};$$

$$P_{[V1,V4]-4} = P_{<R2-T1,R3-T1>} * P_{<R2-T2,R6-T2>} * P_{<R4-T3,R6-T3>} * P_{<0,R6-T4>}$$

$$= (1 + \frac{\lambda_{R2}}{\mu_{R2}} + \frac{\lambda_{R3}}{\mu_{R3}})^{-1} * (1 + \frac{\lambda_{R2}}{\mu_{R2}} + \frac{\lambda_{R6}}{\mu_{R6}})^{-1} * (1 + \frac{\lambda_{R4}}{\mu_{R4}} + \frac{\lambda_{R6}}{\mu_{R6}})^{-1} * (1 + \frac{\lambda_{R6}}{\mu_{R6}})^{-1}.$$

Analogously, $P_{[V1,V4]-1}$, $P_{[V1,V4]-2}$, $P_{[V1,V4]-3}$ can be deduced. In addition, there is only one task e5 in non-critical region and $R_{e5} = [R7]$ means that there is only one available resource, $P_{R7} = (1 + \frac{\lambda_{R7}}{\mu_{R7}})^{-1}$, given by (3). Thus, $P_{cp} = P_{<V1,V4>-4} * P_{R7} = (1 + \frac{\lambda_{R2}}{\mu_{R2}} + \frac{\lambda_{R3}}{\mu_{R3}})^{-1} *$

$$(1+\frac{\lambda_{R2}}{\mu_{R2}}+\frac{\lambda_{R6}}{\mu_{R6}})^{-1}*(1+\frac{\lambda_{R4}}{\mu_{R4}}+\frac{\lambda_{R6}}{\mu_{R6}})^{-1}*(1+\frac{\lambda_{R6}}{\mu_{R6}})^{-1}*(1+\frac{\lambda_{R7}}{\mu_{R7}})^{-1}, \text{ namely it is one of reliability}$$

of resource combination on critical path in DAG(the 4th scheme on the critical region and R7 on the non-critical path). Other P_{cp} can be analogously calculated through the above-mention methodology.

4.2 Main Steps of Algorithm

Step 1. Find out the critical path e in DAG employing the traditional classic algorithm. (We omit them in this paper, to allow for being less related to the topic).

Step 2. Find out the entire critical region [Vi,Vj] on the critical path.

Step 3. While (each critical region)
       { If ($E_{[vi,vj]}$ exist)
               //Discriminance is based on the //relativethreshold condition
        { Compute each $P_{[Vi,Vj]-i}$;
               // ($i \in \{1,2,...m$=the number of //resource combination scheme
               //in [Vi,Vj]})
        E(G)=E(G)- E[vi,vj]
        }
       }

Step 4. If (E(G)≠NULL)
       {WHILE (each task ei)
          //ei $\in$ E(G)
    Compute each reliability of single resource Ri;
         //Ri $\in$ R_{ei} and ei $\in$ E(G)
       }

Step 5. Compute each P_{cp} and each cost of resource combination on the critical path in DAG.

Step 6. Choose a scheme of resource combination on the critical path in DAG, which should satisfy the following condition: $P_{cp} > \alpha$ and minimize the total expenditure.

5 Performance Evaluation

We have performed simulations of the example discussed in Fig.2 and Fig.3, in which QoS requirements is under the α=75% credit level of reliability of resource combination on the critical path in DAG and used related simulation parameters is illustrated as following Table 1.

According to our algorithm and above parameters, we get each value of P_{cp} (the reliability of resource combination on the critical path in DAG) and related total expenditure, as showed in Table 2.

Clearly, scheme ④ of resource combination on the critical path in DAG, i.e. {R2, R3, R4, R6, R7} should be the best preliminary workflow schedule, because it be able to satisfy following condition: Pcp>75% and with lower total expenditure, From Table 2.

Table 1. Simulation Parameters

Resource Ri	λ_{Ri}	μ_{Ri}	$P_{Ri}=\mu_{Ri}/ \; (\lambda_{Ri}+\mu_{Ri})$	c_{Ri}
R1	1/5	5	0. 9615	12
R2	1/6	4	0. 9600	9
R3	1/7	3	0. 9545	5
R4	1/8	2	0. 9412	4
R5	1/12	3	0. 8780	3
R6	1/11	6	0. 9851	13
R7	1/13	7	0. 9891	14

Table 2. Value of P_{cp} and Total expenditure

Scheme of resource	P_{cp}	Total expenditure
①{R1,R3,R4,R5,R7}	0.5638	233
②{R1,R3,R4,R6,R7}	0.7879	353
③{R2,R3,R4,R5,R7}	0.5622	212
④{R2,R3,R4,R6,R7}	0.7854	332

We present the most important part of our simulation and analysis below. Fig.4. illustrates a case of two states of all resources, in which, higher intermittent line attaching to Ri denotes 'abnormal state', while lower intermittent line attaching to Ri denotes the 'normal state'. To scheme ④, in T3, the 'abnormal state' happen to R2, but R2 have already finished e1 task in the first two phase T1 and T2 ; it is R4 and R6 being in the 'normal state' that is required to carry out task e3 and e4, according to Fig.3., R6 keeps on executing e4 and its state keeps on being 'normal state' throughout T4; subsequently, the 'abnormal state' happen to R6 in T5, but R6 have already finished workflow task in T4 and these 'abnormal state' do not affect the entire workflow. Therefore, in all the phase T1-T5, corresponding resources always are being the 'normal state' during the time of executing respective task. Based on these observations, workflow has been carried out successfully. To scheme ③, parallel resource group in the phase T3 is <R4-T3,R5-T3>. Although R4 can complete task e3, the 'abnormal state' happened to R5 in T3, which will make R7 to fail to start e5 on time eventually. Hence, if choose scheme ③, it would not meet the time limit in experiments this time. We have conducted a large number of above experiments under the same conditions, successful workflow execution rate of each scheme is as in Fig.5.

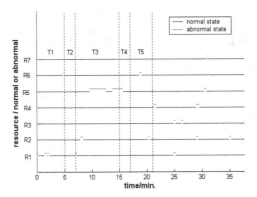

Fig. 4. Two State Alternation of all resource

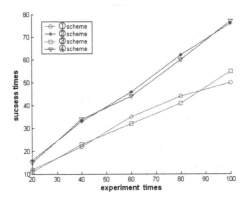

Fig. 5. Successful execution rate of each scheme

Above simulation experiments demonstrate the efficacy of workflow scheduling algorithm. In the Grid computing environment, when there are a few resources which can finish a certain task within the same time limit and whose reliability are different, our algorithm is able to efficiently choose more reliable Grid resource to carry out time-restricted workflow with the lower total expenditure.

6   Conclusion

In this paper, we present an approximation method for computing the reliability of resource combination. This method is constructed based on stochastic processes, finite-state continuous-time Markov process. Simulation experiments show that our approach produces both good execution performance and scheduling results. Assuming that both the 'normal state' and the 'abnormal state' of the Grid resource are exponentially distributed is approximate approach. In our future work, we are going to substitute more appropriate probability density functions for the exponential distribution function to improve Grid workflow scheduling performance.

Acknowledgements

This research is supported by National Natural Science Foundation of China under Grant No. 60563002 and Scientific Research Program of the Higher Education Institution of XinJiang under Grant No. XJEDU2004I03.

References

1. Jia, Y., Rajkumar, B.: A Taxonomy of Workflow Management Systems for Grid Computing. J. Grid Computing 3(3-4), 171–200 (2005)
2. Ullman, J.D.: NP-complete Scheduling Problems. J. Computer and System Sciences 1(10), 384–393 (1975)
3. Jin, H.S., Myoung, H.K.: Improving the performance of time-constrained workflow processing. J. System and Software 58(3), 211–219 (2001)
4. Eunjoung, B., Sungjin, C., Maengsoon, B., et al.: MJSA Markov job scheduler based on availability in desktop grid. Future Generation Computer Systems 23(4), 616–622 (2007)
5. Jia, Y., Rajkumar, B., Chen, K.T.: QoS-based Scheduling of workflow Applications on Service Grids. In: 1st IEEE International Conference one-Science and Grid Computing. IEEE Computer Science Press, Melbourne (2005)
6. Xianhe, S., Lingou, G., Edward, F.W.: Performance modeling and prediction of non-dedicated network computing. IEEE Trans. Comput. 51(9), 1041–1055 (2002)
7. Yu, J., Buyya, R., Tham, C.K.: Cost-based Scheduling of Scientific Workflow Applications on Utility Grids. J. System and Software 233, 236–242 (2005)
8. Hagras, T., Janec, J.: A high performance and lower complexity algorithm for compile-time task scheduling in heterogeneous systems. Parallel Computing 31, 653–670 (2005)
9. Hollinsworth, D.: The Workflow Reference Model. Technical report, Workflow Management Coalition, TC00-1003 (1994)
10. W3C. XML Pipeline Definition Language Version 1.0, http://www.w3.org/TR/2002/NOTE-xml-pipeline-20020228
11. Guang-lu, G.: Applied Stochastic process tutorial, pp. 149–155. Tsinghua University publishing company, Beijing (2004)

A SyncML Middleware-Based Solution for Pervasive Relational Data Synchronization

Haitao Yang[1,2,3], Peng Yang[4], Pingjing Lu[4], and Zhenghua Wang[4]

[1] Guangdong Construction Information Center, Guangzhou 510500, China
yhtyxc@hotmail.com
[2] Institute of Computing Technology,
[3] Graduate University, Chinese Academy of Sciences, Beijing 100080, China
[4] School of Computer Science, National University of Defense Technology,
Changsha 410073, China

Abstract. In ubiquitous data applications, local data replicas are often essential for mobile users to get more reliable and faster access. Referring to the open source-code resource Sync4j for a data synchronization solution of lower price, we design and implement an application-independent SyncML-complied middleware, named GSMS, to synchronize data between heterogeneous Relational Database Management Systems (RDBMSs), which is featured with no interference in the data relation schemas and program logics of existent applications. The performance stability of GSMS is verified through synchronization experiments on different combinations of prevalent RDBMS.

Keywords: Data synchronization, middleware, distributed heterogeneous RDBMS, SyncML, Pervasive computing.

1 Introduction

With the rapid proliferation of pervasive computing, related academic and industrial societies have spent a great deal of effort in infrastructural solutions for data synchronization across distributed diverse devices or autonomous systems. However, all the workable solutions currently still fall short of what we regard as the technology ideal, the Date's famous 12 rules for DDBSs (Distributed Database Systems), particularly, the sixth rule: "data replication transparency" [3]. In practice, to efficiently and effectively fulfill such rules remains one of the most subtle issues in elaborating a generic data synchronization product. As industrial protocols and products are paving the way for the ubiquitous data availability, generic heterogeneous data synchronization solutions are most wanted on a product level.

1.1 Project Background and Related Work

The term *synchronization* (in short *sync* as verb and noun), refers to the process of propagating updates across distributed replicas of data objects, which is often mixed with the "replication" that does not directly refer to timeliness or schedule while *sync* does. Among work about data replication in traditional applications [5, 13] and data

J. Cao et al. (Eds.): NPC 2008, LNCS 5245, pp. 308–319, 2008.

sync in mobile applications [4], we notice several typical techniques that help or enlighten us greatly in shaping a generic, flexible and feasible *sync* solution.

First of all, we refer to the academic literature. As to the consistency aspect, J. Gray at el [6] warned that a synchronous handling mode is unrealistic due to its low success rate, R. Gallersdörfer and M. Nicola [5] suggested relaxing consistency for better performance, and H. Yu and A. Vahdat [16] argued that a service's availability is worthy of its replicas' consistency degradation for most Internet scenarios. On the connectivity aspect, Nikaein and Bonnet [8] and Tan at el [14] pointed out that a tree topology has the privilege of minimum cost of propagation. With respect to sync middleware schema, the middleware implementation frame reported by J.E. Armendáriz-Iñigo et al [2] represents a classical design, in which the middleware as an intermediate layer is plugged in between the application and underlying DBMS, and entailed to intercept all calls to the surrogated DBMS. However, such a framework is not desirable for users and DBMS vendors due to its fatal defects: it imposes a bottle-neck on the hosting DBMS and its implementation is tightly bounded to the extension mechanism of the DBMS.

Then, we turn to the industrial side. Although the main bodies (over 650 leading companies) of the communication industries have jointly promoted a platform-independent data sync standard, the SyncML[1] (Synchronization Markup Language) as a generic framework of information exchange for all devices and applications over any network [12], however, the data sync requirements from commercial and industrial societies are still far from satisfaction [7]. Moreover, to the interest of most medium and small enterprises, it is necessitated to seek data sync solutions featured with low price, easy deployment, free tailoring, and independent from specific vendors of DBMSs.

Finally, we should mention a well-known prototype of SyncML-based data sync middleware, the *sync4j* system [4], which is an open source Java implementation of SyncML. Although *sync4j* has many merits over contemporary products, its applicability is degraded by several non-trivial flaws which include altering data tables to be synced, lacking application verifications, and incapability to sync heterogeneous RDBMSs. Therefore, we ought to develop an effective middleware system free of the above mentioned weakness, and preferably with reference to open source-code resources.

1.2 Our Major Approach

We set forth first the main design principles: 1) using simple and flexible topology connections which have the advantages of fast failure detection, clear exchange targets, light network traffic, and easily-organized access control; 2) interfering least in client applications; 3) easy to add or delete nodes from sync network; 4) applicable for limited resource client devices.

Abiding the above principles we design and implement a SyncML-complied middleware data sync system, which can be extended to any RDBMS by developing the corresponding add-on modules. We assume a middleware framework distinct from

---

[1] Although SyncML is currently referred to as OMA DS and DM (Open Mobile Alliance Data Synchronization and Device Management) we still use the earlier name for the conciseness.

the classical one: it is no longer the agent or entrance of the hosting DBMS, but is purely an add-on just working in parallel with the DBMS. Our sync middleware consists of two parts: 1) the inner DBMS part which is realized with triggers and store procedures, and 2) the outside DBMS part which is coded as Java-programmed software components. We develop two types of sync middleware: server and client. The client is light-weighted, while the server is endowed with much complex capability. The sync add-ons are all based on a RDBMS that supports the standard SQL and provides trigger mechanisms for timely capturing basic data manipulation events.

In general, a sync process mainly has four tasks: data-change capture, change propagation, conflict detection, and conflict reconciliation (ConR). For the former three, often a generic syntax-based model could handle well, whereas it is not feasible to implement a good ConR without sound semantic knowledge of data change. At this point, what we can do best is to lower the chance of conflict occurrence. In our approach, the job of change capture is weighted over others, because if a change is missed, it can not be remedied until the next change occurs at the same object.

2 Sync Model

The sync model can be elucidated by related basic notions, terms, and patterns:

Data Node refers to a device where the data objects of concern reside, which normally has the capability and responsibility for maintaining data locally.

Sync-client, in short *client,* refers to the SyncML protocol implementing role that issues "request" messages [9].

Sync-server, in short *server*, refers to the SyncML protocol implementing role that receives and handles "request" messages, and responds with "response" messages [9].

Sync-node refers to a software instance that acts as a sync-client or sync-server.

In data sync (DS) applications, a data node must be assigned to and thereby synced through a sync-node, and normally they should be located geographically close to each other, e.g. at least in the same LAN. By default, we just use a single word *node* to refer to the tuple of a data node and its sync-node.

Replica refers to homogenous instances of the same data entity, which could be diverse temporarily, but should eventually become identical in content. In relational data models, different replicas of the same data entity must have their attributes one-to-one matched with each other regardless of whether they might be contained in different relations at different nodes.

A basic *sync action* reflects that a pair of nodes is having a sync session with each other. In a sync action, one node must be designated as the *server* according to the SyncML protocol.

Here, we use the term *sync-wave* to refer to a series of adjacent subsequent *sync* actions which just resemble the propagation of a specific version of a replica. The meet of two *sync-waves* will result in a new merged sync-wave which only contains the agreed-on content but unsolved conflicts. The path a *sync-wave* travels is named the *trace* of a *sync-wave*.

To simplify the network management, we assign each node a level, and designate that a sync node is limited to syncing upwards only with one node on the higher lever, thus a tree topology is formed. As each parent node and its children alone in fact form a star topology, in which the center node plays a role of the server while the others act as clients, we call such a topology the *hierarchy-star* to stress the asymmetry and locality. The *Hierarchy-Star* (**HS**) concept reflects that 1) the asymmetry of nodes' capabilities in a sync relation in general; 2) except within the bone-network, the available communication paths for the end user are actually limited hierarchically; and 3) in Internet any loop path is forbidden.

Content transfer method of data-change propagation: the latest content of a replicated object is delivered, also called the *state* transfer mode [13], which is apt for propagating the data changes created by the *Update* and *Insert* manipulations.

Operation transfer method of change propagation: the data manipulation commands are transferred, which is used for transferring the data changes of *delete* operations, to decrease the transfer amount (especially for large records).

Change_log: to record the captured changes of monitored data sets in a separate specific table. This approach has the merit of not altering the data schema of existent applications. And whenever a record of change has been successfully transferred to the sync server node, it can be deleted from the change_log at the client end safely in our **HS** propagation topology. Of course, the merit of a separate change_log is at the cost of a certain redundant store of the changed data record.

Snapshot: given that the local consistency of data sets is guaranteed at each node, the global intermediate state of sync can be reviewed as a series of *snapshots* about each node's state and the *progressive* sync-wave.

Refining change-capture unit: in a relational database, the minimal change units can not be smaller than a single field. Within the trigger mechanism, most of the prevalent DBMSs, e.g., MySQL 5.1(higher), Oracle 8 (higher), provide field determiners such as *New* or *Old* to refer to the values of a target field before or after the *Update* operation respectively. With these delimiters we can refine the unit of change-capture down to the field level, given that the tables do not contain any field of abnormal data type, e.g., LOB in Oracle. In our design, a GUI is served for a sync DBA (database administrator) to select a change capture unit from a field or record.

Configuration to include sync objects: the sync DBA at each node shall be requested to tell the GSMS (generic sync middleware system) which tables of which databases are to be included in or removed from the sync schedule. The table structure is then rendered to the GSMS at this stage, which includes the primary key declaration, as well as the name and data type of fields to be synced.

Synchronization frequency: in general, the quicker the propagation, the lower the degree of replica inconsistency and the rate of conflict, but the higher the complexity and overhead, especially when the application is *write intensive* [13].

Sync Baseline: in the *incremental* mode, only the data units that are known to have changed after the last sync need to be synced, whereas in the *total* mode all data should be replicated.

Mapping table: to cope with heterogeneous fragmentation of sync data objects, at server nodes we have to configure a mapping between the synced fields of each local replica and the corresponding fields of the counterpart.

Table 1. Change_log Schema

Field	description	node
Table_name	The local name of sync table	All
SeqN_change	The sequence number of a table's changes	All
Key_field	The name of a field of the primary key	All
StrValue_kf	The string value of the data field indicated by key_field	All
Change_type	"U, D, N"--Update, Delete, iNsert or New operations	All
Chg_lst_fields	Indicate which fields changed	All
Timestamp	Arrival time of this sync-wave or the time of local change	All
URI_sync	URI of the sync neighbor	Non-leaf
URI _ Origin	URI of this sync-wave's creator	Non-leaf
Birth_time	Birth time of this sync-wave	Non-leaf
Sem	Semaphore for concurrent processes	All

3 Change_log's Design

The schema of the change_log that records local replica changes is shown in Table 1. *SeqN_change* stands for the sequence number of data changes, which are numbered separately for different sync data tables – each time a record is changed the value of the corresponding *SeqN_change* will be increased by one. *change_type* = "U|D|N" stands for "Update|Delete|iNsert" data manipulation operations (DMLs) respectively. Normally, each DML operation creates a set of change records in the change_log, but a Update DMLs that changes the primary key's value will create two sets of change_log records, of which one is responding to a set of change_log records of the Delete(old.*Key*) operation, and the other is equivalent to the Insert (new.*Key*)'s. *chg_lst_fields* note down the list of fields whose values have been changed since the last sync, which is expressed as a bit string with one bit for one field sequentially (a *Null* value indicates all fields). *SeqN_change* will link all fields' values of a primary key instance to a specific data change, which is useful in refining the sync control granularity. *Timestamp* indicates the time that a local data change takes effect. *URI_origin* identifies the creator of the current version of the data record, which is different from *URI_sync* that indicates the neighbor node that passes the current version directly to this node. Fields *URI_origin* and *Birth_time* together mark uniquely the origin of the current change, which is useful for reconciling the conflicts of data versions.

Now, we elucidate how to record a data change in the change_log, and how to form a change propagation message from a set of change_log records (of the same *SeqN_change*). Given that a sync data table has the primary key with an attribute set $\{f_i | 1 \leq i \leq k\}$. Normally DBMSs limit attributes of a primary key must be of a comparable type, which excludes any abnormal types (e.g. Oracle's Lob data type, etc.), i.e. any attribute's value of a primary key can be translated into a string type, and will be stored in the *StrValue_kf* field when the data record has a change – meanwhile the attribute name is stored in *Key_field*. Each change_log record is uniquely identified by the *table_name*, *SeqN_change*, and *Key_field*'s values. Each tuple $(f_i, \text{Str}(f_i))\{1 \leq i \leq k\}$ has a corresponding record in the change_log, where $\text{Str}(f)$ is a function that translate the value of f into a string expression. Therefore, a change of a data record with a primary key of k attributes is separately recorded in k records of the change_log under the same value of *SeqN_change*. When the tuple $\{\text{Str}(f_i) | 1 \leq i \leq k\}$ of the primary key is used to locate the corresponding record in the data table (remote or local), a mapping process is required to revert $Str(f_i)$ $\{1 \leq i \leq k\}$ to the data type of the target DBMS, which is handled by the outer part of a sync middleware. The triggers are responsible for mapping the primary key's value into the change_log.

For setting up the time baseline of sync, it is sufficient to note down the timestamp of last sync at only one node of the synced pair.

In our sync model, a sync action is centred at the local server, which along with the **HS** topology makes the GSMS work well for most cases without precise clock sync among server nodes. This is quite significant, since precise clock syncs may increase the time complexity and space overheads greatly.

Be adaptive to the constrained resource of client-only devices (e.g. PDAs, cell phones), the change_log's records at leaf nodes will be purged after each sync action, whereas those at non-leaf nodes are kept until all involved syncs being fulfilled. To avoid the trouble of tackling new log records created during a sync action, the sync process should note down its start moment, and only synchronize data with a change timestamp before that moment.

4 Sync Session

Regarding the asymmetry of the SyncML protocol, our GSMS provides four sync patterns for choices, named "two-way", "slow", "one-way", and "refresh". The former two are bidirectional, whereas the others are unilateral. The "two-way" and "one-way" patterns correspond to the *incremental* mode while the others belong to the *total* mode. The "slow" pattern exchanges the whole content of replicas between a sync pair, whereas the "refresh" one just overwrites the client's replica with the server's. In GSMS the sync pattern is configurable.

The *one-way* and *refresh* patterns are intended for special scenarios of applications: e.g., where the authority of one node prevails clearly over the other, or when the client belongs to a receiver-only device or is limited to read-access of replicas at the server node, or the case of data restoration.

Normally, bidirectional sync in *total* mode is used to initialize the sync system, where the DBA should designate a fiducial node as the initial data source. Often, people regard the *total* mode of data sync as a kind of maintenance mode, and software in this mode should occupy the maintained objects exclusively. Besides, a sound GSMS should be able to resume an interrupted sync at the save point nearest to the abort point especially for the total mode. This can be achieved if the sync session is processed in a lock-step mode.

Transferring enormous data in a single sync session should be avoided, since deluging data will likely exceed the capability of the middleware-hosting web server, which may result in a serious performance decline or even a crash. These cases often occur during syncing a very large data table in total mode, or a single huge record in any mode, or when a "cache-all and write-once" strategy is used (a routine measure assumed in SyncML documents [10]). Thus, we should divide such a large replication into several sessions so that each is responsible just for a fragment of the data.

In our solution, a large data record transfer only occurs when syncing *Update* or *Insert* operations. An *Update* operation can be substituted by a series of *Update* operations that each exerts on only one field, whereas an *Insert* operation is equivalent to an *Insert* operation with the primary key fields, plus an *Update* operation on the remaining fields, given that the recipient can handle the fields of unknown value, e.g., assign a *Null* value if possible, or a default value temporarily. Since a SyncML message – the smallest self-contained unit conveyed in a SyncML sync action [9, 10, 11] – at least should contain a SyncML operation that corresponds to a DML operation, on the sync protocol level the transfer unit can not be smaller than the set of the primary-key fields plus the largest field involved in an *Update* operation. Further division of a message is up to lower level protocols such as HTTP or WAP, where a message can be separated into smaller units of transmission.

To reduce redundant content transfers, we need to refine the logging granularity of data changes, e.g., data changes are logged down to the field level. However, such a refining measure has a prerequisite – for any specific data record, its different change events shall not reuse any its previous change_log record, i.e., each change event shall be noted down in a distinct set of change_log records, otherwise, it might encounter some problems.

5 Handling Conflict

As the basis of trade-offs, we set up several principles for sync engineering, named **SE** codes:

1. Avoiding any unnoticed overlay among conflict data changes except as the result of explicit regulations.
2. The data version that is more likely preferential on semantics should dominate others.
3. Facilities for manual reconciliation of conflicts.
4. Detected change conflicts should not automatically disappear except through a ConR procedure.
5. A detectable conflict is better than a loss of data changes.
6. Manual ConRs should be separate from the sync session.

SE line 2 links to the auto reconciliation of conflicts (**AuRC**); however, its implementation depends on use-cases. To be practical, we suggest several basic rules:

1) Jurisdiction priority.
2) Diligent clients dominate lazy ones.
3) Server wins.
4) Client wins.
5) Last-writer wins, also known as the Thomas's write rule [13].

AuRC rule 1 can be applied when a jurisdiction table is available. A jurisdiction table indicates the jurisdiction of a data object belongs to which nodes -- the *principal*, and such nodes (if existing) shall always dominate their data objects. AuRC rule 2 suggests the node that syncs with the server more frequently should win. The interval of the last two syncs of a client can be used to indicate the sync frequency, which we refer to as "the shorter interval wins". Other rules are self-explanatory.

The key aim of using AuRC is to avoid interfering in the applications on high levels, smooth and speed up the conflict reconciliation, which are essential for a data sync infrastructure. However, no AuRCs can get rid of rationality exceptions, e.g. even for the most believable rule 1, a bad AuRC scenario can occurs when the principal's update is incorrect while others' are right. The application of AuRC rules is situation-dependent, in other words, you need to select and prioritize them basing what you stress. Normally, we insist on using AuRC rule 1 first, and recommend other by the list order -- but it is still up to whether the responsibility or the data freshness is stressed, for the former you can select AuRC rule 3 or 4, for the later you might use AuRC rule 2 or 5.

It should be cautious to apply those AuRC rules except rule 1 since their effects are not guaranteed. For instance, the latest writer that seldom syncs with its server probably updates the data replica based on a stale version of the data -- this update does not reflect the due status of corresponding entity objects. In such cases, we shall apply the "the shorter interval wins" instead. Whereas in some cases, AuRC rule 3 may lead to an "early-writer wins" phenomenon since the earlier update from a client has become the server's version.

Before applying the rule "server wins" we had better know where the server version of a data object originates from: the server itself, or a client at a previous sync. In many cases the "server wins" rule equals the "the shorter interval wins" rule, whereas in some other cases, these two rules may have different results.

For a generic AuRC solution, the best we can do is to construct a framework with AuRC options that can simplify the AuRC process. It is clear that no versatile AuRC rules ever exists, manually handling of conflicts is often the last resort, therefore we furnish GSMS with basic manually-handling facilities.

6 Sync Networking

Sync can be described as a distributed progressive version-merging transaction (DPVT). For DPVTs a snapshot showing many intermediate replica versions on the way implies nothing than higher frequencies of data changes and relative lags of change propagation. In this section, we discuss the DPVT issue from the view of networking. To this end, a few concepts are introduced:

- *Unilateral policy of ConR*:
A node autonomously determines the local result of ConR.
- *Peer reconciliation of conflict*: either node in a sync pair assumes a unilateral policy of ConR.
- *Sync graph* consists of
  1) Nodes that host replicas.
  2) Directed edges, each connecting a pair of nodes, and indicating only a unilateral propagation of data changes along the directed edge.
  3) Undirected edges, each indicating a bidirectional propagation of data changes between the two nodes it connects.
  4) Arrows – degenerate directed edges, of which the tail node is deleted, indicating the node pointed to is a source of data changes.

- A sync graph is called **acyclic** if it contains no simple loop of length three or more (an undirected edge is equivalent to two directed edges).
- **Oblivious sync action**: when a sync-wave is passed through an edge of a sync graph, the recipient gets its replica refreshed with the version the sync-wave carries, and discards the sync-wave's origin information. Although a version identity can be attached to identify an individual sync-wave, it is hard to devise a proper version identity that is easily maintained and capable of sufficient description, since potentially any distributed change sources can create their new versions independently [1]. The edge undergoing an oblivious action is called *oblivious edge*.

With the above definitions, we can get:

Lemma 1. Conflicts can only occur at nodes with in-degree greater than 1.

Theorem 1. If a sync graph contains a directed cycle of length three or more, and the cycle includes at least an oblivious edge, then any sync process may suffer retroversion, even worse the progressive consistency may become impossible.

Corollary 1. To ensure the progressive consistency, sync-wave traces should be acyclic.

Apparently, only the tree *sync* topology can tolerate oblivious edges -- our **HS** *sync* topology has this advantage, which can be planned as a spanning tree of the network graph [15].

7 Mobile Access

A mobile client should remember the last sync server when it syncs with a new one somewhere else. If the client's update on the previous server $s(p)$ has not been propagated to the current server $s(c)$, the client may trigger a new sync-wave from $s(p)$ to $s(c)$, which is referred to as MiTS (Motion ignited Third-Sync). A MiTS may be guided through a frond of a **HS** tree, which is referred to as a frond-MiTS. A frond-MiTS may break the topology of **HS** temporarily. Seemingly, when a MiTS has a trace of length greater than 1 (measured by the length of the corresponding shortest path within the **HS** tree), named *indirect* MiTS, there is an option that deletes the edge that connects node $s(p)$ to its parent node, and replaces it with the frond connecting $s(p)$ to $s(c)$, such that the sync graph is still of **HS** type. But this approach may involve a lot of complex work, including the topology change's notice to every node that should be informed and the initialization task for this new joined sync relation. Though the initialization can be much easier if we set the sync baseline at the time a sync pair first connects each other, i.e., subsequent incremental syncs will not consider those changes that occur before the baseline, which, however, implies the need to forget the previous diversity including the recent changes uploaded by the client to its former server.

To this point, we shall recall the design of server nodes, in which all received sync-waves with their origin information are recorded in the change_log with an arrival timestamp, and the last sync time is also kept for each synced node. This enables two servers to exchange changes only that are from specific sources and satisfy a given time condition. For an *indirect* MiTS, such processing is applicable if no changes from other sources have ever overridden the data that the mobile client just uploaded – this is normally true in a well-designed mobile user information application (subject to Date's 5th rule: data fragmentation transparency), where each client has its proprietary data fragmentation for sync. In general, for an indirect MiTS, both the $s(p)$ and $s(c)$ nodes must be aware of the directions of the path connecting them in the **HS** tree, which needs very complicated algorithms [15].

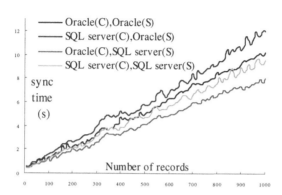

Fig. 1. Sync time of different DBMS combinations

8 Experiments

To evaluate GSMS's performance, we devised a test scheme as follows: first, compare the sync time between homogeneous and heterogeneous distributed DBMSs; second, test the stability of GSMS's sync performance on varied data record lengths; third, compare GSMS's performance and Sync4j's for homogenous DBMSs considering Sync4j can not support heterogeneous DBMS syncs, and that commercial products for heterogeneous DBMS sync are very expensive and their resource requirements are very high – we believe it is unfair to compare them with GSMS, a low-price-oriented sync product. To see whether sync performance is asymmetric, we used the same OS and hardware for both server and client nodes: Windows XP; Pentium 4 (2.66 GHz) CPU, 1G Memory. We tested GSMS for syncs of different combinations of Oracle 9i and SQL server 2000, Sybase ASE 15. Representative parts of the test results are presented in Fig.1, Fig.2, and Fig.3, where, symbol (C) or (S) indicates a DBMS configured as a sync client or server respectively.

The results of experiments show that, 1) the sync time is obviously linear to the amount of data being synced, which is similar for different record lengths; 2) the sync speed of heterogeneous DBMS is comparative to that of homogeneous DBMS; 3) there is no significant asymmetry for GSMS's sync time; 4) GSMS has better sync performance and stability than Sync4j.

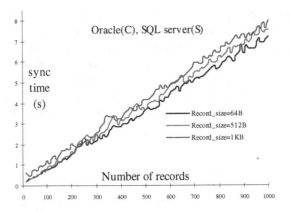

Fig. 2. Sync time of different record lengths

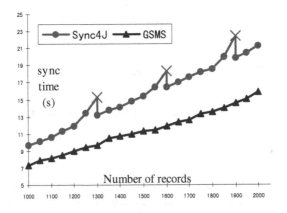

Fig. 3. Sync comparison of GSMS and Sync4j

9 Conclusion

Better generality, flexibility and interoperability, as well as stable performance and lower cost of time or space are on top of the list of GSMS's goals. To these ends, we developed GSMS by means of the SyncML protocol, platform independent languages (SQL, XML and Java), a **HS** sync topology, granularity controlling on sync objects, logging techniques, hybrid scheme of content and operation transfers, and exception handling, etc. Now GSMS is capable to sync prevalent DBMS products, such as Oracle, SQL server, and Sybase -- the list can be easily extended in future. The key innovation here is the GSMS middleware's working frame which is parallel to the hosting DBMS. Subject to SyncML and based on a relaxed consistency, our solution is oriented for data syncs between mobile units as well as static nodes, and is particularly suitable for the applications where the data references to mobile entities are shared and updated anytime and anywhere when the data availability is more crucial than their version consistency.

Acknowledgement. This work is supported in part by the Science and Technology Program of Guangzhou Municipal Government Grant No. 2006Z3-D3031.

References

1. Almeida, P.S., Baquero, C., Fonte, V.: Version stamps – decentralized version vectors. In: 22nd Int. Conf. on Dist. Comp. Sys. (ICDCS), Vienna, Austria, pp. 544–551 (2002)
2. Armendáriz-Iñigo, J.E., Decker, H., González De Mendívil, J.R., Muñoz-Escoí, F.D.: Middleware-Based Data Replication: Some History and Future Trends. In: 2nd Int. Workshop on High Availability of Distributed Systems, Krakow, Poland, 4–8 September, pp. 390–394. IEEE-Computer Science Press, Los Alamitos (2006)
3. Date, C.J.: An Introduction to Database Systems, 7th edn. Addison-Wesley, MA (2000)
4. FUNAMBOL mobile open source project (Sync4j),
   `http://www.funambol.com/opensource/`
5. Gallersdörfer, R., Nicola, M.: Improving performance in replicated database systems through relaxed coherency. In: Proc. of the 21st VLDB conference, pp. 445–456 (1995)
6. Gray, J., Helland, P., O'neil, P., Shasha, D.: The dangers of replication and a solution. ACM SIGMOD Record 25(2), 173–182 (1996)
7. Bowling, T., Licul, E.D., Hammond, V.: Global Data Synchronization — Building a flexible approach. IBM Business Consulting Services (2007), `ftp://ftp.software.ibm.com/software/integration/wpc/library/ge-5103990.pdf`
8. Nikaein, N., Bonnet, C.: Topology management for improving routing and network performances in mobile ad hoc networks. Mob. Netw. Appl. 9(6), 583–594 (2004)
9. OMA: SyncML Representation Protocol (Candidate Version 1.2). Open Mobile Alliance (June 01, 2004)
10. OMA: DS Protocol (Approved Version 1.2). Open Mobile Alliance (July 10, 2006)
11. OMA: SyncML Representation Protocol–Data Synchronization Usage (Approved Version 1.2). Open Mobile Alliance (July 10, 2006)
12. OASIS: The SyncML Initiative. Technology reports hosted by OASIS (April 29, 2003),
    `http://xml.coverpages.org/syncML.html`
13. Saito, Y., Shapiro, M.: Optimistic replication. ACM Computing Surveys 37(1), 42–81 (2005)
14. Tan, G.Z., Han, N.N., Liu, Y., Li, J.L., Wang, H.: Wireless Network Dynamic Topology Routing Protocol Based on Aggregation Tree Model. In: Int. Conf. on Netw., Int. Conf. on Systems and Int. Conf. on Mobile Comm. and Learning Tech (ICNICONSMCL 2006), pp. 128–132 (2006)
15. Gerard, T.: Introduction to Distributed Algorithms, 2nd edn., pp. 560–561. Cambridge University Press, Cambridge (2000)
16. Yu, H., And Vahdat, A.: The costs and limits of availability for replicated services. ACM Transactions on Computer Systems 24(1), 70–113 (2006)

An Efficient Authentication and Key Agreement Protocol in RFID System

Eun-Jun Yoon[1] and Kee-Young Yoo[2,*]

[1] School of Electrical Engineering and Computer Science,
Kyungpook National University,
1370 Sankyuk-Dong, Buk-Gu, Daegu 702-701, South Korea
ejyoon@tpic.ac.kr
[2] Department of Computer Engineering, Kyungpook National University,
1370 Sankyuk-Dong, Buk-Gu, Daegu 702-701, South Korea
Tel.: +82-53-950-5553; Fax: +82-53-957-4846
yook@knu.ac.kr

Abstract. Due to the very limited computing resource, storing space and electric power supply of tag, it is a great challenge for us to design a practical RFID protocol which is security, efficient and can be used in the low-cost tag. In 2007, He et al. proposed an authentication and key agreement protocol which is used in the process of communication between the low-cost tag and reader. They also proved the security of the protocol through the extended strand space model. This paper presents a more efficient authentication and key agreement protocol for RFID system than He et al.'s protocol. Compare with He et al.'s protocol, the proposed protocol reduces the computational costs as well as protocol communication rounds to agree a shared session key between the reader and the tag.

Keywords: Security protocol, RFID system, Authentication, Key agreement, Session key.

1 Introduction

Recently, Radio Frequency Identification (RFID) [1,2,3,4,5,6,7,8,9,10,11,12] has become a new spotlight technology for supporting ubiquitous computing environments. In the current open network environment, RFID identifies an object by using the radio frequency technology which is a kind of non-contact automatic identification technique. It can automatically read the information from a great deal of tags instantly. Therefore, RFID technology has been widely used by manufacturing management, custody control, management of humans and farm animals, arrangement of books at some libraries, etc.

The important key problem of the current RFID systems is the information security. It means that the current RFID systems have several security problems and challenges. In the normal RFID systems, the communication channel

---

* Corresponding author.

J. Cao et al. (Eds.): NPC 2008, LNCS 5245, pp. 320–326, 2008.

between the reader and the backend database is considered to be secure. However, because the communication channel between the RFID tag and the reader is not secure channel, it can be easily attacked by passive or active attackers. Therefore, secure RFID systems must be able to resist any kind of attack, such as wiretap, active attack, tracking etc., and also solve the three basic security problems including secrecy, identification and untraceability [1,2,3,4,12].

In general, RFID tags have very limited computing ability, storing space and electric power supply. Due to these characteristics and a lot of restrictions, it is very difficult to design of the security mechanism of the RFID system. Currently, the most common design method is to use secure one-way hash function, bit-wise exclusive-or (XOR) operation, PRNG (pseudo-random number generator) etc. Up to now, most RFID authentication protocols are based on these cryptographic operations. Therefore, in the RFID system, it is an important challenge to design an efficient and secure protocol which can be used in the low-cost tag [1,2,3,4,12].

In 2007, He et al. [12] proposed an authentication and key agreement (AKA) protocol which is used in the process of communication between the low-cost tag and reader. They also proved the security of the protocol through the extended strand space model [13,14,15]. This paper presents a more efficient authentication and key agreement (AKA) protocol which is used in the process of communication between the low-cost tag and reader for RFID system than He et al.'s AKA protocol. Compare with He et al.'s AKAP protocol, the proposed AKA protocol reduces the computational costs as well as protocol communication rounds to agree a shared session key between the reader and the tag.

This paper is organized as follows: In Section 2, we briefly review previous He et al.'s AKA protocol. In Section 3, we presents our proposed efficient AKA protocol for RFID system. In Sections 4 and 5, we analyze the security and the efficiency of our proposed AKA protocol, respectively. Finally, our conclusions are presented in Section 6.

2 Review of He et al.'s AKA Protocol

This section reviews He et al.'s AKA protocol [12]. The notations used throughout the paper can be summarized as follows:

- A: the tag.
- B: the reader.
- ID_A: the identity of the tag.
- ID_B: the identity of the reader.
- k_{AB}: the shared key between the reader and the tag.
- S: the shared secret counter between the reader and the tag which increases after authentication.
- SK: the shared session key between the reader and the tag.
- $H(x)$: the secure one-way hash value of x
- $x \oplus y$: the bit-wise XOR operation of x and y.
- M: the plaintext message exchanged between the reader and the tag.

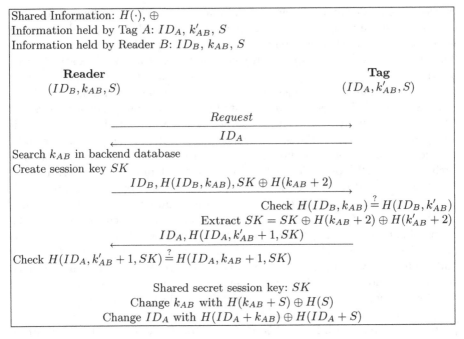

Shared Information: $H(\cdot)$, $\oplus$
Information held by Tag A: ID_A, k'_{AB}, S
Information held by Reader B: ID_B, k_{AB}, S

$$\textbf{Reader} \qquad\qquad\qquad\qquad\qquad\qquad\qquad \textbf{Tag}$$
$$(ID_B, k_{AB}, S) \qquad\qquad\qquad\qquad\qquad\qquad (ID_A, k'_{AB}, S)$$

$$\xrightarrow{\hspace{2cm} Request \hspace{2cm}}$$
$$\xleftarrow{\hspace{2cm} ID_A \hspace{2cm}}$$

Search k_{AB} in backend database
Create session key SK
$$\xrightarrow{\hspace{0.5cm} ID_B, H(ID_B, k_{AB}), SK \oplus H(k_{AB} + 2) \hspace{0.5cm}}$$

Check $H(ID_B, k_{AB}) \overset{?}{=} H(ID_B, k'_{AB})$
Extract $SK = SK \oplus H(k_{AB} + 2) \oplus H(k'_{AB} + 2)$
$$\xleftarrow{\hspace{0.5cm} ID_A, H(ID_A, k'_{AB} + 1, SK) \hspace{0.5cm}}$$

Check $H(ID_A, k'_{AB} + 1, SK) \overset{?}{=} H(ID_A, k_{AB} + 1, SK)$

Shared secret session key: SK
Change k_{AB} with $H(k_{AB} + S) \oplus H(S)$
Change ID_A with $H(ID_A + k_{AB}) \oplus H(ID_A + S)$

Fig. 1. He et al.'s AKA protocol

He et al.'s AKA protocol is shown in figure 1 and performs as follows:

1. $B \rightarrow A$: *Request*
   B sends request message to A.
2. $A \rightarrow B$: ID_A
   A sends its identity ID_A to B.
3. $B \rightarrow A$: $ID_B, H(ID_B, k_{AB}), SK \oplus H(k_{AB} + 2)$
   After receiving ID_A from A, B searches the secret key k_{AB} in the backend
   database and creates session key SK. Then, B sends out $\{ID_B, H(ID_B, k_{AB}),$
   $SK \oplus H(k_{AB} + 2)\}$ to A.
4. $A \rightarrow B$: $ID_A, H(ID_A, k'_{AB} + 1, SK)$
   After receiving $\{ID_B, H(ID_B, k_{AB}), SK \oplus H(k_{AB} + 2)\}$ from B, A computes $H(ID_B, k'_{AB})$ by its saved k'_{AB}. If $H(ID_B, k_{AB}) = H(ID_B, k'_{AB})$,
   the A successfully authenticates B and calculates $H(k_{AB} + 2)$ to get SK;
   If $H(ID_B, k_{AB})) \neq H(ID_B, k'_{AB})$, authentication fails. Then, A sends out
   $\{ID_A, H(ID_A, k'_{AB} + 1, SK)\}$ to B.
5. After receiving $\{ID_A, H(ID_A, k'_{AB} + 1, SK)\}$ from A, B computes $H(ID_A,$
   $k_{AB} + 1, SK)$ to see whether they are equal or not. If they equal, the authentication and the agreement on SK succeed.
6. After successful agreement on SK, both A and B change k_{AB} with $H(k_{AB} +$
   $S) \oplus H(S)$. The following communication adopts encrypt mode, ciphertext
   $C = M \oplus H(SK)$.
7. After the communication, both A and B change the tag A's identity ID_A
   with $H(ID_A + k_{AB}) \oplus H(ID_A + S)$ and destroy the SK.

Shared Information: $H(\cdot)$

Information held by Tag A: ID_A, k_{AB}, S
Information held by Reader B: ID_B, k'_{AB}, S

Reader	**Tag**
(ID_B, k_{AB}, S)	(ID_A, k'_{AB}, S)

Generate random number r_B

$$\xrightarrow{\quad ID_B, Request, r_B \quad}$$

Compute $SK = H(ID_A, ID_B, k'_{AB}, r_B)$

$$\xleftarrow{\quad ID_A, H(ID_A, k'_{AB}, SK) \quad}$$

Search k_{AB} in backend database
Compute $SK = H(ID_A, ID_B, k_{AB}, r_B)$
Check $H(ID_A, k'_{AB}, SK) \overset{?}{=} H(ID_A, k_{AB}, SK)$

$$\xrightarrow{\quad ID_B, H(ID_B, k_{AB}, SK) \quad}$$

Check $H(ID_B, k_{AB}, SK) \overset{?}{=} H(ID_B, k'_{AB}, SK)$

Shared secret session key: $SK = H(ID_A, ID_B, k_{AB}, r_B)$
Change k_{AB} with $H(k_{AB}, S)$
Change ID_A with $H(ID_A, k_{AB}, S, SK)$

Fig. 2. Proposed AKA protocol

3 Proposed AKA Protocol

This section proposes an efficient AKA protocol than Lie et al.'s AKA protocol. The proposed AKA protocol is shown in figure 2 and performs as follows:

1. $B \to A$: $ID_B, Request, r_B$
   B generates a random number r_B and sends out a request message $\{ID_B, Request, r_B\}$ to A.
2. $A \to B$: $ID_A, H(ID_A, k'_{AB}, SK)$
   After receiving request message $\{ID_B, Request, r_B\}$ from B, A computes session key $SK = H(ID_A, ID_B, k'_{AB}, r_B)$ and then sends out $\{ID_A, H(ID_A, k'_{AB}, SK)\}$ to B.
3. $B \to A$: $ID_B, H(ID_B, k_{AB}, SK)$
   After receiving $\{ID_A, H(ID_A, k'_{AB}, SK)\}$ from A, B searches the secret key k'_{AB} in the backend database and computes session key $SK = H(ID_A, ID_B, k_{AB}, r_B)$. Then, B computes $H(ID_A, k_{AB}, SK)$. If $H(ID_A, k'_{AB}, SK) = H(ID_A, k_{AB}, SK)$, the B successfully authenticates A and agreements session key SK; If $H(ID_A, k'_{AB}, SK) \neq H(ID_A, k_{AB}, SK)$, authentication fails. Finally, B sends out $\{ID_B, H(ID_B, k_{AB}, SK)\}$ to A
4. After receiving $\{ID_B, H(ID_B, k_{AB}, SK)\}$ from B, A computes $H(ID_B, k'_{AB}, SK)$. If $H(ID_B, k_{AB}, SK) = H(ID_B, k'_{AB}, SK)$, the A successfully authenticates B and agreements session key SK; If $H(ID_B, k_{AB}, SK) \neq H(ID_B, k'_{AB}, SK)$, authentication fails.
5. After successful agreement on SK, both A and B change k_{AB} with $H(k_{AB}, S)$.

The following communication adopts encrypt mode, ciphertext $C = M \oplus H(SK)$.

6. After the communication, both A and B change the tag A's identity ID_A with $H(ID_A, k_{AB}, S, SK)$ and destroy the SK.

4   Security Analysis

This section provides the proof of correctness of the proposed AKA protocol.

1. *Mutual authentication and key agreement*: In steps 3 and 4, by using the secure one-way hash function $H(\cdot)$ [16], the reader and the tag always verify whether the received massage authentication values ($H(ID_A, k'_{AB}, SK)$ and $H(ID_B, k_{AB}, SK)$) are legal corresponding party's sending message. Therefore, the proposed AKA protocol provides the two-way mutual authentication and guarantees the secrecy of the reader and the tag.

2. *Untraceability*: In step 6, after finish the message communication, both the reader and the tag always change the tag A's identity ID_A with $H(ID_A, k_{AB}, S, SK)$ and then destroy the shared session key SK. Therefore, the proposed AKA protocol ensures the untraceability of the tag.

3. *Computing complexity*: Compared with the Hash-Lock protocol and Hash chain protocol [1,2,3,4,5,6,7,8,9,10,11], the proposed AKA protocol simply uses secure one-way hash function without PRNG(Pseudo-Random Number Generator) on the tag. Only involving one hash function module, it efficiently controls the cost of the tag. The computing complexity in the proposed AKA protocol is at the same level of Hash-Lock protocol. Therefore, the proposed AKA protocol is also suitable for the low-cost RFID system.

4. *Replay attacks*: In steps 5 and 6, both the reader and the tag always change the key k_{AB} and tag's identity ID, the proposed AKA protocol can avoid the replay attacks.

5   Efficiency Analysis

This section discusses the efficiency features of the proposed AKA protocol. The computational costs of the proposed AKA protocol in the reader and the tag are summarized in Table 1.

In He et al.'s AKA protocol, the computational overhead of the reader is 7 hash operations, 3 Bit-wise XOR($\oplus$) operations, and 1 random number generations. The computational overhead of the tag is 7 hash operations and 3 Bit-wise XOR($\oplus$) operations. He et al.'s AKA protocol needs 4 communication rounds for mutual authentication and session key agreement.

In our proposed AKA protocol, the computational overhead of the reader is 5 hash operations and 1 random number generations. The computational overhead of the tag is 5 hash operations. Our proposed AKA protocol needs 3 communication rounds for mutual authentication and session key agreement.

Obviously, the proposed AKA protocol is more efficient than He et al.'s AKA protocol.

Table 1. Computational costs of the proposed AKA protocol

	Reader	Tag	Communication Rounds
He et al.'s AKA protocol	7 Hash + 3 Xor + 1 Ran	7 Hash + 3 Xor + 0 Ran	4
Proposed AKA protocol	5 Hash + 0 Xor + 1 Ran	5 Hash + 0 Xor + 0 Ran	3

Hash: Hash operation; Xor : Bit-wise XOR($\oplus$) operation;
Ran: Random number generation.

6   Conclusions

This paper presented a more efficient authentication and key agreement (AKA) protocol which is used in the process of communication between the low-cost tag and reader for RFID system than He et al.'s AKA protocol. In the proposed AKA protocol, the numbers of communication rounds are reduced that can be executed in seven messages and three rounds, respectively. As a result, compare with He et al.'s AKA protocol, the proposed AKA protocol has same security and is more computationally efficient and communication round efficient to agree a shared session key between the reader and the tag.

Acknowledgements

Kee-Young Yoo was supported by the MKE(Ministry of Knowledge Economy) of Korea, under the ITRC support program supervised by the IITA(IITA-2008-C1090-0801-0026). Eun-Jun Yoon was supported by the 2nd Brain Korea 21 Project in 2008.

References

1. Sarma, S.E., Weis, S.A., Engels, D.W.: Radio-frequency Identification: Secure Risks and Challenges, RSA Laboratories Cryptobytes, pp. 2–9 (June 2003)
2. Ohkubo, M., Suzuki, K., Kinoshita, S.: Hash-chain Based Forward-secure Privacy Protection Scheme for Low-cost RFID. In: Proceedings of the 2004 Symposium on Cryptography and Information Security (SCIS 2004), Sendai, pp. 719–724 (2004)
3. Avoine, G., Oechslin, P.: A Scalable and Provably Secure Hash-based RFID Protocol. In: Proceedings of the 2nd IEEE International Workshop on Pervasive Computing and Communication Security(PerSec 2005), Washington. DC, USA, pp. 110–114 (2005)

4. Zhou, Y.B., Feng, D.G.: Design and Analysis of Cryptographic Protocols for RFID. Chinese Journal of Computers, 582–589 (April 2006)
5. Avoine, G., Dysli, E., Oechslin, P.: Reducing Time Complexity in RFID Systems. In: Preneel, B., Tavares, S. (eds.) SAC 2005. LNCS, vol. 3897, pp. 291–306. Springer, Heidelberg (2006)
6. Kinoshita, S., Hoshino, F., Komuro, T., Fujimura, A., Ohkubo, M.: Low-cost RFID Privacy Protection Scheme. IPSJ 45(8), 2004–2021 (2007)
7. Ohkubo, M., Suzuki, K., Kinoshita, S.: Cryptographic Approach to "privacy-friendly" tags. In: RFID Privacy Workshop (2003)
8. Saito, J., Sakurai, K.: Owner Transferable Privacy Protection Scheme for RFID Tags. In: CSS 2005. IPSJ Symposium Series, pp. 283–288 (2005)
9. Han, D.G., Takagi, T., Kim, H.W., Chung, K.I.: New Security Problem in RFID Systems Tag Killing. In: Gavrilova, M.L., Gervasi, O., Kumar, V., Tan, C.J.K., Taniar, D., Laganá, A., Mun, Y., Choo, H. (eds.) ICCSA 2006. LNCS, vol. 3982, pp. 375–384. Springer, Heidelberg (2006)
10. Rhee, K., Kwak, J., Kim, S., Won, D.: Challenge-response based RFID Authentication Protocol for Distributed Database Environment. In: Hutter, D., Ullmann, M. (eds.) SPC 2005. LNCS, vol. 3450, pp. 70–84. Springer, Heidelberg (2005)
11. Osaka, K., Takagi, T., Yamazaki, K., Takahashi, O.: An Efficient and Secure RFID Security Method with Ownership Transfer. In: International Conference on Computational Intelligence and Security, 2006, pp. 1090–1095 (2006)
12. He, L., Gan, Y., Li, N.N., Cai, Z.Y.: A Security-provable Authentication and Key Agreement Protocol in RFID System. In: International Conference on Wireless Communications, Networking and Mobile Computing, 2007, vol. 1(1), pp. 2078–2080 (2007)
13. Fabrega, F.J.T., Herzog, J.C., Guttman, J.D.: Strand Spaces: Proving Security Protocols Correct. Journal of Computer Security, 191–230 (July 1999)
14. Thayer, F.J., Herzog, J.C., Guttman, J.D.: Strand Spaces: Why is a Security Protocol Correct. In: Proceedings of the 1998 IEEE Symposium on Security and Privacy, pp. 160–171. IEEE Computer Society Press, Los Alamitos (1998)
15. Shen, H.F., Xue, R., Huangn, H.Y., Chen, Z.X.: Extending the Theory of Strand Spaces. Journal of Software, 1785–1789 (October 2005)
16. Schneier, B.: Applied Cryptography Protocols, Algorithms and Source Code in C, 2nd edn. John Wiley & Sons Inc., Chichester (1995)

Grid Service Discovery Based on Cross-VO Service Domain Model

Jing-Ya Zhou, Jun-Zhou Luo, and Ai-Bo Song

School of Computer Science and Engineering, Southeast University,
210096 Nanjing, P.R. China
{jyz,jluo,absong}@seu.edu.cn

Abstract. The diversity of grid service originates from heterogeneous and dynamic nature of grid, and it poses a great challenge to grid service discovery. How to discover services satisfying users' multiple requests meanwhile avoiding negative effect derived from requests and updates becomes increasingly important in grid environment. This paper proposes a Cross-VO (Visual Organization) service domain model for compensating deficiencies that traditional approaches exhibit in flexibility of discovery. Service domain is developed to make advantage of similarity among services. In this model each service domain is constructed through all services that have similar function in VOs and nodes in service domain connect according to unstructured P2P system. It breaks through resource restriction in a VO and satisfies users' requests in great extent while achieves favorable scalability and flexibility. Both theoretical analysis and experimental results indicate that this model performs efficiently in high discovery success ratio, low average hops and messages even with low density and small TTL. Compared with non-domain grid system via the same discovery success ratio, our model outperforms it in both average hops and messages.

Keywords: Service Discovery, Service Domain, P2P.

1 Introduction

OGSA (Open Grid Service Architecture) [1] is a service oriented grid architecture that derives from computational grid and combining with Web Services forms a grid service oriented hierarchical integration architecture. In OGSA the virtualization of resources is embodied in the form of grid services and these services distribute in large scale grid environment. Hence, how to discover grid service satisfying users' requirements effectively becomes key issue in grid study.

VO is defined as a set of individuals and/or institutions defined by sharing rules and they share resources and cooperate with each other through a way of under controlled [2]. According to the collaboration, the service type provided by local VO usually meet users' requirements in higher probability, but service instances may not satisfy requirements due to resource restriction in one VO or higher requirements addressed by users. There are a large number of grid services with same type or similar functional property across VOs, but traditional discovery approaches do not take this case into account. Consequently, we propose Cross-VO service domain model for grid service

J. Cao et al. (Eds.): NPC 2008, LNCS 5245, pp. 327–338, 2008.

discovery. Service domain is composed of many services with similar functions. Efficient discovery strategy is designed based on the model too. Both theoretical analysis and experimental results indicate that the model we proposed can reduce updating load effectively and increase discovery success ratio.

The rest of this paper is organized as follows: Section 2 gives related work on service/resource discovery in grid environment. Section 3 introduces Cross-VO service domain model, then service discovery strategy is described. In section 4 we make performance analysis on theory. The experimental results and analysis is present in section 5. In section 6 we conclude the paper and look forward to future work.

2   Related Work

Grid service/resource discovery is somewhat special because of high dynamics in grid environment. Many studies have made their efforts to solve this problem.

Globus [3] uses MDS (Monitoring and Discovery Service) [4] to realize tree-like metadata directory service based on LDAP [5]. MDS is in charge of monitoring and discovery of grid resources, however, it focuses on service data query while lack of support for service type discovery. UDDI (Universal Description Discovery and Integration) is a specification for distributed Web-based information registries for Web services [6]. It allows services to be published, and subsequently searched, based on their interface, but it does not an automatic mechanism for updating the registry as services change. A. ShaikhAli, etc. present UDDIe as an extension to UDDI, which supports QoS (Quality of Service) dynamic registry and enable discovery of services based on QoS [7]. Unfortunately, it is a centralized model, in which central server in charge of all queries and inclines to failure in case of overload. Meanwhile frequent QoS update results in huge network overhead due to dynamic nature of grid. In this paper, we suggest that similar services should be aggregated together in a service domain, and then multitude dynamic update is restricted within the range of domain.

P2P shares many common features with grid, for example, both of them are large scale system constructed for the purpose of resource sharing; resources or services in system exhibit characteristics of strong autonomy, heterogeneity and high dynamics; nodes may participate or withdraw at any moment. P. Trunfio, etc. propose that two systems be converged for the discovery research, and three kinds of P2P systems are also analyzed in [8]. As to unstructured P2P system, A. Iamnitchi, etc. propose a fully decentralized P2P architecture for resource discovery in grid environment. In this architecture all nodes are equivalent and no one act as central server. The discovery process is the execution of traversal among all nodes, because of no central server it avoids single-point failure, nevertheless, it will appear high latency as the growth of network size. Chord [9, 10] is the first structured P2P system to be proposed. The discovery process emulates the binary search, thus requires O (logN) hops and messages. Compared with unstructured P2P system, structured P2P system is more scalable in terms of traffic load, but need to have strong self-organization capabilities in order to be able to maintain rigid structure. Hybrid P2P system has been proposed to overcome the drawbacks of aforesaid two systems while retaining their benefits. Hybrid P2P system is composed of two kinds of nodes: ordinary nodes and super nodes, in which several ordinary nodes are administrated by one super node and super nodes constitute a fully decentralized structure. There is no central server storing index structure, so it is no need to worry about the appearance of server bottleneck. Compared with unstructured P2P system, it has much faster speed for synchronization of index information and does not result in large traffic. Y. Gong, etc. put forward VEGA resource discovery framework in [11]. In this framework, several resource routers constitute management domain and are connect to backbone through border router. VEGA constructs a hybrid-like hierarchical P2P structure, and uses layered clustering approach to aggregate resource information. Through interaction between layers resource information are updated continuously. This architecture brings enlightening significance to our study. The concept of management domain is similar to VO in management perspective, however, it lacks of consideration for clustering management of similar resources.

3   Cross-VO Service Domain Model

3.1   Introduction to the Model

Service domain aggregates many types of service with similar function. It is similar to the conception of VO in architectural perspective, whereas, other than VO the former pays more attention to clustering of service providers of specific application field. Cross-VO service domain model is a hybrid hierarchical P2P structure. In the model, VO can be composed of several service domains while single service domain may be covered by several VOs. There are a VOSR (VO Service Registry) and many LDSRs (Local Domain Service Registry) located in VO. LDSR takes charge of registry of service information belong to a certain type, so LDSR represents a kind of service type, and the service information here is the detailed service description including static and dynamic information. As to provisional services we use factory pattern for registry, namely providers only register service handle for activating factory to LDSR, but no context and resources are allocated. The service handle associate with service type, and create service instances when needed. For further description of similarity, we introduce service compatibility to depict the substitutable relationship between different service types. If service type A is compatible with service type B, it indicates that user's requirements for instance of A can also be satisfied by instance of B. Apparently the introduction of service compatibility enhances discovery performance. In addition, it is notable that compatibility has no reflexivity. VOSR takes charge of recording and maintaining service type etc. static information gathered from LDSRs in local VO. LDSRs belong to a service domain are collected together to constitute a complete service domain. In service domain, LDSRs as nodes connect with one another according to unstructured P2P system.

Figure 1 shows an example of Cross-VO service domain model. Service domain III is covered by three VOs namely VO A, B and C, while VO A is composed of part of three service domains namely service domain I, II and III. On the VO level of this model, VOSRs of all VOs constitute an unstructured P2P system, then they correspond to super nodes in hybrid P2P system. In each VOSR we set a cache for recording

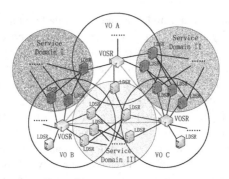

Fig. 1. Cross-VO Service Domain Model

service domain information published from neighbors and publish information of its own to neighbors periodically.

3.2 Service Discovery Strategy

In service discovery process, service request is dealt with according to distributed transmit strategy and describes as follows:

1. Users send request to local VOSR via LDSR.
2. VOSR receives request and makes some analysis, then lookup in service type list to determine if there exists item that match service domain that required service belongs to, if true, forward it to corresponding LDSR and go on, or else go to 5.
3. LDSR receives request and compares it with its own registry service type to determine whether they are the same or the registry service type is included in the compatibility list of required service, if not true, go to next step, or else continue to carry out service instance match in LDSR according to QoS etc. state information, if match success, then return discovery success and service information, otherwise, go to next step.
4. If request forwarding hops exceed TTL (Time To Live) return failure, otherwise, forward request to all its neighbors and go to 3.
5. Lookup cache for further match, if there exist item matching the required service domain, then forward request to the corresponding neighbor and go to 2, or else forward request to all neighbors and go to 2.

The above discovery strategy can be divided into two parts: discovery on VO level and discovery within service domain. The first part aims at finding service domain that required service belongs to. As service domain crosses VOs, each LDSR can be regarded as entrance from VO to service domain, it is equivalent to say that service domain has entrances among multiple VOs. It not only improves discovery success ratio, but avoids instability caused by node failure. After finding the service domain, it will go to the second part. The second part is responsible for finding satisfied service instance in service domain according to service type, state requirement etc.. It breaks through service resources restriction in a VO, meanwhile, it also solves the problem of single-point failure and load balancing. When VOSR of VO A fails or overloads,

LDSR 1 belonging to A will sends request to any of its neighbor LDSR 2 in the same domain instead of forwarding to VOSR of A, then LDSR 2 sends request to its own VO B and continue the following discovery process.

4 Performance Analysis

It is demonstrated that Internet topology follows power-law [12]. We assume that both inter-VO topology and intra-domain topology in Cross-VO service domain model obey power-law and theoretical analysis is given below.

Table 1. Symbols and Definitions

Symbol	Definition
N_{VO}	Number of VOs
N_D	Number of service domains
$N_{D\text{-}LDSR}$	Average number of LDSRs in a service domain
$P_{SUC}(h,t)$	Discovery success ratio within h+t hops
$T(h,t)$	Average hops under discovery success
$M(h,t)$	Average messages forwarded by single request
$P_{VO}(h)$	The probability of finding service domain that required within h hops
$P_D(t)$	The probability of finding satisfied service instance within t hops
$T(h)$	Average hops under service domain discovery success within h hops
$T'(t)$	Average hops in domain under service discovery success within t hops
$M(h)$	Average messages forwarded by single request within h hops on VO level
$M'(t)$	Average messages forwarded by single request within t hops in domain

Firstly, we take the first part of discovery process into consideration. According to lemma 2 in [12], the number of edges E on VO level, can be estimated as a function of N_{VO} and the rank exponent R: $E = \dfrac{1}{2(R+1)}(1 - \dfrac{1}{N_{VO}^{R+1}})N_{VO}$, then substitute it into

$d = \dfrac{2E}{N_{VO}}$, it goes into $d = \dfrac{N_{VO}^{R+1} - 1}{(R+1)N_{VO}^{R+1}}$. d represents average degree on VO level, it can

be seen that when $N_{VO} \to +\infty$, d tends to be constant $\dfrac{1}{R+1}$. Supposing that we search service with certain type x and x belongs to domain I. There are two possibilities to find domain I, let us donate by P_I the possibility that I is in the service type list, and P_{IC} the possibility of finding I in cache. Then, the possibility of finding I on VO level is shown to be:

$$P_{VO\text{-}I} = 1 - (1 - P_I)(1 - P_{IC}) \tag{1}$$

Since I is covered by n_I VOs, we have: $P_I = \dfrac{n_I}{N_{VO}}$. The cache size of VOSR is set as

its degree, we have got d, so $1 - P_{IC} = \dfrac{\binom{N_D - 1}{d}}{\binom{N_D}{d}} = \dfrac{N_D - d}{N_D}$, substitute it to equation (1),

we obtain:

$$P_{VO-I} = 1 - \frac{(N_{VO} - n_I)(N_D - d)}{N_{VO} N_D} \tag{2}$$

We use the following equation to calculate $P_{VO}(h)$:

$$P_{VO}(h) = 1 - (1 - P_{VO-I})(1 - P_{VO}(h-1))^d = 1 - (1 - P_{VO-I})^{\frac{d^{h+1} - 1}{d - 1}} \tag{3}$$

Equation (3) shows that $P_{VO}(h)$ initially increases quickly as TTL h increases, then as $P_{VO}(h)$ approaches 1 the increase amplitude slow down gradually. Meanwhile, the increasement of P_{VO-I} brings higher $P_{VO}(h)$, and we can improve P_{VO-I} via heightening n_I, so n_I is also proportional to $P_{VO}(h)$. Let p_i donate the probability of finding service domain at exactly the ith hop, then $P_{VO}(h)$ is given by: $P_{VO}(h) = \sum_{i=0}^{h} p_i$. Now consider the probability of finding service domain at exactly the ith hop under service domain discovery success within h hops should be $p_i / P_{VO}(h)$, we have:

$$T(h) = \sum_{i=1}^{h} i \frac{p_i}{P_{VO}(h)} = \frac{1}{P_{VO}(h)} \left(\sum_{i=1}^{h-1} i p_i + h p_h \right) = \frac{1}{P_{VO}(h)} (P_{VO}(h-1)T(h-1) + h p_h)$$

Substitute $p_h = P_{VO}(h) - P_{VO}(h-1)$ to above equation and replace $P_{VO}(h)$ with equation (3), we obtain:

$$T(h) = h - \frac{h}{P_{VO}(h)} + \frac{1}{P_{VO}(h)} \sum_{i=1}^{h} (1 - P_{VO-I})^{\frac{d^i - 1}{d - 1}} \tag{4}$$

By analyzing equation (4), we conclude that both h and P_{VO-I} have relationship with T(h), increasing h exclusively may not always lead to continuous increase of T(h).

When the required service domain appears in service type list, discovery process go to the second part——intro-domain discovery, and then there is no messages generated on VO level, if matching in cache, a message is forwarded to corresponding neighbor. Otherwise, messages are forwarded to all neighbors. We let $a = 1 - P_{VO-I}$, so M(h) is given by:

$$M(h) = 1 \cdot (1 - P_I)P_{IC} + (d + dm(h-1))a \tag{5}$$

where m(h-1) are messages generated within the following h-1 hops and can be calculated by following equations:

$$m(h-1) = 1[(1-P_I)P_{IC} + (d + dm(h-2))a = \sum_{i=0}^{h-1}(ad)^i(1+b) - 1$$

and we rewrite equation (5) as:

$$M(h) = b + \frac{ad((ad)^h - b - 1)}{ad - 1} \tag{6}$$

Equation (6) indicates that node degree corresponds to an exponential number of messages, and degree of node in WAN tends to constant, so decreasing messages requires reducing TTL h. But on basis of analysis on equation (3), reducing h may result in drop of success ratio largely. Therefore, we need to take both factors into consideration.

Given that we find service domain, then we reach intra-domain discovery process. Different from VO level, we do not set cache in LDSR for considering similarity of services in domain and update load. According to lemma 4 in [12], the average number of nodes within t hops is the function of hot-plot exponent H, where E' is the average number of edges in domain:

$$NN(t) = \frac{N_{D\text{-}LDSR} + 2E'}{N_{D\text{-}LDSR}} t^H - 1$$

Supposing that the required service type was S, and the number of nodes that provide this kind of service was N_S, then the density of type S is $D_S = \frac{N_S}{N_{D\text{-}LDSR}}$. We let m_c as the number of service types that are compatible with S. The probability that request can find at least one satisfied service instance within t hops is given by:

$$P_D(t) = 1 - (1 - P_M)^{NN(t)\sum_{i=1}^{m_c+1} D_i} \tag{7}$$

where P_M represents the probability of instance match. $P_D(t)$ shares the same change trend with $P_{VO}(h)$ in equation (3). Combining equations (3) and (7) we obtain:

$$P_{SUC}(h,t) = 1 - (1 - P_{VO\text{-}I}P_D(t))^{\frac{d^{h+1}-1}{d-1}} \tag{8}$$

From equation (8), it is known that increasing match probability P_M, service density D_S, and number of compatible services m_c will increase $P_D(t)$, and further increase $P_{SUC}(h,t)$.

In terms of approaches for calculating average hops on VO level, we calculate intra-domain average hops as:

$$T'(t) = t - \frac{t}{P_D(t)} + \frac{1}{P_D(t)}\sum_{i=1}^{t}(1 - P_M)^{\frac{d^i-1}{d-1}} \tag{9}$$

Average hops under discovery success are described as:

$$T(h,t) = h + T'(t) - \frac{1}{P_{SUC}(h,t)} \square \sum_{i=1}^{h-1} P_{SUC}(i,t) \qquad (10)$$

$T'(t)$ and t in equation (9) are not strictly inverse proportion relationship, $T'(t)$ will keep stable on a range as $P_D(t)$ increases, and then as to $T(h,t)$ we pay more attention to the impact of $T(h)$.

When service request be satisfied, a success message will be returned, or else return failure message. Average messages within t hops are given by:

$$M'(t) = 1\square P_M + (d' + d'm'(t-1))(1 - P_M)$$

Where $m'(t-1)$ are messages generated within the following $h-1$ hops and d' is average degree in domain. Let $a' = 1 - P_M$, with a boundary of condition, we have:

$$m'(t-1) = (a'd')^{t-1} + \frac{(a'd')^{t-1} - 1}{a'd' - 1}\square(a'd' + 1 - a')$$

and then

$$M'(t) = 1 - a' + a'd'(1 + m'(t-1)) = \frac{2(a'd')^{t+1} - a'(a'd')^t - a'd' + a' - 1}{a'd' - 1} \qquad (11)$$

Through decreasing a', namely increasing P_M, we can get smaller average messages. In terms of above approaches, overall average messages is calculated by:

$$M(h,t) = P_{VO-I}M'(t) + (1 - P_{VO-I})(d + dg(h-1))$$

where $g(h-1) = P_{VO-I}M'(t) + (1 - P_{VO-I})(d + dg(h-2))$

then

$$M(h,t) = P_{VO-I}M'(t) + \frac{ad((ad)^h - P_{VO-I}M'(t) - 1)}{ad - 1} \qquad (12)$$

Above theoretical analysis indicates that discovery ratio, average hops and average messages are all mainly determined by three factors: node degree d or d', TTL h or t and probability of service instance match P_M. As network scale enlarge, node degree tends to be constant, if instance match probability keep unchanged, then it will be needed to choose suitable TTL to keep balance between discovery success ratio and average hops and messages.

5 Experiment

In this section, experimental environment is presented including our parameters setup. We also present metrics as well as the experimental results for performance evaluation.

5.1 Experimental Environment

SEUGrid is a grid system established for AMS-02 (Alpha Magnetic Spectrometer-02) project [13]. The AMS project is a large scale international collaborative project with the goal of searching in space for missing matter, antimatter and dark matter on the international space station. SEUGrid currently is used to deal with minitype vast data processing in MC (Monte Carlo) production. MC production aims at producing mass simulated data for particles analysis. Because there are many kinds of services is offered for different particles analysis, service discovery is needed to guarantee performance. All machines registered in SEUGrid are equipped with one or more type(s) of services. Cross-VO service domain model proposed in this paper is implemented in SEUGrid, and a service discovery strategy based on the model is also applied to it. We conduct our experiment in SEUGrid environment.

We divide experiment into two parts, the first part is used for performance comparison among different parameters in our model, only a kind of service type is considered; in the second part we compare our model with non-domain grid system, and requests are generated randomly without service type restriction. As to compatibility, parts of service types have one or two compatible service types.

Network topology affects performance of discovery strategy to some extent. We construct inter-VO topology according to power-law formula in [14] $f_d = \exp(8.03) * d^{-2.489}$ and intra-domain topology according to $f_d' = \exp(6.47) * d^{-2.489}$ and the node degree ranges from 2 to 10. Ten kinds of domains with two types of service in each one is registered to each VO, then there are 10*2=20 LDSRs included in each VO. Each LDSR is registered with a type of service instances, and the number of instances distributes in the range of 10 to 20.

$$N_{VO} = \sum_{d=2}^{10} f_d \approx 1000 \qquad N_{D\text{-}LDSR} = \sum_{d=2}^{10} f_d' \approx 200$$

The number of VOs is about 1000, and we set up 100 domains, hence, the average number of LDSRs:

$$N_{D\text{-}LDSR}=(1000*10*2)/100=200$$

We perform MC production on specified machines with high performance and divide generated data into many data blocks according to certain rule, then data blocks are transferred to several machines in each VO. Some of these machines are chosen randomly as request nodes every time.

5.2 Metrics

Three metrics are considered in the experiment. The former two are from user's perspective, while the latter is from the system's perspective.

1. Discovery Success Ratio: the percentage of satisfied requests of total requests, and can be divided into service domain discovery success ratio and intra-domain discovery success ratio respectively.
2. Average Hops: the mean of hops under service discovery success. We use average hops instead of response time as metrics to express search efficiency. It is divided into average hops on VO level and intra-domain average hops.
3. Average messages: the mean of messages generated by single request. We also divide it into average hops on VO level and intra-domain average hops.

5.3   Results

In order to avoiding influence of randomness, each group of experiment repeats for 100 times and all results are averaged. The discovery process is divided into two parts. Figure 3 shows that discovery success ratio of both parts initially increase quickly as TTL increases, when TTL reaches a certain value, the increase amplitude slow down and keep stable. This is because the number of domains arrived increases as TTL increases at initial time, afterward, the overlapping of service domains strengthened as TTL increases. Then the increase amplitude of number of domains slow down. When conduct intra-domain discovery, we set compatibility number as 1, and make comparisons between different densities. We find that the higher density the higher success ratio is, and success ratio become 1 when t is 3. Accordingly, when t comes to 3, overall success ratio is mainly dependent on service domain discovery success ratio.

The average hops in Figure 4 has the same trend with what Figure 3 reflects, and the points that change the trend are same too. This result is consistent with theoretical

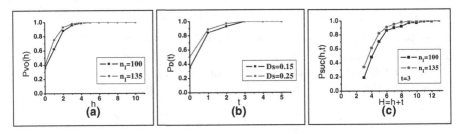

Fig. 2. Success Ratio and TTL

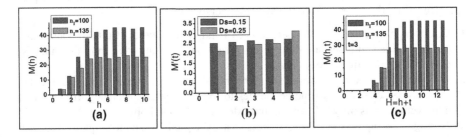

Fig. 3. Average Hops and TTL

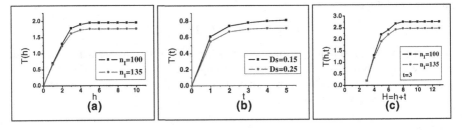

Fig. 4. Average Messages and TTL

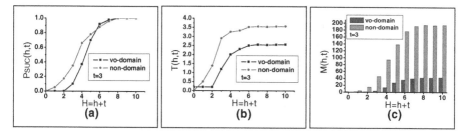

Fig. 5. Cross-VO Service Domain vs. Non-domain grid system

analysis. Compared with Figure 5 (a) and (b), we find that increasing density is one of the effective ways to reduce average messages, especially for large number of services and wide distribution.

In the second part, as to non-domain grid system, we conduct searching by flooding on VO level and set cache size as node degree, but take no consideration of compatibility, in addition, we set t as 3. The other settings including topology and services information registered are same with service domain model. As Figure 6 describes, in (a) when H≤5, non-domain grid system keeps higher success ratio. The reason can be concluded that h is limited to 2 which do not arrive at equilibrium point, after exceeding the point, our model exhibits better performance. (b) indicates that non-domain grid system requires larger average hops under same discovery success ratio. Meanwhile, in service domain model, forwarding requests are restricted in a domain constructed by services with compatibility. This consequently reduces average messages greatly as (c) shown.

6   Conclusion and Future Work

This paper introduces service domain into grid system to make advantage of similarity among services as well as avoiding single-point failure and appearance of massive messages, and proposes Cross-VO service domain model. The whole discovery process is composed of service domain discovery and intra-domain discovery. The introduction of compatibility enhances discovery power of potential similar service resources, thus achieves favorable flexibility. We analyze factors on performance, and do experiment in SEUGrid to evaluate these factors, and compare it with non-domain grid system. The experimental results show that Cross-VO service domain model we proposed can achieve high discovery success ratio, low average hops and messages.

Grid environment equipped with high dynamics requires updating frequently for correctness guarantee, especially for information in cache in our model. The performance impact of cache update will become our future work.

Acknowledgments. This work is supported by National Natural Science Foundation of China under Grants No. 90604004 and 60773103, Jiangsu Provincial Natural Science Foundation of China under Grants No. BK2007708, Jiangsu Provincial Key Laboratory of Network and Information Security under Grants No. BM2003201 and Key

Laboratory of Computer Network and Information Integration (Southeast University), Ministry of Education under Grants No. 93K-9.

References

1. Foster, I., Kesselman, C., Nick, J., et al.: The physiology of the grid: An open grid services architecture for distributed systems integration (2002), http://www.globus.org/research/papers/ogsa.pdf
2. Foster, I., Kesselman, C., Tuecke, S.: The Anatomy of the Grid: Enabling Scalable Virtual Organizations. International Journal Supercomputer Applications 15(3), 200–222 (2001)
3. Globus Toolkit, http://www.globus.org
4. Czajkowski, K., Fitagerald, S., Foster, I., Kesselman, C.: Grid Information Services for Distributed Resource Sharing. In: International Symposium on High Performance Distributed Computing (HPDC 2001), Proceedings, Redondo Beach (2001)
5. Howes, T., Smith, M.: A scalable, deployable directory service framework for the internet. Technical report, Michigan (1995)
6. Universal Description Discovery and Integration (UDDI), http://www.uddi.org/pubs/IruUDDITechnicalWhitePaper.pdf
7. ShaikhAli, A., Rana, O., Al-Ali, R., Walker, D.: UDDIe: An extended registry for web services. In: The Workshop on Service Oriented Computing: Models, Architectures and Applications, pp. 85–89 (2003)
8. Trunfio, P., Talia, D., Papadskis, H., et al.: Peer-to-Peer resource discovery in Grids: Models and systems. Future Generation Computer Systems 23(7), 864–878 (2007)
9. Stoica, I., Morris, R., Karger, D., et al.: Chord: A scalable Peer-to-Peer lookup service for internet applications. In: ACM Conference on Applications, Technologies, Architectures, and Protocols for Computer Communication (SIGCOMM 2001), pp. 149–160 (2001)
10. Krishnamurthy, S., El-Ansary, S., Aurell, E., Haridi, S.: A Statistical Theory of Chord Under Churn. In: Castro, M., van Renesse, R. (eds.) IPTPS 2005. LNCS, vol. 3640. Springer, Heidelberg (2005)
11. Gong, Y., Dong, F., Li, W., Xu, Z.: VEGA Infrastructure for Resource Discovery in Grids. Journal of Computer Science & Technology 18(4), 413–422 (2003)
12. Faloutsos, M., Faloutsos, P., Faloutsos, C.: On power-law relationship of the internet topology. In: ACM Conference on Applications, Technologies, Architectures, and Protocols for Computer Communication (SIGCOMM 1999), pp. 251–262 (1999)
13. Fisher, P., Klimentov, A., Mujunen, A., Ritakari, J.: AMS Ground Support Computers for ISS mission. AMS Note 2002-03-01 (2002)
14. Lu, D., Dinda, P.: Synthesizing Realistic Computational Grids. In: ACM/IEEE Supercomputing Conference (SC 2003), Phoenix (2003)

Ontology-Based Semantic Method
for Service Modeling in Grid

Bin Cheng [1,2,*], Xingang Wang [1,3], and Weiqin Tong [1]

[1] School of Computer Engineering and Science, Shanghai University,
Shanghai 200072; China
[2] College of Mathematics, Physics and Information Engineering, Zhejiang Normal
University, Zhejiang Jinhua 321000, China
[3] College of Information Engineering, Zhejiang University of Technology,
Hangzhou 310014, China
cb@shu.edu.cn, wxg@zjut.edu.cn, wqtong@mail.shu.edu.cn

Abstract. Grid is a newly developed technology for complex system with large-scale resource sharing, wide-area communication, multi-institutional collaboration, etc. A service-based approach for Grid can improve the extensibility and interoperability. In this paper, Service Oriented Grid Hierarchical Architecture is proposed within the OGSA framework, which gives a new approach to build the Grid. The need of semantic component in Grid to discover and describe the resources is analyzed and a Star Model of Ontology is introduced to describe services semantically. A Grid Service Matchmaking Semantic method is presented on the base of the ontology.

Keywords: Grid service, Ontology, Grid.

1 Introduction

Grid is a newly developed technology for complex system, which has been widely adopted in scientific and technical computing. It enable us to share, exchange, discover, select and aggregate geographical or Internet-wide distributed heterogeneous resources-such as sensors, computers, databases, visualization devices and scientific instruments. In Grid where resources are generally owned by different people, obtaining and managing these resources is not a simple task for communities or organizations with varied administration policies and capabilities. And the resource sharing and the problem solving in dynamic multi-institutional virtual organizations are difficult[2].

Grid technologies have been evolving toward an Open Grid Services Architecture (OGSA) in which a Grid provides an extensible set of services that virtual organizations can aggregate in various ways[1]. However, OGSA has not indicated how to build the Grid architecture and the platform directly based on service. A novel hierarchical structure of grid is proposed in this paper which can be described as an extension of the current Grid. It is a service oriented architecture in which entities provide services to one another under various forms of contract. The services are given well defined meaning, better enabling computers and people to work in cooperation semantically under ontology.

---

[*] Corresponding author.

J. Cao et al. (Eds.): NPC 2008, LNCS 5245, pp. 339–348, 2008.

The rest of the paper is organized as follows: Section 2 proposed the service-oriented hierarchical structure of Grid. The critical technologies of the service layer are discussed in Section 3, such as the Grid Ontology, the service discovering, the capability evaluating and the service composing. Section 4 concludes the paper highlighting the advantages and future scope of this research work.

2 Service Oriented Grid Hierarchical Architecture

Open Grid Service Architecture (OGSA)[1], oriented Grid Service (GS), discussed in Global Grid Forum (GGF) has been evolving since it was proposed in the early 2002. According to [1], the service abstraction may be used to specify the access to computational resources, storage resources, and networks, in a unified way. But it does not discuss how to model the Grid architecture based on service. We present a novel approach to integrate Web service and Grid computing by researching the Grid functional model and OGSA[4].

First, Grid is concerned with coordinated resource sharing and problem solving in dynamic, multi-institutional virtual organizations. Protocols are the building block of the function sharing and cooperation. And the service mechanism is the approach to achieve the protocols. So the service is an ideal form of resource abstraction.

Second, the Service Oriented Architecture (SOA) is introduced to manage the resources in the virtual organizations (VOs). SOA builds a uniform environment of service computing, which is composed of the resource service, the common service and the application service, in the VO layer of Grid. And the resource sharing transforms to a mapping from an abstract resource to a resource service. The cooperation becomes the interaction among different service entities. The job scheduling converts into the lifecycle management of service entities, such as creation, maintenance and negotiation.

Third, the method of workflow modeling based on Web service emphasizes the ability of the need description and studies the description language of Grid job. It works for adapting the request of application and the environmental change.

Last, the mechanism of the Grid Service security and the combination of QoS and OGSA are set up, and implements the credible Grid environment based on safe Grid Service and satisfies the request of Grid application.

The Service Oriented Grid Hierarchical Architecture (Fig.1) introduces a method to build a Grid system based on service semantically and analyzes the relationship of every layer. It describes further details of the Grid functional model based on the Grid Service technology.

(1) Resource Layer
Resources are the infrastructure of the Grid computing and the execution of the scientific task finally[7]. Resources not only include the physical resources such as sensors, computers, databases, scientific instruments, etc., but also the logical resources such as network bandwidth, software, application service, etc. So the resource layer highlights the distributed, autonomous and heterogeneous characteristic of the Grid environment.

(2) Service Layer
The service layer focuses on solving the resource sharing and cooperation for supporting the service oriented development, assignment, processing and testing of Grid application. The detailed components of the Services layer are presented as follows:

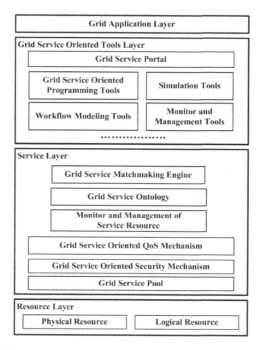

Fig. 1. Service Oriented Grid Hierarchical Architecture

a) Grid Service Pool

It includes all the elementary services or complex services, which are registered, and builds the environment of the Grid Service, e.g. the uniform description of service.

b) Grid Service Oriented Security Mechanism

It offers such function as the security support, such as identification, authorization, access control, secure communication, etc. to the Grid Service.

c) Grid Service Oriented QoS Mechanism

It provides the QoS guarantee to the VOs directly and the QoS negotiation to the services. It can satisfy the nonfunctional request, e.g. service capability, reliability, management, etc.

d) Monitor and Management of Service Resource

It can analyze the service request, break apart the computing task, cooperate and schedule the subtask, offer the information service, etc. It also can provide some common functions such as instantiation of the service, internal status maintenance, lifecycle negotiation and so on.

e) Grid Service Ontology

It is consisted of a global ontology and several local ontologies. Every local ontology records the local services' concepts and the relationships of these concepts. If it is difficult to solve a problem by one ontology, a global mapping mechanism is used to integrate the semantic information of other ontologies. It is helpful to improve the accurate service matchmaking and support the user or service to maintain and search the local ontologies.

f) Grid Service Matchmaking Engine

It supports the service discovering, the capability evaluating, the queuing strategy and the service composing semantically. The mapping from the task to the service is under the ontology. It coordinates the interaction among the services and embodies the cooperative solution of multiple services.

(3) Grid Service Oriented Tools Layer

It offers the user interface and the uniform access interface, e.g. Grid Service portal. There are programming model, test and simulation tools, monitoring and management tools and workflow modeling tools in this layer. All the tools and API can simplify the development, assignment, test and management of the Grid application.

(4) Grid Application Layer

This layer is based on service. These applications are not limited to scientific computing and mass data processing.

3   Critical Technologies of Grid Service Layer

The Service Layer is the core layer of the system in the Fig.1. The heterogeneous and distributed services, which are viewed as the standard software components, can be discovered, issued, composed and scheduled by the uniform programming environment[2][10]. The protocol group of Web service makes the open, scalable and standard infrastructure implement and interact among the services[6]. We introduce the domain ontology to improve the ability of automatic discovery and accurate location and solve the semantic heterogeneity. The global ontology and the local ontologies are integrated to share the semantic information. The service is described by OWL-S. UDDI and WS-Inspection are extended semantically to realize the service discovery and dynamic binding. We implement the service scheduling based on SOAP and its security extension. The system supports the cooperation in security based on WS-Inspection specification. And the service composing is realized under ontology technology. Compared with the 5-layer Grid system[1], the service is viewed as the unified resources in Fig.1. The novel architecture presented in the paper combines with the previous work of Web service. It is built in the autonomous and credible Grid Service environment and solves the resource connection, sharing and assembling.

3.1 Grid Ontology Architecture

The concept of Ontology, which originates from philosophy, has been widely employed by several research communities[8][9]. The use of ontology for the explication of implicit and hidden knowledge is a possible approach to overcome the problem of semantic heterogeneity. The interoperability and the semantic information integration are the key application of ontology[11][5]. An ontology provides semantics by defining concepts and properties, and by describing axioms. It includes machine-interpretable definitions of basic concepts in the domain and their relations. And it has features of domain-specificity, standardization, and evolution.

Now the research on distributed, heterogeneous Grid Service has begun to exploit ontologies in order to support semantic interoperability, because lots of Grid Service providers issue their Grid Service in a distributed environment. The shared definitions and understanding are required to discover a Grid Service [13]. It will be convenient to combine the simple Grid Services into a complex Grid Service and evaluate the capability of the Grid Service based on the ontology[14][15].

Ontology is built in the following ways and we choose the last one to model the ontology, which is called the Star Model of Ontology (Fig.2c)[8]:

1. Single ontology approach (Fig.2a): a typical example of this app roach is SIMS. This approach is susceptible to change in the information sources which can affect the conceptualization of the domain represented in the ontology.

2. Multiple ontology approach (Fig.2b): the OBSERVER system is an example of this app roach. In practice the inter-ontology mapping is very difficult to define, because of the many semantic heterogeneity problems which may occur.

3. Hybrid ontology approach (Fig.2c): a combination of the two preceding approaches is used. A local ontology is built for each source schema, which is not mapped to other local ontologies, but to a global shared ontology. It avoids the disadvantages of single ontology or multiple ontology approaches.

Definition 1 (Ontology). Ontology is built on OWL(web ontology language). It is expressed as a 4-tupel: O={C, R, I, A}, where C is a finite set of concepts; R is a finite set of relations; I is a set of instances; A is a set of axioms, expressed in a logical language over T which is T=C$\cup$R$\cup$I, and it can be used to infer knowledge from an existing one.

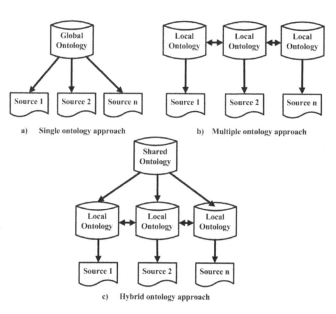

Fig. 2. The three possible ways for using ontologies

Definition 2 (Grid Service). Grid Service is a special Web service. It is expressed as a 4-tuple: GS={CA, UA, IN, OUT}, where CA is a set of common attributes that all Grid

Services have, e.g. service name, service providers, edition, URI; UA is a set of unique attributes that a service has individually; IN is a set of parameters, describing the input interface; OUT is a set of p parameters, describing the output interface.

We can describe the semantic character of an essential service by binding the interface and the service attributes. The service provider and the service requester can be ensured to call the Grid Service based on semantic.

Definition 3 (Service associating). Given two Grid Services GS1 and GS2, IN1⊆OUT2 indicates that GS1 is associated with GS2, expressed as GS1←GS2. The symbol ⊆ means the set IN1 covered by the set OUT2. And the SD(GS1, GS2) is the degree of the association between GS1 and GS2 based on semantic.

Definition 4 (Ontology mapping). Ontology mapping is the task of finding semantic relationships between entities (i.e. concept, attribute, and relation) of two ontologies. The ontology mapping system is a 3-tuple OM={G, L, M}

(1)G is the global conceptual schema, expressed over an alphabet Ag. It defines the global semantics and provides the global view for users.

(2)L is the local conceptual schema, expressed over an alphabet As. L defines the local semantics for data source.

(3)M is the mapping between G and S, constituted by a set of assertions which define the relationship between global conceptual schema and local conceptual schema.

The similarity of two entities among different ontologies or between the registered and requested concepts is defined as a similarity function: $sim(e_i, e_j) \in [0, 1]$ (0 means e_i is different from e_j, 1 means they are synonymous). If there are more than one matching candidates in several ontologies for e_i, the one with the highest similarity is selected as its matched entity.

Since the ontologies evolve as time goes by, the global ontology and the local ontologies for the Grid Services should have a flexible infrastructure that has an ability to reflect the changes in ontologies[8][12].

A flexible ontology management approach is proposed for discovery and description of Grid Service capabilities supporting ontology evolution whose goal is to enhance the interoperability among Grid Services. In this approach, concepts and descriptions in an ontology are defined independently, and they are connected by relationships. In addition, the relationships are updated based on real-time evaluations of ontology users in order to flexibly support ontology evolution. A bottom-up ontology evolution means such environment that allows ontology users to evaluate impact factors of concepts in an ontology and that results of the evaluation are reflected to the modification of the ontology. So the ontology management framework not only enables semantic discovery and description of a Grid Service capability but also supports a bottom-up ontology evolution based on the evaluations.

3.2 Grid Service Matchmaking Semantically

The matchmaking approach proposed in this paper adds semantics to the Grid Service concepts through OWL-S. The service matchmaking algorithm infers knowledge from the description to discover closely related services. We use user-defined weighted QoS

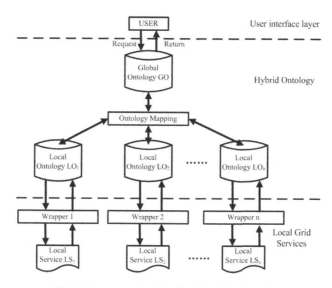

Fig. 3. Framework of the Star Model of Ontology

factors to evaluate the capability and obtain the suitable services, then combine these elementary services as a complex one that meets the user's requirements.

The matchmaking approach has 3 modules, which are discovering module, evaluating module and composing module, based on semantics.

(1) Discovering module
We use the semantic similarity between the requested capability and that of the registered ones to discover the service initially. The semantic similarity is determined among concepts from different ontologies directly, named SIM. SIM = Σ(NCS, ACS, SRS) = sim(e1, e2), where NCS is the similarity in the name of concept, ACS is the similarity in the attribute of concept, SRS is the similarity of semantic relation and sim is defined in Definition 4. Semantic relation includes two kinds of relationships. They are hierarchical relation and inhierarchical relation. The service discovering module can eliminate irrelevant services from being compared and improve the accuracy of the final results.

(2) Evaluating module
The chief criterion for evaluating whether the Grid Service is practicable is the Quality of Service(QoS). Users may have different QoS requirements with respect to the service requested. So we use weighted QoS factors to evaluate the capability. Six important factors are extracted to describe the QoS needed by a service requester, which are CPU cycles(CPU), network bandwidth(NB), memory space(MS), system reliability(SR), packets lost(PL), I/O bandwidth(IOB). These factors can be computed, e.g. NB=1 − (RequiredNB/AvailableNB). RequiredNB is the minimum network bandwidth and AvailableNB is the network bandwidth available at the service provider. Therefore, the value of RequiredNB/AvailableNB must be low. It means the service provider can offer a good QoS for bandwidth.

The parameters required by the service request such as RequiredNB are obtained from the service requester. The requester specifies the priorities of every QoS parameters, i.e. weights (W). Then computes overall QoS requested by the user as shown:

$$AQoS = \Sigma(w1*CPU, w2*NB, w3*MS, w4*SR, w5*PL, w6*IOB)$$

The user can choose the single service or the complex service which has the maximum value of AQoS.

(3) Composing module

The ability to compose services (and applications) based on currently available services, current context, and dynamically defined objectives and goals is critical[3][14]. While the existing systems do address many aspects of composition, they do not completely address the challenges of dynamic service composition based on semantic. We present a dynamic composition model which is to autonomically synthesize the Grid Services from the pool of available services, which are chosen after service discovery and QoS evaluation, to satisfy dynamically defined composition objectives, policies and constraints.

Definition 5 (Directed Constraint Graph). Directed constraint graph (DCG) is a directed chart G=<V,E>. And V={GS1, GS2,..., GSn} is the set of the nodes, which represent Grid Services, in the graph. E is the set of directed edges. Every (vi, vj) E indicates that there is a directed association between vi and vj. And the value of the edge is SD. The first node of the graph is the element IN of the request service. And the last node is the element OUT of the request service.

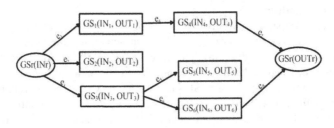

Fig. 4. Directed Constraint Graph

So the service composing can be described in the form of DCG through service associating analysis. And choose one pathway, which can satisfy the user's request and the constraints of the directed graph, to be the composed service. This model is based on the semantic similarity of concepts and the semantic relativity of the service under ontology. It can not only meet the function of service request, but also has high efficiency.

For example, GSr is the Grid Service of the request service(Fig.4). We find the GS1, GS2 and GS3 are associated with GSr by computing SD. So there are e1, e2 and e3 to indicate the association and the values are SDs. The other nodes and edges of the DCG are analogized in this way. Then it is found that there are 2 pathways (e1→e4→e5, e3→e6→e8) that can reach the end point GSr(OUTr), which is the request out. We choose one of them that has high ΣAGoS. ΣAGoS is the sum of all nodes' AGoS in the pathway.

4   Conclusions and Future Work

In this paper Service Oriented Grid Hierarchical Architecture is proposed within the OGSA framework. Its supporting environment and the critical technologies are introduced. The ontology technique is used to solve the problem of describing and discovering Grid Services semantically in a heterogeneous grid environment. Then we can discover the suitable Grid Service quickly and accurately and compose the elementary service into the complex service under ontology. The service composing is a method that finds a suitable pathway in a directed graph. We discuss the problems associated with managing ontologies in Grid and present the mapping mechanism to share the semantic information in distributed environment. There are still many problems that need to be solved, such as learn local ontology from data source, semi-automatic ontology mapping, similarity computing optimization, validity checking on Grid Service composition, etc. Future work will investigate these issues more deeply.

References

1. Foster, I., Kesselman, C.: Grid services for distributed system integration. Computer 35(6), 37–46 (2002)
2. Chaol, K.-M., Younas, M.: Analysis of grid service composition with BPEL4WS. In: 18th International Conference on Advanced Information Networking and Applications, AINA 2004 V1, pp. 284–289 (2004)
3. Derong, S., Ge, Y., et al.: Heterogeneity resolution based on ontology in web services composition. In: Proceedings of the IEEE International Conference on E-Commerce Technology for Dynamic E-Business, CEC-East 2004, Proceedings of the IEEE International Conference on E-Commerce Technology for Dynamic E-Business, CEC-East 2004, pp. 274–277 (2004)
4. Chun-Ming, H., Jin-Peng, H.: Web Service-based Grid Architecture and Its Supporting Environment. Journal of Software 15(7), 1064–1073 (2004)
5. Le-Yun, P., Xiao-qiang, L.: Evaluation of Multistrategy Classifiers for Heterogeneous Ontology Matching On the Semantic Web. Journal of Dong Hua University 22(2), 55–61 (2005)
6. Zou, D., Qiang, W.: A formal general framework and service access model for service grid. In: Proceedings - 10th IEEE International Conference on Engineering of Complex Computer Systems, pp. 349–356 (2005)
7. Wolfgang, M., Julio, A.J., Ricardo, A.: An ontology- and resources-based approach to evolution and reactivity in the semantic web. In: Meersman, R., Tari, Z. (eds.) OTM 2005. LNCS, vol. 3761, pp. 1553–1570. Springer, Heidelberg (2005)
8. Pernas, A.M., Dantas, M.A.R.: Using ontology for description of grid resources. In: Proceedings - 19th International Symposium, pp. 223–229 (2005)
9. Tangmunarunkit, H., Decker, S.: Ontology-based Resource Matching in the Grid[EB/OL] (2006), http://epicenter.usc.edu/docs/iswc03.pdf
10. Ludwig Simone, A., Reyhani, S.M.S.: Semantic approach to service discovery in a Grid environment. Web Semantics 4(1), 1–13 (2006)
11. Ling, L., Yu-jin, H., et al.: Semantic-based clustering method to build domain ontology from multiple heterogeneous knowledge sources. Journal of Donghua University (English Edition) 23(2), 1–7 (2006)

12. Changjun, H., Xiaoming, Z., et al.: Ontology-Based Semantic Integration Method for Domain-Specific Scientific Data. In: Eighth ACIS International Conference on Software Engineering, Artificial Intelligence, Networking, and Parallel/Distributed Computing, pp. 772–777 (2007)
13. Pastore, S.: Introducing semantic technologies in web services-based application discovery within grid environments. In: Fourth European Conference on Universal Multiservice Networks, pp. 22–31 (2007)
14. Xiandi, Y., Ning, H.: Ontology based approach of semantic information integration. Journal of Southeast University (English Edition) 23(3), 338–342 (2007)
15. Rajagopal, S., Thamarai Selvi, S.: Semantic grid service discovery approach using clustering of service ontologies. In: IEEE Region 10 Conference, pp. 414–553 (2007)

A Scalable and Adaptive Distributed Service Discovery Mechanism in SOC Environments

Xiao Zheng, Junzhou Luo, and Aibo Song

School of Computer Science and Engineering, Southeast University,
210096 Nanjing, P.R. China
{xzheng,jluo,absong}@seu.edu.cn

Abstract. Current researches on service discovery mainly pursue fast response and high recall, but little work focuses on scalability and adaptability of large-scale distributed service registries in SOC. This paper proposes a solution using an agent based distributed service discovery mechanism. Firstly an unstructured P2P based registry system is proposed in which each peer is an autonomous registry center and services are organized and managed according to domain ontology within these registry centers. Secondly, an ant-like multi-agent service discovery method is proposed. Search agents and guide agents cooperate to discover services. Search agents simulate the behaviors of ants to travel the network and discover services. Guide agents are responsible to manage a service routing table consisting of pheromone and hop count, instructing search agents' routing. Experimental results show that the suggested mechanism is scalable and adaptive in a large-scale dynamic SOC environment.

Keywords: multi-agent system, P2P network, service discovery, ant algorithm.

1 Introduction

In Service-Oriented Computing (SOC), in order to discover and locate a target service efficiently, services should be published to a service registry. The registry stores metadata documents of Web services, including functions, parameters and providers. The service registry is a bridge between service consumers and service providers.

Currently used services registries, for example those based on UDDI standard, often adopt a centralized or hierarchical architecture, which are not suitable for very large SOC environments for their intrinsic poor scalability features. The design of decentralized registry systems is therefore urgent. Recent UDDI v3 [1] introduces a mechanism of registry affiliation. Affiliated registries could share data with each other in a controlled environment. Peer-to-peer(P2P) based registry is also suggested[2-6] to support distributed service discovery. The P2P registry architectural style has no centralized registry to store the metadata of services. Each peer in the P2P registry is a registry center that maintains data independently, and data can be shared among peers. Recent researches almost focus on data partition and management among peers, and designing a high efficient service discovery algorithm. Little work considers scalability and adaptability of the registry system when thousands of

J. Cao et al. (Eds.): NPC 2008, LNCS 5245, pp. 349–360, 2008.
© IFIP International Federation for Information Processing 2008

peers exist in it. However, the problem of scalability and adaptability must be solved for distributed computing.

Under an environment consisting of thousands of registries, service discovery would involve locating the correct registry in the first place and then locating the appropriate service within that registry. This paper focuses on solving the first challenge of finding appropriate registries. We propose an adaptive distributed services discovery mechanism for large-scale dynamic SOC environments. The main contributions in this paper are:

(1) We propose an agent based distributed service registry system, which is based on unstructured P2P architecture. Moreover, domain ontology is adopted to partition and manage services in registry centers.

(2) We examine a decentralized and self-organizing approach inspired by ant behaviors. According to dynamic variable pheromone level, agents can adapt to the changes of registry topology and registered services.

2 Related Work

Distributed service publication and discovery models have been extensively studied in previous work. Many researches [2-6] suggest using P2P network as the infrastructure of service registries. Current P2P systems can be classified into two types, namely unstructured and structured. Structured designs are likely to be less resilient in the face of a very transient user population, precisely because the structure required for routing is hard to maintain when nodes joining and leaving at a high rate. In contrast, the unstructured networks are ad-hoc and the placement of data is completely unrelated to the overlay topology. The advantage of such systems is that they can easily accommodate a highly transient node population. In addition, unstructured networks support many desirable properties such as simplicity, robustness, low requirement for network topology and supporting semantic searching.

METEOR-S [2] is a scalable P2P infrastructure of registries for semantic publication and discovery of Web services. This work uses an ontology-based approach to organize registries into domains, enabling domain based classification of all Web services. The mapping between UDDI registry and ontology is used to organize a P2P network. Under this mechanism, the content of the registry is tightly coupled with the topology of P2P network, which leads to their synchronization and less flexibility. Reference [3] suggests a P2P and semantic web based service discovery mechanism where deployment and publication of a Web service are bound together. This mechanism omits obvious publication process of services, and could get dynamic various QoS of services in time. However, due to lacking registry, the response time of service discovery certainly delays, and its efficiency must lower. Reference [4] proposes a P2P based service discovery mechanism by creating an agent called P2P Registry as a middleware within DNS and peers. Each peer is able to register and discover desirable services automatically through current DNS within a short duration. In this scheme, centralized DNS is used to locate the target, which is similar to the super node in hybrid P2P systems.

3   A P2P-Based Distributed Service Registry System

In order to support dynamic adaptive service discovery, an agent based unstructured P2P registry system is introduced, which is illustrated in figure 1. The whole registry system is composed of numerous self-organized registry centers that are interconnected through unstructured P2P network style. Three types of agents are used to manage registry centers and discovery services, namely registry agent, search agent and guide agent (RA, SA, GA for short respectively). RA, resided in registry centers, is responsible for registering and indexing service metadata, etc.. SA is a kind of mobile agent, accepting discovery task and responsible for searching target services over the registry system. GA, also resided in a registry center, is a guide who helps SA to select a best route. GA maintains a service routing table which records routes from the local registry to service domains.

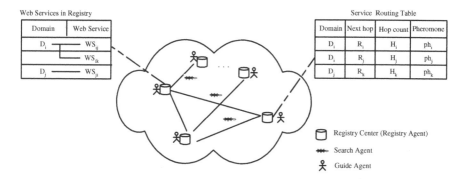

Fig. 1. An overview of the distributed service registry system

Widely adoptive UDDI standard only supports keyword-based search. However, the accepted view is that semantic organization and management should be supported in near future, which should guarantee the accuracy of search result and offer foundation to automatic service composition based on semantics. Our suggested registry center adopts a domain ontology based two-level structure.

Domain ontology could support the common understanding about domain knowledge, and eliminate different meanings of the same word or sentence [8]. In SOC, a service always belongs to one or more particular domains. For example, car rental services belong to a traffic and transport domain, and hotel booking services belong to a travel domain. Consequently, registered services can be categorized in terms of which domain them belong to. Each registry center manages and clusters services by means of domain ontology.

A service can be defined as $WS = (I, O)$. I is a set of inputs, and O is a set of outputs. For $WS_i(I_i, O_i)$, if I_i and O_i belong to domain D_i semantically, WS_i will be registered in D_i. Once the registry center does not contain such D_i, a new domain D_i will be added. As illustrated in figure 1, registered services are organized as a directory tree. When querying a service WS_{ij}, a conclusion can be drawn rapidly through judging whether it belongs to one domain of the registry center or not. Consequently, the query process can be divided into two stages. At the first stage, which domain the target service belonging to should be judged; at the second stage, the service could be queried within its domain. Index technique can be used to improve the speed of query. Semantic technique can be used to judge similarity between a service and a domain. All of these techniques can be referred in the study of information retrieval and semantic web, which will not be studied in this paper.

4 Agent-Based Ant-Like Service Discovery

Ant algorithm, based on behaviors of the real ant, is initially applied to find the shortest paths in a graph [7] and, later on, successfully applied to combinatorial problems [9] or network routing [10]. The principle of this class of artificial ant algorithm is to translate into algorithmic models some of the real ants' biological principles. They use pheromone remaining in paths to indirectly exchange the path information between ants, whereas former ants passing by the path, which represents some experience knowledge, deposit such pheromone. In ant algorithm, the positive feedback of global updating reduces the search scope, and the hidden negative feedback retains the scope.

Our work also follows these thoughts. For each query request, n SAs are generated which emulate ants to execute a query task. In distributed service registry architecture, different service providers usually register many services with the same functions but different QoS properties. Service consumers do not generally find one particular service, but a number of services belonging to a given service class, so that they can subsequently select the service which is the best suited for their applications. A service class can be seen as a set of services satisfying a given set of syntactic and semantic constraints on the values of service metadata parameters. The objective of SAs is therefore to find target services as many as possible under particular constraints.

4.1 Behaviors of Agents

SA roams over the P2P network and queries the services belonging to its own ontology domain. Each SA carries some property information including a target service, TTL(Time to live), hop count and Tabu (tabu table). TTL records the life-span of SA, and hop count is the number of nodes (registry centers) that a SA has passed after discovering the latest target service. Tabu contains all nodes having been visited. SA's behaviors are described as follows. Corresponding algorithms will be introduced in section 4.2.

(1) Roam. In order to find target services, SA moves among nodes by a predefined routing policy. Each node maintains a service routing table that directs SA to select next hop. As illustrated in figure 1, a service routing table includes four fields, namely target domain, next hop, hop count and pheromone. The first record in service routing table showed in figure 1 represents that if target services belong to domain D_i, R_i will be the next hop where the distance from local to the node having D_i is hop count H_i, and the amount of pheromone on this exit is ph_i. In order to avoid visiting the same node again, SA records the visited nodes in its Tabu. At last the hop count is updated.

(2) Querying services. SA queries target services at the visited node. The two stage query approach has been simply introduced above.

(3) Generating and sending pheromone updating messages. A message includes service domain and hop count. There are two different kinds of updating messages. If SAs having found successfully, the massage of reporting a target service registered in this node is going to be flooded to all its neighbors. In addition, if SA's hop count is not equal to zero, a message containing this hop count will be sent to the local GA.

(4) Life-span control. SA has a life-span, which could control the number of SAs roaming in the network and insure there are no more SAs moving ceaselessly after a query is over. When a SA is created, its TTL is set to an initial life value. After this, TTL will be updated by a particular rule. The number of SAs roaming over the network can therefore be controlled. In addition, by adjusting the initial life value, SA's searching radius can be increased or decreased. Because SA can destroy itself after its TTL is decreased to zero, its life-span could be managed by itself.

GA mainly maintains the service routing table. Its behaviors are described as follows:

(1) Listening and receiving updating messages. GA always listens in pheromone updating messages from SAs or neighbor nodes' GAs.

(2) Managing service routing table. Updating messages are accepted and analyzed. If the service domain specified in the message could be found in the routing table, pheromone and hop count in the corresponding item will be updated. Conversely, if the domain does not exist, a new item will be added. Hop count contained in the accepted updating message will replace the hop count in the current item. Due to the dynamic variety of service availability, pheromone is always decreased periodically. The pheromone, which does not increase after a long time, would be given out at last. It denotes that no service exists in the corresponding routing, or no requirements about searching this kind of services exist. If an item's pheromone is zero, it will be deleted from the table.

(3) Diffusion of pheromone updating message. When resided node joins a network, or a new service is registered successfully, GA floods messages to all its neighbors with hop count equal to 1.

4.2 Ant-Like Service Discovery Approach

4.2.1 Search Agent Routing Policy

When SA queries the current service routing table, two cases would appear. The first case is that target services do not belong to any service domains in the table. In such situation, SA would select a neighbor randomly. The second case is that one or more domains can match the target services. Here SA would make a decision in terms of the amount of pheromone and hop count in corresponding items. The amount of pheromone denotes the number of ever-successful search along the route, and hop count denotes the distance to target services. SA moving to the neighbor with more pheromone may get higher success rate, and selecting less hop count may get shorter response time. Therefore, two factors should be considered together. Because pheromone represents rather a probability than certain knowledge, a roulette wheel selection algorithm [11] is used to select a neighbor. After adopting this method, the path with fewer pheromones also has the chance to be chosen, even if the probability is smaller.

In the second case, the probability of SA k at node i choosing to move to neighbor j is defined as

$$p_k(i,j) = \begin{cases} \dfrac{ph(i,j)(1/hops(i,j))^\lambda}{\sum_{u\in N} ph(i,u)(1/hops(i,u))^\lambda}, & j \in N \\ 0 & , & j \notin N \end{cases} \tag{1}$$

$$let \quad N = \{t[Nexthop] | t \in RT_i \wedge s \in t[Domain]\} - Tabu(k)$$

where $ph(i,j)$ denotes the amount of pheromone from node i to node j, $hops(i,j)$ denotes the hop count which is the distance to target service domain while selecting j as the next hop, and $\lambda > 0$ is a parameter which determines the relative importance of pheromone versus distance. s denotes the target service, RT_i denotes the service routing table in node i, $t[Domain]$ denotes the projection on field $Domain$, $t[Nexthop]$ denotes the projection on field $Nexthop$. $Tabu(k)$ is the Tabu of SA k.

4.2.2 Pheromone Generation and Updating

Pheromone, which directs SA to select routing, plays an important role in SA routing. Thus, how to generate and update pheromone is a key to influence algorithm performance. In the following cases, pheromone will be generated or updated.

(1) SA will deposit pheromone on the path passed by if it has discovered a target service. Its generated new pheromone will be added to the pheromone remained on the path previously. Assume that SA enters local node i from neighbor n, and let $ph(i,n)$ denotes the pheromone amount on the path from local node i to neighbor n, a updating rule is give by formula (2)

$$ph(i,n) = \alpha \cdot ph(i,n) + (1-\alpha)\Delta p_1 \tag{2}$$

where $\alpha \in (0,1)$ and Δp_1 is a constant.

(2) When having found a target service at node n, SA would diffusion pheromone to all neighbors. Receiving a message of pheromone updating, GA positioned on its neighbor would update pheromone in the corresponding item of its service routing table by formula (3).

$$ph(m,n) = \beta \cdot ph(m,n) + (1-\beta)\Delta p_2, \quad m \in J(n) \tag{3}$$

where $\beta \in (0,1)$ and Δp_2 is a constant. m is a element of the set of node n's neighbors. $J(n)$ is the set of node n's neighbors.

(3) For each item of the service routing table, an update process will be done in period by formula (4).

$$ph(i,n) = \rho \cdot ph(i,n) \tag{4}$$

where $\rho \in (0,1)$ is pheromone decay parameter. Thus if a neighbor is always not be visited, its pheromone level will be closer to zero.

(4) If a new node enters the P2P network or new services have been registered in a node, the local GA will send update messages to all its neighbors. In this situation, neighbors' service routing tables will be updated by formula (3).

4.2.3 SA's Hop Count Updating

When SA searches a target service, it records the hop count from latest discovered service to current position. The initial value of SA's hop count is zero, which represents it has not discovered any target services. When SA finds a target for the first time, it will set hop count to 1. Hereafter, once discovering a target service at a node, SA will reset hop count to 1; otherwise add 1 to current hop count. Such hop count is contained in pheromone updating messages and is used to update service routing table. Hop count HC_k is updated by (5)

$$HC_k = \begin{cases} 0, & HC_k = 0 \wedge s_k \notin C(i) \\ 1, & s_k \in C(i) \\ HC_k + 1, & HC_k > 0 \wedge s_k \notin C(i) \end{cases} \qquad (5)$$

where s_k denotes the target service of SA k, and $C(i)$ denotes the service set of node i.

4.2.4 Life-Span Control

Our algorithm uses TTL to control SA's life-span. When a SA is created, its TTL will be set to an initial value. Hereafter at each visiting node, the SA's TTL will be updated. If SA does not find target services, its TTL will be decreased; otherwise it will not be changed so that the SA can visit more nodes. If all neighbors are in the Tabu, the SA's TTL will be set to zero. Such SA will not move any more and be killed. When SA k at node i, the update rule of its TTL_k is:

$$TTL_k = \begin{cases} TTL_k - 1, & s_k \notin C(i) \\ TTL_k, & s_k \in C(i) \\ 0, & J(i) \subseteq Tabu(k) \end{cases} \qquad (6)$$

where the meanings of s_k and $C(i)$ are similar to formula (5).

Based on discussion above, the routing selection algorithm is described as follows.

Algorithm 1. Routing selection algorithm. SA runs this algorithm at each node.

```
1:   Input Seach Agent SA, target servies WS, local node
lnode, pheromone increment ph1 and ph2;
2:   SendUpdatePheromoneMessage to lnode with
SA.HopCount and ph1;
3:   SA.UpdateHopCount;
4:   SA.Tabu.Add(lnode);
5:   IF Other SAs having the same task had arrived THEN
6:       SA.TTL--;
7:   ELSE
8:       SA.Query(WS);
9:       IF (NoFound) THEN
10:          SA.TTL--;
11:      ELSE
12:          FOREACH node_i IN lnode.neighbour
13:              SendUpdatePheromoneMessage to node_i with
msg.hc=1 and ph2;
14:      END IF
```

```
15:  END IF
16:  IF All lnode.neighbour in SA.Tabu THEN
17:     SA.TTL=0;
18:  ELSE
19:     SA.Nexthop =RouletteSelect(lnode);
20:  END IF
```

5 Simulation and Performance Analysis

This section evaluates performance of our approach. For the sake of focusing on SA's search performance over the P2P based registry, assume that once SA reaches a node owning target services, it could discover all of them.

Repast 3(REursive Porus Agent Simulation Toolkit) [12] is a multi-agent simulation platform for large-scale systems. Our simulation program is based on Repast and implemented in C#. Simulated network topology is a Power-law random graph[13]. Each registry center has at most 20 kinds of service domains, and each domain has at most 50 kinds of services. 200 services are randomly generated and registered in each registry center. The class of ant-based algorithms often uses a number of tuning parameters. Unfortunately, these parameters are not directed by scientific rigor theory until now [14]. According to repeating experimentation and guidelines in reference [15], the parameters are set as $\alpha=0.9, \beta=0.85, \rho=0.95, \Delta p_1=0.25$, and $\Delta p_2=0.35$ in our algorithm. Parameter λ determines whether pheromone or hop count more affects routing selection. In a static environment, where network topology and metadata of registered services are generally stable, hop count could truly reflect the position of registered services. In contrast, the mechanism of updating pheromone plays an important role for adapting the algorithm to dynamic environments. Therefore, in static simulations, λ is set to 0.5, in order to magnify the effect of hop count, but $\lambda=2$ in dynamic simulations. The simulation is based on a discrete time model and all events are executed in discrete time steps, called tick.

Two groups of experiments are designed to evaluate our algorithm roundly. The first group examines the performance of the algorithm, and how the number of SAs and TTLs affect its performance. The second compares our algorithm to two classical resource discovery algorithms in P2P systems.

We focus on scalability and adaptability in a large-scale dynamic environment, and use the following metrics:

- *Recall* is the ratio of the number of discovered target services to the total number of target services, which shows the algorithm's search capability.
- *Search performance-price ratio* is average number of target services discovered by a search agent or query message. It is calculated as (number of discovered target services)/(number of query messages or SAs).

5.1 Performance Analysis

First experiments run in a static system in which the number of registry center, network topology, and the kind and number of services are invariable. Figure 2 shows a scenario, in which there lacks pheromone initially, and SAs repeatedly search a same target service later. There are 175 target services randomly distributed in the system of 1000 registry centers. 15 SAs with initial TTL=20 are generated to search target services. A search round is the span from the generation to death of all SAs for the same target. Figure 2(a) is a real-time statistic graph, which shows the trend of the number of SAs and discovered services along with running time. At the first search round, recall is very low and reaches 26%. However from the second round, a higher recall can be reached in few time steps. At the tenth round, a recall of about 83% can be reached. This is because at the beginning there is no pheromone in the service routing table, so SA blindly selects routing. After several rounds, pheromone has accumulated which could direct SA to search the registry with higher probability of owning target services. Summing up the data in figure 2(a), figure 2(b) shows the comparison between recalls of different rounds. Because Figure 2 illustrates that a fast convergence and a high recall can be reach in a short time in our algorithm.

Figure 3 shows how different system size affects the recall. As the number of registry centers increasing, recall decreases slowly. Because the number and initial TTL of SAs do not change, the degressive trend is rational. Figure 4 shows how the number and initial TTL of SAs affect the recall when the number of registry centers is 4000. Increasing the number of SAs can improve search scope, and increasing initial TTL can increase search radius. One of approaches of improving recall is therefore to increase the number and initial TTL of SAs, especially when the system size increases. Figure 2, 3, and 4 show that our algorithm is feasible for large-scale service discovery systems.

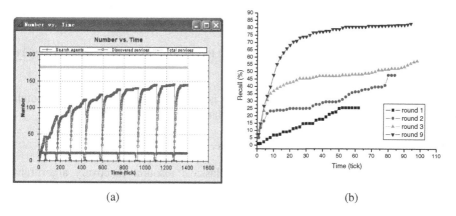

(a)   (b)

Fig. 2. Results of repeated running. (a) Trend of the number of discovered services and SAs. (b) Comparison between recalls of different rounds.

In order to examine the performance of our algorithm in dynamic environments, the experiment simulates a dynamic system where the number of registry centers is varying. For the sake of getting stable statistic, assume that there are no changes during a search round and randomly increase or decrease 10% registry centers between search rounds. Figure 5 is a dynamic output graph of the simulation program when the number of registry centers is 500. It shows the changing number of discovered services and total services after 10% registry centers having been increased. Figure 5(b)

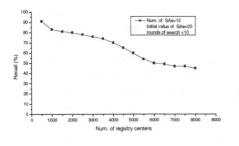
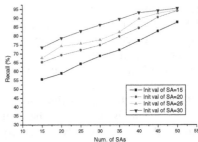

Fig. 3. Recall versus the number of registry centers

Fig. 4. Recall versus the number of SAs

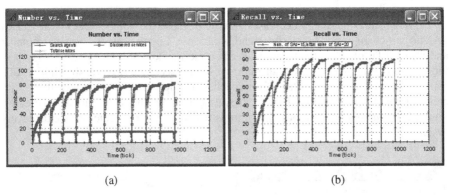

(a)   (b)

Fig. 5. Experiments in a dynamic environment. (a) Process of multi-round search. (b) Trend of recall.

shows that the recall decreases to 85%, but is back to former 90% after 3 rounds. Obviously, our algorithm is adaptable to the change of the system scale.

5.2 Comparison with Classical Algorithms

Gnutella[16] and Random Walks[17] are classical resource discovery algorithms, which are often used to P2P based service discovery model. Figure 6(a) shows the comparison of search performance-price ratio under different system scales. Since Gnutella's flooding style generate many new SAs at each node, and k-Random Walks generate k-1 new SAs, numerous SAs will be generated in order to get high recall. As a result, their search performance-price ratio is very low. Conversely, as our algorithm does not generate new SAs during the process of searching, a high search performance-price ratio is easily gained.

Again, as showed in Figure 6(b), through the pheromone-based instruction, our algorithm can obtains high recall after visiting about 30% registry centers. However, the other two algorithms' recall is geometric proportion to visited registry centers. This is because our algorithm has the knowledge about which registry probably having target services. The other algorithms only depend on magnifying search scope to improve recall.

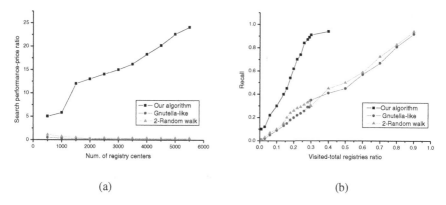

Fig. 6. Comparison between three algorithms. (a)Search performance-price ratio versus the number of registry centers. (b) Recall versus the visited to total ratio of registry centers.

6 Conclusions and Future Work

This paper proposes an agent based distributed service discovery mechanism for a P2P based registry. Under this model, search agents and guide agents cooperate to discover services. Search agent simulates the behaviors of ant to travel the network and discover services. Guide agent is responsible to manage a service routing table. The self-organizing and decentralized nature of the involved algorithms, along with the analysis of performance results obtained with variable system sizes, shows that the proposed mechanism is scalable and adaptive and can be adopted in a large-scale dynamic computing environment.

Recently some two layered and virtual domain based P2P models have been suggested to construct a distributed registry, which try to organize and manage services more efficiently. A service discovery approach under such infrastructure will be studied and implemented in near future.

Acknowledgments. This work is supported by National Natural Science Foundation of China under Grants No. 90604004 and 60773103, Jiangsu Provincial Natural Science Foundation of China under Grants No. BK2007708, Jiangsu Provincial Key Laboratory of Network and Information Security under Grants No. BM2003201 and Key Laboratory of Computer Network and Information Integration (Southeast University), Ministry of Education under Grants No. 93K-9.

References

1. Clement, L., Hately, A., Riegen, C.V., Rogers, T.: Universal Description Discovery & Integration (UDDI) 3.0.2 (2004), http://uddi.org/pubs/uddi_v3.htm
2. Verma, K., Sivashanmugam, K., Sheth, A., Patil, A., Oundhakar, S., Miller, J.: METEOR-S WSDI: A Scalable P2P Infrastructure of Registries for Semantic Publication and Discovery of Web Services. Journal of Information Technology and Management 6(1), 17–39 (2005)

3. Chen, D.W., Xu, B.C., Yue, R., Li, J.Z.: A P2P Based Web Service Discovery Mechanism with Bounding Deployment and Publication. Chinese Journal Of Computers 28(4), 615–626 (2005)
4. Chen, C.W., Gan, P.S., Yang, C.H.: A Service Discovery Mechanism with Load Balance Issue in Decentralized Peer-to-peer Network. In: 11th International Conference on Parallel and Distributed System(ICPADS 2005), pp. 592–598. IEEE Press, New York (2005)
5. Liu, Z.Z., Wang, H.M., Zhou, B.: A Two Layered P2P Model for Semantic Service Discovery. Journal of Software 18(8), 1922–1932 (2007)
6. Guo, D.K., Ren, Y., Chen, H.H., Luo, X.S.: A QoS-Guaranteed and Distributed Model forWeb Service Discovery. Journal of software 17(11), 2324–2334 (2006)
7. Dorigo, M., Gambardella, L.M.: Ant Colony System: A Cooperative Learning Approach to the Traveling Salesman Problem. IEEE Trans. on Evolutionary Computation 1, 53–66 (1997)
8. Arpinar, I.B., Zhang, R.Y., Aleman-Meza, B., et al.: Ontology-Driven Web Service Composition Platform. In: Proc. of the Int'l Conf. on E-Commerce Technology, San Diego, pp. 146–152. IEEE Press, New York (2004)
9. Bonabeau, E., Dorigo, M., Theraulaz, G.: Swarm Intelligence: From Natural to Artificial Systems. Oxford University Press, New York (1999)
10. Caro, G.D., Dorigo, M.: Antnet: Distributed Stigmergetic Control for Communications Network. Journal of Artificial Intelligence Research 9, 317–365 (1998)
11. Baker, J.E.: Reducing Bias and Inefficiency in the Selection Algorithm. In: The Second International Conference on Genetic Algorithms and their Application, pp. 14–21 (1987)
12. North, M.J., Collier, N.T., Vos, J.R.: Experiences Creating Three Implementations of the Repast Agent Modeling Toolkit. ACM Trans. on Modeling and Computer Simulation 1, 1–25 (2006)
13. Adamic, L.A., Lukose, R.M., Puniyani, A.R., Huberman, B.A.: Search in Power Law Networks. Phys. Rev. E64, 46135–46143 (2001)
14. Ridge, E., Curry, E.: A Roadmap of Nature-inspired Systems Research and Development. Multiagent and Grid Systems 3, 3–8 (2007)
15. Parunak, H.V.D., Brueckner, S.A., Matthews, R., Sauter, J.: Pheromone Learning for Self-Organizing Agents. IEEE Trans. on Systems, Man, and Cybernetics-Part A: Systems and Humans 35(3), 316–326 (2005)
16. Gnutella website, http://www.gnutella.com
17. Lv, Q., Cao, P., Cohen, E., Li, K., Shenker, S.: Search and Replication in Unstructured Peer-to-peer Networks. In: The Int'l Conf. on Measurements and Modeling of Computer Systems, pp. 84–95 (2002)

Author Index

Lecture Notes in Computer Science

Sublibrary 1: Theoretical Computer Science and General Issues

For information about Vols. 1– 4978
please contact your bookseller or Springer

Vol. 5132: P.J. Bentley, D. Lee, S. Jung (Eds.), Artificial Immune Systems. XIV, 436 pages. 2008.

Vol. 5131: H.J. van den Herik, X. Xu, Z. Ma, M.H.M. Winands (Eds.), Computers and Games. XII, 275 pages. 2008.

Vol. 5130: J. von zur Gathen, J.L. Imaña, Ç.K. Koç (Eds.), Arithmetic of Finite Fields. X, 205 pages. 2008.

Vol. 5126: L. Aceto, I. Damgård, L.A. Goldberg, M.M. Halldórsson, A. Ingólfsdóttir, I. Walukiewicz (Eds.), Automata, Languages and Programming, Part II. XXII, 730 pages. 2008.

Vol. 5125: L. Aceto, I. Damgård, L.A. Goldberg, M.M. Halldórsson, A. Ingólfsdóttir, I. Walukiewicz (Eds.), Automata, Languages and Programming, Part I. XXIII, 896 pages. 2008.

Vol. 5124: J. Gudmundsson (Ed.), Algorithm Theory – SWAT 2008. XIII, 438 pages. 2008.

Vol. 5123: A. Gupta, S. Malik (Eds.), Computer Aided Verification. XVII, 558 pages. 2008.

Vol. 5117: A. Voronkov (Ed.), Rewriting Techniques and Applications. XIII, 457 pages. 2008.

Vol. 5114: M. Bereković, N. Dimopoulos, S. Wong (Eds.), Embedded Computer Systems: Architectures, Modeling, and Simulation. XVI, 300 pages. 2008.

Vol. 5104: F. Bello, E. Edwards (Eds.), Biomedical Simulation. XI, 228 pages. 2008.

Vol. 5103: M. Bubak, G.D. van Albada, J. Dongarra, P.M.A. Sloot (Eds.), Computational Science – ICCS 2008, Part III. XXVIII, 758 pages. 2008.

Vol. 5102: M. Bubak, G.D. van Albada, J. Dongarra, P.M.A. Sloot (Eds.), Computational Science – ICCS 2008, Part II. XXVIII, 752 pages. 2008.

Vol. 5101: M. Bubak, G.D. van Albada, J. Dongarra, P.M.A. Sloot (Eds.), Computational Science – ICCS 2008, Part I. XLVI, 1058 pages. 2008.

Vol. 5092: X. Hu, J. Wang (Eds.), Computing and Combinatorics. XIV, 680 pages. 2008.

Vol. 5090: R.T. Mittermeir, M.M. Sysło (Eds.), Informatics Education - Supporting Computational Thinking. XV, 357 pages. 2008.

Vol. 5084: J.F. Peters, A. Skowron (Eds.), Transactions on Rough Sets VIII. X, 521 pages. 2008.

Vol. 5083: O. Chitil, Z. Horváth, V. Zsók (Eds.), Implementation and Application of Functional Languages. XI, 272 pages. 2008.

Vol. 5073: O. Gervasi, B. Murgante, A. Laganà, D. Taniar, Y. Mun, M.L. Gavrilova (Eds.), Computational Science and Its Applications – ICCSA 2008, Part II. XXIX, 1280 pages. 2008.

Vol. 5072: O. Gervasi, B. Murgante, A. Laganà, D. Taniar, Y. Mun, M.L. Gavrilova (Eds.), Computational Science and Its Applications – ICCSA 2008, Part I. XXIX, 1266 pages. 2008.

Vol. 5065: P. Degano, R. De Nicola, J. Meseguer (Eds.), Concurrency, Graphs and Models. XV, 810 pages. 2008.

Vol. 5062: K.M. van Hee, R. Valk (Eds.), Applications and Theory of Petri Nets. XIII, 429 pages. 2008.

Vol. 5059: F.P. Preparata, X. Wu, J. Yin (Eds.), Frontiers in Algorithmics. XI, 350 pages. 2008.

Vol. 5058: A.A. Shvartsman, P. Felber (Eds.), Structural Information and Communication Complexity. X, 307 pages. 2008.

Vol. 5050: J.M. Zurada, G.G. Yen, J. Wang (Eds.), Computational Intelligence: Research Frontiers. XVI, 389 pages. 2008.

Vol. 5045: P. Hertling, C.M. Hoffmann, W. Luther, N. Revol (Eds.), Reliable Implementation of Real Number Algorithms: Theory and Practice. XI, 239 pages. 2008.

Vol. 5038: C.C. McGeoch (Ed.), Experimental Algorithms. X, 363 pages. 2008.

Vol. 5036: S. Wu, L.T. Yang, T.L. Xu (Eds.), Advances in Grid and Pervasive Computing. XV, 518 pages. 2008.

Vol. 5035: A. Lodi, A. Panconesi, G. Rinaldi (Eds.), Integer Programming and Combinatorial Optimization. XI, 477 pages. 2008.

Vol. 5029: P. Ferragina, G.M. Landau (Eds.), Combinatorial Pattern Matching. XIII, 317 pages. 2008.

Vol. 5028: A. Beckmann, C. Dimitracopoulos, B. Löwe (Eds.), Logic and Theory of Algorithms. XIX, 596 pages. 2008.

Vol. 5022: A.G. Bourgeois, S.Q. Zheng (Eds.), Algorithms and Architectures for Parallel Processing. XIII, 336 pages. 2008.

Vol. 5018: M. Grohe, R. Niedermeier (Eds.), Parameterized and Exact Computation. X, 227 pages. 2008.

Vol. 5015: L. Perron, M.A. Trick (Eds.), Integration of AI and OR Techniques in Constraint Programming for Combinatorial Optimization Problems. XII, 394 pages. 2008.

Vol. 5011: A.J. van der Poorten, A. Stein (Eds.), Algorithmic Number Theory. IX, 455 pages. 2008.

Vol. 5010: E.A. Hirsch, A.A. Razborov, A. Semenov, A. Slissenko (Eds.), Computer Science – Theory and Applications. XIII, 411 pages. 2008.

Vol. 5008: A. Gasteratos, M. Vincze, J.K. Tsotsos (Eds.), Computer Vision Systems. XV, 560 pages. 2008.

Vol. 5004: R. Eigenmann, B.R. de Supinski (Eds.), OpenMP in a New Era of Parallelism. X, 191 pages. 2008.

Vol. 5000: O. Grumberg, H. Veith (Eds.), 25 Years of Model Checking. VII, 231 pages. 2008.

Vol. 4996: H. Kleine Büning, X. Zhao (Eds.), Theory and Applications of Satisfiability Testing – SAT 2008. X, 305 pages. 2008.

Vol. 4988: R. Berghammer, B. Möller, G. Struth (Eds.), Relations and Kleene Algebra in Computer Science. X, 397 pages. 2008.

Vol. 4985: M. Ishikawa, K. Doya, H. Miyamoto, T. Yamakawa (Eds.), Neural Information Processing, Part II. XXX, 1091 pages. 2008.

Vol. 4984: M. Ishikawa, K. Doya, H. Miyamoto, T. Yamakawa (Eds.), Neural Information Processing, Part I. XXX, 1147 pages. 2008.

Vol. 4981: M. Egerstedt, B. Mishra (Eds.), Hybrid Systems: Computation and Control. XV, 680 pages. 2008.